全国14家国家特色服务出口基地（语言服务）联合推荐
新文科语言服务学术文库

翻译质量评估

从原则到实践

Translation Quality Assessment

From Principles to Practice

Joss Moorkens / Sheila Castilho /
Federico Gaspari / Stephen Doherty ● 编

林 旭 ● 导读

上海外语教育出版社
SHANGHAI FOREIGN LANGUAGE EDUCATION PRESS

图书在版编目（CIP）数据

翻译质量评估：从原则到实践：英文/乔斯·
穆尔肯斯（Joss Moorkens）等编；林旭导读. —上海：
上海外语教育出版社，2024
（新文科语言服务学术文库/王立非总主编）
ISBN 978-7-5446-7902-2

Ⅰ.①翻…　Ⅱ.①乔…②林…　Ⅲ.①翻译—质量
评价—研究—英文　Ⅳ.①H059

中国国家版本馆CIP数据核字（2023）第200515号

First published in English under the title
Translation Quality Assessment: From Principles to Practice
edited by Joss Moorkens, Sheila Castilho, Federico Gaspari and Stephen Doherty,
edition: 1.

出版发行：上海外语教育出版社
　　　　　（上海外国语大学内）　邮编：200083
电　　话：021-65425300（总机）
电子邮箱：bookinfo@sflep.com.cn
网　　址：http://www.sflep.com
责任编辑：潘　敏

印　　刷：上海宝山译文印刷厂有限公司
开　　本：635×965　1/16　印张19.75　字数442千字
版　　次：2024年1月第1版　2024年1月第1次印刷

书　　号：ISBN 978-7-5446-7902-2
定　　价：68.00元

本版图书如有印装质量问题，可向本社调换
质量服务热线：4008-213-263

"新文科语言服务学术文库"专家委员会

顾问：
李宇明（北京语言大学）
王继辉（北京大学）

主任：
王立非（北京语言大学）

委员：（姓氏笔画为序）
王传英（南开大学）
王华树（北京外国语大学）
王宗琥（首都师范大学）
王铭玉（天津外国语大学）
文　军（北京航空航天大学）
艾　斌（上海财经大学）
冯光武（广东外语外贸大学）
司显柱（北京第二外国语学院）
吕世生（北京语言大学）
任虎林（北京科技大学）
刘　宏（大连外国语大学）
刘和平（北京语言大学）
孙　玉（上海外语教育出版社）
李　梅（同济大学）
杨明星（郑州大学）
张　政（北京师范大学）

张天伟（北京外国语大学）

张法连（中国政法大学）

张慧玉（浙江大学）

罗慧芳（当代中国与世界研究院）

屈哨兵（广州大学）

赵蓉晖（上海外国语大学）

胡开宝（上海外国语大学）

俞敬松（北京大学）

祝朝伟（四川外国语大学）

贺永中（美国蒙特雷高等国际研究院）

高明乐（北京语言大学）

高　霄（华北电力大学）

郭英剑（中国人民大学）

黄立波（西安外国语大学）

曹　进（西北师范大学）

崔启亮（对外经济贸易大学）

蒙永业（北京悦尔信息技术有限公司）

蔡基刚（复旦大学）

穆　雷（广东外语外贸大学）

Arle Lommel（美国 CSA 咨询公司）

前　言

语言服务兴起于 20 世纪 90 年代的欧美。2010 年，中国翻译协会首次正式在我国提出"语言服务"的概念。语言服务指以语言能力为核心，以促进跨语言、跨文化交流为目标，提供语际信息转化服务和产品，以及相关研究咨询、技术研发、工具应用、资产管理、教育培训等专业化服务的现代服务业。

根据统计，尽管全球经济不断受到挑战，但语言服务行业依然保持增长，2022 年，全球语言服务产值突破 600 亿美元。我国对外开放、中外人文交流和"一带一路"建设不断促进我国的语言服务市场增长。2022 年，我国的翻译公司和各类型的语言服务企业总计超过 42 万家，总产值突破 554 亿元人民币。语言服务发展的同时也带来巨大的人才需求。

语言服务教育在我国是一个新生事物，目标是培养行业需要的口笔译、语言技术和项目管理人才。2007 年，我国开办翻译硕士专业学位教育，为语言服务行业培养翻译人才。近年来，部分高校通过开设研究方向或独立设置二级学科点等方式，招收本地化管理、技术传播、翻译项目管理、医学语言服务、国际语言服务研究生，培养"语言＋技术""语言＋专业"和"语言＋管理"的复合型和应用型人才。部分高校成立了语言服务研究院所、应急语言服务基地（中心），召开语言服务论坛，编写语言服务研究报告等。2020 年，中国英汉语比较研究会批准成立语言服务研究专业委员会，出版《语言服务研究》集刊。2022 年，商务部、教育部、中国外文局等部委批准成立特色语言服务出口基地，国家发改委和商务部批准语言服务进入鼓励外商投资产业目录。以上举措有力地促进了语言服务的发展。

　　为了帮助广大师生了解国外语言服务领域学术研究和行业发展动态，满足高校语言服务学科建设、人才培养、教学科研的需要，上海外语教育出版社组织专家精心策划了"新文科语言服务学术文库"，从国外原版引进多种语言服务学术著作。本文库涵盖翻译及语言服务的职业技能和企业管理两个方面，包括翻译教学、技术文档写作、本地化技术、质量管理、服务管理、众包翻译管理等，体系完整，内容丰富，值得推荐。同时，为了方便读者理解重点，文库各书还专门配有中文导读和推荐阅读书目。

　　本文库可用作研究生教材，也适合语言服务行业人士和对语言服务感兴趣的广大社会读者作为参考书使用。希望文库的出版能为我国的语言服务发展贡献一份力量。

专家委员会主任

王立非

2023 年 12 月

导　读

一、本领域概述

（一）机器翻译

　　机器翻译（machine translation，MT）是利用计算机把一种语言转换成另一种语言的过程。美国数学家 Warren Weaver 最先于 1947 年提出机器翻译的设想，并将之记录在 1949 年 7 月发表的名为《翻译》的备忘录中。历经 70 多年的发展，机器翻译从研发到应用均取得了重大进步。机器翻译技术的发展通常被归纳为三个阶段：基于规则的机器翻译、基于统计的机器翻译和神经网络机器翻译。基于规则的机器翻译是最早的阶段，主要由词典和规则库构成知识源，一般分为语法型、语义型、知识型和智能型，其中的技术差别主要体现在转换平面的不同。基于统计的机器翻译方面，1993 年，IBM 的 Peter Brown 和 Della Pietra 等人提出了第一个可行性模型，主要基于词对齐的翻译模型和语料库。基于统计的机器翻译的提出，标志着现代机器翻译方法的长足发展。2006 年，谷歌翻译正式发布，带来了基于统计的机器翻译研究的一大波热潮。神经网络机器翻译于 2013 年逐渐兴起，开启了深度学习用于翻译技术的新时代。谷歌公司在 2016 年发布了神经机器翻译系统（Google Neural Machine Translation，GNMT），此后，国内外多家技术公司开始研发基于神经网络的机器翻译系统。机器翻译逐渐在多领域广泛运用，并最终发展成当今翻译工作中一个不可或缺的生产环境。目前的机器翻译软件已经可以实现几十种语言的实时互译、屏幕取词、文字扫描翻译、离线翻译等多种翻译形式。

（二）翻译质量评估

翻译质量评估是翻译研究和翻译实践的重要组成部分。在机器翻译大规模应用之前，针对翻译质量的评估主要是通过理论研究的方式进行。著名的理论有清代翻译家严复提出的"信、达、雅"，美国翻译家 Eugene A. Nida 提出的"功能对等"理论，德国翻译家 Hans J. Vermeer 提出的"目的论"，等等。这些理论对翻译实践及翻译标准产生了深远的影响，一定时期内也被用作评估翻译质量好坏的准则。翻译标准是衡量译文好坏的重要尺度，也是翻译质量评估不可或缺的部分。据统计，国际标准化组织（International Organization for Standardization，ISO）目前已经发布了 18 项有关翻译的标准，涵盖口译、笔译、翻译服务、机器翻译译后编辑、法律翻译、医疗口译等方面。

随着机器翻译的大量应用，翻译开启了大规模、多领域的行业应用时代，机器翻译的质量评估也成为机器翻译研发与实践的重点。针对机器翻译质量的评估，主要采用人工评估和自动评估两种方式。人工评估包括忠实度/流利度评分、等级排序、错误分类等（贾艳芳，孙三军 2022）。自动评估通常脱离语言的外壳，主要由基于编辑距离、准确率、召回率、综合指标的方法组成，包括 BLEU、NIST、GTM、METEOR、TER、HTER 等（贾艳芳，孙三军 2022）。面对日益增多的翻译需求，能够集合细分领域、文本类型、工作流程及终端用户的多角度、综合性翻译质量评估体系的研发与应用呼之欲出，也成为学术界、语言服务行业及相关机构的关注点。

二、作者简介

本书有四位编者。Joss Moorkens 博士是爱尔兰都柏林城市大学（Dublin City University）应用语言学与跨文化研究学院副教授，主要研究方向为翻译技术、翻译伦理、翻译社会学、机器翻译等，独立撰写或与人合著了 50 多篇关于翻译技术、机器翻译译后编辑、机器翻译评估和翻译伦理的期刊文章、图书章节和会议论文。Sheila Castilho 博士与 Federico Gaspari 博士为都柏林城市大学计算机学院 ADAPT 中心研究员，Stephen Doherty 博士为澳大利亚新南威尔士大学（The University of New South Wales）教授。

三、内容概要

（一）本书概况

本书英文原版 2018 年由施普林格（Springer）出版发行。全书以翻译产品为切入点，从学术研究、使用机构、产业发展三个角度探讨了覆盖人工翻译和机器翻译的翻译质量评估体系构建原则。本书以大量真实案例作为支撑，充分讨论了翻译质量评估体系的使用场景、研制原则及使用现状，并针对机器翻译在语言产业中大规模使用的现状，专门介绍了适用于神经网络机器翻译的质量评估及相关案例。本书为翻译学术研究及翻译行业发展提供了新视角、新思路，为后续开展相关研究和体系研发奠定了理论和实践基础，还可为翻译从业人员、翻译专业师生及语言服务行业管理者提供多角度参考。

（二）本书结构

除绪论外，本书分为三个部分，共包含 11 篇文章，具体如下：

第一部分（Part Ⅰ）主要介绍了翻译质量评估的最新现状，收录了 4 篇文章。文章 1 介绍了人工翻译和机器翻译质量评估的前沿方法，文章 2 主要介绍欧盟的翻译质量管理机构和管理标准，文章 3 介绍众包翻译质量评估，文章 4 探讨翻译质量评估的教学和训练。

第二部分（Part Ⅱ）围绕翻译质量评估模型的研制，收录了 4 篇文章。文章 5 从错误分类的角度介绍了翻译质量评估的标准，文章

6 探讨机器翻译质量评估标准及错误分类，文章 7 探讨机器翻译质量评估的新进展，文章 8 介绍视听翻译的质量评估标准。

第三部分（Part Ⅲ）通过实证方式，验证第二部分的相关指标。本部分共有 3 篇文章。文章 9 探讨机器翻译质量评估的应用和未来展望，文章 10 讨论机器翻译与译后编辑对学术写作质量提升的支持，文章 11 主要讨论神经网络机器翻译的质量评估。

（三）各篇概要

文章 1　人工翻译与机器翻译质量评估方法现状介绍

本文从学术研究、教育教学及行业发展等角度，对目前已有和正在研发的人工翻译和机器翻译质量评估方法进行综述。几位作者对目前流行的机器翻译质量自动评估指标进行了介绍，同时对翻译质量评估中存在的问题，如翻译标准化和译文一致性等，展开深入讨论。在翻译质量评估方面，本文从人工评估和自动评估两个方面，对现有的翻译质量评估体系进行梳理。人工评估主要包含准确性、流利性、可读性、接受度、等级排序、可用性等，自动评估主要有 WER、TER、HTER、BLEU、NIST 等模型框架。此外，本文还梳理了适用于"机器翻译＋译后编辑"的质量评估体系的研究现状。本文的相关结论为阅读文章 4 提供了背景。

文章 2　翻译质量、质量管理及管理机构：欧盟翻译司的原则与实践

本文以欧盟翻译司为研究对象，从学术研究和质量控制实践的角度，详细介绍了欧盟翻译司在翻译质量评估和管理方面的做法与经验。Drugan（2013）的研究将学术研究、理论构建与行业方法结合，提出了评估与提升翻译质量的方法，对行业场景下的翻译质量评估进行了有效分析。在本文中，Drugan 重点介绍了欧盟翻译司对翻译质量的特殊要求。在欧盟，所有语言的官方法律文本都被认为是等效的，而欧盟成员国众多，译员成分复杂，既有公务员，又有自由译者，这为翻

译质量的评估和把控带来极大挑战。本文详细介绍了这一问题的解决方式及欧盟翻译司采用的标准化体系。作者通过研究发现，在类似欧盟翻译司这样的翻译机构内，翻译质量不仅指译文本身的好坏，还关乎伦理、权力关系及专业素养。

文章 3　众包翻译与翻译质量：语言产业及翻译研究新动向

本文主要探讨众包翻译下的翻译质量评估。作者 Jiménez-Crespo 讨论了众包翻译中质量把控责任的分解。众包翻译的质量控制应覆盖众包翻译的全过程，而非仅局限在语言服务提供者层面，即众包平台上的所有参与者都应该担负起翻译质量控制的责任。本文对众包翻译的工作流程进行了详细梳理，从业务内容和翻译过程自动化的角度，对众包翻译的质量控制进行了探讨。作者认为，众包翻译下的翻译质量评估需要囊括一些特殊的评估指标，比如众包选取的标准、译前测试、工作社区建设等。众包翻译中，每个环节都是翻译质量控制的"第一责任人"。

文章 4　翻译质量评估教育与培训

本文内容主要分为两方面：一是对第一部分（Part Ⅰ）的回顾，涉及其中提到的一些关键概念，尤其是翻译质量评估的学术研究情况；二是针对翻译质量评估教育与培训的探讨。通过研究，本文得出结论：让翻译专业的学生充分学习目前的翻译质量评估方法和评估工具，对他们将来的职业发展非常有利。学生可以掌握关于翻译质量标准和评估的知识与技能，以便将来能够利用所学知识，从事与语言服务行业相关的工作流程设计、项目准备、机器翻译模型训练及数据选择等工作。此外，学生还需通过学习翻译质量评估手段，了解并掌握提升翻译质量的方法与技巧，以适应翻译行业的需求。因此，本文在最后呼吁将翻译质量评估作为翻译课程的一部分。

文章 5　翻译质量评估指标：以错误分类标准化为例

从本文开始，全书进入第二部分（Part Ⅱ），考察翻译质量评估指标和相关应用的研发。本文主要从机器翻译中的错误分类入手，探讨翻译质量评估指标的构建。文章作者 Lommel 一直以来致力于翻译和本地化产业的质量评估与标准化建设。在本文中，作者对以往的翻译错误分类进行了综述，梳理了"多维质量标准"（Multidimensional Quality Metrics，MQM）和"动态质量框架"（Dynamic Quality Framework，DQF）这两个翻译质量评估框架的构建背景。这两个评估框架在 2014 年之后逐渐合流，形成一套较为成熟的翻译质量评估体系。作者同时介绍了合流之后的评估框架的等级、维度、赋分情况及相关规范。

文章 6　机器翻译质量评估错误分类与分析

本文主要围绕机器翻译质量评估中的错误分类与分析展开，介绍了自动标注、人工标注和计算机辅助标注下的机器翻译错误分类，依次比较了不同的机器翻译系统，并为机器翻译开发者提供诊断依据。人工标注对于原文中的错误标注最为细致深入，但标注尺度会因人而异，造成标注标准不一。自动标注则会准确、一致地标注翻译错误。此外，作者还梳理了机器翻译错误类型的演进，并对不同的质量分析框架实验做了介绍。本文通过分析指出，应整合不同的机器翻译评估模型，提升整体的一致性。本文作者认为，机器翻译质量评估错误分类具有广阔的研究和创新前景。

文章 7　机器翻译质量展望

本文是作者 Way 对其前序研究的延伸。Way（2013）介绍了机器翻译的用例，考察了机器翻译对翻译成本的影响。研究表明，机器翻译正逐渐在更多的翻译工作中得到应用，同时，机器翻译译后编辑也成为主流（Lommel and DePalma 2016）。在本文中，作者进一步探讨了前述观点，阐释了机器翻译、人工评估指标和自动评估指标三者之间的关系，同时考察了基于任务的机器翻译评估。本文还讨论了自动评估的缺点和机器翻译系统的变化，并在文末梳理了目前机器翻译系统的部署方式，指出了目前机器翻译质量评估存在的问题，提出了未来展望。本文结论认为，机器翻译与翻译记忆库携手，将会积极推进翻译行业的发展，但目前人工评估仍具有重要作用。

文章 8　字幕翻译质量评估：人工翻译与机器翻译视角

本文主要探讨视听翻译的质量评估。一直以来，针对翻译质量评估的相关研究均未包含视听翻译产品，机器翻译译后编辑在视听翻译领域的应用尤其遭到忽视。本文针对这一话题进行了探讨。作者先梳理了视听翻译的现状，接着探讨基于传统的功能主义翻译理论产出的视听翻译产品与观众需求之间的差异情况，以此引出有关视听翻译质量评估的探讨。作者指出，视听翻译通常对翻译质量有着特殊的需求（Ivarsson and Carroll 1998），但这些特殊需求受制于译者的时间和空间因素，无法完全与传统的翻译质量评估标准（如准确性）吻合。本文研究表明，语言技术与视听翻译应该是互补的关系，研究人员应基于这种互补性和已有的翻译认知研究，提出一套完整可行的评估指标，利用传统指标和新指标的整合与互补，来评估视听翻译产品的质量。

文章 9　机器翻译质量评估：应用与展望

本文围绕机器翻译质量评估体系的应用展开，探讨了机器翻译质量评估（Machine Translation Quality Estimation，MTQE）的历史背景及前景。MTQE 的目的是对单一机器翻译输出的译文进行质量评估。在本文中，作者介绍了多种句法层面的质量评估手段及应用情况，如针对译后编辑情况的预测，在多个机器翻译工具产生的译文中挑选喜好的译文，选择有效的机器翻译训练数据，利用错误分类构建人工评估模型，通过实验考察质量评估在研究环境下的有效性，等等。本文认为，MTQE 将继续成为机器翻译的热点话题。虽然 MTQE 仍存在不少问题，但它提升了机器翻译的易用性，为终端用户在多领域场景的应用提供了便利。

文章 10　机器翻译及自动译后编辑对学术写作的助力：基于质量提升的探索

本文围绕机器翻译和自动译后编辑对提升学术写作质量的作用这一话题展开讨论。作者选取了一系列重要的质量评估因素进行考察，包括被试者观念、时间投入以及被试者用母语进行学术摘要写作时的修改要求等。研究共选取 10 位被试者，要求他们写一篇本专业领域的文献摘要。其中，5 位被试者直接用英语写作，另外 5 位先用母语写作，再由机器翻译和自动译后编辑工具译成英语并进行处理。对比研究表明：机器翻译和译后自动编辑工具处理后的文献摘要质量较好，但对术语的把握不够准确。被试者对采用机器翻译进行学术写作的可行性存在一定的分歧。本文为学术写作研究提供了新视角，也为减少国际论文发表中的语言障碍提供了一种解决方案。

文章 11　神经网络机器翻译应用于文学翻译的质量分析

本文主要围绕神经网络机器翻译在文学作品翻译中的质量评估进行讨论。机器翻译面临的最大挑战就是文学作品翻译。本文从小说入手，评估机器翻译在文学作品翻译层面的质量。作者构建了一个用于文学翻译的神经网络模型（Neural Machine Translation，NMT），并将之与基于短语规则的机器翻译系统（Phrase-Based Statistical Machine Translation，PBSMT）进行对比。本文采用 BLEU 自动评估指标展开研究，发现 NMT 的翻译质量比 PBSMT 显著提升，其提升率约为11%。此外，经人工评估得知，通过 NMT 翻译的作品，约有 17%—34% 被目标读者认为与人工翻译的质量相同，而 PBSMT 翻译作品的受认同比例为 8%—20%。

林　旭

参考文献

Abdallah K (2017) Three-dimensional quality model: the focal point of workflow management in organisational ergonomics. Paper presented at Translating and the Computer 39, London

Drugan J (2013) Quality in professional translation: assessment and improvement. Bloomsbury, London

Graham Y, Baldwin T, Moffat A, Zobel J (2017) Can machine translation systems be evaluated by the crowd alone? J Nat Lang Eng (JNLE) 23(1):

3–30

Ivarsson J, Carroll M (1998) Subtitling. TransEdit, Simrishamn

Lommel A, DePalma DA (2016) Europe's leading role in machine translation. Common Sense Advisory, Boston

Suojanen T, Koskinen K, Tuominen T (2015) User-centred translation. Routledge, London

Vermeer HJ (1978) Ein Rahmen für eine allgemeine Translationstheorie. Lebende Sprachen 23(3): 99–102

Way A (2013) Traditional and emerging use-cases for machine translation. Paper presented at Translating and the Computer 35, London

贾艳芳，孙三军（2022）机器翻译译后编辑难度测量体系构建研究. 中国外语（3），16–24

推荐阅读

Angelone E, Ehrensberger-Dow M, Massey G (2020) The Bloomsbury companion to language industry studies. Bloomsbury, London and New York

O'Hagan M (2020) The Routledge handbook of translation and technology. Routledge, London and New York

Wilks Y (2009) Machine translation: its scope and limits. Springer, New York

Joss Moorkens • Sheila Castilho
Federico Gaspari • Stephen Doherty
Editors

Translation Quality Assessment

From Principles to Practice

Acknowledgements

We would like to thank the contributors to this volume for their hard work and dedication to improving translation quality for us all. We would also particularly like to thank Series Editor (and contributor) Prof. Andy Way, for allowing us to produce the inaugural volume of this new series as co-editors, and for his many pieces of valuable advice along the way. We are also very grateful to our editors at Springer, Jolanda Voogd and Helen van der Stelt, for their trust and support.

The two anonymous peer reviewers left us detailed reviews that improved individual chapters and the volume as a whole – thank you for your time, care, and attention to detail. We also gratefully acknowledge the advice and backing of our colleagues, near and far, and our supportive families and friends. Finally, we also thank those who created the metrics and methodologies, translators, researchers, and developers, cited and uncited, on which the content of this book is based.

Contents

Contributors

Sheila Castilho ADAPT Centre/School of Computing, Dublin City University, Dublin, Ireland

Stephen Doherty School of Humanities and Languages, The University of New South Wales, Sydney, Australia

Joanna Drugan School of Politics, Philosophy, Language and Communication Studies, University of East Anglia, Norwich, UK

Federico Gaspari ADAPT Centre/School of Computing, Dublin City University, Dublin, Ireland

University for Foreigners "Dante Alighieri" of Reggio Calabria, Reggio Calabria, Italy

Marie-Josée Goulet Université du Québec en Outaouais, Gatineau, QC, Canada

Miguel A. Jiménez-Crespo School of Arts and Sciences, Rutgers University, New Brunswick, NJ, USA

The State University of New Jersey, New Brunswick, NJ, USA

Jan-Louis Kruger Department of Linguistics, Macquarie University, Sydney, Australia

North-West University, Vanderbijlpark, South Africa

Arle Lommel Common Sense Advisory (CSA Research), Indiana University, Bloomington, IN, USA

Joss Moorkens ADAPT Centre/School of Applied Language and Intercultural Studies, Dublin City University, Dublin, Ireland

Sharon O'Brien ADAPT Centre/School of Applied Language and Intercultural Studies, Dublin City University, Dublin, Ireland

Maja Popović Department of English and American Studies, Humboldt University of Berlin, Berlin, Germany

Kashif Shah eBay Research, San Jose, CA, USA

Michel Simard National Research Council, Ottawa, ON, Canada

Lucia Specia Department of Computer Science, University of Sheffield, Sheffield, UK

Ingemar Strandvik Directorate-General for Translation, European Commission, Brussels, Belgium

Antonio Toral Faculty of Arts, Center for Language and Cognition, University of Groningen, Groningen, The Netherlands

Erkka Vuorinen Directorate-General for Translation, European Commission, Brussels, Belgium

Andy Way ADAPT Centre/School of Computing, Dublin City University, Dublin, Ireland

Abbreviations

AEM	Automatic Evaluation Metric
AL	Active Learning
ASR	Automatic Speech Recognition
AVT	Audiovisual Translation
BLEU	Bilingual Evaluation Understudy
CAF	Common Assessment Framework
CAT	Computer-Aided Translation
CL	Controlled Language
CMS	Content Management System
DARPA	USA Defence Advanced Research Projects Agency
DGT	Directorate General for Translation, European Commission
DQF	Dynamic Quality Framework
EEG	Electroencephalography
EFL	English as a Foreign Language
EMNLP	Empirical Methods on Natural Language Processing
EU	European Union
FL	Foreign Language
FPER	F-SCORE Position-Independent Word Error Rate
GTM	General Text Matcher
HCI	Human-Computer Interaction
HPER	PRECISION Position-Independent Word Error Rate
HT	Human Translation
HTER	Human-Targeted Translation Edit Rate
IATE	Interactive Terminology for Europe
ISO	International Standards Organization
IT	Information Technology
LISA	Localization Industry Standards Association
LM	Language Model
LSP	Language Service Provider
MAE	Mean Absolute Error
MOOC	Massive Open Online Courses

MQM	Multidimensional Quality Metrics
MT	Machine Translation
MTE	MT Evaluation
MTQE	Machine Translation Quality Estimation
NMT	Neural Machine Translation
PBSMT	Phrase-Based Statistical Machine Translation
PE	Post-Editing
PER	Position-Independent Word Error Rate
POS	Part of Speech
QA	Quality Assessment
QC	Quality Control
QE	Quality Estimation
RBMT	Rule-Based Machine Translation
SAE	Society of Automotive Engineers
SMT	Statistical Machine Translation
TBX	TermBase eXchange
TEP	Translation Edit Publish
TER	Translation Edit Rate
TM	Translation Memory
TQA	Translation Quality Assessment
TQM	Total Quality Management
TS	Translation Studies
TSP	Translation Service Provider
TT	Target Text
TTR	Type-Token Ratio
WER	Word Error Rate
XLIFF	XML Localisation Interchange File Format

Introduction

Joss Moorkens, Sheila Castilho, Federico Gaspari, and Stephen Doherty

Abstract The continuing growth in digital content means that there is now significantly more linguistic content to translate using more diverse workflows and tools than ever before. This growth necessitates broader requirements for Translation Quality Assessment (TQA) that include appropriate methods for the domain, text type, workflow, and end-user. With this in mind, this volume sheds light on TQA research and practice from academic, institutional, and industry settings in its unique combination of human and machine translation evaluation (MTE). The focus in this book is on the product, rather than the process, of translation. The contributions trace the convergence of post-hoc TQA methods, with cross-pollination from one translation method to another: New error typologies are being taken on for MTE; the concept of 'fitness for purpose' when raw or post-edited MT is considered 'good enough' is now also used for crowdsourced translation. The state-of-the-art evinces a pragmatic focus, calibrated to a targeted end-user group. Understanding translation technologies and the appropriate evaluation techniques is critical to the successful integration of these technologies in the language services industry of today, where the lines between human and machine have become increasingly blurred and adaptability to change has become a key asset that can ultimately mean success or failure in a competitive landscape.

J. Moorkens
ADAPT Centre/School of Applied Language and Intercultural Studies, Dublin City University, Dublin, Ireland
e-mail: joss.moorkens@dcu.ie

S. Castilho
ADAPT Centre/School of Computing, Dublin City University, Dublin, Ireland
e-mail: sheila.castilho@adaptcentre.ie

F. Gaspari
ADAPT Centre/School of Computing, Dublin City University, Dublin, Ireland

University for Foreigners "Dante Alighieri" of Reggio Calabria, Reggio Calabria, Italy
e-mail: e-mail:federico.gaspari@adaptcentre.ie

S. Doherty
School of Humanities and Languages, The University of New South Wales, Sydney, Australia
e-mail: s.doherty@unsw.edu.au

The continuing exponential growth in primarily digital content means that there is now significantly more linguistic content to translate using more diverse workflows than ever before. This growth necessitates broader requirements for Translation Quality Assessment (TQA) that include appropriate methods for the domain, text type, workflow, and end-user. With this in mind, this volume sheds light on TQA research and practice from academic, institutional, and industry settings in its unique combination of human and machine translation evaluation (MTE). Understanding translation technologies and the appropriate evaluation techniques is critical to the successful integration of these technologies in the language services industry of today, where the lines between human and machine have become increasingly blurred and adaptability to change has become a key asset that can ultimately mean success or failure in a competitive landscape. This tumultuous environment affects all translation stakeholders, from students and educators to project managers and language services professionals, including in-house and freelance translators, as well as, of course, translation scholars and researchers.

At a high level, translation providers may try to ensure trust in translation quality levels by following standard approaches and workflows, such as the International Standards Organisation (ISO) 17100 translation process standard,[1] or the 18587 process for the human post-editing of MT output.[2] Another approach is to measure quality using traditional definitions of post-hoc quality, and it is these that we focus on to a greater extent in this volume.[3] Both approaches are used in tandem in the world's largest translation service, the European Commission Directorate-General for Translation (DGT), as described in detail in the chapter by Drugan et al. Not only is the DGT process the gold standard for translation quality, but it is an unusual example of moving beyond formal equivalence to a scenario in which each language version may be considered the 'original' text, due to legal effect, in that these texts "create rights, obligations and legitimate expectations" (ibid.).

What becomes clear when reading the following chapters is the convergence of post-hoc TQA methods, with cross-pollination from one translation method to another. New standard error typologies (see Lommel, in this volume), introduced to replace the previous TQA models, are being taken on for machine translation (MT) evaluation, as described by Popović. The concept of 'fitness for purpose' when raw or post-edited MT is considered 'good enough' for a notional translation end-user, as discussed by Way (this volume), is now also used for crowdsourced translation, as described by Jiménez-Crespo (this volume). Crowdsourced evaluation is becoming more common within the MT research community, particularly for large-scale competitive shared tasks (Graham et al. 2017).

---

[1] https://www.iso.org/standard/59149.html

[2] https://www.iso.org/standard/62970.html

[3] Abdallah (2017) suggests that an all-encompassing quality model should include not only process and product, but also social quality, as the interactions and work practices of those in a translation network are likely to affect process and product quality (see also Sect. 6.4, in Castilho et al.). Drugan et al. consider this in their contribution.

Consideration of the (usually assumed) requirements of a translation's end-user is not novel, and follows in the tradition of the functionalist approaches to translation, and in particular Skopos theory (Vermeer 1978). However, the sheer amount of text to translate and the number of language pairs and directions has led to a new level of pragmatism in large translation service providers, whereby a sharpened focus on a targeted end-user (as detailed in Suojanen et al. 2015) has added a new meticulously calibrated variability to translation quality requirements. These may be expressed using vague, relatively undefined terms, such as the prescriptive guidelines for light or medium post-editing, the exacting requirements of detailed error typology evaluations with an elaborate system of associated penalties, or a combination of approaches tailored for a translation client.

The subtitle of this volume is *From Principles to Practice*, and some of the principles of TQA are only of use in an academic context, or in the case of error typologies have been too unwieldy to apply at scale, tend to be difficult to explain to translation clients, and were for many years at a developmental standstill. For this reason, we hope to bring principles and practice together in this volume, with descriptions of highly complex use-cases for many text and translation process types (Drugan et al. and Way), novel empirical applications of translation technology and evaluation (O'Brien et al.; Toral and Way; Specia and Shah), and considerations of broadened future TQA applications (Doherty and Kruger; Jiménez-Crespo).

The first part of the book examines the state-of-the-art in TQA, beginning with a chapter by Castilho et al., who provide a historical background and an overview of established and developing approaches to human and machine TQA. In this opening chapter, the most popular automatic MT evaluation metrics are described in detail. This is followed by an in-depth discussion of the leading current issues in TQA, including problems with standardisation and consistency, particularly in relation to translator education and training, a topic returned to in a later chapter of the book (see Doherty et al.).

Drugan, Strandvik, and Vuorinen bring experience and expertise from both academia and translation quality in an institutional setting. Drugan (2013) has previously combined academic, theoretical and professional approaches to measuring and improving translation quality, offering a critical analysis of their effectiveness especially in industrial scenarios. This chapter focuses on the particular quality requirements of the European Commission DGT, wherein legislative texts in all official EU languages are considered equivalent and equally authentic. Defining translation quality and consistently managing quality expectations are challenging tasks when trying to balance legal compliance and maintain consistency among a huge and geographically dispersed cohort of translators, with varied translation processes and working conditions as either public servants or freelance workers. This chapter details the complex and interconnected TQA methodologies employed within the DGT. The authors also consider implications of these processes beyond translation for institutional and (increasingly) freelance translators to whom European Commission work is outsourced, with regard to power, agency, professionalism, and values.

Jiménez-Crespo describes how the relatively novel practice of crowdsourcing has impacted the notion of translation quality by expanding the *fitness-for-purpose* model (see also Way, in this volume), introduced with the growth in digital content and the need for fast (and, one may add, low-cost) translations. The author discusses the distribution of responsibility to different agents, that is, how the responsibility for the translation quality may shift from language providers and translators to participants from crowd platforms. Jiménez-Crespo presents an overview of workflow practices in these crowd platforms inspired both by professional context and translation automation. Translation crowdsourcing also introduces some particular TQA measures, such as crowd selection, embedded translator testing, and community-building.

In the final chapter of this part, Doherty et al. revisit some of the key issues addressed in the volume, focusing on academic applications of TQA. Firstly, teaching of contemporary evaluation methodologies provides translation graduates with skills that we can already see prove valuable, with graduates moving on to advisory roles in the language industry, using their expertise to take on such tasks as workflow design, project preparation, and MT training data selection. Secondly, familiarity with TQA measures prepares translation graduates for the standards that will be applied and the quality expectations in the translation industry. For these reasons, we advocate adding both of these applications of TQA to translation curricula.

In the second part of the book, we look at developing applications of TQA. Lommel has a long history of vital contributions to quality issues and standards in the translation and localization industry. His chapter provides a historical context for translation error typologies (also known as *typologies* and *classifications*), mostly used in the translation industry, and the background to recent influential developments in the area, namely the Multidimensional Quality Metrics (MQM) and Dynamic Quality Framework (DQF). While these two approaches began independently, they were harmonised in 2014. Lommel describes the hierarchy, dimensions, scoring, and specifications of this recent systematic standard approach to assessing translation quality. Popović describes the state-of-the-art for automatic, human, and computer-aided annotation of MT errors according to various error typologies as a way to compare MT systems or as a diagnostic tool for MT developers. Human-annotated translations can give deep insight, but tend to suffer from low inter-annotator agreement, especially when error classes are not clearly defined. Popović explains why automatic tools struggle to accurately identify very specific error types and tend to confuse mistranslations, omissions, and additions. She also discusses the evolution of MT error typologies, and describes experiments with different analysis methods (including the MQM, described in detail in Lommel's chapter), such as attempts to employ linguistic check-points to identify specific linguistic phenomena that cause particular problems. This chapter brings up the need to consolidate disparate MT evaluation typologies, in order to improve consistency. One particularly interesting suggestion is that widespread use of MQM for MT evaluation would allow subsets of a single unified metric to be used for both human and MT evaluation. As an alternative, Popović suggests a unified metric based on a number of typologies used in previous studies.

Way (2013) described use-cases appropriate for MT based on the perishability of texts, but increases in quality, coupled with economic considerations, mean that MT is being pressed into action in more workflows, and MT post-editing has gone mainstream (Lommel and DePalma 2016). Cognisant of this, Way updates his assessment of MT today in his contribution, explaining the "proper place" of MT, human and automatic evaluation metrics, and task-based MT evaluation. He addresses the weaknesses of automatic evaluation, and describes the changing nature of MT systems. Finally, he examines how MT is currently deployed, and considers associated questions of MT quality expectations and perception, and his prediction of its continued use as a production tool alongside translation memory.

Audiovisual translation (AVT) is absent from contemporary discussions of TQA, especially in the context of translation technologies of MT and post-editing. Doherty and Kruger remedy this with a comprehensive overview of the state-of-the-art in computer-aided AVT, and the difficulties of assessing whether translated media, consumed using a wide range of media devices, translated employing a functionalist approach, meet the needs of a heterogeneous audience. The authors consider the difficulties of merging the distinct AVT quality needs, usually prescriptively imposed (see Ivarsson and Carroll 1998), with concepts in TQA (such as accuracy) when spatial and temporal constraints may require the subtitler to substantially reformulate a target segment. They believe that the fields of language technology and AVT are (and should be) convergent and that this convergence, along with insights from cognitive translation studies, will help to show a holistic way in which traditional and new metrics can be used complementarily for measuring AVT quality.

The chapters in Part III present empirical studies, employing novel applications of TQA. One suggestion from Way's contribution on quality expectations of MT is "system-internal confidence measures". Relatedly, in this chapter, Specia and Shah discuss the historical background, and "promising practical uses" of MT quality estimation (QE). The purpose of QE is to provide an indicator of quality for individual MT outputs in use, where reference segments are not available. The authors describe several possible applications of sentence-level QE, such as to predict post-editing effort, to select a preferred translation from several produced by different MT systems, to choose effective MT training data, or to identify samples for human evaluation using an error typology (rather than sampling randomly), and provide experiment results to show to what extent QE has worked in a research environment. MTQE is very much an active research topic today, and the authors are clear that this is "far from a solved problem". However, they envisage that successful deployment of MTQE has "immense potential to make MT more useful to end-users of various types".

O'Brien, Simard and Goulet explore the potential of using MT and self-post-editing as a second-language academic writing aid. The authors choose an interesting range of quality assessment measures, comparing participant perceptions, temporal effort (time spent), and revisions required when participants write an academic abstract in their first language, then machine translate and self-post-edit it, and when they write the abstract in English (their L2). Results are also compared using an automatic grammar- and style-checking tool. Participants were generally impressed with the quality of MT output, but some had difficulty in finding the appropriate terminology in their native language, as they were used to using English language terms. This study demonstrates the potential for reducing the cognitive burden of authors when accessing international academic publishing via the current *lingua franca* of English.

A recent, novel approach to MT using neural network models is introduced by Toral and Way. Although Way advises the use of MT for highly perishable texts in his other contribution, with Toral he investigates the results when that advice is completely disregarded, translating a non-perishable and difficult content type. They apply neural MT to literary texts and perform a quality assessment comparing a portion of the output to that from statistical MT systems and published human translations, showing surprisingly promising results, especially considering the challenging text type.

At an extremely dynamic time for the translation industry, where the pressures of technology and economy have accelerated change (not only for the better) in work processes and working conditions, we consider that it is essential to continually update knowledge of technology and process, in order to maximise one's agency as a translator, student, teacher, researcher, or process manager. As an aid for such a purpose, we, the editors, believe that this volume covers the dominant methods from various translation scenarios, providing a comprehensive collection of contributions by leading international experts in human and machine translation quality and evaluation who can situate current developments and chart future trends of significant interest to the translation community as a whole.

References

Abdallah K (2017) Three-dimensional quality model: the focal point of workflow management in organisational ergonomics. Paper presented at Translating and the Computer 39, London

Drugan J (2013) Quality in professional translation: assessment and improvement. Bloomsbury, London

Graham Y, Baldwin T, Moffat A, Zobel J (2017) Can machine translation systems be evaluated by the crowd alone? J Nat Lang Eng (JNLE) 23(1):3–30

Ivarsson J, Carroll M (1998) Subtitling. TransEdit, Simrishamn

Lommel A, DePalma DA (2016) Europe's leading role in machine translation. Common Sense Advisory, Boston

Suojanen T, Koskinen K, Tuominen T (2015) User-centred translation. Routledge, London

Vermeer HJ (1978) Ein Rahmen für eine allgemeine Translationstheorie. Lebende Sprachen 23(3):99–102

Way A (2013) Traditional and emerging use-cases for machine translation. Paper presented at Translating and the Computer 35, London

Part I
Scenarios for Translation Quality Assessment

Approaches to Human and Machine Translation Quality Assessment

1

Sheila Castilho, Stephen Doherty, Federico Gaspari, and Joss Moorkens

Abstract In both research and practice, translation quality assessment is a complex task involving a range of linguistic and extra-linguistic factors. This chapter provides a critical overview of the established and developing approaches to the definition and measurement of translation quality in human and machine translation workflows across a range of research, educational, and industry scenarios. We intertwine literature from several interrelated disciplines dealing with contemporary translation quality assessment and, while we acknowledge the need for diversity in these approaches, we argue that there are fundamental and widespread issues that remain to be addressed, if we are to consolidate our knowledge and practice of translation quality assessment in increasingly technologised environments across research, teaching, and professional practice.

Keywords Translation quality assessment · Principles to practice · Translation industry · Translation metrics · Translation studies · Machine translation · Human translation · Professional translation

S. Castilho
ADAPT Centre/School of Computing, Dublin City University, Dublin, Ireland
e-mail: sheila.castilho@adaptcentre.ie

S. Doherty
School of Humanities and Languages, The University of New South Wales, Sydney, Australia
e-mail: s.doherty@unsw.edu.au

F. Gaspari
ADAPT Centre/School of Computing, Dublin City University, Dublin, Ireland

University for Foreigners "Dante Alighieri" of Reggio Calabria, Reggio Calabria, Italy
e-mail: federico.gaspari@adaptcentre.ie

J. Moorkens
ADAPT Centre/School of Applied Language and Intercultural Studies, Dublin City University, Dublin, Ireland
e-mail: joss.moorkens@dcu.ie

1 Background

Translation is a complex cognitive, linguistic, social, cultural, and technological process. Defining the translation process and assessing the quality of its outputs reflects this complexity and has rendered the concept of translation quality difficult to operationalise and measure. Consequently, definitions of translation quality attempt to capture these dimensions and their interactions to devise a means of formally assessing translation quality for a given purpose.

Given its importance, it is not surprising that translation quality assessment (TQA) has been a topic of much debate in translation studies and translation technology in particular, as well as throughout the translation and localisation industry. Even though there are commonalities in the theoretical discussion of translation quality in the dichotomy between the source-oriented concept of accuracy (or adequacy) and the target-oriented concept of fluency, in practice resource constraints mean that TQA processes vary considerably and have limitations. At the same time, the evolution and widespread adoption of translation technologies, especially machine translation (MT), have resulted in a plethora of differently operationalised definitions of translation quality (Gaspari et al. 2015). Drawing upon an industry survey that involved almost 500 translation and localisation buyers and vendors, where respondents could select one or more options, Doherty et al. (2013) identify a strong preference among respondents for human TQA (69%) over automatic evaluation (22%) and customised in-house measures (13%), when participants were asked to state which evaluation methods they used, including all the ones that applied to them.

This overview of methodologies and approaches to human and machine TQA is by no means exhaustive; rather it is intended to serve to highlight the diversity of its applications from fundamental and applied research projects to everyday industry pricing and public consumption. We do not attempt to criticise or reduce the diversity of these methodologies and approaches; rather, we provide a contemporary inventory of TQA which then develops to identify a number of universal issues, especially in the technologised environments of today and tomorrow, where the border between human and machine translation is being obfuscated (see O'Hagan 2012; Doherty 2016).

Accordingly, this chapter first reviews a wide range of approaches to TQA in the context of human translation (HT) from translation studies and industry literature. It then moves to examine MT quality and its assessment, highlighting the strengths and weaknesses of the various approaches that are discussed. Finally, it identifies several open issues which, we contend, should be addressed if we are to advance TQA in research, educational, and industrial contexts.

2 Notions of Translation Quality and Its Assessment

Although TQA is recognised as a key topic in the area of translation and localisation, academia and industry differ greatly when it comes to defining and evaluating translation quality. As Drugan (2013) aptly puts it, "theorists and professionals overwhelmingly agree there is no single objective way to measure quality". While researchers and academics tend to focus on theoretical and pedagogic concerns related to translation quality, in most sectors of the industry TQA is broadly limited to the application of somewhat arbitrary 'one-size-fits-all' error typology models that aim to give quantitative indicators of quality (Lommel et al. 2014; for a discussion of some relevant developments, see the contributions by Lommel and Popović in this volume).

Approaches and practices in TQA tend to differ at both the micro and macro level, as the meaning of quality can vary considerably for different individuals, groups, and contexts. Further variability is added as the nature and purpose of an evaluation are likely to change depending on whether it takes place as part of a production process or a research study. In industry, the aim of TQA is to ensure that a specified level of quality is identified, measured, and delivered to the client, buyer, end-user, etc., of translated content. In research, the aim is typically to obtain a measure that can show a demonstrable change in quality, most usually an improvement, from previous work or between different translation processes. The commercial interest in research and development of MT systems has also contributed to the debate, with alternative ways of assessing quality, e.g. by using automatic evaluation metrics and measuring post-editing (PE) effort. When considering the issue of translation quality, academia and industry are effectively "pursuing different goals and asking different questions" (Drugan 2013), and an agreement on an objective way to measure translation quality seems desirable (Koby et al. 2014).

We contend that the boundaries between HT and MT (and, to some extent, also those between translation as understood in academia versus in the industry) are increasingly blurring; this is apparent, in particular, in software and web localisation as well as in a wide range of technical and specialised domains, where MT (often supported by PE) is becoming widely used alongside the now commonplace computer-assisted translation (CAT) software such as translation memories, especially for projects involving major languages as source or target, or for language pairs with substantial commercial interest. The classical strict separation between (professional) HT on the one hand, and MT on the other, seems to become increasingly indistinct today; one need only think about PE, interactive MT, and the related techniques and tools which are becoming progressively more efficient. This trend is set to extend to a growing number of domains, as parallel corpora and natural language processing tools required to build customised and domain-adapted statistical and neural MT systems become available for new language pairs, additional text types, and further subject matters. In addition, more and more technological solutions are being adopted to support translation efforts e.g. in crowdsourcing and shared or collaborative projects (see Jiménez-Crespo in this volume).

In such a complex and fascinating scenario, it seems legitimate to argue that, even though so far the notions of quality have differed for HT and MT, the methodologies and approaches used for TQA may at some point converge, and possibly be unified, as a result of this increasing integration between different ways of translating.

2.1 TQA in Translation Studies

This section situates TQA with respect to key theories and major paradigms that have guided the development of Translation Studies since it first emerged as a separate independent discipline. Early definitions of translation quality from the time when translation studies started moving its own first steps as an offshoot of linguistics, such as those provided by Nida (1964) and Holmes (1988), focus on translation criticism rather than empirical measurement. Taking stock of the substantial progress made by Translation Studies over the decades, House (2001) calls for a move away from subjective quality evaluation to assessment of functional equivalence, but crucially admits that an evaluator "will always be forced to flexibly move from a macro-analytical focus to a micro-analytical one", thus suggesting an inherent shortcoming in this approach.

For Drugan (2013, emphasis in the original), "within translation studies, theorists disagree even on how many *categories* of models there are"; this in itself suggests that research-oriented TQA models are heavily theoretically motivated, reflecting the assumptions, and to some extent the biases, of those who propose or adopt them.[1] As a matter of fact, several researchers, such as House (1997), Schäffner (1997), Secară (2005), and Fields et al. (2014), have argued that evaluation is directly associated with the underlying translation theory that one subscribes to, so that inevitably "different views of translation lead to different concepts of translational quality, and hence different ways of assessing it" (House 1997).

The "equivalence" approach defines translation as a reproduction of the source text in the target-language, that is, "the attempt to reproduce the source text as closely as possible" (Lauscher 2000). Criticism of this approach relates to the fact that "the target text can never be equivalent to the source text on all levels" (ibid.), and over time theorists have indeed differentiated between types of equivalence (Nida 1964; Catford 1965; Baker 1992; Pym 2010). One of the first systematic models for TQA comes from Reiss (1971), who builds on the concept of equivalence, suggesting specific translation methods according to text types. In her

---

[1] For a comprehensive review on translation theories in relation to quality see Munday (2008); Pym (2010); Drugan (2013); House (2015).

model, "a translation is deemed good if it achieves optimal equivalence" (Lauscher 2000). Critics of this approach claim that the notion of "optimal equivalence" is too vague, and that there is no convincing explanation as to how text and language functions should be classified comparing the source and the target sides of the translation (see House 2015).

The descriptive and markedly target-oriented approach introduced by Toury (1995) rejects the prescriptive notion of equivalence and sees the target text as the starting point for a translation analysis (Williams 2013). For House (2015), the descriptive theory has an overly broad view of what translation is, "which makes it impossible [. . .] to clearly define criteria for translation quality assessment".

In the functionalist (or Skopos) approach (Reiss and Vermeer 1984), "it is the purpose of a translation that determines the translation strategy and the shape it takes in the host culture" (Williams 2013). That is, the purpose is the most important factor in translation. However, House (2015) does not consider the functionalist approach particularly useful for TQA, since it is not clear "how one can determine whether a given translation fulfils its skopos".

For Munday (2008), even though there has been a move away from prescriptive approaches to translation, new perspectives to translation have continued to emerge in recent years, "each seeking to establish a new 'paradigm' in translation studies" (ibid.). The author affirms that translation methodology has evolved and has become more sophisticated, but there is still "considerable divergence", as the object of study has changed over time from translation as connected to pedagogy to the "study of what happens in and around translation, translating and now translators" (ibid.). For Munday, this shift of the object of study of translation has allowed for a framework in which the choice of theory and methodology is crucial and "depends on the goals of the research and the researchers" (ibid.).

2.2 TQA in the Translation Industry

To provide a complementary perspective to the one sketched above concerning the conceptualisation of TQA viz. major theoretical streams in translation studies over the decades, this section focuses specifically on the role of TQA in the translation and localisation industry. While recognizing that translation covers very multifaceted and diverse business sectors across the world, here we consider in particular technical and specialised domains, as they represent ideal areas for the application of agreed and standardised TQA procedures, in which most of the professional translators work. Of course, the translation industry as a whole also includes a wide range of literary and non-fiction texts (e.g. biographies, travel literature, academic essays, etc.), which are subject to specific TQA processes (e.g. revision by senior translators or subject matter experts). However, in the interest of providing a more cohesive and focused discussion, we limit the brief overview presented in this section to the technical and specialised domains within the translation and localisation industry (for a novel appraisal of the potential of neural MT to provide quality translations of literary texts, see Toral and Way, this volume).

A common view in the translation industry is that quality is largely related to customer opinion (e.g. Drugan 2013), while O'Brien (2012) argues that quality evaluation in the translation industry is "managed by gatekeepers in the supply and demand chain who work with static evaluation models [. . .] applying penalties and maintaining thresholds with little, if any, input from customers". The rise of MT, which is now increasingly integrated into CAT work environments for an ever increasing range of technical and specialised texts as well as language pairs, has also contributed to making TQA a much-debated topic in the translation and localisation industry, since "human and machine translation [. . .] quality evaluation methods have been fundamentally different in kind, preventing comparison of the two" (Lommel et al. 2014).

Language Service Providers (LSPs) carry out TQA at the process level, where workflow steps are pre-defined, concurrently with translation work, using standalone or inbuilt CAT tool error checking software, or post-hoc using one of several evaluation models. Concurrent error checking tools that check for errors in respect of terminology, consistency, punctuation, formatting, number values, and tags include ApSIC XBench, Yamagata QA Distiller, ErrorSpy, Okapi CheckMate, and Acrocheck, to name but a few. Debove et al. believe that these tools constitute a "crucial step in the translation workflow" (2011) that work efficiently, although they also tend to generate a lot of false positives or incorrectly identified errors.

The evaluation models used in the industry are predominantly error-based, where errors found in (samples of) the translated text are counted, classified and weighted according to their severity by a senior translator or reviewer. This entails that the errors (and their severity weightings) must be predetermined according to some logical or hierarchical criteria. Interestingly, this is a common assessment approach in academic translator training programmes as well, even though lecturers tend to grade entire translation assignments or exams of their students (as opposed to samples or extracts). Other factors are also typically considered in TQA conducted as part of academic translator training, like the expected bilingual expertise (whether this concerns particularly the source or the target-language) on the part of the students, especially when the trainees translate into their non-native language (see, e.g. Stewart 2012, 2013; Tang 2017). These issues of language competence are less relevant in professional translation, as there is often an expectation that this should be performed only into the translator's native language. However, no matter how desirable this requirement is, in several parts of the world the sociolinguistic and economic reality is such that this principle is not upheld consistently, especially for language pairs where the demand for translations into a certain language (most notably English) exceeds the supply of native speakers of the target-language who are also proficient in the (local) source-language (see e.g. Campbell 1998; Adab 2005; Pokorn 2005).

With regard to specific TQA methodologies used in the industry, lists of error types to evaluate translations and localisation projects began to be widely used in localisation in the late 1990s. One particularly influential model has been the Localisation Industry Standards Association (LISA) QA Model, which has continued to be used in a variety of adaptations even after LISA ceased its operations in 2011. The LISA QA model consists of a list of types of errors categorised as 'minor', 'major' or 'critical', in the opinion of whoever performs the evaluation. Each segment of the translated text is assigned a score depending on the type(s) of error(s) it contains, which leads to an overall score for the whole evaluation task. A translation receives the status of 'pass' or 'fail' depending on the threshold defined by the evaluator, who decides how demanding and strict he/she wants to be in the overall evaluation of the translation product (i.e. how many errors of which severity can be tolerated in the evaluated text, for it not to be rejected). Many company-specific TQA models are customised from the original LISA model (O'Brien 2012); however, as pointed out by Lommel et al. (2014), among others, one of the major limitations of this type of TQA model is its underlying 'one-size-fits-all' philosophy: if, on the one hand, this offers a degree of standardisation, on the other it makes adaptability to the specifications of individual translation and localisation projects rather difficult.

The tendency to quantify, and thus increasingly standardise, TQA at the process level has gained traction in recent times, with the development of an ISO certification of translation parameters, namely, the ISO/TS 11669:2012. The ISO 11669 is a guideline standard that "provides guidance concerning best practices for all phases of a translation project" (ISO/TS 11669:2012) and features a framework for a structured translation specification consisting of 21 translation parameters in five categories: source content, requirements for the target, production tasks, environment, and relationships. Translation quality is defined by the standard as follows: "When both requesters and TSPs [Translation Service Providers] agree on project specifications, the quality of a translation – from a workflow and final delivery perspective – can be determined by the degree to which the target content adheres to the predetermined specifications." (ISO/TS 11669:2012).

For Muegge (2015), the standard is "a major evolutionary step forward", especially when compared to previous standards such as the ASTM F2575,[2] since it devotes a great space to terminology management. In contrast, for Muzii (2014), the ISO 11669 is a long list of parameters that builds upon "vague, blurry, and subjective criteria for quality assessment from the archetypal academic scenario" of a traditional "error-catching approach" (ibid.).[3] Such opposing views on this particular ISO standard confirm the difficulty of proposing effective solutions to long-standing problems in the industry due to the lack of recognised approaches to successfully measure and reward quality, even though this is taken for granted both by clients and providers.

---

[2] http://www.astm.org/Standards/F2575.htm

[3] A new ISO proposal was accepted in 2017 and is under development at the time of writing. The new standard is ISO/AWI 21999 "Translation quality assurance and assessment – Models and metrics". Details are at https://www.iso.org/standard/72345.html

Interestingly, Koby et al. (2014) disagree on a single definition of translation quality, offering both a broad and a narrow definition in its place. In the broad view, specifications relating to the readers and users as well as to the purpose of the translation should be made explicit whenever possible: that is, requesters and providers should negotiate requirements and discuss the end-users' needs upfront, and state them as specifications before the translation process even begins. This broad view is predicated on the assumption that there cannot be absolute specifications that are applicable once and for all to translation projects in general, and is reminiscent especially of the tenets of Skopos theory (Reiss and Vermeer 1984) and, more in general, of functionalist approaches to translation (e.g. Kussmaul 1995; Nord 1997), discussed in Sect. 2.1. In contrast, Koby et al.'s (2014) narrow definition categorises translation as text-centric, that is, activities such as summarisation, localisation, etc., are not considered to be translation. This narrow view suggests that explicit specifications are often unnecessary, because requesters and end-users do not always know what specifications a project requires, thus proposing a radically different view from that adopted in their broad definition. Interestingly, one key point on which there is agreement is that a method for measuring translation quality "should emphasise identifying problems that can be corrected" and that "any effort to measure translation quality is doomed to confusion without an explicit definition of translation quality" (Koby et al. 2014).

The Translation Automation User Society (TAUS) is a translation industry think-tank that has been attempting to develop and benchmark indicators of effective TQA for a few years, involving major stakeholders in the industry. In a 2011 report (O'Brien et al. 2011), TAUS considers a range of variables such as communicative function, end-user requirements, context, mode of translation (HT, raw MT output, and post-edited MT), as well as content profiling and quality estimation (see Specia and Shah, this volume) as precursors to TQA. One of the noteworthy points of the Dynamic Quality Framework (DQF) developed by TAUS (O'Brien et al. 2011) is that rather than dealing with problems after the translation process, quality issues should be considered before the actual translation process begins (for subsequent efforts to integrate the DQF within a broader translation quality metric, see Lommel, this volume). Work in the same area has also been conducted by QTLaunchPad, an EU-funded collaborative research project which aimed at standardising TQA, by identifying quality barriers in translation and language technologies and preparing steps for overcoming them (Doherty et al. 2013). This initiative has then developed into QT21, a large-scale initiative focusing on the identification of quality barriers in MT and systematic improvements to address them.[4]

One of the major outcomes of QTLaunchPad was the Multidimensional Quality Metrics (MQM) framework, which creates a shared quality metric for both HT and MT quality evaluation, based on the identification of textual features and specific types of issues that can be selected by the users, depending on the project they are working on, their priorities in the evaluation, etc. It should be noted that the MQM

---

[4]http://www.qt21.eu/

can be applicable to professional translations as well as to MT output, i.e. the metric is designed to evaluate the translation product, regardless of how the target text is generated. Interestingly, even though the MQM incorporates many principles from the LISA QA Model, it was developed to address the widely recognised limitations in previous quality evaluation models adopted in the translation industry, providing the flexibility to accommodate other standards. The DQF and the MQM are the most recent large-scale initiatives attempting to standardise TQA, bringing together approaches that originally developed independently in research and in the industry, and their integration is described in detail by Lommel (this volume).

In sum, as this overview shows, several efforts have been made to achieve effective quality evaluation models that combine, and to some extent reconcile, different views of translation quality, including, crucially, the expectations of end-users. This is a widely felt need in the translation and localisation industry, and we commend such worthwhile attempts to provide reliable TQA methodologies that promote quality. As such, we agree with Koby et al. (2014), who argue that translation studies and the translation industry "need a way to compare different sorts of translation as objectively as possible, with an emphasis on identifying problems", and the metrics adopted to this end should be "built on a well-defined foundation including at least clearly stated definitions of translation, quality, and translation quality" (ibid.). The rest of this chapter and indeed the entire volume attempt to disentangle and shed further light on these crucial issues from multiple perspectives, which should be of benefit both to the translation industry and to the research and academic community, including in particular translator trainers (the chapter by Doherty et al. in this volume, in particular, is devoted to teaching-oriented and pedagogic issues in the area of TQA).

3 TQA Performed by Humans

A range of measures exist for TQA performed by humans in research and in industry. In these scenarios, TQA is most commonly carried out looking at adequacy and fluency, although secondary measures can also be employed to assess the readability, comprehensibility, usability and acceptability of translations, especially MT output (see also Way, this volume), including with comparative approaches based on ranking of multiple renditions of the same input (not necessarily an entire text, as it is quite customary to evaluate individual segments or sentences in this way). Such TQA is carried out by evaluators in a range of scenarios, where performance-based measures and user-centred approaches are more recent additions. The rest of this section discusses in turn the main approaches to TQA performed by humans especially to evaluate MT output, highlighting their main strengths and weaknesses; finally, Sect. 3.6 considers the key issues concerning the evaluators who perform these various types of human TQA.

3.1   Adequacy and Fluency

Adequacy (also called accuracy or fidelity in certain studies devoted to MT evaluation, MTE) is a well-established TQA measure for MT output (Koehn 2009: 218ff), and is typically defined as the extent to which the translation transfers the meaning of the source-language unit into the target. Adequacy judgements are often used alongside those concerning fluency, which instead focuses on the target text and is typically defined as the extent to which the translation follows the rules and norms of the target-language (regardless of the source or input text). Arnold et al. (1994) note that fluency (using the term intelligibility, which may have other specific meanings in other contexts) is "affected by grammatical errors, mistranslations and untranslated words", a view that Reeder (2004) substantiates in experimental conditions which identified predictors as incorrect pronouns, inconsistent prepositions, and incorrect punctuation.

Adequacy and fluency are typically assessed using ordinal scales in the form of Likert scales (see Fig. 1). This assessment is normally conducted at sentence (or segment) level, without considering extended context, to evaluate MT output. The assessment of adequacy requires some degree of bilingual proficiency, while – at least in principle – fluency requires only proficiency in the target-language; both professional and amateur evaluators can be employed in TQA tasks adopting this double integrated approach (see Sect. 3.6 for a more detailed discussion of the key issues concerning evaluators).

3.2   Readability and Comprehensibility

The study of readability is well established, with relevant measures being refined for over a century, e.g. to define the features of linguistic complexity of a text in a particular language that make it suitable for intended readers of a certain age and/or level of formal education. Broadly, readability relates to the ease with which a given text can be read by one or more person(s). Many different measures of readability exist, and they are typically based on linguistic features such as word frequency and sentence length, in addition to extra-linguistic features such as formatting and spacing. Several of these measures have stood the test of time and remain popular today, including Flesch-Kincaid (Flesch 1948; Kincaid et al. 1975)

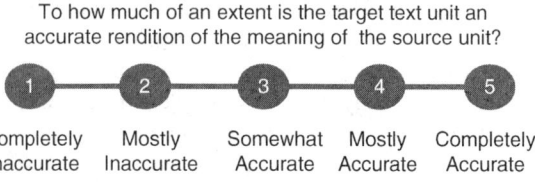

To how much of an extent is the target text unit an
accurate rendition of the meaning of the source unit?

1 — 2 — 3 — 4 — 5

Completely   Mostly   Somewhat   Mostly   Completely
Inaccurate   Inaccurate   Accurate   Accurate   Accurate

Fig. 1   An example of an operationalised measure of adequacy from a TQA task in an MT research project

and Dale-Chall (1948). A similar approach to the measurement of readability has also been applied to interlingual readability measures, e.g. LIX (Björnsson 1971). These measures, also known as readability metrics or indices, are available from within word processing software and online, and have also been integrated into MT systems with reports of relative success (e.g. Stymne et al. 2013).

In the context of TQA, measures of readability are typically used to assess the complexity of the source or target text, where the latter is the most common usage scenario. TQA using readability measures can rely on these measures with or without end-user ratings of the readability of a translation. Typical examples of this can be found in MTE (e.g. Doherty 2012) and community translation (Karwacka 2014) contexts.

Following Van Slype (1979), comprehensibility represents an attribute of the (source or target) text which indicates how understandable it is for a reader. In other words, while readability as described above is inherently dependent on the text itself, comprehensibility can vary depending on the specific reader of the text (e.g. their degree of education and familiarity with reading certain kinds of texts).

Doherty (2012) identifies an inconsistency in the literature, whereby comprehensibility and readability are either grouped together, where one is subsumed by the other, or where both concepts and their measurements are separate. Smith and Taffler (1992) find that "comprehensibility can be different to readability and the latter might frequently be used erroneously as a proxy for the former". Harrison (1980), for example, reiterates that readability is a characteristic of the text, while comprehensibility depends on the reader. On the other hand, Jones (1988) argues that comprehensibility is reflected in readability as the former is not possible without the latter. Finally, Van Slype (1979) holds that comprehensibility and intelligibility are actually synonymous and refer to the "ease with which a translation can be understood, its clarity to the reader".

When intended as a discrete concept, comprehensibility can be measured in the source text and in the target text. Much like readability, we typically see comprehensibility being applied to the target text in TQA scenarios, especially when evaluating MT output. As there are no unified prescriptive measures of comprehensibility, TQA applications using this measure rely on Likert scales (similarly to what happens with adequacy and fluency, as discussed in Sect. 3.1) and cloze testing (or gap-filling, which is used extensively in foreign language learning and testing; for an application of the cloze procedure to MTE, see Somers and Wild 2000). Another technique that can be utilised to specifically assess comprehensibility is recall testing, which derives from cognitive psychology and is related to how much of (the information given in) a text the experimental subjects can remember. Recall testing can be conducted in various ways, depending on the constraints that are applied in the experimental set-up and on the type of interaction with the evaluators (i.e. free recall, cued recall and recognition tasks).[5]

---

[5]The notion of 'recall' intended here is borrowed from cognitive psychology, and it should not be confused with the concept of 'recall' (as opposed to 'precision') more commonly used to assess

3.3 Acceptability

The term 'acceptability' has been used in various fields including linguistics, translation, and human-computer interaction (HCI), and so different definitions have been assigned to the term. In the context of TQA, it refers to the degree to which the target or output text meets the needs and expectations of its reader(s) or user(s). Chomsky (1969) views acceptability as a matter of degree(s) that can be specified through various operational tests. Applied to translation, De Beaugrande and Dressler (1981) state that acceptability concerns "the text receiver's attitude that the set of occurrences should constitute a cohesive and coherent text having some use or relevance for the receiver, e.g. to acquire knowledge or provide co-operation in a plan", and such attitudes of the text users "involve some tolerance toward disturbances of cohesion or coherence, as long as the purposeful nature of the communication is upheld" (ibid.) – a notion that is reminiscent of the functionalist approaches in translation theory reviewed in Sect. 2.1.

With specific reference to MT, Van Slype (1979) defines acceptability, somewhat tautologically, as "a subjective assessment of the extent to which a translation is acceptable to its final user" that "can be effectively measured only by a survey of final users" (ibid.), although the author does not specify the type of survey questions to be put to the user. Several studies attempted to measure the acceptability of MT, drawing on Van Slype's definition, including Coughlin (2003), Lassen (2003) and Roturier (2006). For Roturier (2006), "acceptability does not only refer to the relevance a text has for its receiver, but also to the manner in which its textual characteristics are going to be accepted, tolerated, or rejected by its receivers", and, therefore, "users will find machine-translated documentation acceptable when they tolerate some of the textual disturbances caused by an MT process". The author concludes that it is "essential that the evaluation of documents is performed by genuine users of such documents to maximise the ecological validity of the study" (ibid.); while we concur that this is desirable in principle, particularly in research settings it is often impractical to conduct extensive acceptability tests with the real intended users of MT output, and for example students or evaluators from crowdsourcing platforms are involved as feasible alternatives (see Sect. 3.6 for a more detailed discussion of evaluators).

Acceptability is also a relevant concept in HCI. For Nielsen (1993), system acceptability "is the question of whether the system is good enough to satisfy all the needs and requirements of the users and other potential stakeholders, such as the users' clients and managers". In his model of system acceptability, Nielsen considers usability to be a narrow concern of the system acceptability model. Castilho (2016) measures the acceptability of machine-translated instructional

---

natural language processing tasks and, in particular, the performance of MT systems, e.g. with automatic evaluation metrics, which are discussed in more detail in Sect. 4 (for an introduction to the role of precision and recall in automatic MTE metrics, see Koehn 2009: 222).

content using the concept of acceptability, following Nielsen (1993), De Beaugrande and Dressler (1981), as well as Roturier (2006). In this view, acceptability is composed of various categories, and is measured via usability, satisfaction and quality. Castilho (2016) states that users will find a translation to be more acceptable if they are able to use it to perform tasks, regardless of any flaws it may contain, or "they will find the text less acceptable if the flaws in the translation affect their ability to use the text to some extent".

3.4 Ranking

Ranking is typically used in research contexts and to comparatively evaluate output from different MT systems originating from the same source text. In such scenarios, evaluators are asked to rank the given sentences in the target-language against given criteria or general concepts, e.g. fluency. As shown in Fig. 2, a source-text unit is provided and two or more MT outputs are listed anonymously, normally in an unpredictable, randomly scrambled order. The evaluators then either pick the single best translation in their opinion, or put the target-language options in order from best to worst, according to some specific criteria. This approach to TQA, which has the advantage of providing easy-to-interpret outcomes while being relatively fast and efficient, is popular in large-scale MTE campaigns such as the well-established shared tasks conducted within the Workshop in Machine Translation (WMT) series.[6]

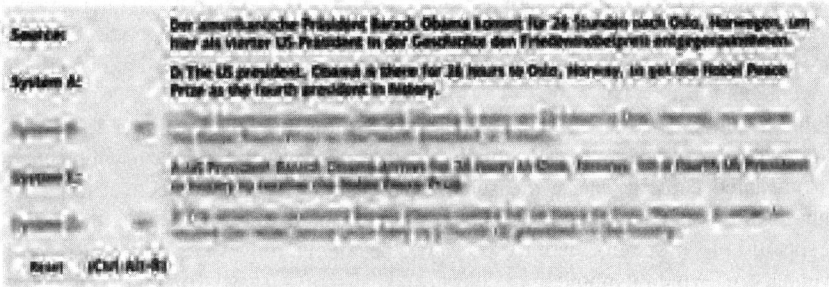

Fig. 2 An example of a ranking task in Appraise (Federmann 2012)

---

[6]See http://www.statmt.org/

3.5 Usability and Performance

The usability of translated content is rarely considered from a TQA perspective.[7] While it is often the case that the usability of products and services containing translated or localised content is assessed and tested with real users, e.g. for software and web-based applications, few studies have measured the usability of translated content in isolation (cf. Byrne 2006). In terms of overall usability of products and services, Sacher et al. (2001) identify the macro-level of language and culture as being of importance, rather than focusing on a 'translation problem'. Similarly, Proctor et al. (2002) identify translation as being one aspect of usability and state that translated content "should not lose its meaning through translation", but unfortunately further details to this are not provided.

Studies such as Roturier (2006), Stymne et al. (2012), Doherty and O'Brien (2014), Castilho et al. (2014), Klerke et al. (2015), and Castilho and O'Brien (2016) have specifically investigated the usability or usefulness of MT output, and measures of efficiency, accuracy, and user satisfaction are typically used in assessing the usability of natural language processing applications more generally (e.g. Dybkjær et al. 2004). In addition to such an approach, Gaspari (2004) evaluates the expectations and success rates of users when they use popular free online MT systems for the first time, examining the extent to which such web-based systems enable users to learn how to use them effectively.

Doherty and O'Brien (2014) identify an inconsistency in terminology and operationalisation in usability studies and call for the adoption of international standards, in this case, the ISO/TR 16982, which defines usability as "the extent to which a product can be used by specified users to achieve specified goals with effectiveness, efficiency, and satisfaction in a specified context of use" (International Organization for Standardisation 2002). Here, again, the emphasis is placed on the product in a generic sense, rather than specific aspects of its contents, e.g. technical documentation.

In a similar vein, performance-based measures are also employed in TQA contexts to assess how users actually use the product or service in which there is translated content. These measures can be objective and subjective: objective measures typically measure time (e.g. time spent on a webpage or window to find a specific piece of information), browsing behaviour (e.g. visits and revisits to a webpage or window, number of 'likes' and 'shares' on social media); subjective measures ask users for their opinions on the content, e.g. checking whether the

---

[7]The notion of 'usability' discussed here is different from that of 'adequacy' covered in Sect. 3.1, as it involves aspects of practical operational validity and effectiveness of the translated content, e.g. whether a set of translated instructions enable a user to correctly operate a device to perform a specific function or achieve a particular objective (say, update the contact list in a mobile phone, adding a new item).

webpage was what the user was actually looking for, getting the user to rate their level of satisfaction, asking the user whether they would recommend the content to friends or colleagues.

These performance-based measures focus on the users of the final product or service and involve collecting real usage data. This approach is more feasible and common in the localisation industry, especially for video games, software, websites and online services, and provides an indirect method for TQA under the assumption that negative results indicate errors or unsatisfactory quality, while positive results indicate high quality.

3.6   Evaluators

By way of conclusion of this discussion of the main approaches to TQA performed by humans, including the respective pros and cons, this final section examines some key issues concerning the evaluators themselves. TQA can involve both professional and amateur evaluators, depending on the scenario: while, intuitively, professionals can be assumed to provide more reliable results, amateurs may be equally helpful in some TQA tasks; professional translators and linguists are more frequently involved in TQA in the industry (cf. Sect. 2.2), but recent approaches that incorporate crowdsourcing techniques have included amateur evaluators (for a comprehensive discussion of this new phenomenon, see Jiménez-Crespo, this volume). In MT research contexts, in particular, professional evaluators tend to be the exception, rather than the rule: resource constraints may make it difficult for researchers to access trained professional evaluators. There is therefore a tendency to rely on students and amateur evaluators, sometimes with an undefined (or self-rated) proficiency in the languages involved, an unknown expertise with the text type and requirements of the TQA task at hand, and no formal or extended training in the use of TQA measures or error typologies employed in the task (Doherty 2017).

TQA tasks may be conducted individually, in groups, and in crowds. On an individual level, the evaluator typically assesses HT or MT against the given criteria and provides the results. Group-based TQA involves several evaluators conducting the assessment in this way and the averaging of their scores, to moderate strong positive or negative personal biases. On a larger scale, groups of amateur evaluators take part in crowdsourced TQA evaluation campaigns for research and industry-related purposes. The reason why group-based and crowd-based TQA mostly involves (often volunteer) amateurs is that the quantity of evaluators is supposed to, at least partially, make up for their lower level of expertise when eliciting judgements on quality; in contrast, it is very unusual to engage groups of professionals or experts (e.g. senior translators or trained linguists) to assess the same translation or MT output, also because it would be very expensive. Unfortunately, very few studies actually provide the specifications of human TQA tasks and it appears from the data available that professional or trained evaluators are the exception in MTE tasks, rather than the rule (e.g. Doherty 2017).

One approach that is worth mentioning is user-centred translation (UCT, Suo-janen et al. 2015), in which users have a central role to play in the production and evaluation of the translation. UCT examines usability research approaches from the perspective of translation in order to develop a model in which the end-user is considered consistently throughout the translation process (cf. Sect. 3.5). Suojanen et al. (2015) argue that traditional TQA practices suffer from 'end-of-the-line' problems, that is, TQA mostly "focusses on measuring the end product" in which "any changes can be costly both financially and in terms of missed deadlines". They also claim that UCT can be an alternative basis for evaluation as it "concentrates on imagining what kind of a process will produce a variety of successful translations to serve the needs of different commissions" (ibid.). Errors, especially translation mistakes in comparison to the source text, are evaluated according to their relevance in terms of functionality and usability. Although UCT's position for offering the model is academic, the model is also claimed to be a framework for TQA in the translation industry as due to the competitive market situation, companies have to become more flexible and innovative and the user-centred approach allows translation companies to create "new value for customers" and redefine "the products and services offered" (ibid.).

4 Automated TQA

The need to assess MT systems via their output has existed since the early days of MT, and it is no surprise that MTE has been studied extensively. It has even been famously claimed by Wilks (1994) that "MT evaluation is, for all its faults, probably in better shape than MT itself". One would be forgiven for thinking that this statement appears much harsher, and less accurate in its paradoxical nature, today than it did when it was first put forward. MT has certainly made significant strides since the mid-1990s, and MTE methodologies have substantially improved in parallel. In spite of this general progress, however, MT quality can be assessed in a wide range of different ways and no single approach or metric is sufficient to address all evaluation purposes and scenarios (Hovy et al. 2002).

Several researchers have worked on the problem of measuring translation quality for MT. The Defense Advanced Research Projects Agency (DARPA) MTE project represented one of the earliest formalised efforts in this area in the 1990s. The DARPA MT initiative lasted 4 years and aimed at developing new approaches and methodologies for evaluating MT systems (White et al. 1994). Another notable past effort aimed at tackling MTE issues was the Framework for the Evaluation of MT (FEMTI), that aimed at drawing an overall perspective of all the MTE metrics according to the evaluation purpose; the ultimate goal of FEMTI was to "build a coherent picture of the various features and metrics that have been used in the past, to offer a common descriptive framework and vocabulary, and to unify the process of evaluation design" (Hovy et al. 2002). More recently, the WMT events, held annually since 2006, have included extensive manual and automatic evaluations of commercial and experimental MT systems (Callison-Burch et al. 2007).

One initial, and rather basic, distinction that can be useful to explore the MTE space is that MT quality can be assessed manually or automatically. On the one hand, automatic evaluation is generally recognised as being objective and cheap, although it has been claimed that it is less comprehensive than manual evaluation and does not readily indicate the type of problems that the translated text contains (Uszkoreit and Lommel 2013). On the other hand, manual evaluation is often claimed to be subjective and can be slow as well as expensive to perform (Bojar et al. 2011; Callison-Burch et al. 2011), and inter-annotator agreement can be an issue, when evaluations are performed involving multiple judges, which is clearly desirable in principle; however, manual approaches have the benefit of being useful to assess complex linguistic phenomena, going beyond mere adequacy and fluency (described in more detail in Sect. 3.1), but focusing also, for example, on error types (see Popović in this volume for an overview of error typologies for MTE), provided that the evaluators have a good grounding in translation and linguistics. Manual approaches also vary with regard to the skills of the evaluators: while, for example, grammaticality and fluency can be evaluated by looking only at the target text (hence requiring, at least potentially, thorough familiarity exclusively with the target-language), judgements of accuracy and adequacy assume bilingual competence (see Sect. 3.6). All these factors can have an impact on the cost, length and overall complexity of human MTE.

In light of these apparent shortcomings, automatic MTE metrics may offer a valuable alternative. Automatic MTE is a thriving research area at present, with many scholars working on evaluating and improving the relevant automatic metrics as well as proposing new ones. The main purpose of state-of-the-art automatic evaluation metrics is to compare the output of an MT system (the so-called translation hypothesis) to one or several reference translations, which are assumed to be good, because they are human quality. Therefore, essentially automatic MTE metrics try to measure how close the output of a given MT system is to the reference translation(s), computing a score to quantify this similarity (Koehn 2010).

The first automatic metrics used in MTE came from the field of automatic speech recognition, as was the case for Word Error Rate (WER) used by Nießen et al. (2000); this error rate computes the insertions, deletions and substitutions required for the MT output to match the reference translation, normalised by the length of the reference translation. Other automatic evaluation metrics such as Translation Error Rate (TER, Snover et al. 2006) and the variant Human-targeted TER (HTER), have also become relatively popular. Bilingual Evaluation Understudy (BLEU, Papineni et al. 2002) has gained substantial popularity by showing good correlation with human judgement, and it eventually became the official metric of the MTE campaigns of the National Institute of Standards and Technology (NIST, Doddington 2002).

Other common automatic metrics that are also based on error counting viz. (multiple, when available) reference human translations include General Text

Matcher (GTM, Turian et al. 2003) and METEOR (Lavie and Agarwal 2007). Although several new metrics have been developed and individual researchers use different ones, BLEU is the de facto standard for most research purposes, in a prevailing position compared to METEOR and TER. An interesting, and more recent, automatic MTE metric is CHRF (Popović 2015), which is based on the use of character n-gram F-score: this metric has been shown to offer a number of advantages, as it takes into account some morpho-syntactic phenomena while being language-independent and tokenisation-independent; crucially, it also shows good correlations with human judgments both on the system- and on the segment-level. In addition, comparisons of the different metrics have found that new-generation metrics can outperform BLEU in terms of correlation with human judgements (Callison-Burch et al. 2009), which is the case for ULC (Giménez and Màrquez 2008), MaxSim (Chan and Ng 2008) and RTE (Padó et al. 2009) when translating into English; and for TERp (Snover et al. 2006) and wpBleu (Popović and Ney 2009) when translating into other languages. These results demonstrate that the debate on the best approaches and automatic metrics for evaluating MT quality is far from settled.

One of the main arguments for using automatic metrics is that they have the advantage of requiring minimal human labour, therefore supposedly being more objective. As opposed to human assessments, they circumvent the need for (bilingual) evaluators to assess the translation, which tends to make the assessment much more cost-effective, possibly however with the risk of losing granularity. It is important to note that translators are needed in order to create the reference translation(s) used in the process; this in itself introduces a more subtle element of subjectivity and variability. In addition, the gold standard quality of the human reference is assumed, but often not verified. And, crucially, the quality of the MT output is judged on the basis of how closely it resembles the specific reference translation(s), while even a basic understanding and experience of translation suggest that for a given source text or input sentence there can be multiple good, or equally valid, renditions into one target-language. Hence, one can claim that automatic MTE metrics provide scores that appear to be objective and reliable, but the way in which they work is based on a number of assumptions that can raise some concerns as to their actual value (see Way in this volume).

Automatic MTE also provides rapid feedback and is often used on an ongoing basis throughout development to test changes in a given MT system and gather valuable indications as to how its performance could be improved. However, another problem with automatic metrics is that at present their ability to assess syntactic and semantic equivalence in MT output is severely limited, since they lack linguistic analysis and understanding, and face just as many challenges as MT itself. Although METEOR allows for non-exact matches such as synonyms and paraphrases, the processing of complex and subtle levels of syntactic, semantic and pragmatic equivalence between any source and target-languages remains a serious challenge for automatic MT quality metrics. To overcome this limitation, a number of automatic metrics exploiting deeper linguistic analysis have been proposed, e.g.

Owczarzak et al. (2007), Giménez and Màrquez (2008), Padó et al. (2009), Liu et al. (2011). Crucially, however, as is the case for METEOR, even when evaluation metrics can incorporate such rich linguistic knowledge, this increased possibility to analyse and factor in linguistic variation relies on rather sophisticated technologies, resources and language processing tools, which are available only for a limited, although admittedly increasing, number of well-supported languages (see Rehm and Uszkoreit 2012).

Finally, automatic metrics have been recently proposed that evaluate MT at the document level, rather than at the sentence/segment level, which could lead to a more precise way of measuring the coherence of an automatically translated text. These include, for example, Giménez et al. (2010), who propose to use coreference and discourse relations in MT metrics, Wong and Kit (2012), who apply lexical cohesion to existing sentence-level evaluation metrics, and Guzmán et al. (2014), who incorporate discourse structures to complement existing automatic MTE metrics.

5 TQA in Integrated HT-MT Workflows

In providing this inventory of contemporary TQA techniques and metrics, we argue that the boundary between HT and MT has become increasingly blurred in recent years, largely due to the development of CAT tools and technologised workflows (see O'Hagan 2012; Doherty 2016). In the context of TQA, it consequently becomes more difficult to identify the agent of a translation, and even if a human agent is identified, unless we are operating in a research environment where independent variables can be controlled and manipulated, it is typically unknown to what extent MT or other translation technologies and tools have been involved in the process. We therefore suggest here that the traditional separation of human and machine is no longer valid, and drawing an arbitrary line between HT and MT no longer serves us in research, teaching and professional practice. With this in mind, we now focus on TQA in the context of integrated HT-MT workflows, which are now commonplace in the translation industry and will continue to develop as translation technologies become more sophisticated, especially in the area of PE.

PE consists in the practice of modifying raw MT output so that a specific quality level is achieved. There are generally two distinct main types of PE: so-called 'light PE' and 'full PE' (Allen 2003). Light PE has a quick turn-around and only essential errors are corrected, which makes it more appropriate for short-lived translated texts for internal circulation; in contrast, full PE requires more corrections for a higher quality, with a slower turn-around, and is typically employed to disseminate high-visibility or sensitive texts (O'Brien et al. 2009) – the aim of PE is to achieve publishable quality for the final revised MT output. Quite clearly, a large number of options are possible between these two extremes, depending on the circumstances in which the translation is needed and the resources that are available in given specific situations.

In seminal work in this area, Krings (2001) divided PE effort into three categories: temporal, technical, and cognitive, where temporal effort is the time spent doing PE, technical effort is the number of edits made by the post-editor, and cognitive effort is measured using eye-tracking, keyboard logging, pause-to-word ratios, or other similar methods. Many subsequent studies have built upon Krings' ground-breaking work and, in recent years, the task and process of PE have received significant attention (e.g. De Almeida and O'Brien 2010; Depraetere 2010; Plitt and Masselot 2010; Sousa et al. 2011; Specia 2011; Koponen 2012; O'Brien et al. 2012, 2013, 2014; Guerberof 2014; Lacruz and Shreve 2014; Carl et al. 2015; Daems et al. 2015; Moorkens et al. 2015), particularly as MT systems gain space in the translation and localisation industry. Although it is possible to say that there have been great advances in MT, PE of MT output is still the norm for achieving publication quality.

Several approaches have been attempted to understand the level of cognitive effort involved in PE, while clarifying what the effort indicators are and what they can be used for. Snover et al. (2006) have measured PE effort in terms of an edit distance, that is, the amount of edit operations (e.g. insertions, deletions, substitutions, shifts, etc.) that transform the raw MT output into its post-edited version. Tatsumi (2009) and O'Brien (2011) attempt to determine if automatic metrics correlate with human judgements. Results from both studies suggest that even though there is some correlation between PE effort and automatic metrics, it is not a linear one. Sousa et al. (2011) compare the time spent on PE with (i) subjective assessments of effort and quality, and (ii) the scores of automatic MTE metrics such as BLEU, METEOR and HTER. The results show that sentences requiring less PE time to achieve optimal (i.e. publishable) quality are more often tagged by humans as demanding low effort. In addition, PE time has shown positive correlation with BLEU, METEOR and HTER scores, that is, sentences that required less time to be post-edited scored better for those metrics.

Specia (2011) uses PE effort classified in terms of time, subjective scores and PE distance to predict the quality of an MT system. Results show that using those effort indicators to train the confidence estimation models produces rankings of translations that reliably reflect their required PE effort. Daems et al. (2015) examine the impact of different types of MT errors on PE effort indicators from English into Dutch with the help of an eye-tracker device. Their results show that average MT error weights are good predictors of six different PE effort indicators, i.e. average number of production units, average duration per word, average fixation duration, average number of fixations, pause ratio, and average pause ratio.[8]

---

[8]In Daems et al. (2015), the average number of production units refers to the number of production units of a segment divided by the number of source text words in that segment. The average time per word indicates the total time spent editing a segment, divided by the number of source text words in that segment. The average fixation duration is based on the total fixation duration (in milliseconds) of a segment divided by the number of fixations within that segment. The average number of fixations results from the number of fixations in a segment divided by the number of source text words in that segment. The pause ratio is given by the total time in pauses (in milliseconds) for a

An important evaluation-oriented use of PE consists of the collection of information that can help to measure MT quality and diagnose translation problems. Several tools have been developed in order to capture this information, such as Post-Editing Tool (PET, Aziz et al. 2012), Translog-II (Carl 2012), Cognitive Analysis and Statistical Methods for Advanced Computer Aided Translation (CASMACAT, Alabau et al. 2013), and iOmegaT (Moran et al. 2014). One of the major concerns in the translation industry is how to quantify the amount of effort that is necessary for MT PE, based on the initial quality of the raw output, in relation to the final needs and expectations of the end-users. The purpose of this is to pre-determine whether MT output PE would be time- and cost-effective when compared to translating the text from scratch, which in turn would guide pricing decisions, while also optimising the turnaround time; these are all crucial factors to be competitive in an increasingly pressurised translation market, in which budget-conscious clients regularly ask translators to meet tight deadlines, but are hardly ever prepared to compromise on the final quality of the translation product they receive. The possibility of reliably assessing the expected PE effort has become indispensable, given that it enables LSPs to optimise their translation processes.

6 Discussion

In this chapter we have provided a broad overview of the established and developing approaches to TQA across HT and MT workflows. Our discussion of contemporary approaches and methods has covered TQA performed by both humans and automatic metrics, considering research and educational contexts as well as typical scenarios in the translation and localisation industry. In addition to pointing out differences and similarities across these different sectors, we have also examined the strengths and weaknesses of the various techniques and metrics under review. This enables us to articulate several fundamental issues that remain to be addressed in research, education, and professional practice in this concluding discussion. In this spirit, the remaining part of this overview summarises these key issues, grouping them into four main areas; this serves as a prelude to the subsequent chapters of the volume, which will expand on the main issues that have been introduced in this opening overview.

---

segment divided by the total editing time (in milliseconds) for that segment and, finally, the average pause ratio is the average time per pause in a segment divided by the average time per word in a segment.

6.1   Lack of Standardisation in TQA Usage

First and foremost, the investigation presented in this chapter shows there is a serious lack of standardisation in TQA for both HT and MT. While specific sectors of the industry have developed their own standardised measures of TQA, these remain isolated cases and tend to focus on overall products and services, rather than on the translated content itself. Further issues can be found in the lack of internal standardisation in terms of designing, conducting, and reporting on TQA tasks.

Drawing from industry data, Ray et al. (2013) argue that "buyers and suppliers often disagree on what translation quality means" as there is a significant lack of agreement on the definition and measurement of TQA, which inevitably leads to internal and external issues of mismatched expectations and even conflict. They highlight the problem of there being "no generally accepted standards" in TQA, where "quality expectations tend to follow prices up but not down" (ibid.). The same issues persist in research involving TQA, notably in the recruitment of inappropriate evaluators, the lack of transparency and reporting on TQA specifications and procedures, and the reliance on one measure over a holistic approach that is less prone to the issues inherent in any one human or machine TQA measure.

6.2   Inherent Inconsistency in TQA

Related to the first point, a lack of standardisation at the macro and micro level of TQA has yielded great inconsistency in human TQA procedures most especially. DePalma and Kelly (2009), perhaps somewhat simplistically, describe TQA in the industry as "boiling down to the opinion of one person over that of another" with "too much time in arbitration mode". Although there will always be some degree of variance in human judgement, White et al. (1994) attest that "evaluation must exploit intuitive judgments while constraining subjectivity in ways that minimise idiosyncratic sources of variance in the measurement". In an effort to address this issue, Doherty (2017) proposes a set of guidelines to improve the validity, reliability, and consistency of TQA, with a focus on the adoption of psychometric principles from the psychological and cognitive sciences, also suggesting an investment in evaluator training and materials.

6.3   The Relationship Between Human and Automatic Measures

Given the above issues in standardisation and consistency, it is unsurprising that there is considerable variation in the correlations between human and machine TQA (see, e.g. Labaka et al. 2014; Doherty 2017). Results from any TQA measure may vary considerably depending on the specifications and context and should therefore be interpreted with care. Popular automatic metrics such as BLEU have occasionally been shown not to correlate well with other TQA measures (see, for example, Callison-Burch et al. 2006), yet continue to be widely used due to their relative ease and low cost, especially when compared to human TQA, as explained in Sect. 4. It is easy to see that inconsistencies and lack of correlation with human judgements may be dependent, at least to some extent, on the language pairs and on the text types involved in the specific evaluation tasks. Indeed, recent reviews hold that it is still "often the case that the results of manual and automatic evaluations do not agree" (Labaka et al. 2014). Far from calling into question the importance and usefulness of TQA, this observation should encourage us to pursue more advanced and refined procedures that minimise these shortcomings.

6.4 Social Quality and Risk

Changes in work practices due to rationalisation and cost-cutting have seen a widespread move towards the vendor model and contingent work in the translation industry (Abdallah 2012; Kushner 2013; Moorkens 2017). Drugan et al. (in this volume) note that this move to outsourcing is occurring in the Directorate-General for Translation (DGT), and consider the social, ethical, and qualitative implications. This social aspect of translation necessarily affects the process and product of translation, and, according to Abdallah (2012), should be considered in a three-dimensional quality model with process and product quality. Abdallah (ibid.) argues that "quality is a multidimensional concept which also includes ethical issues", as it would in any chain of production. While we focus (in this chapter and in this book) on the product of translation, TQA in practice necessitates consideration of the social.

Also outside of the scope of this chapter is consideration of risk. Any TQA method aims to minimise risk, whether this is a risk to communication, to reputation, or a risk of injury or death. Inherent in the notion of acceptability or 'good enough' translation is a permitted level of acceptable risk. A high-level consideration of TQA requires evaluation of risks, assignment of responsibility, and risk management. This is considered for crowdsourcing by Jimenéz-Crespo in this volume, and elsewhere by Pym (2015) and Canfora and Ottmann (2016).

6.5 Education and Training

Finally, we argue that education and training in TQA underpin all of the above issues and represent effective solutions, even if admittedly in the long term. This includes not only the provision of accessible education and training for suppliers and buyers of language services, but also for amateur translators and evaluators, public users of translation services, and the relevant policy makers.

Such education and training should focus on providing knowledge of the strengths and limitations of human and machine TQA measures, thus enabling all stakeholders in the TQA process to critically choose and assess the appropriateness of TQA in a given context. Some of these issues are revisited in more detail in the chapter by Doherty et al. in this volume in a specific teaching-oriented perspective. Lastly, with regard to those conducting TQA, researchers and practitioners need to be educated in transparent design and reporting of their TQA specifications and results.

In closing, we are confident that by combining multiple perspectives and covering a wide range of topics, the chapters in this volume provide a significant step forward in addressing these issues and consolidate our current knowledge and practice across the length and breadth of TQA in research, industry and education.

Acknowledgments This work has been partly supported by the ADAPT Centre for Digital Content Technology which is funded under the SFI Research Centres Programme (Grant 13/RC/2106) and is co-funded under the European Regional Development Fund.

References

Abdallah K (2012) Translators in production networks. Reflections on Agency, Quality and Ethics. Dissertation, University of Eastern Finland

Adab B (2005) Translating into a second language: can we, should we? In: Anderman G, Rogers M (eds) In and out of English for better, for worse? Multilingual Matters, Clevedon, pp 227–241

Alabau V, Bonk R, Buck C, Carl M, Casacuberta F, García-Martínez M, González J, Koehn P, Leiva L, Mesa-Lao B, Ortiz D, Saint-Amand H, Sanchis G, Tsoukala C (2013) CASMACAT: an open source workbench for advanced computer aided translation. Prague Bull Math Linguist 100(1):101–112

Allen J (2003) Post-editing. In: Somers H (ed) Computers and translation: a translator's guide. John Benjamins, Amsterdam, pp 297–317

Arnold D, Balkan L, Meijer S, Lee Humphreys R, Sadler L (1994) Machine translation: an introductory guide. Blackwell, Manchester

Aziz W, Sousa SCM, Specia L (2012) PET: a tool for post-editing and assessing machine translation. In: Calzolari N, Choukri K, Declerck T, Doğan MU, Maegaard B, Mariani J, Moreno A, Odijk J, Piperidis S (eds) Proceedings of the eighth international conference on language resources and evaluation, Istanbul, pp 3982–3987

Baker M (1992) In other words: a coursebook on translation. Routledge, London

Björnsson CH (1971) Læsbarhed. København, Gad

Bojar O, Ercegovčević M, Popel M, Zaidan OF (2011) A grain of salt for the WMT manual evaluation. In: Proceedings of the 6th workshop on Statistical Machine Translation, Edinburgh, 30–31 July 2011, pp 1–11

Byrne J (2006) Technical translation: usability strategies for translating technical documentation. Springer, Heidelberg

Callison-Burch C, Osborne M, Koehn P (2006) Re-evaluating the role of BLEU in machine translation research. In: Proceedings of 11th conference of the European chapter of the association for computational linguistics 2006, Trento, 3–7 April, pp 249–256

Callison-Burch C, Fordyce C, Koehn P, Monz C, Schroeder J (2007) (Meta-)evaluation of machine translation. In: Proceedings of the second workshop on Statistical Machine Translation, Prague, pp 136–158

Callison-Burch C, Koehn P, Monz C, Schroeder J (2009) Findings of the 2009 workshop on Statistical Machine Translation. In: Proceedings of the 4th EACL workshop on Statistical Machine Translation, Athens, 30–31 March 2009, pp 1–28

Callison-Burch C, Koehn P, Monz C, Zaidan OF (2011) Findings of the 2011 Workshop on Statistical Machine Translation. In: Proceedings of the 6th Workshop on Statistical Machine Translation, 30–31 July, 2011, Edinburgh, pp 22–64

Campbell S (1998) Translation into the second language. Longman, New York

Canfora C, Ottmann A (2016) Who's afraid of translation risks? Paper presented at the 8th EST Congress, Aarhus, 15–17 September 2016

Carl M (2012) Translog – II: a program for recording user activity data for empirical reading and writing research. In: Calzolari N, Choukri K, Declerck T, Doğan MU, Maegaard B, Mariani J, Moreno A, Odijk J, Piperidis S (eds) Proceedings of the eight international conference on language resources and evaluation, Istanbul, 23–25 May 2014, pp 4108–4112

Carl M, Gutermuth S, Hansen-Schirra S (2015) Post-editing machine translation: a usability test for professional translation settings. In: Ferreira A, Schwieter JW (eds) Psycholinguistic and cognitive inquiries into translation and interpreting. John Benjamins, Amsterdam, pp 145–174

Castilho S (2016) Measuring acceptability of machine translated enterprise content. PhD thesis, Dublin City University

Castilho S, O'Brien S (2016) Evaluating the impact of light post-editing on usability. In: Proceedings of the tenth international conference on language resources and evaluation, Portorož, 23–28 May 2016, pp 310–316

Castilho S, O'Brien S, Alves F, O'Brien M (2014) Does post-editing increase usability? A study with Brazilian Portuguese as target language. In: Proceedings of the seventeenth annual conference of the European Association for Machine Translation, Dubrovnik, 16–18 June 2014, pp 183–190

Catford J (1965) A linguistic theory of translation. Oxford University Press, Oxford

Chan YS, Ng HT (2008) MAXSIM: an automatic metric for machine translation evaluation based on maximum similarity. In: Proceedings of the MetricsMATR workshop of AMTA-2008, Honolulu, Hawaii, pp 55–62

Chomsky N (1969) Aspects of the theory of syntax. MIT Press, Cambridge, MA

Coughlin D (2003) Correlating automated and human assessments of machine translation quality. In: Proceedings of the Machine Translation Summit IX, New Orleans, 23–27 September 2003, pp 63–70

Daems J, Vandepitte S, Hartsuiker R, Macken L (2015) The Impact of machine translation error types on post-editing effort indicators. In: Proceedings of the 4th workshop on post-editing technology and practice, Miami, 3 November 2015, pp 31–45

Dale E, Chall JS (1948) A formula for predicting readability: instructions. Educ Res Bull 27(2): 37–54

De Almeida G, O'Brien S (2010) Analysing post-editing performance: correlations with years of translation experience. In: Hansen V, Yvon F (eds) Proceedings of the 14th annual conference of the European Association for Machine Translation, St. Raphaël, 27–28 May 2010. Available via: http://www.mt-archive.info/EAMT-2010-Almeida.pdf. Accessed 10 Jan 2017

De Beaugrande R, Dressler W (1981) Introduction to text linguistics. Longman, New York

Debove A, Furlan S, Depraetere I (2011) A contrastive analysis of five automated QA tools (QA distiller. 6.5.8, Xbench 2.8, ErrorSpy 5.0, SDLTrados 2007 QA checker 2.0 and SDLX 2007 SP2 QA check). In: Depraetere I (ed) Perspectives on translation quality. Walter de Gruyter, Berlin, pp 161–192

DePalma D, Kelly N (2009) The business case for machine translation. Common Sense Advisory, Boston

Depraetere I (2010) What counts as useful advice in a university post-editing training context? Report on a case study. In: Proceedings of the 14th annual conference of the European Association for Machine Translation, St. Raphaël, 27–28 May 2010. Available via: http://www.mt-archive.info/EAMT-2010-Depraetere-2.pdf. Accessed 12 May 2017

Doddington G (2002) Automatic evaluation of machine translation quality using n-gram co-occurrence statistics. In: Proceedings of the second international conference on human language technology research, San Diego, pp 138–145

Doherty S (2012) Investigating the effects of controlled language on the reading and comprehension of machine translated texts. PhD dissertation, Dublin City University

Doherty S (2016) The impact of translation technologies on the process and product of translation. Int J Commun 10:947–969

Doherty S (2017) Issues in human and automatic translation quality assessment. In: Kenny D (ed) Human issues in translation technology. Routledge, London, pp 154–178

Doherty S, O'Brien S (2014) Assessing the usability of raw machine translated output: a user-centred study using eye tracking. Int J Hum Comput Interact 30(1):40–51

Doherty S, Gaspari F, Groves D, van Genabith J, Specia L, Burchardt A, Lommel A, Uszkoreit H (2013) Mapping the industry I: findings on translation technologies and quality assessment. Available via: http://www.qt21.eu/launchpad/sites/default/files/QTLP_Survey2i.pdf. Accessed 12 May 2017

Drugan J (2013) Quality in professional translation: assessment and improvement. Bloomsbury, London

Dybkjær L, Bernsen N, Minker W (2004) Evaluation and usability of multimodal spoken language dialogue systems. Speech Comm 43(1):33–54

Federmann C (2012) Appraise: an open-source toolkit for manual evaluation of MT output. Prague Bull Math Linguist 98:25–35

Fields P, Hague D, Koby GS, Lommel A, Melby A (2014) What is quality? A management discipline and the translation industry get acquainted. Revista Tradumàtica 12:404–412. Available via: https://ddd.uab.cat/pub/tradumatica/tradumatica_a2014n12/tradumatica_a2014n12p404.pdf. Accessed 12 May 2017

Flesch R (1948) A new readability yardstick. J Appl Psychol 32(3):221–233

Gaspari F (2004) Online MT services and real users' needs: an empirical usability evaluation. In: Frederking RE, Taylor KB (eds) Proceedings of AMTA 2004: 6th conference of the Association for Machine Translation in the Americas "Machine translation: from real users to research". Springer, Berlin, pp 74–85

Gaspari F, Almaghout H, Doherty S (2015) A survey of machine translation competences: insights for translation technology educators and practitioners. Perspect Stud Translatol 23(3):333–358

Giménez J, Màrquez L (2008) A smorgasbord of features for automatic MT evaluation. In: Proceedings of the third workshop on Statistical Machine Translation, Columbus, pp 195–198

Giménez J, Màrquez L, Comelles E, Catellón I, Arranz V (2010) Document-level automatic MT evaluation based on discourse representations. In: Proceedings of the joint fifth workshop on Statistical Machine Translation and MetricsMATR, Uppsala, pp 333–338

Guerberof A (2014) Correlations between productivity and quality when post-editing in a professional context. Mach Transl 28(3–4):165–186

Guzmán F, Joty S, Màrquez L, Nakov P (2014) Using discourse structure improves machine translation evaluation. In: Proceedings of the 52nd annual meeting of the Association for Computational Linguistics, Baltimore, June 23–25 2014, pp 687–698

Harrison C (1980) Readability in the classroom. Cambridge University Press, Cambridge

Holmes JS (1988) Translated! Papers on literary translation and translation studies. Rodopi, Amsterdam

House J (1997) Translation quality assessment. A model revisited. Gunter Narr, Tübingen

House J (2001) Translation quality assessment: linguistic description versus social evaluation. Meta 46(2):243–257

House J (2015) Translation quality assessment: past and present. Routledge, London

Hovy E, King M, Popescu-Belis A (2002) Principles of context-based machine translation evaluation. Mach Transl 17(1):43–75

International Organization for Standardisation (2002) ISO/TR 16982:2002 ergonomics of human-system interaction—usability methods supporting human centred design. International Organization for Standardisation, Geneva. Available via: http://www.iso.org/iso/catalogue_detail?csnumber=31176. Accessed 20 May 2017

International Organization for Standardisation (2012) ISO/TS 11669:2012 technical specification: translation projects – general guidance. International Organization for Standardisation, Geneva. Available via: https://www.iso.org/standard/50687.html. Accessed 20 May 2017

Jones MJ (1988) A longitudinal study of the readability of the chairman's narratives in the corporate reports of a UK company. Account Bus Res 18(72):297–305

Karwacka W (2014) Quality assurance in medical translation. JoSTrans 21:19–34

Kincaid JP, Fishburne RP Jr, Rogers RL, Chissom BS (1975) Derivation of new readability formulas (automated readability index, Fog count and Flesch reading ease formula) for navy enlisted personnel (No. RBR-8-75). Naval Technical Training Command Millington TN Research Branch

Klerke S, Castilho S, Barrett M, Søgaard A (2015) Reading metrics for estimating task efficiency with MT output. In: Proceedings of the sixth workshop on cognitive aspects of computational language learning, Lisbon, 18 September 2015, pp 6–13

Koby GS, Fields P, Hague D, Lommel A, Melby A (2014) Defining translation quality. Revista Tradumàtica 12:413–420. Available via: https://ddd.uab.cat/pub/tradumatica/tradumatica_a2014n12/tradumatica_a2014n12p413.pdf. Accessed 12 May 2017

Koehn P (2009) Statistical machine translation. Cambridge University Press, Cambridge

Koehn P (2010) Enabling monolingual translators: post-editing vs. options. In: Proceedings of human language technologies: the 2010 annual conference of the North American chapter of the ACL, Los Angeles, pp 537–545

Koponen M (2012) Comparing human perceptions of post-editing effort with post-editing operations. In: Proceedings of the seventh workshop on Statistical Machine Translation, Montréal, 7–8 June 2012, pp 181–190

Krings HP (2001) Repairing texts: empirical investigations of machine translation post-editing processes. Kent State University Press, Kent

Kushner S (2013) The freelance translation machine: algorithmic culture and the invisible industry. New Media Soc 15(8):1241–1258

Kussmaul P (1995) Training the translator. John Benjamins, Amsterdam

Labaka G, España-Bonet C, Marquez L, Sarasola K (2014) A hybrid machine translation architecture guided by syntax. Mach Transl 28(2):91–125

Lacruz I, Shreve GM (2014) Pauses and cognitive effort in post-editing. In: O'Brien S, Balling LW, Carl M, Simard M, Specia L (eds) Post-editing of machine translation: processes and applications. Cambridge Scholars Publishing, Newcastle-Upon-Tyne, pp 246–272

Lassen I (2003) Accessibility and acceptability in technical manuals: a survey of style and grammatical metaphor. John Benjamins, Amsterdam

Lauscher S (2000) Translation quality assessment: where can theory and practice meet? Translator 6(2):149–168

Lavie A, Agarwal A (2007) METEOR: an automatic metric for MT evaluation with high levels of correlation with human judgments. In: Proceedings of the workshop on Statistical Machine Translation, Prague, pp 228–231

Liu C, Dahlmeier D, Ng HT (2011) Better evaluation metrics lead to better machine translation. In: Proceedings of the 2011 conference on empirical methods in natural language processing, Edinburgh, 27–31 July 2011, pp 375–384

Lommel A, Uszkoreit H, Burchardt A (2014) Multidimensional Quality Metrics (MQM): a framework for declaring and describing translation quality metrics. Revista Tradumàtica 12:455–463. Available via: https://ddd.uab.cat/pub/tradumatica/tradumatica_a2014n12/tradumatica_a2014n12p455.pdf. Accessed 12 May 2017

Moorkens J (2017) Under pressure: translation in times of austerity. Perspect Stud Trans Theory Pract 25(3):464–477

Moorkens J, O'Brien S, da Silva IAL, de Lima Fonseca NB, Alves F (2015) Correlations of perceived post-editing effort with measurements of actual effort. Mach Transl 29(3):267–284

Moran J, Lewis D, Saam C (2014) Analysis of post-editing data: a productivity field test using an instrumented CAT tool. In: O'Brien S, Balling LW, Carl M, Simard M, Specia L (eds) Post-editing of machine translation: processes and applications. Cambridge Scholars Publishing, Newcastle-Upon-Tyne, pp 128–169

Muegge U (2015) Do translation standards encourage effective terminology management? Revista Tradumàtica 13:552–560. Available via: https://ddd.uab.cat/pub/tradumatica/tradumatica_a2015n13/tradumatica_a2015n13p552.pdf. Accessed 2 May 2017

Munday J (2008) Introducing translation studies: theories and applications. Routledge, London

Muzii L (2014) The red-pen syndrome. Revista Tradumàtica 12:421–429. Available via: https://ddd.uab.cat/pub/tradumatica/tradumatica_a2014n12/tradumatica_a2014n12p421.pdf. Accessed 30 May 2017

Nida E (1964) Toward a science of translation. Brill, Leiden

Nielsen J (1993) Usability engineering. Morgan Kaufmann, Amsterdam

Nießen S, Och FJ, Leusch G, Ney H (2000) An evaluation tool for machine translation: fast evaluation for MT research. In: Proceedings of the second international conference on language resources and evaluation, Athens, 31 May–2 June 2000, pp 39–45

Nord C (1997) Translating as a purposeful activity. St. Jerome, Manchester

O'Brien S (2011) Towards predicting post-editing productivity. Mach Transl 25(3):197–215

O'Brien S (2012) Towards a dynamic quality evaluation model for translation. JoSTrans 17:55–77

O'Brien S, Roturier J, de Almeida G (2009) Post-editing MT output: views from the researcher, trainer, publisher and practitioner. Paper presented at the Machine Translation Summit XII, Ottawa, 26 August 2009

O'Brien, S, Choudhury R, Van der Meer J, Aranberri Monasterio N (2011) Dynamic quality evaluation framework. Available via: https://goo.gl/eyk3Xf. Accessed 21 May 2017

O'Brien S, Simard M, Specia L (eds) (2012) Workshop on post-editing technology and practice (WPTP 2012). In: Conference of the Association for Machine Translation in the Americas (AMTA 2012), San Diego

O'Brien S, Simard M, Specia L (eds) (2013) Workshop on post-editing technology and practice (WPTP 2013). Machine Translation Summit XIV, Nice

O'Brien S, Balling LW, Carl M, Simard M, Specia L (eds) (2014) Post-editing of machine translation: processes and applications. Cambridge Scholars Publishing, Newcastle-Upon-Tyne

O'Hagan M (2012) The impact of new technologies on translation studies: a technological turn. In: Millán C, Bartrina F (eds) The Routledge handbook of translation studies. Routledge, London, pp 503–518

Owczarzak K, van Genabith J, Way A (2007) Evaluating machine translation with LFG dependencies. Mach Transl 21(2):95–119

Padó S, Cer D, Galley M, Jurafsky D, Manning CD (2009) Measuring machine translation quality as semantic equivalence: a metric based on entailment features. Mach Transl 23(2–3):181–193

Papineni K, Roukos S, Ward T, Zhu W (2002) BLEU: a method for automatic evaluation of machine translation. In: Proceedings of the 40th annual meeting on Association for Computational Linguistics, Philadelphia, pp 311–318

Plitt M, Masselot F (2010) A productivity test of Statistical Machine Translation post-editing in a typical localisation context. Prague Bull Math Linguist 93:7–16

Pokorn NK (2005) Challenging the traditional axioms: translation into a non-mother tongue. John Benjamins, Amsterdam

Popović M (2015) ChrF: character n-gram F-score for automatic MT evaluation. In: Proceedings of the 10th workshop on Statistical Machine Translation (WMT-15), Lisbon, 17–18 September 2015, pp 392–395

Popović M, Ney H (2009) Syntax-oriented evaluation measures for machine translation output. In: Proceedings of the fourth workshop on Statistical Machine Translation (StatMT '09), Athens, pp 29–32

Proctor R, Vu K, Salvendy G (2002) Content preparation and management for web design: eliciting, structuring, searching, and displaying information. Int J Hum Comput Interact 14(1):25–92

Pym A (2010) Exploring translation theories. Routledge, Abingdon

Pym A (2015) Translating as risk management. J Pragmat 85:67–80

Ray R, DePalma D, Pielmeier H (2013) The price-quality link. Common Sense Advisory, Boston

Reeder F (2004) Investigation of intelligibility judgments. In: Frederking RE, Taylor KB (eds) Proceedings of the 6th conference of the Association for MT in the Americas, AMTA 2004. Springer, Heidelberg, pp 227–235

Rehm G, Uszkoreit H (2012) META-NET White Paper Series: Europe's languages in the digital age. Springer, Heidelberg

Reiss K (1971) Möglichkeiten und Grenzen der Übersetzungskritik. Hueber, Munich

Reiss K, Vermeer HJ (1984) Grundlegung einer allgemeinen Translationstheorie. Niemeyer, Tübingen

Roturier J (2006) An investigation into the impact of controlled English rules on the comprehensibility, usefulness, and acceptability of machine-translated technical documentation for French and German users. Dissertation, Dublin City University

Sacher H, Tng T, Loudon G (2001) Beyond translation: approaches to interactive products for Chinese consumers. Int J Hum Comput Interact 13:41–51

Schäffner C (1997) From 'good' to 'functionally appropriate': assessing translation quality. Curr Issue Lang Soc 4(1):1–5

Secară A (2005) Translation evaluation: a state of the art survey. In: Proceedings of the eCoLoRe/MeLLANGE workshop, Leeds, 21–23 March 2005, pp 39–44

Smith M, Taffler R (1992) Readability and understandability: different measures of the textual complexity of accounting narrative. Account Audit Account J 5(4):84–98

Snover M, Dorr B, Schwartz R, Micciulla L, Makhoul J (2006) A study of translation edit rate with targeted human annotation. In: Proceedings of the 7th conference of the Association for Machine Translation in the Americas: "Visions for the future of Machine Translation", Cambridge, 8–12 August 2006, pp 223–231

Somers H, Wild E (2000) Evaluating Machine Translation: The Cloze procedure revisited. Paper presented at Translating and the Computer 22, London

Sousa SC, Aziz W, Specia L (2011) Assessing the post-editing effort for automatic and semi-automatic translations of DVD subtitles. Paper presented at the recent advances in natural language processing workshop, Hissar, pp 97–103

Specia L (2011) Exploiting objective annotations for measuring translation post-editing effort. In: Proceedings of the fifteenth annual conference of the European Association for Machine Translation, Leuven, 30–31 May, pp 73–80

Stewart D (2012) Translating tourist texts into English as a foreign language. Liguori, Napoli

Stewart D (2013) From pro loco to pro globo: translating into English for an international readership. Interpret Transl Train 7(2):217–234

Stymne S, Danielsson H, Bremin S, Hu H, Karlsson J, Lillkull AP, Wester M (2012) Eye-tracking as a tool for machine translation error analysis. In: Calzolari N, Choukri K, Declerck T, Doğan MU, Maegaard B, Mariani J, Moreno A, Odijk J, Piperidis S (eds) Proceedings of the eighth international conference on language resources and evaluation, Istanbul, 23–25 May 2012, pp 1121–1126

Stymne S, Tiedemann J, Hardmeier C, Nivre J (2013) Statistical machine translation with readability constraints. In: Proceedings of the 19th Nordic conference of computational linguistics, Oslo, 22–24 May 2013, pp 375–386

Suojanen T, Koskinen K, Tuominen T (2015) User-centered translation. Routledge, Abingdon

Tang J (2017) Translating into English as a non-native language: a translator trainer's perspective. Translator 23(4):388–403

Tatsumi M (2009) Correlation between automatic evaluation metric scores, post-editing speed, and some other factors. In: Proceedings of MT Summit XII, Ottawa, pp 332–339

Toury G (1995) Descriptive translation studies and beyond. John Benjamins, Amsterdam

Turian JP, Shen L, Melamed ID (2003) Evaluation of machine translation and its evaluation. In: Proceedings of MT Summit IX, New Orleans, pp 386–393

Uszkoreit H, Lommel A (2013) Multidimensional quality metrics: a new unified paradigm for human and machine translation quality assessment. Paper presented at Localisation World, London, 12–14 June 2013

Van Slype G (1979) Critical study of methods for evaluating the quality of machine translation. Bureau Marcel van Dijk, Bruxelles

White J, O'Connell T, O'Mara F (1994) The ARPA MT evaluation methodologies: evolution, lessons and future approaches. In: Technology partnerships for crossing the language barrier, Proceedings of the first conference of the Association for Machine Translation in the Americas, Columbia, pp 193–205

Wilks Y (1994) Stone soup and the French room. In: Zampolli A, Calzolari N, Palmer M (eds) Current issues in computational linguistics: in honour of Don Walker. Linguistica Computazionale IX–X:585–594. Reprinted in Ahmad K, Brewster C, Stevenson M (eds) (2007) Words and intelligence I: selected papers by Yorick Wilks. Springer, Heidelberg, pp 255–265

Williams J (2013) Theories of translation. Palgrave Macmillan, Basingstoke

Wong BTM, Kit C (2012) Extending machine translation evaluation metrics with lexical cohesion to document level. In: Proceedings of the 2012 joint conference on empirical methods in natural language processing and computational natural language learning, Jeju Island, 12–14 July 2012, pp 1060–1068

Translation Quality, Quality Management and Agency: Principles and Practice in the European Union Institutions

2

Joanna Drugan, Ingemar Strandvik, and Erkka Vuorinen

Abstract Translation quality and translation quality management are key concerns for the European Commission's Directorate-General for Translation (DGT), and the European Union institutions more broadly. Translated texts are often legally binding, politically sensitive, confidential or important for the image of the institutions. For legislative texts, an important principle of EU law is that there is no 'original': all language versions are equivalent and equally authentic. Consistency in translation strategies and in the approach to quality is therefore critical.

In this contribution, we first outline the context in which translation takes place in the EU institutions, focusing on challenges for quality. We illustrate how translation quality is managed in practice, identifying two guiding principles: consistency of approach, and consistency of quality. We explain how DGT's quality management policy defines quality and how it should be managed, then demonstrate why achieving 'equivalent' quality across all language versions, translators, and institutions is hard. We examine how translated texts are dealt with in the attempt to achieve this goal. Last, we widen the focus to consider what these challenges and the EU approach mean for translators and their status and agency. Issues of translation quality are also issues of ethics, power relations and professional values.

Keywords Translation quality assessment · Principles to practice · European Union · Legal translation · Translation management · Translation policy · Translators · Translation profession · Translator status · Translation ethics

The opinions expressed here are those of the authors and should not be considered to represent the European Commission's official position.

J. Drugan
School of Politics, Philosophy, Language and Communication Studies, University of East Anglia, Norwich, UK
e-mail: j.drugan@uea.ac.uk

I. Strandvik · E. Vuorinen
Directorate-General for Translation, European Commission, Brussels, Belgium
e-mail: Ingemar.strandvik@ec.europa.eu; Erkka.vuorinen@ec.europa.eu

1 Introduction

Translation at the EU institutions has been widely documented and discussed by
scholars and leading EU practitioners (Dollerup 2001; Šarčević 2001; Wagner et al.
2002; Correia 2003; Tosi 2003; Koskinen 2008; Robertson 2012, 2016). This is true
at both macro and micro levels, with some studies taking a broad-brush approach
to translation across multiple institutions, while others have narrowed the focus to
specific aspects (e.g. revision and editing; cf. Martin 2007). Some attention has also
been paid to translation quality in the EU (Wagner 2000; Xanthaki 2001; Strandvik
2012, 2014b; Drugan 2013). However, the issue of translation quality *management*
(or translation quality *assurance*)[1] has become increasingly important recently. This
is true both inside the EU institutions and in the translation industry more broadly,
associated with the development of international standards (Corpas Pastor 2009).
Translation quality management is as yet comparatively unexplored by translation
studies academics, however, in contrast to more specific features such as quality
assessment (QA)[2] or quality control (QC).[3] In this chapter, we seek to contribute to
bridging this gap in understanding via a collaboration between EU experts and an
academic specialist in professional translation quality management.

2 Why Is Translation Quality Important for the EU?

Translation quality[4] and quality management are highly significant concerns for the
EU and for the European Commission as one of its key institutions. Why?

---

[1]In this contribution, we use 'quality management' to refer to the totality of policies, methods,
processes and procedures designed and implemented to achieve the product and service quality
objectives set. 'Quality assurance', which is part of quality management, refers, in a wide sense, to
operations taking place before, during and after translation (and involving both source and target
texts) to ensure the desired quality of the product. We use the term 'quality assurance' in full
to avoid possible confusion with 'quality assessment', as both may be abbreviated to QA in the
literature.

[2]Methods and procedures used to judge whether, and to what extent, a translation product meets
the established quality requirements. In the EU context, quality assessment is mostly, but not
exclusively, performed on outsourced translations.

[3]The DGT definition of 'quality control' (QC) is "making sure that a translation complies with
the required quality standards for the intended use and the text type concerned". QC relies on
revision (systematic comparison of the original and the translation) and *review* (target-text-focused
checking of the translation to ensure its suitability for the agreed purpose); see DGT's tender
specifications for the OMNIBUS-15 outsourcing call for tender, Sect. 5.1 below; see also the ISO
17100:2015 standard – Requirements for translation services).

[4]In the *DGT Quality Management Framework*, 'quality' is defined, drawing on ISO standards
for quality management, as "the degree to which a set of characteristics fulfils stated or implied
needs or expectations". Hence, DGT's notion of quality is customer-focused. Defined in this way,
translation quality is never absolute but depends on both context and situation. It is the sum of
various quality aspects that may need to be prioritised and it concerns both products and services,
as well the processes involved.

There are two main underlying reasons: efficiency and efficacy. First, it goes without saying that optimising the efficiency of processes is a must and a continuous concern in a context where thousands of in-house translators interact with each other and with hundreds of different internal and external stakeholders in complex work-flows. Second, in terms of efficacy, translation is a key instrument in communicating the entire EU project to the European citizens. In 23 out of the EU's 24 official languages, communication takes place through translations. Translation is therefore a fundamental element in putting the EU's multilingualism policy[5] into practice; as Koskinen (2008) points out, the institutions both carry out translation and depend on translation in order to function. Poor-quality translation would seriously undermine not only the multilingualism policy, but also the institutions themselves. Efficacy matters particularly in the EU context because translated EU legal acts have a legal effect: they create rights, obligations and legitimate expectations. All language versions, once they are adopted, are equally authentic. They are expected to convey the same meaning and produce the same legal effect in all languages and all legal orders. Those using, applying and interpreting the legal acts, be they national authorities, businesses, courts of law, experts or citizens, need to be able to have full confidence in the correctness of the language versions, first of all because, for most EU legislative texts, national courts must be able to "interpret and smoothly apply [them] even when the EU text is the only source of relevant law available to national judges" (Xanthaki 2001). Second, individuals, companies and other parties are now directly affected by, and must comply with, "complex EU legislation affecting a huge chunk of their lives and ranging from equal employment rights to sex equality and from the determination of technical standards for products sold within the EU to the accountancy obligations of EU companies" (ibid.). High-quality translations are essential if the stakeholders are expected to do this. Moreover, in the legislative process, the EU institutions are interdependent and rely on the quality of each other's translations. For instance, in the ordinary legislative procedure,[6] the European Parliament and the Council of the European Union have to be able to trust that the Commission's proposal has been translated reliably; and later, when the two institutions try to reach a mutual agreement, they must be able to trust the quality of any additional translation or revision work done by one of them (Strandvik 2014b). Once adopted, EU legislation must also be enforced effectively. This involves reporting, correspondence, infringement handling, etc. which all require good-quality translation.

---

[5] See Communication from the Commission to the Council, the European Parliament, the European Economic and Social committee and the Committee of the Regions – A New Framework Strategy for Multilingualism. COM(2005) 596 final. http://eur-lex.europa.eu/legal-content/EN/TXT/?qid= 1512987626500&uri=CELEX:52005DC0596

[6] This is the main decision-making procedure used for adopting EU legislation. It mainly involves the European Commission, the European Parliament and the Council of the European Union. For a more detailed illustration of the procedure, see e.g. http://www.europarl.europa.eu/external/html/ legislativeprocedure/default_en.htm

In all this and more, the EU's image is at stake. The European project also needs to be communicated effectively. As Gouadec puts it, a defining feature of any institutional translation is that some of the translation carried out will be *"for the benefit of* institutions" (2010; our emphasis). In addition to regulating, the EU must 'sell' its idea – through information materials, press releases, leaflets, brochures, websites, etc. – in order to gain or retain legitimacy and acceptance. This selling is largely done through translations.

Consistency in both the approach to translation quality and in the quality of the different language versions is therefore critical. This means that effective translation quality management has become a central concern for the EU.

3   The EU Translation Context

European Union translation is unusual in several key ways. First, it does not take place in one location, in one central translation service, but separately in different EU institutions. Second, it happens on a very large scale and across an unusually wide, and stable, range of language pairs.[7] Third, EU translation is embedded in an ongoing cycle, with a long history, a huge mass of pre-existing translated texts, and a far-reaching impact in legal and political terms. Of course, on a day-to-day basis, translation is experienced as a multitude of one-off requests or stand-alone jobs, but the institutions and their substantial translation resources are ever present as the background context. Fourth, all the above factors mean that translation *policy* receives unusual attention in the EU. Decades of experience in organising translation has resulted in substantial internal understanding, resources, and attention paid to translation quality. Furthermore, there is a requirement to obtain consistent levels of quality as well as value for money in publicly funded bodies. Policy makers therefore have an interest in and impact on translation quality and its assurance.

The EU institutions producing translations include the European Commission, the Council of the European Union, the European Parliament, the Court of Justice of the European Union, the European Court of Auditors, the European Economic and Social Committee and the European Committee of the Regions, and the European Central Bank. They all have their own translation services (the two Committees

---

[7]Theoretically, as far as the EU's official languages are concerned, there are 552 (i.e. 24×23) potential language pairs to deal with. In practice, the number of language combinations is considerably smaller, as English is now the overwhelmingly dominant source-language: In the Commission, in 2016, more than 80% of all documents were translated from English. Translation agencies on the market also deal with high numbers of language pairs, of course, but their dependence on client demand and market developments leads to significant fluctuations, with agencies regularly obliged to source new suppliers for previously unheard-of languages at very short notice.

share a joint one), located in either Brussels, Luxembourg or Frankfurt. In the EU legislative process some of these institutions are in closer contact than others. This is particularly true for the Commission, the Parliament and the Council. These three must base their work on each other's translations. In the legislative process, the Commission drafts and translates a proposal, thereby doing the groundwork, not least for terminology. The proposal is then transferred to the Parliament and the Council, the actual legislators, for discussion, negotiation and adoption, and the Commission's translation serves as the basis on which the translation services of the two institutions build their respective translation work, as they translate proposed amendments, modifications or additions. The need for a consistent approach to quality in this endeavour is evident, both within each language and across languages.

The translation volumes are massive. In 2016, for instance, DGT alone received some 73,000 language service requests and produced 2.2 million pages of translations in 24 languages. In total, approximately 1,600 in-house translators and 700 other staff were needed to do the job. Over the years, millions of pages have been translated into every official language, and even the more recently joined member states now have hundreds of thousands of pages of translated documents. This also means that practically all new documents assigned for translation are based on or related to pre-existing documents and texts, and often to multiple different ones. Complex intertextual relations emerge, particularly in the case of legislation. Existing texts set various, and tight, constraints on new ones, in terms of aspects such as consistent formulations, terminology, and definitions of terms. A further important feature in this context is that, with the exception of the Council, the translation services of the EU institutions outsource a considerable share of their production. In 2016, for instance, DGT sent out more than 650,000 pages, i.e. almost 30% of its translation volume, to be translated by freelancers. Under current plans, the proportion of translations outsourced could increase to as much as 40% of the total volume.

As a result of earlier translation work, a very large common central translation memory database, Euramis, with a total of more than one billion memory segments in the EU's official languages, is in place. New translation tasks retrieve information from Euramis so there is an inherent need to ensure the database is fit for purpose and reliable. Each new translation memory segment exported into Euramis should fulfil agreed quality requirements, so as to avoid 'contamination' of future translation memories retrieved from the database. Due to the sheer volume of the database, it is a challenging task to ensure that its design and maintenance are managed efficiently. The need for quality content is arguably more important than ever as the database continues to grow at a rapid pace (as memory tools are used extensively and are expected to produce productivity gains), and in a context of increased outsourcing (since outsourced translations are subject to standard industry practices such as paying translators lower rates for fuzzy matches). Euramis also serves as the basis for MT engines, which are now widely and increasingly used as support tools by EU translators.

4   Consistency of Approach

How can a consistent approach to quality be ensured in such a complex setting? First of all, there has to be a shared understanding of how EU legislative and other documents should be translated and what constitutes good quality in the EU context. Secondly, this idea has to be operationalised in a coordinated manner, both interinstitutionally and within the individual institutions, translation departments, and units. For legislative documents in particular, there must also be sufficient common ground on what quality means between the translators in the translation units and the lawyer-linguists in the institutions' legal services.[8] The common ground must cover notions of both drafting quality and translation quality, since according to Regulation 1/58 "Regulations and other documents shall be *drafted* in the official languages" (our emphasis) and in 23 languages this drafting takes place via translation. In practice, this means that the drafting-through-translation of legislative documents is in effect shared by two groups of people who typically have different educational and professional backgrounds and, arguably, different statuses within the organisation (Strandvik 2014a). This is also a setting where power relations come into play. Namely, in the interinstitutional legislative process, the lawyer-linguists have the final word on the translations and can overrule the translators' choices. Likewise, the lawyer-linguists have traditionally played and are playing a dominant role in setting the norms and conventions for EU legal translation.

Interinstitutionally, the shared understanding of quality finds its expression in a number of common EU norm sources and guidelines. These include:

- the *Interinstitutional Style Guide* (drafted and translated jointly by the institutions);
- the *Joint Handbook for the Presentation and Drafting of Acts Subject to the Ordinary Legislative Procedure* (drafted and translated jointly by the legal services of the European Parliament, the Council and the Commission);

---

[8]In the EU institutions, the legal services constitute independent organisational entities, separate from the translation and other services. One of the principal tasks of an EU lawyer-linguist is to ensure that all EU legislation has the same legal meaning in every official language. Lawyer-linguists must therefore be able to discern precisely the intention of EU legislation and make sure that this intention is accurately conveyed in their native language. A degree in law is a prerequisite for the job. In addition, sound linguistic abilities and experience in drafting or translating, checking or revising legal texts are emphasised as professional skills, but no formal degree in languages, linguistics or translation is required (Correia 2003; Strandvik 2014a). However, today this description applies particularly to the European Parliament and Council lawyer-linguists. The role of the Commission's lawyer-linguists, now called legal revisers, has changed over the years. While still doing some translation revision, mostly of translations of the Commission's autonomous acts, they now concentrate mainly on the legislative quality of the original documents, and much less on the quality of translations. As for the European Court of Justice, the translators, who are all lawyers, are titled lawyer-linguists.

- the *Joint Practical Guide of the European Parliament, the Council and the Commission for Persons Involved in the Drafting of European Union Legislation* (drafted and translated jointly by the legal services of the European Parliament, the Council and the Commission, and now also annexed to the Joint Handbook listed above); and
- the *Manual of Precedents for Acts Established within the Council of the European Union* (the Council's own set of guidelines, but also used as reference by other institutions; the manual largely overlaps with the *Joint Handbook* referred to above).

These guides and handbooks are *drafting* guidelines, but through their translations into the EU's official languages, and the fact that they contain explicit references to translation, they also become normative *translation* guidelines. They express the institutional intent, how the institutions want to draft legislation in the different languages. They contain both general principles and (partly language-specific) detailed drafting rules and formulae and are meant to serve as reference tools for legislative drafting and other written works for the EU institutions, bodies, and organisations. For instance, the *Joint Practical Guide* (JPG) was drawn up as a result of Declaration No. 39 on the quality of the drafting of Community legislation (1993), annexed to the final act of the Amsterdam Treaty, and the subsequent common guidelines adopted by the European Parliament, the Council, and the Commission in their 1998 Interinstitutional Agreement. According to the JPG (2015),

> In order for Community legislation to be better understood and correctly implemented, it is essential to ensure that it is well drafted. Acts adopted by the Community institutions must be drawn up in an intelligible and consistent manner, in accordance with uniform principles of presentation and legislative drafting, so that citizens and economic operators can identify their rights and obligations and the courts can enforce them, and so that, where necessary, the Member States can correctly transpose those acts in due time.

In fact, for every new EU translator, professional and institutional socialisation is largely a process of learning and internalising the rules and practices enshrined in the common norm sources, and the – largely juridical – way of thinking underlying them (Strandvik 2014a).

In addition to the common norm sources, the shared understanding of quality is maintained and reproduced interinstitutionally through the EU's technological resources and tools. Euramis, the central translation memory database, suggests memory segments – including normative ones – retrieved from earlier translations to be used in new ones. Similarly, the EU's terminology database IATE (InterActive Terminology for Europe) contains (normative) terminology fed and validated by the institutions' translation services. Further cooperation channels and fora include the European Institutions Linguistic Information Storage and Exchange[9] (ELISE) database, which supports rapid exchange of information on individual translations

---

[9]http://ec.europa.eu/dpo-register/details.htm?id=35571

or translation packages amongst translators working on the same file, and the more formal Interinstitutional Committee for Translation and Interpretation (ICTI) which deals with more general issues of common interest to the various translation and interpretation services, including quality.

A significant driver of interinstitutional knowledge-sharing and cooperation on translation quality is increased contact between the different institutions. Since the entry into force of the Lisbon Treaty in 2009, the translation services and legal services of the European Parliament and the Council have worked in closer contact with each other in the context of the ordinary legislative procedure, coordinating the translation, revision, and finalisation work related to legislative proposals received from the Commission (Directorate-General for Translation 2010). Interinstitutional cooperation, and thereby negotiation and reproduction of common quality norms, also takes place through personal contacts and more or less formal language-specific groups. For example, soon after Finland joined the EU in 1995, Finnish translators and lawyer-linguists formed an informal Finnish language group to discuss problematic language- and terminology-related questions of common interest and to issue recommendations on jointly agreed solutions, preferences, and practices. The group, which consists of members from all Finnish translation units and legal services in the Institutions plus the EU Publications Office, still exists, though it now convenes less frequently (usually once a year) than during the early days of Finland's EU membership. Today, such networks are common practice in the EU language communities.

At the **intrainstitutional** level (i.e. internally within a single institution), the framework for ensuring a common and consistent approach to quality assurance is more detailed and complex.

Unlike the Council's *Manual of Precedents* mentioned above, there is no set of general multilingual guidelines at the Commission. There is, however, a common set of drafting rules, namely the *Drafters' Assistance Package* (DAP) developed by the Commission's Legal Service on the basis of the JPG and used as an electronic drafting aid. This internal tool offers step-by-step guidance on how to draft legal acts and provides useful links and suggested wordings but exists only in English and French. Several of the Commission's individual Directorates-General have their own drafting guidelines, such as DG Communication's *Guidelines for Press Material* and DG Trade's *DG Trade Communications Manual*. In these guidelines, the institution explains how it wants to communicate through different types of text. Besides the drafting language, the principles expressed in such guidelines also apply to translations (of press releases, competition documents, and so on).

Another Commission-wide quality effort is the Clear Writing Campaign launched in 2010 as a joint initiative by five Commission departments: the Secretariat-General, the Legal Service, DG Human Resources, DG Communication and DGT. The campaign features training and clear writing awards for drafters, among other measures. In 2011, it published a booklet entitled *How to Write Clearly* (European Commission 2015) to serve as a quick guide for administrative drafting in general. The guide has been translated and adapted into 22 official languages, so it has become a language-specific reference document for good writing.

The various guidelines mentioned above serve, above all, as technical reference materials: they define the textual and linguistic norms and conventions to be applied for legislative documents in particular, in order to write correctly and meet the EU standard. But they leave many quality-related questions unanswered, especially with regard to what good quality means in practice for text types/genres other than legislation, how good quality can be achieved and ensured, how quality should be monitored and assessed, and how efforts to guarantee quality should be reflected in the operations of the whole organisation (Strandvik 2014a).

4.1 DGT's Quality Management Model

In 2006, DGT launched a large-scale quality management project to address the challenges listed above. The project focused on processes relevant for the quality of translation services. More than 20 quality-related topics were identified and analysed, including pre-processing of texts for translation; translation briefs and feedback for freelancers; standards for the evaluation of freelance translations (including training, error quantification, and tools for evaluation); increased awareness about the nature and purpose of the texts to be translated; mapping of subject matter competence; contacts with experts within and outside the Commission; improvement of workflow tools for better capacity monitoring; collecting and soliciting feedback; and more structured approaches to quality management in each language department. Following this initiative, DGT launched a more comprehensive Total Quality Management project in 2008, during which all the relevant workflow processes of the organisation, not just those directly related to translation, were assessed by applying the Common Assessment Framework (CAF), a European quality management methodology for public sector organisations.[10] After several years of work, DGT presented a comprehensive three-layer quality management model (as shown in Fig. 1) consisting of:

1. An overall *DGT Quality Management Framework* (Directorate-General for Translation 2014). This document defines the key concepts and principles for quality management and outlines the structure of quality management-related work, including the main contributors and processes involved.
2. Two sets of Guidelines, which operationalise the DGT Quality Management Framework:

    (a) *DGT Translation Quality Guidelines* (Directorate-General for Translation 2015): a document providing guidance on translation, quality control and risk assessment; and

---

[10]See http://www.eipa.eu/en/topic/show/&tid=191

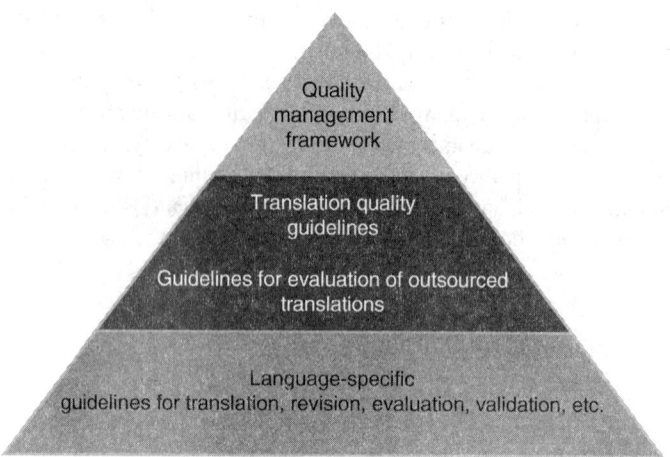

Fig. 1 DGT's three-layer reference model for quality management

(b) *Guidelines for Evaluation of Freelance Translations* (Directorate-General for Translation 2016a): a document describing the process of evaluation, marking, and quality control of outsourced translations.

3. Various language-specific guidelines, drafted and maintained by the individual language departments, for translation, revision, evaluation, and so on.

The DGT Quality Management Framework builds on the EN 15038:2006 standard for translation services and adopts a clearly functionalist approach to translation quality. According to the Framework document:

> As regards delivery of products and services, the key quality concept at operational level is fitness for purpose ('suitability for purpose' as expressed in the standard of the translation service provision).
>
> A translation is fit for purpose when it is suitable for its intended communicative use and satisfies the expressed or implied needs and expectations of our direct customers (requesting DGs), our partners in the other EU institutions, the end-users and any other relevant stakeholders.

In this definition, translation is seen as a purpose-oriented activity which serves the needs and objectives of the Commission and its Directorates-General and, ultimately, the end users. Hence, the products of translation, the translations, are not independent objects with independent quality attributes but their quality is ultimately determined by how successfully they can be used to fulfil the requirements set by the processes and goals of the Commission and the EU at large.

The DGT Translation Quality Guidelines are an attempt at operationalising the functionalist approach defined in the DGT Quality Management Framework. They classify the EU documents typically submitted for translation into four main categories according to their use and purpose:

(a) legal documents;
(b) policy and administrative documents;
(c) information for the public;
(d) input for EU legislation, policy formulation and administration.

Based on the classification, each text category (divided into further sub-categories, as appropriate) is described, focusing on the purposes, legal statuses, and other characteristic features of these texts and the ensuing requirements for translation, the risks involved in cases of poor quality, aspects and issues that should receive particular attention in the translation process, and the recommended minimum level of quality control. The document categorisation and the descriptions are also used as part of the translation briefs provided to freelance translators.[11]

The Guidelines for Evaluation of Freelance Translations aim to operationalise the principles defined in the DGT Quality Management Framework and the DGT Translation Quality Guidelines to ensure efficient, fair and consistent handling and evaluation of outsourced translations. They include practical instructions on quality requirements, error types, marking principles, quality marks and their distinctions, as well as on text samples to be evaluated and feedback to be given, to help in-house translators in their decisions when they act as evaluators. Outside the reference model for quality management, but closely linked to the evaluation guidelines, DGT also has a more comprehensive *Outsourcing Framework* (Directorate-General for Translation 2016b). The Framework, which consists of several modules, addresses, among other things, key quality assurance aspects for outsourcing, such as ensuring quality through communication, more specifically through specifications, translation briefs, and feedback.

Finally, the language-specific guidelines include various documents and instruction materials produced and maintained at the language department level to establish standard linguistic practices in a specific language, to give guidance on recurring linguistic problems and to define preferred (and non-preferred) usages. Such specific guidelines are needed, because the aim of ensuring DGT-wide consistency of approach necessarily has its limits. Since languages differ in their structures and text type conventions and the challenges faced by translators (e.g. gender and cases), each language department must also provide guidelines and instructions according to the individual needs of their respective language: it would not make sense for English translators to use the same guidance on these issues as Italian translators. Moreover, since the overwhelming majority of Commission documents are now drafted in English as the source-language, DGT's English translators have an inverted document flow compared to the other languages. They translate most of the incoming documents that are used as input for the Commission's administrative, legislative, and monitoring work. The guidelines and instructions are hence not uniform across DGT's language departments.

---

[11] https://ec.europa.eu/info/files/translation-resources-translation-quality-info-sheets-contractors_en

4.2 Practical Quality Management at DGT Level

Alongside the above guidelines provided to operationalise the principles expressed
in the more abstract DGT Quality Management Framework, practical implementation of DGT's quality assurance takes place through human action, interaction, and
processes at different organisational levels.[12] There are many contributors beyond
the translators, both before texts reach the translators, and after they leave their
hands (as shown in Fig. 2). The main ones include, first of all, management levels:
senior management (Director-General, Deputy Director-General and Directors)
sets and enables strategic objectives related to quality while **middle management**
(heads of language departments and heads of translation units) has an important
role to play in terms of risk assessment and allocation of resources to translation,
quality control, and evaluation tasks. Other key actors are the four directorate-level
quality managers. They coordinate, as a team, quality management actions at DGT
level and deal with cross-cutting quality management initiatives, such as monitoring
the implementation of the corporate quality management system and promoting
a common understanding of quality-related issues. They also analyse individual
departments' project reports and report on findings, advise senior management in
quality matters, draft policy papers dealing with quality, maintain a web forum
for quality-related matters, test quality assurance tools, and more. The quality
managers work in a matrix structure together with the **quality officers** (see also
Sect. 4.3), one per language department, who coordinate quality matters within their
respective departments and cooperate with their counterparts in the other language
departments, following up on incidents, ensuring that relevant knowledge sharing
takes place, and carrying out joint projects, such as ex-post quality analyses[13] of
translation samples (see also Castilho et al. and Lommel in this volume).

DGT's horizontal (non-translating) units and sectors also have a role to play
in practical quality management. The **Editing Unit**, which edits some of the
Commission's documents and texts at the drafting stage, helps to improve linguistic
quality before texts are sent for translation. The **Demand Management Unit**,
and its **Planning Sector** in particular, which acts as the interface between DGT's
clients (i.e. the Commission Directorates-General requesting translations) and
the language departments, has a key role in negotiating sustainable translation
deadlines, assuring the technical quality of source documents, and acquiring relevant
background information related to translation requests – all prerequisites for high-
quality translations. **DGT's Corrigenda Sector**, also placed under the Demand

---

[12]See DGT's organisation chart at https://ec.europa.eu/info/departments/translation_en

[13]'Ex-post quality analysis' refers to post-production analyses of translations after they have left
DGT. Typically, a sample of translations is collected, and a certain number of pages are analysed to
examine various aspects of quality. Different quality aspects may be focused on from one analysis
to another.

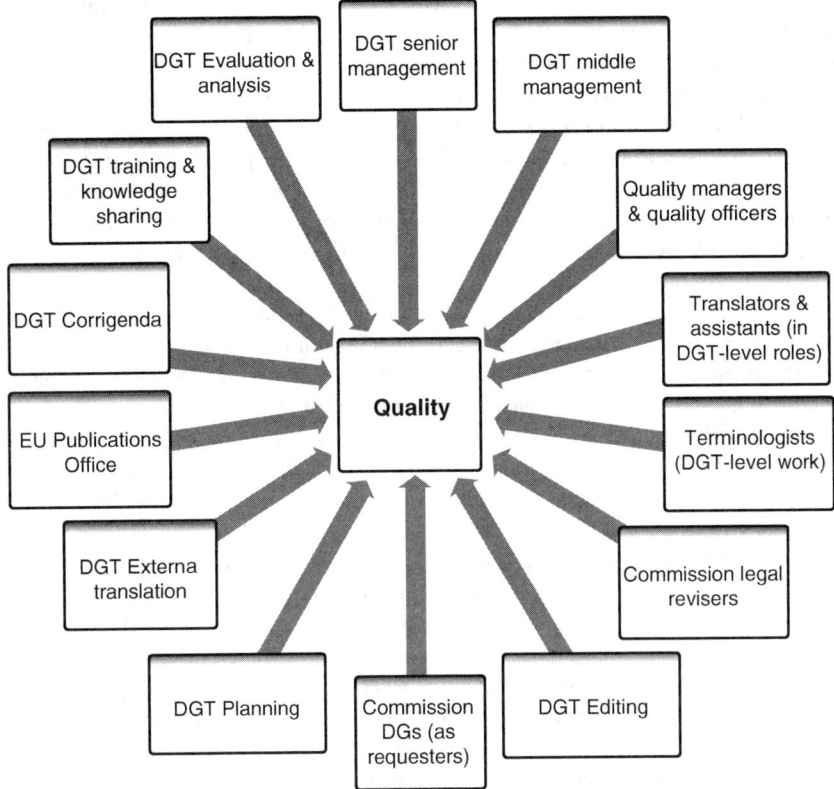

Fig. 2 Quality management at DGT level: potential contributors

Management Unit, has responsibility for corrigenda and correcting acts.[14] In addition to handling corrigenda requests, it drafts regular reports on the corrigenda cases and their numbers, organises meetings with the language departments' corrigenda correspondents and may bring up recurrent quality issues and give recommendations. The **External Translation Unit** deals with external contractors, also in matters related to (non-optimal) quality. The **Evaluation and Analysis Unit** conducts business process analyses and suggests areas for improvement. The unit runs regular customer satisfaction surveys among DGT's clients and also collects

---

[14] A *corrigendum* is a formal document (a list of errors and their corrections), used to correct a legal act or other official document or their translations, when the errors detected do not affect the essential substance of the adopted act or document (in other words when they are non-substantive, e.g. because they are obvious). When the errors detected *do* affect the substance of an act (i.e. are substantive), a *correcting act* must usually be drafted. In such cases, an adoption procedure similar to that applied when the act was initially adopted must be followed.

data on so-called unsolicited general feedback, i.e. feedback on DGT's translations sent by stakeholders, such as national authorities, other EU institutions, businesses or private citizens on their own initiative, without any specific request by DGT or the Commission as part of the standard drafting/legislative process. DGT **staff in charge of training and knowledge sharing**, including DGT Library, help organise training events and, more generally, provide for knowledge resources and *domain competence management*, in collaboration with senior and middle management and the translation departments. Domain competence, in this context, includes both knowledge of the Commission's policies and EU legislation and knowledge of specific fields (such as chemistry or economics), and is considered important for translation efficiency and the avoidance of errors especially in cases of highly technical or unclear source texts (Directorate-General for Translation 2017).

The most relevant individual staff roles in relation to practical quality management are naturally linked to translation activities, but also to training and specialist skills. **Translators and assistants** act at the DGT level in quality-related tasks such as freelance correspondents, training correspondents, corrigenda correspondents, language technology correspondents, lead translators (i.e. file coordinators for important translation files), performers of joint technical quality checks, and a host of *ad hoc* activities (e.g. as members of working groups). **Terminologists**, in cooperation with DGT's **Terminology Coordination Unit**, carry out DGT-wide common terminology projects and ensure the reliability of the joint IATE terminology database. Last but certainly not least, as an external party, the **legal revisers** in the Commission's Legal Service monitor whether the 'originals' comply with the legislative drafting guidelines before translation, revise some of DGT's translations, provide translation models and templates for legislative documents, and give advice in cases of translation problems with (potential) legal implications. Finally, an external role in quality control is also played by the **requesting Directorates-General** and the by the **EU's Publications Office**. DGs may ask internal or external experts to revise the translated language versions, and the Publications Office's proof-readers check legal acts and other documents and written materials before publication, eliminating spelling errors, formatting problems and obvious linguistic errors.

4.3   Practical Quality Management in DGT's Language Departments and Translation Units

Practical quality management involves processes as well as roles and responsibilities, as outlined in the previous section. Quality management and assurance measures at the level of individual language departments and translation units can take many forms, depending on the specific situation of each department/unit. We now outline the typical minimum procedures, shown graphically in Fig. 3. First, as would be expected, is the aspect of quality management many non-specialists

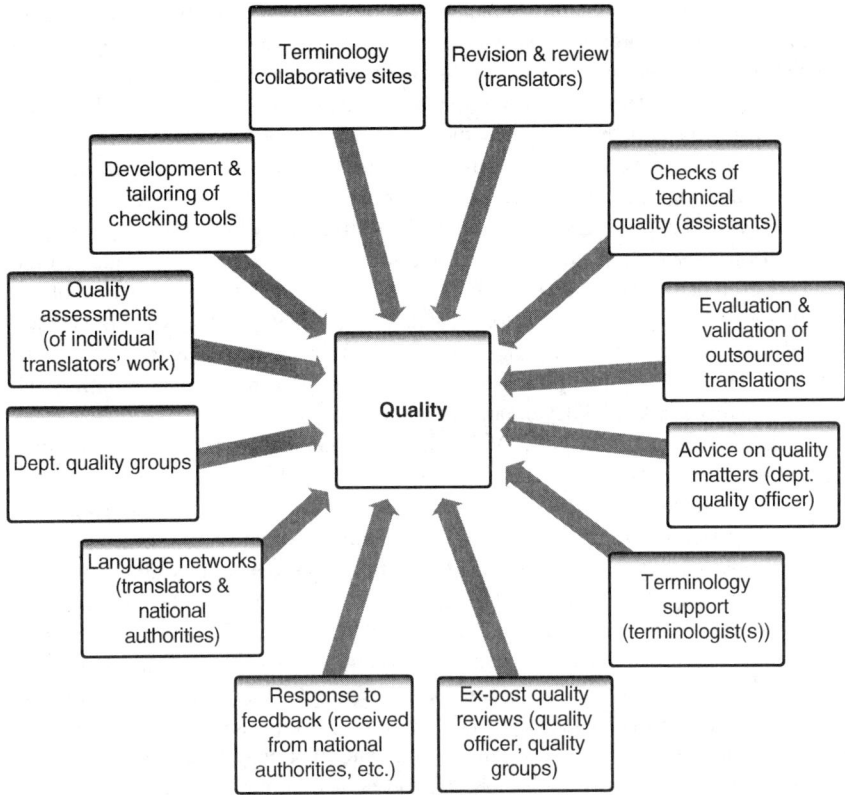

Fig. 3 Quality management in DGT's language departments and translation units: measures, processes and contributors

recognise as relevant, namely **revision and review of translations**. The translations produced are systematically quality-controlled, usually by fellow translators but in some exceptional cases also by external (national) experts. The quality control may be carried out using variable combinations of comparative revision and target-text-focused review. The decisions concerning the quality control to be applied are made on the basis of risk assessments, mainly by the heads of translation units. In cases where the risks are considered minor (e.g. where a translation is intended for internal use only, or it is largely based on earlier, quality-checked translations or model translations/templates), quality control may be done with a lighter touch. Revision and review also have a training and knowledge sharing function, especially for the benefit of new translators and trainees, as well as for those having to translate texts with unfamiliar subject matters. **Checks of the technical quality of translations** are in addition to revision and review. These are made mainly by assistants, observing specific checklists for technical details, such as formats, numbering and integrity of content, that have to be in order in the finalised translation.

Another element of quality management which might be expected to figure prominently in any organisation which outsources a significant percentage of the translation task is **evaluation and validation of outsourced translations**. A sample of every outsourced translation submitted by any external contractor is evaluated by an in-house translator to verify whether the language department has received a product that meets the quality requirements set in DGT's tender specifications.[15] In the evaluation, the translation is examined with regard to a set of quality attributes (see Sect. 5.1). The evaluation is then validated by one of the department's validators to ensure fair and consistent marking, and feedback is provided to the external contractor. The marks given are taken into account in the ranking of the contractor on the list of contractors, calculated according to a dynamic ranking system determining the order in which translation assignments are offered to the contractors. The language department's freelance correspondent monitors the average quality marks and developments in the ranking.

All language departments in DGT must nominate a quality officer who coordinates quality-related matters and, depending on the department's needs and the person's competence profile, gives **advice and support** to translators **on linguistic and quality-related matters**, analyses issues related to quality (also in cooperation with national experts), drafts language-specific recommendations and guidelines and posts and updates them on the department's intranet website, and gives or organises quality-related training within the department. Moreover, every DGT translation department must allocate at least the equivalent of two full-time members of staff in resources per year to **terminology support**, one of them by a full-time terminologist. Translators usually send terminology enquiries to the department's main terminologist who then consults sources and experts to find a solution to the problem. The results of such discussions and consultations are fed into the IATE terminology database, as appropriate, to ensure correct and uniform usage.

Ex-post quality reviews conducted within the language department are more or less regular post-production analyses of various quality aspects of samples of texts translated and revised in the translation units. The findings of the quality reviews are reported on, and training events may be organised to follow up on them; similar analyses may also be carried out as joint projects involving all DGT language departments. **Response to quality-related feedback** is distinct from such quality reviews because it is based on feedback such as corrigenda and correction requests or comments, suggestions or criticisms received from clients (requesting DGs), end users of translations (e.g. national authorities) or other stakeholders in conjunction with the translation/legislative process. The feedback is dealt with according to standard procedures and, if necessary, steps are taken to put the matter right. It also includes the so called unsolicited general feedback (see Sect. 4.2 above).

---

[15]DGT's outsourcing is based on multiannual framework contracts concluded with external contractors. The contracts result from a tendering procedure in which a set of tender specifications defined by DGT are applied. In the tendering process, aspiring contractors' offers are assessed as a function of the quality of the service proposed and the price quoted, with a weighting of 70% for quality and 30% for price.

In addition to the standard measures listed above, DGT's individual language departments may carry out a number of supplementary activities aimed at assuring and maintaining quality, according to their specific situations and needs (the list here is not exhaustive). They often create **networks between EU translators and national authorities**, such as ministries, specialised agencies, academic institutions, expert bodies, or language authorities. Depending on the language and country in question, such networks may have varying degrees of formality and focus on more general cooperation in language matters or everyday exchange of information on matters of terminology, linguistic questions, or quality-related feedback. As examples of such initiatives, the Swedish and Finnish networks of cooperation and feedback may be mentioned, both having informal, non-hierarchical, but well-organised structures. In addition, language departments may have bilateral relations and contacts, e.g. in matters of terminology and quality assurance, with external experts or specialised national agencies dealing with individual policy sectors, such as aviation, food safety, safety of medicinal products, or financial supervision. Alongside these external expert links, the establishment of **departmental quality groups** supports quality internally. Such groups may exist on a permanent basis or be formed for *ad hoc* assignments. They may, for instance, conduct quality-related analyses, identify and record good practices for quality assurance, or help draft translation guidelines for certain text types or genres. They may also act as consultative bodies, for example by commenting on new linguistic recommendations, guidelines or model translations.

Language departments may also carry out **assessments of the quality of individual translators' work**. Translations produced by in-house translators may be subjected to regular quality assessment carried out by the quality officer or a head of unit or department, as part of the Commission's annual career appraisal process and in order to monitor the overall level of quality of the work done within the translation department.

Tools and resources figure at departmental level as well as at DGT, institutional or interinstitutional levels. Departments may take responsibility for tool-related training or for the **development and tailoring of checking tools**, for example applications developed to detect frequent errors in translations (e.g. deviations in certain standard expressions or dates and numbers). The development and tailoring is typically language-specific as some languages lend themselves to error checking more easily than others.

To help to achieve consistency of terminology, **departmental terminology wikis** may be set up as collaborative sites for discussing and recording terminology and references during individual translation assignments. Such terminology wikis may then be made available to the translation services of other institutions for their further work on the same document or document package and the terms may be validated and fed into the IATE terminology database.

4.4 Consistency of Approach: Challenges

As we have seen, translation and quality assurance, which at first sight might seem to be rather straightforward institutional operations, actually involve a multitude of different processes. The multi-layered quality management system described above includes a large number of different principles, guidelines, procedures, workflows, and participants contributing to the overall goal. The assumption is that when the rules, principles, and practices are adhered to, and everyone involved in the different processes works correctly and according to agreed standards, good quality will be achieved. One of the key elements in the system is therefore constant *coordination* between the processes and the participants. Without it, the required efficiency, uniformity, and consistency would inevitably be lost.

One of the challenges for the current framework is to ensure sufficient communication and coordination between the numerous participants in the processes. To address this issue within the Commission, DGT has created a system with lead translators, who act as file coordinators or project managers for important translation files, channelling and centralising the communication between all translators and the requester. For major files, such as large translation packages with hundreds of pages, a multitude of questions may be channelled from the translators to the requesters. As an illustration, in the context of a recent package, more than 300 questions were sent to the authors. The replies received from them provided the expert clarifications the translators needed to carry out the work with a common understanding of the source text. A third of the questions led to corrections in the source text and to new document versions, while another third had to do with issues that did not warrant corrections or new versions. A major challenge is also to ensure that this information flow is not hampered when texts are outsourced.

In the interinstitutional setup, the challenges may multiply. For instance, in the ordinary legislative procedure, the following actors are typically involved as a minimum: drafters/translation requesters in the Commission Directorate-General in charge of the legislative proposal; the Commission's Legal Service; DGT Planning (which receives and transmits further the translation assignment); assistants, translators, revisers, and terminologists in DGT translation units; national experts (consulted in case of need or commenting on translations at the preparatory stage); the Commission's Secretariat General (which transfers the translated documents to other institutions); translators, terminologists, assistants and other administrators in the European Parliament and the Council; lawyer-linguists in the Parliament and the Council; Members of Parliament (in the European Parliament) and national authorities and their representatives (in the Council) negotiating the final version of the act to be adopted; and the Publications Office. If, for instance, changes that Parliament/Council lawyer-linguists working 'downstream' in the process make in translations – possibly because of demands made by national authorities – do not come to the attention of the translators/revisers further 'upstream', the same errors or non-preferred usages may be repeated over and over again. A case from one language department provides a telling example: the name of a new EU initiative was coined by the language department in DGT after consultations with all institutions. However, when the document reached the Council and Parliament a year later, national authorities proposed another name to the lawyer-linguists. Since the proposed alternative name was fully correct and possible, it was accepted and became the formal denomination. In the meantime, though, more than 300 other documents, featuring the name which had been agreed on initially, had been translated. They were now outdated as far as the name of the initiative was concerned. All relevant information concerning the initial process of establishing the name had been duly documented in the ELISE database, which follows all interinstitutional files throughout the workflow, but because of time pressure the database was not consulted at later stages.

Secondly, documents or texts may bypass DGT and the standard quality assurance processes, if those who need translations decide to produce or outsource them themselves. In Commission Directorates-General, translations are sometimes requested from their own in-house staff with a knowledge of the target-language (but not necessarily any experience in translation), or, if speakers of the target-language are not available, MT may be used, sometimes with no subsequent quality control or post-editing. Similarly, materials to be translated may be sent to external translation service providers without DGT playing any role in the process, and the self-outsourced translations may not be subject to any quality control. The results may thus deviate considerably from the normal quality standards of the Commission. Sometimes, end products from such self-translation/outsourcing may be combined with other texts translated earlier by the institution's own translation service (for instance on websites), and the result may be patchy, inconsistent, and often difficult to correct afterwards.

In more general terms, basically any translation intervention which bypasses the standard processes and/or is unforeseen and unannounced poses a significant quality risk. This is illustrated well by cases in which, to achieve efficiency gains, those needing translations are increasingly tempted to use automatically generated translations for snippets of text that occur frequently in different documents and contexts. Such snippets may include, for instance, dates to be inserted into texts, or words, headings or labels for web pages. The 'universal' translations to be used for automatic generation may be created by either having them first translated by the institution's translation service, as ordinary translation assignments, and then storing them for future use, or by extracting them from existing translations. However, their inherent problem is, besides that of possibly extracting wrong forms in the first place, the unpredictability of their future uses: through automatic generation the translations may end up in contexts where they do not fit at all. And since the automatic generation takes place outside DGT, the end results cannot usually be checked by translators, so they are largely uncontrollable and can only be corrected afterwards, and not necessarily even then. A non-standard approach poses risks for any language, but especially for the case-rich, agglutinative, and inflectional ones, such as Hungarian, Estonian, or Finnish, which tolerate automatic generation of text elements very badly. Increasing use of MT could lead to a further escalation of this problem.

A third challenge is the tension between harmonisation and flexibility. In a workflow with so many processes, tools, participants, and large translation volumes, there is a natural and well-founded wish to harmonise processes and working methods. However, as Mossop (2007) says, translation and revision are not rule-based activities. Instead, they are activities based on principles, and principles are things you do, unless there is a reason to do something else. The interactions between the various participants take place if there is a need for them to take place. If a translator has a doubt, he or she consults the terminologist, the quality officer, the requester, the lawyer-linguists, or a colleague, depending on a number of things that may not be easily harmonised in an efficient way. What gives rise to a problem in one language might not be an issue in other languages. Competence profiles of the people involved may vary (domain competence, IT competence, etc.). Language departments may be more or less able to access experts in national administrations for terminology inquiries. Freelance markets are not the same, neither in size nor in maturity. In other words, an efficient translation workflow is not a standardised linear workflow, but one where certain processes are activated only if and when they are needed and readily available.

5   Consistency of Quality

What remains to be discussed is how translation quality is evaluated and managed in practice across DGT and its language pairs. How can consistent quality be attained across two dozen languages? To understand this, and the challenges involved, we need to have a look at DGT's translation quality assessment model.

5.1   DGT's Model for Translation Quality Assessment

According to DGT's mission statement, DGT provides the Commission with high-quality translation. The specifications of what this means in practice are laid down in the DGT Translation Quality Guidelines described above. The basic quality requirements are also presented in a compact form in the tender specifications[16] for DGT's most recent call for tenders for outsourced translations (OMNIBUS-15). According to the specifications,

> The quality of the translations must be such that they can be used as they stand upon delivery, without any further formatting, revision, review and/or correction by the contracting authority.
>
> To this end, the contractor must thoroughly revise and review the entire target text, ensuring inter alia that:

---

[16]https://infoeuropa.eurocid.pt/files/database/000064001-000065000/000064078_2.pdf

Error type	Code	Relevance	
		Low	High
Mistranslation + unjustified addition	SENS		
Unjustified omission or non-translation	OM		
Wrong or inconsistent EU usage or terminology	TERM		
Reference documents/material not used; norm sources or job-specific instructions not adhered to	RD		
Clarity, register and text-type conventions	CL		
Grammar	GR		
Punctuation	PT		
Spelling	SP		

Table 1 DGT's quality grid

- it is complete (without unjustified omissions or additions);
- it is an accurate and consistent rendering of the source text;
- references to documents already published have been checked and quoted correctly;
- the terminology and lexis are consistent with any relevant reference material and internally;
- appropriate attention has been paid to the clarity and register and text-type conventions;
- it contains no syntactical, spelling, punctuation, typographical, grammatical or other errors;
- the formatting of the original has been maintained (including codes and tags if applicable);
- any specific instructions given by the authorising department are followed; and
- the agreed deadline (date and time) is scrupulously respected.

As for linguistic and textual quality, the aspects of quality listed reflect the following quality grid used by DGT (Table 1).

A distinction is made between 'low-relevance' and 'high-relevance' errors, a high-relevance error being one that seriously compromises the usability of the text for its intended purpose.

In addition to the aspects of quality listed in the table, EU translations have a further 'institutional' quality requirement, namely that of equivalence or consistency between (or equal value of) all language versions. In the EU (legislative) context, this equivalence has also been termed 'multilingual concordance' or 'multilingual consistency', in order to describe a situation where there are a number of language versions (instead of only one source text and one target text) which may have different linguistic equivalence relations vis-à-vis the source text and vis-à-vis each other, but which should still produce the same legal effect.

5.2 Consistency of Quality: Challenges

As with the consistency of approach, the basic assumption is that if the above-mentioned linguistic and textual quality requirements are perceived and observed in an appropriate and coherent manner by all those involved, there will be good and consistent quality. This is, of course, possible only if the translation demand and the organisation's resources match each other. If translators do not have time to read through their translations before sending them to revision and/or if quality assurance and control procedures must be skipped altogether or reduced significantly due to workload, consistency of quality is at risk. With the high translation demand in the Commission and diminishing translation resources, it is a real challenge to carry out workflow and translation processes in such a way that efficiency gains are achieved without professional working methods being distorted (Strandvik 2018). Similarly, if the domain competence required by specific translation jobs does not exist or cannot be allocated, consistency of quality may be difficult to achieve, or assess. And further, increased outsourcing may also contribute to such risks. For instance, in-house field-specific domain competence may be gradually lost if all or most of the documents dealing with a particular field are systematically outsourced. This, in turn, may entail difficulties in maintaining consistency of quality through the evaluation and revision of the outsourced translations.

The multilingual and multicultural organisation also presents certain in-built challenges. While language-specific aspects of quality (such as grammar, punctuation, and spelling) are relatively clear-cut, others are more vague (in particular clarity, sense, and omission). For instance, what is considered clear writing in one target culture may not coincide with the clarity ideals of another. Norms and conventions of good administrative language, as reflected in sentence and paragraph lengths and structures, use of rhetorical devices and such, are very different in, say, Sweden and France (Strandvik 2012). Pym (2000), trying to explain debates in the Finnish press concerning the EU and its (presumed negative) effects on the Finnish language after Finland's accession to the EU in 1995, even suggests that there is a:

> significant divide here between the north and south of Europe, and more especially along the lines of partition brought about by the sixteenth-century Reformation and Counter-Reformation. Protestant Europe has long sought to bring the word of authority close to the language of the people; it has long encouraged the individual to reason with the law alone. Catholic Europe, on the other hand, has traditionally understood sacred texts through a mediating institution; it is relatively unperturbed by the idea that priest-like experts might exist for the interpretation and application of complex language. The analogy is perhaps forced. But it does point to the depth of the traditions involved.

The fact that translators from different countries have different training backgrounds may also play a role. For instance, when Greece joined the EU in 1981, there was no translator training available in the country. As a result, many of the Greek translators recruited by the EU came from engineering backgrounds. Similarly, in some countries, Translation Studies has a long history as an independent academic discipline whereas in others it has traditionally been a sub-component of philology (Biel 2011). This may have an impact on translators' perceptions as to their role, task and room for manoeuvre as mediators and communicators (linguistics-based/source-text-oriented vs. functionalist/target-text-oriented paradigm). Different perceptions and attitudes can have an impact on multilingual consistency, as translators may approach their task with different preconceptions and mind-sets. They may also be the source of differing views on what constitutes a high-relevance error, e.g. in terms of what translators can add to or take away from a text (cf. Pym 2000). Similarly, these differences may affect 'professional visions' of whether translators, in their translation approach and strategies, should look rather inward towards their institutions or outward towards the users and receivers of their translations (*ibid*.; see also Suojanen et al. 2014).

One factor that is challenging for the consistency of quality is that the EU's legislative translations, on the one hand, and its other translations, in particular those of more informative and persuasive texts targeted at the public, on the other, have to meet different demands. While legislative translations, aiming at the same legal effect, have to conform to strict norms with regard to form and content, translations of other texts can – and actually should (see DGT Translation Quality Guidelines) – pursue their intended effects with a more varied set of tools, particularly with regard to form but also, to some extent, to content elements (localisation). If in the case of the latter, different approaches are adopted in different language pairs, so that in some language pairs a strategic decision is made to stick very close to the source text in all its aspects, but others choose a more target-oriented and text-manipulative approach, then consistency of quality between the language versions may not be achieved. An attempt to reproduce the source text form and content as fully as possible may also result in what might be called 'synoptic equivalence'. Synoptic equivalence means that on the surface a language version may look very much the same as the source text but, exactly for this reason, it may differ considerably as to the extent that it achieves the intended communicative effect in comparison with the source text. Attempts to ensure such synoptic equivalence are then potentially counter-productive, as they may prefer formal correspondence to effective communication through translation. Related to the above, the EU's language regime also creates a somewhat tricky situation in that the same translation may have to serve more than one member state (for instance French translations serve France and Belgium). This means that some language versions can be tailored less to local needs than others, which may have an effect on multilingual consistency.

It is also worth noting that in certain situations different EU translation norms may be in conflict with each other, and this may have an effect on quality. A case in point is the so-called *sentence rule* which is applied in EU legislative translation. According to the rule, the sentence boundaries in the enacting terms (articles) of a legal act must be the same in all its language versions. This facilitates later references to the provisions of the act. But it also means that a conflict with the quality dimension 'clarity' may emerge, if the source text includes (excessively) long sentences. At the same time, as typical and recommended sentence lengths vary in different national (legal) languages, the forced reproduction of the sentence boundaries in all language versions is potentially conducive to inconsistency of quality.

Finally, technical constraints may manifest themselves in consistency of quality issues. For example, translating an EU text, such as a Commission press release, in the current XML format may effectively limit certain textual operations needed to optimise quality in certain languages, or at least make such optimisation more difficult. As the limiting effects on different languages may vary, inconsistency of quality may ensue. Similarly, new content types and content management systems may have a 'decontextualisation effect', forcing translators to work on isolated strings of text instead of coherent wholes (see Drugan 2013). This, too, may have different consequences for different languages in terms of quality.

6   The Impact and Implications of Translation Quality Management

These issues and challenges, and the associated response by DGT (i.e. the adoption of a translation quality management policy) have effects beyond translation quality alone. In such a large diverse multilingual and multicultural workplace 'ecosystem', introducing any wide-ranging policy on management of course has significant consequences, both intended and unforeseen. The DGT translation quality management approach also raises questions relating to ethics, economics, politics, technology, professionalism, culture, and values. Significant questions include the implications for individual translators; issues relating to their agency,[17] power, and status within the EU institutions; issues relating to agency, power, and status beyond the EU in the wider translation industry; and ultimately questions of culture, values, and professionalism. Some of the most important are now briefly discussed from the bottom up, i.e. from the individual translator, to the EU institutions, to the translation industry generally, and finally to professional culture and values.

What does a consistent policy on translation quality management mean for individual translators' experiences of working for the EU institutions? Based on the discussion in the previous sections, it could be concluded that DGT's quality management policy empowers and motivates translators by giving them opportunities and responsibilities for taking action to ensure, maintain or improve quality (including through acting in different quality-related roles). The fact that most translations do not undergo any further quality control in the requesting Commission Directorates-General after they leave DGT is also likely to add to translators' ownership and responsibility. But at the same time, the comprehensive quality framework, with its strict norms, conventions, and standard procedures and processes, obviously limits translators' margin for manoeuvre.

Some likely outcomes are suggested by evidence from large-scale empirical studies of Total Quality Management approaches across a broad range of industries and sectors, though these have not thus far included the translation industry. Early research on the effects of Total Quality Management concentrated on the

---

[17]Buzelin defines agency in general terms as "the ability to exert power in an intentional way" (2011). Kinnunen and Koskinen define it as "willingness and ability to act" (2010). See also Moorkens (2017) for a discussion of freelance translators' agency.

organisational level, assessing productivity, operational performance, and financial aspects (Agus and Abdullah 2000; Nair 2006). However, more recent work has shifted the focus to the individual. Studies have measured how Total Quality Management affects staff workloads, sense of belonging, stress and well-being, for example (Liu and Liu 2012). This work has found not only the improved quality and efficiency which might have been expected, but also: enhanced staff well-being, particularly where "team- and empowerment-oriented" TQM practices are chosen; an increased sense of well-being related to job satisfaction when staff have responsibility for promoting TQM practices; the creation of a "climate of communication in the workplace", due to the greater levels of interaction and feedback among workers required by TQM approaches; and at the higher level, greater "autonomy, meaningfulness and connectedness" (see Liu and Liu 2012 for a summary of these findings across multiple studies). These impacts were observed even though staff were found to work harder under TQM approaches.

However, the various studies which Liu and Liu assessed to identify these broad findings focused on *employees*. As we note above, a significant and growing proportion of translation work in the EU institutions is outsourced and thus performed by freelance workers, who may have no direct connection to the institutions if the work is further subcontracted by an external translation service provider, the standard industry model. In a context where management of translation quality is formalised and operationalised as outlined above, there is asymmetric access to understanding of the quality management policy among freelance and in-house, or novice and experienced translators. What is each individual's place in the quality management ecosystem and do they always understand this? Or even, in the case of freelance providers, know that the quality management policy exists? What access do freelance translators have to quality management processes and policy? An important feature of TQM approaches is the feedback loop, so that the policy evolves based on learning from practice and as practice itself changes; but this depends here on the inclusion of a large cohort of freelance translators, who may be well-placed to provide relevant feedback (for example, translators working for the EU on a freelance basis may have decades of high-level experience working for the institutions or even be former in-house translators). What do elements such as consistency of approach mean in practice for those who deliver it via their individual translations? Who makes decisions where conflicts arise? For instance, when questions of cost or efficiency come into conflict with translators' concerns around time or translation quality, does the common approach to quality management help in adjudicating or have a role in protecting quality standards? Empirical studies of TQM approaches have also repeatedly emphasised the importance of co-worker support for effective implementation (e.g. Joiner 2007), but freelance translators typically work remotely and with little if any contact with their peers or in-house staff: how can they access such 'co-worker' support? In a discussion of general freelance translation contexts, Moorkens (2017) links freelance translators' general lack of supportive co-workers to lowered social capital, and hence lower job and life satisfaction, and subjective well-being. It is not clear whether TQM approaches can or do make an impact on this less positive broader setting. These questions do not have clear or uniform answers but highlight areas for further research and development of TQM approaches in evolving work contexts.

Moving up a level from the individual translator to consider the broader context within the institutions, questions of status, power and agency are present in relation to the translation quality management policy. An empirical study by Dam and Korning Zethsen (2008) singled out EU translators as those who may have an "assumed higher status" in a profession which was more generally considered low-status, including by translators themselves. Translator power and influence were assessed by asking in-house translators and other employees in Denmark to state whether they had, or might be expected to attain, "an executive office or managerial position" (*ibid.*). The EU institutions' development of more powerful roles in quality management might support the hypothesis of "assumed higher status" in these terms. However, power and influence at the EU must also be seen in the broader context of the status of translators and quality managers in relation to multiple other (powerful) actors such as lawyer-linguists, elected representatives, or officials in national administrations. As outlined above, translators' choices and decisions are subject to review and can be overridden by lawyer-linguists, among others. Not only this, but the strong institutional history and existence of approved prior translations and reference documents mean that translators must accept recognised translations that are not necessarily their own preferred version. Of course, this is no different to most other professional translation contexts; but it can clearly come into conflict with a strong emphasis on translation quality. Here we see a good illustration of how translation quality is not absolute, but can be viewed differently at the level of the individual and of the system. For instance, in a given individual translation situation, it may be fully justified to accept a choice or solution which is not ideal in terms of quality, because doing something else, and thereby deviating from earlier usage or practice, could eventually lead to a more serious quality issue. Strandvik (2014b) describes how different actors in the workflow have different needs and expectations, and hence different views on what translation quality is. Dollerup (2001) highlights a further question of status which is relevant for quality at the institutional level: the different statuses of EU languages, with 'official', 'working', and 'other' languages and, arguably, English as an exceptional case. How do the different internal statuses of EU languages play out in practice in relation to the 'no original' and 'equivalent value' principles for legislative texts, and how can a broad translation quality management policy handle any conflicts which arise here?

Moving up one step further, to the level of the translation industry more generally, other questions of status, power and agency arise, particularly in relation to outsourcing. In common with many other sectors, translation is increasingly subject to the drive to outsource provision of services, and the EU institutions too are sending out a large and growing proportion of translation work. The logic of such changes may seem apparent, for maintaining large in-house divisions is expensive whereas outsourced models pass substantial costs (e.g. equipment, holiday pay) on to the providers. The outsourcing model can have undesirable and hard-to-predict effects for quality, however, and can thus come into conflict with the quality management approach. As an example, it makes sense for organisations to outsource translation provision in terms of cost and, to some extent, administration upstream; but this has consequences downstream for assessment and control of translation quality. In-house staff must spend increasing time away from producing their own translations to monitor and check other providers' work, among other effects. This means internal expertise and motivation (and hence, quality) can be placed at risk in the longer term, making it all the more important that attention continues to be focused on quality management at the strategic level so that unforeseen side-effects or new issues can be spotted and addressed as they transpire.

What impact does quality management have at the more abstract level of professional culture and values? Although there is little research in relation to quality management in the translation industry, several decades of research into the effects of TQM in management and business studies contexts indicate some potentially relevant findings here (e.g. Adam et al. 1997; Kaynak 2003). A leading empirical evaluation of the effects of TQM across multiple sectors and organisations concluded that the three TQM practices which have direct effects on operating performance were supplier quality management, product/service design, and process management (Kaynak 2003).[18] Performance was also affected by management leadership, training, employee relations, and quality data and reporting, and by 'top-down' approaches, with researchers stressing that "Quality should not be directed from the outside the individual and the organisational unit, but inside both of them" (Lee and Lazarus 2007).

In DGT, processes and their actors are critical in achieving this 'insider' direction. As Strandvik has argued (2014a), "roles might be clear-cut in theory but overlap in practice", so "the different actors quite heavily depend on each other for the end product to be of high quality". The very fact of formally paying attention to quality management, and having dedicated quality managers and quality officers whose role and responsibility it is, sends a clear signal of high-level encouragement of a professional culture, developing and supporting a strong community of practice. There is space to discuss strategic challenges and review the effects of responding to them; for instance, do measures work as intended, and if not, what might work better? This speaks to debates in Translation Studies around the need for greater professionalisation or even regulation of the sector (e.g. Gouadec 2010), and provides hope that the isolated freelance translator may be better integrated in a coherent community, including resources, support, feedback loops with associated opportunities for ongoing self-development, and recognition of their contribution. Agency in this view is not the preserve of the translator, but shared by other important parties including drafters of legislative texts, quality managers who see the bigger picture across the institutions, and ultimately translation users (cf. work by Suojanen et al. (2014) on User-Centred Translation), particularly appropriate in the democratic EU context.

---

[18] In DGT terms, this would mean translation supplier management, translation/translation service design, and translation process management.

The EU has a leading role to play at this higher level of professional values and ethics. In a context of increased outsourcing, an emphasis on translation quality management offers a way to balance rational deployment of limited resources, quality, and professionalism. One indication of the EU institutions' values is that, in their outsourcing tenders, they emphasise quality over price, as witnessed by the Commission's (DGT's) quality/price weighting of 70/30 (see footnote 15). A quality management strategy can also deliberately address some negative effects of the way the industry is increasingly structured. For example, in a situation where public sector contracts are being dominated by a very small number of huge Language Service Providers, the European Court of Justice explicitly offers opportunities for individual freelancers, in addition to larger LSPs. Currently, 80% of their external providers are in fact individual translators, without intermediaries. Another case in point, outside the EU, is translation tenders published by the Swiss Federal Chancellery which have for many years observed a minimum price level. Any bids below this stipulated price level are excluded as ineligible. TQM approaches also emphasise the importance of communication between suppliers, clients, employees, and managers, and so they may offer effective ways to introduce greater peer (if not directly 'co-worker') support for freelance translators as feedback loops develop over time. Achieving this would be directly in line with TQM goals and likely to have positive effects on translation quality, as Kayak concludes (2003) (translations being the relevant 'material' here):

> Establishing an effective system for collecting and disseminating quality data throughout the organisation in a timely manner is necessary to realise improvements in supplier quality management, product/service design, and process management. Then, firms can focus on developing cooperative relationships with their suppliers to improve the quality of incoming materials and to involve them in the buyer firms' product/service design and process management activities. Coordination and cooperation among employees who participate in product/service design and process management are essential to improving quality performance of firms.

One recent example of such good practices is the VW Language service which was awarded the German Hieronymus Prize in 2014, precisely in recognition of its supplier management model.[19]

Last, but not least, in a context of competing online sources of (dis)information, political opposition to the very idea of the EU, and populist media with an anti-EU agenda and deep pockets, there is a greater need than ever to communicate the EU project to citizens as effectively as possible. This will of course have to be achieved through quality translations.

---

[19]See   http://bdue.de/de/fuer-presse-medien/presseinformationen/pm-detail/auszeichnung-vw-erhaelt-bdue-hieronymus-preis-2014/

References

Adam EE Jr, Corbett LM, Flores BE, Harrison NJ, Lee TS, Rho BH, Ribera J, Samson D, Westbrook R (1997) An international study of quality improvement approach and firm performance. Int J Operat Prod Manag 17:842–873

Agus A, Abdullah M (2000) Total quality management practices in manufacturing companies in Malaysia: an exploratory analysis. Total Qual Manag 11(8):1041–1051

Biel Ł (2011) Training translators or translation service providers? EN 15038:2006 standard of translation services and its training implications. JoSTrans 16:61–76

Buzelin H (2011) Agents of translation. In: Gambier Y, van Doorslaer L (eds) Handbook of translation studies, vol 2. John Benjamins, Amsterdam, pp 6–12

Corpas Pastor G (2009) Translation quality standards in Europe: an overview. In: Miyares Bermúdez E, Ruiz Miyares L (eds) Linguistics in the 21st century. Cambridge Scholars Press, Newcastle-Upon-Tyne, pp 47–58

Correia R (2003) Translation of EU legal texts. In: Tosi A (ed) Crossing barriers and bridging cultures: the challenges of multilingual translation for the European Union. Multilingual Matters, Clevedon, pp 38–44

Dam HV, Korning Zethsen K (2008) Translator status. Translator 14(1):71–96

Directorate-General for Translation (2010) Study on lawmaking in the EU multilingual environment. Research report by Cielito Lindo Kommunikációs Szolgáltató Bt. Hungary. Available via: http://www.termcoord.eu/wp-content/uploads/2013/08/Study_on_lawmaking_in_the_EU_multilingual_environment.pdf. Accessed 15 Jan 2017

Directorate-General for Translation (2014) DGT quality management framework, Ares(2014)799428

Directorate-General for Translation (2015) DGT translation quality guidelines. Ares(2015)5389770

Directorate-General for Translation (2016a) DGT guidelines for evaluation of outsourced translation. Ares(2016)3157529

Directorate-General for Translation (2016b) DGT outsourcing framework 2016–2020. Ares(2016)2986797

Directorate-General for Translation (2017) Report on domain competence management. Ares(2017) 552533

Dollerup C (2001) Complexities of EU language work. Perspect Stud Translatol 9(4):271–292

Drugan J (2013) Quality in professional translation. Bloomsbury, London

European Commission (2015) How to write clearly. Publications Office of the European Union, Luxembourg. Available via: https://publications.europa.eu/en/publication-detail/-/publication/725b7eb0-d92e-11e5-8fea-01aa75ed71a1. Accessed 20 Jan 2017

Gouadec D (2010) Translation as a profession. John Benjamins, Amsterdam

Interinstitutional Style Guide (2017) Available online at: http://publications.europa.eu/code/en/en-000100.htm. Accessed 12 Jan 2017

International Organization for Standardization (ISO) (2015) ISO 17100:2015 translation services – requirements for translation services

Joiner T (2007) Total quality management and performance: the role of organization support and co-worker support. Int J Qual Reliab Manag 24(6):617–627

Joint Handbook for the Presentation and Drafting of Acts Subject to the Ordinary Legislative Procedure (2016) Available via: http://www.consilium.europa.eu/en/council-eu/decision-making/ordinary-legislative-procedure/#. Accessed 12 Jan 2017

Joint Practical Guide of the European Parliament, the Council and the Commission for persons involved in the drafting of European Union Legislation (2015) Available via: http://eur-lex.europa.eu/content/techleg/EN-legislative-drafting-guide.pdf. Accessed 12 Mar 2017

Kaynak H (2003) The relationship between total quality management practices and their effects on firm performance. J Oper Manag 21:405–435

Kinnunen T, Koskinen K (eds) (2010) Translators' agency. Tampere University Press, Tampere. Available via: http://tampub.uta.fi/bitstream/handle/10024/65639/978-951-44-8082-9.pdf?sequence=1&isAllowed=y. Accessed 20 Jun 2016

Koskinen K (2008) Translating institutions: an ethnographic study of EU translation. St. Jerome, Manchester

Lee KY, Lazarus H (2007) Uses and criticisms of Total quality management. J Manag Dev 12(7): 5–10

Liu N-C, Liu W-C (2012) The effects of quality management practices on employees' well-being. Total Qual Manag Bus Excell 25(11–12):1247–1261

Martin T (2007) Managing risks and resources: a down-to-earth view of revision. JoSTrans 8: 57–63

Moorkens J (2017) Under pressure: translation in times of austerity. Perspect Stud Trans Theory Pract 25(3):464–477

Mossop B (2007) Revising and editing for translators. St. Jerome, Manchester

Nair A (2006) Meta-analysis of the relationship between quality management practices and firm performance – implications for quality management theory development. J Oper Manag 24:948–975

Pym A (2000) The European Union and its future languages. Questions for language policies and translation theories. Across Lang Cult 1(1):1–17

Robertson C (2012) The problem of meaning in multilingual EU legal texts. Int J Law Lang Discourse 2(1):1–30

Robertson C (2016) Multilingual law. A framework for analysis and understanding. Routledge, Abingdon

Šarčević S (2001) Preserving multilingualism in an enlarged European Union. Terminologie et Traduction 2:34–49

Strandvik I (2012) Legal harmonization through legal translation - texts that say the same thing? In: Baaij CJW (ed) The role of legal translation in legal harmonization. Kluwer Law International, Alphen aan den Rijn, pp 25–49

Strandvik I (2014a) Is there scope for a more professional approach to EU multilingual lawmaking? Theory Pract Legis 2(2):211–228

Strandvik I (2014b) On quality in EU multilingual lawmaking. In: Šarčević S (ed) Language and culture in EU law: multidisciplinary perspectives. Ashgate, London, pp 141–164

Strandvik I (2018) What do we mean by quality and why does it matter? Towards a more structured approach to quality assurance. In: Prieto Ramos F (ed) Institutional translation for international governance: enhancing quality in multilingual legal communication. Bloomsbury, London

Suojanen T, Koskinen K, Tuominen T (2014) User-centred translation. Routledge, London

Tosi A (2003) Crossing barriers and bridging cultures: the challenges of multilingual translation for the European Union. Multilingual Matters, Clevedon

Wagner E (2000) Quality of written communication in a multilingual organisation. Terminologie et Traduction 1:5–16

Wagner E, Bech S, Martinez JM (2002) Translating for the European Union institutions. St Jerome, Manchester

Xanthaki H (2001) The problem of quality in EU legislation: what on earth is really wrong? Common Mark Law Rev 38(3):651–676

Crowdsourcing and Translation Quality: Novel Approaches in the Language Industry and Translation Studies

3

Miguel A. Jiménez-Crespo

Abstract Crowdsourcing involves the outsourcing of processes previously conducted by professionals in structured ways to communities and crowds using innovative workflows in order to achieve the best possible results. This chapter deals with the way in which the notion of quality has been impacted by the crowdsourcing revolution in translation. After defining the scope of what crowdsourcing is in translational contexts, it delves into the impact of crowdsourcing in terms of how the industry and translation studies conceptualise and implement quality. The main issues reviewed will be the consolidation of process-based approaches to guarantee quality, the expansion of the *fitness for purpose* model, and the distribution of responsibility to different agents that participate in the translation event. The chapter ends with an exploration of novel practices and workflows to guarantee quality inspired both by professional approaches and by MT research in existing crowdsourcing initiatives.

Keywords Translation quality assessment · Principles to practice · Community translation · Fitness for purpose · Translation process · Translation workflows · Translation studies

1 Introduction

The twenty-first century has witnessed the rise of crowdsourcing in all sorts of realms and domains. Crowdsourcing entails outsourcing cognitive tasks and problem-solving activities for free, or for low rates, to large crowds of motivated participants (Brabham 2013). This technological revolution has been made possible by new platforms and technologies that allow large groups of people to cooperate

M. A. Jiménez-Crespo
School of Arts and Sciences, Rutgers University, New Brunswick, NJ, USA

Rutgers, The State University of New Jersey, New Brunswick, NJ, USA
e-mail: jimenez.miguel@rutgers.edu

at a scale unimaginable decades ago. The continued evolution of technologies has meant that during recent times we have witnessed the rise in (i) the number of tasks and problem-solving activities to which crowdsourcing is applied, (ii) the output volume of crowdsourcing in all realms, and (iii) the volume of participants. The tasks that crowdsourcing has been applied to are many and varied in nature; from drafting the Icelandic constitution (Siddique 2011) to creating computer operating systems (Arjona Reina et al. 2013); from providing solutions to scientific problems with Innocentive,[1] to identifying stars and galaxies with GalaxyZoo,[2] or even collaboratively translating its spinoff website Zoouniverse (Michalak 2015). This boom in crowdsourcing has also led to a considerable increase in scholarly interest (Estellés et al. 2015): Google Scholar shows that in 2005 only 50 papers mentioned crowdsourcing, while in 2015 alone this term was mentioned in almost 15,000 papers, chapters, and books. Given the paradigm shift in which task completion and problem-solving have moved from being performed in professional contexts, to outsourcing to large crowds of non-professionals working collaboratively using distinct workflows, one basic question or concern of professional communities and researchers alike is often the quality of the output. The innovation in terms of workflows to harness the power of the crowd is also applied innovatively to guarantee the highest possible level of quality.

In this context, this chapter deals with the implications of crowdsourcing for translation quality. It delves into the ways in which this phenomenon introduces novel approaches both in Translation Studies (TS) and the language industry. It is intended to help bridge the gap between the industry and TS following recent initiatives with the involvement of both interested parties, in order to standardise metrics or models such as the TAUS DQF or MQM (i.e. Görög 2014a; Lommel et al. 2014 and Lommel in this volume). The goals of these initiatives are to establish common frameworks and also to enable the evaluation and comparison of quality for all types of translation output that exist today: professional, non-professional, crowdsourced, MT, post-edited MT, or hybrid approaches. It goes without saying that professional approaches in the industry and in TS (i.e. Gouadec 2007; Drugan 2013 and Drugan et al. in this volume), as well as quality evaluation in MT (see Castilho et al. in this volume), have been and will no doubt continue to be widely researched. Nevertheless, crowdsourcing of translation quality has not been sufficiently researched to date. A number of studies have been produced within the MT literature (Zaidan and Callison-Burch 2011; Zbib et al. 2013; Yan et al. 2015 and many others), while the number in TS is still relatively modest but growing (i.e. Jiménez-Crespo 2013, 2016, 2017a; Deriemaeker 2014; Klaus 2014; Mitchell et al. 2014; Mitchell 2015; Persaud and O'Brien 2017). This comes as no surprise given that crowdsourcing in general is a phenomenon that can be considered to be "still in its infancy" (Estellés and González 2012). This is also due to the fact that TS has been concerned primarily with the question of motivation of participants, rather

---

[1] https://www.innocentive.com/

[2] https://www.galaxyzoo.org/

than with quality or other issues (i.e. Mesipuu 2012; McDonough-Dolmaya 2012; Olohan 2014; Jiménez-Crespo 2017a).

In general, two trends emerge in a first analysis of existing approaches to crowdsourced translation quality. On the one hand, the large influence of MT and language automation research: issues such as the focus on segmental processing, the prioritisation of the development of workflows to secure quality (Morera-Mesa 2014) or the search for automatic quality measurements. At the opposite end of the spectrum, certain practices implemented in crowdsourcing are applications of existing professional approaches in the language industry: this can be perceived in the replication of translation-edit-publish (TEP) approaches in certain non-profit crowdsourcing initiatives, or in the use of quality metrics and error scales developed for human translation in professional settings. No matter whether the approach to crowdsourcing translation quality is closer to one or the other, the diverse range of approaches have in common the need to adapt, combine, or merge existing practices, or even to develop new hybrid ones, given the involvement of a wide range of participant populations: from professionals to para-professionals, all the way to bilinguals or even monolinguals (Hu et al. 2011; Mitchell et al. 2014; Koponen and Salmi 2015).

In order to tackle the issue of quality in translation crowdsourcing, this chapter consists of three sections with interrelated goals. The first section reviews the notion of crowdsourcing from an epistemological perspective and delimits the scope of what is – and what is not – translation crowdsourcing. The second section reflects on the main issues of interest brought up in the analysis of crowdsourcing quality evaluation, such as the reliance on process-based approaches to quality, the consolidation and expansion of the *fitness for purpose* models, and the distribution of responsibility to make decisions on quality. The third section provides an overview of workflow practices in order to guarantee quality, categorised according to whether they are inspired by professional or MT approaches.

2 Defining Crowdsourcing

In general terms, crowdsourcing implies the outsourcing of any cognitive tasks that could in principle be completed by employees or professionals to a collective of online users (Brabham 2013). One of the most complete definitions can be found in the seminal paper *Towards an Integrated Crowdsourcing Definition* (Estellés and González 2012). This study identified and synthesised shared elements in 40 existing definitions from different perspectives. As a result of this exercise, the paper proposed one of the most widely used definitions in the research community:

> [A] type of participative online activity in which an individual, an institution, a non-profit organization, or company proposes to a group of individuals of varying knowledge, heterogeneity, and number, via a flexible open call, the voluntary undertaking of a task. The undertaking of the task, of variable complexity and modularity, and in which the crowd should participate bringing their work, money, knowledge and/or experience, always

entails mutual benefit. The user will receive the satisfaction of a given type of need, be it economic, social recognition, self-esteem, or the development of individual skills, while the crowdsourcer will obtain and utilize to their advantage what the user has brought to the venture, whose form will depend on the type of activity undertaken. (Estellés and González 2012)

If this definition is taken as a point of departure, "translation crowdsourcing" can be defined as "collaborative translation processes performed through dedicated web platforms that are initiated by companies or organisations and in which participants collaborate with motivations other than strictly monetary" (Jiménez-Crespo 2017a). Translation crowdsourcing is primarily characterised by the existence of a call by an organisation, institution, or collective, to a large undefined community via the web to perform a translation task in a collaborative manner (Estellés and González 2012; Brabham 2013). The organisations and collectives can be either for- or non-profit, and this entails differences in the types of motivations the participants might have. It is also defined by distinctive technological platforms and workflows that allow an organisation to harness the collective intelligence to provide translations (Morera-Mesa 2014; Jiménez-Crespo 2017b). It is productive to separate the recent subdivision into "free" or "volunteer" crowdsourcing and "paid translation crowdsourcing" (Garcia 2015). The latter refers to crowdsourcing models that include payments for completing micro-tasks. The payments in these crowdsourcing efforts vary depending on the targeted participant (Garcia 2015): from language learners to bilinguals, continuing all the way to professional translators that may receive higher compensation for participating in micro-task crowdsourcing at the segment level. Paid translation crowdsourcing is incorporated in definitions in the literature, where "the existence of a platform and a volunteer community/crowd willing to translate with low payment (if any) content which is submitted online" (Anastasiou and Gupta 2011) is envisaged.

This varied nature of translation crowdsourcing, spanning from volunteers providing translation equivalents of terminology to be used in the improvement of MT engines (Shimohata et al. 2001), all the way to paid crowdsourcing in which collectives of vetted participants are compensated slightly below market rates, represents one of the main innovative issues surrounding the analysis of quality in crowdsourcing. Paid crowdsourcing has also demonstrated that even when the origins of crowdsourcing are primarily based on free participation, it has now expanded to include calls for professionals with specific experience, credentials, or professional status. Crowdsourcing can thus no longer be simply associated with non-professional level quality outcomes, as different sectors have extended these practices to include the entire spectrum of possible participants, from lay people to highly skilled professionals, depending on the initiative.

The emergence of paid crowdsourcing and the expansion of crowdsourcing to professionals represents one of the main impacts on the translation profession: companies such as Unbabel[3] and Stepes[4] have taken the evolution of crowdsourcing to a

---

[3]https://unbabel.com/

[4]https://www.stepes.com/

professional setting in which micro-task translation workflows are accessed through smartphones (DePalma 2015; Jiménez-Crespo 2017c). These paid crowdsourcing models are innovative, in that they attempt to provide the highest possible quality using professional communities, and in utilising a combination of the micro-task segmentation approach and the immediacy of ubiquitous smartphone connectivity, to attempt to deliver the fastest possible translations. Such recent innovations have consistently attempted to take advantage of translation crowdsourcing developments over the years to challenge the classic conundrum of the translation quality triangle: Language Service Providers (LSPs) that use traditional professional workflows cannot provide a combination of high quality, short turnaround time, and low cost (Jiménez-Crespo 2017c).

It should also be kept in mind that due to the novel and dynamic nature of crowdsourcing phenomena in general, and translation in particular, there is a definitional fuzziness since "sometimes the boundaries of what is and what is not crowdsourcing are not completely clear" (Estellés et al. 2015). In translation, the main issue in this regard is related to whether the activity refers to crowdsourcing or to "online collaborative translations" (Fernandez Costales 2011; Jiménez-Crespo 2017a), such as collective subtitling of multimedia materials such as movies or rom files,[5] or translation hacking of videogames. Crowdsourcing implies that there is an organisation, company, collective, or institution that makes a call for participation and that the locus of control is firmly within the initiating organisation. This organisation is ultimately responsible for setting up the mechanisms, workflows, and initiatives, in order to achieve the highest possible level of quality given the constraints in terms of time, skills of participants, motivation to participate, economic issues, technology constraints, content prioritisation, or prioritisation of different components of quality, etc. It is also responsible for approving the final translations that are published or distributed. In contrast, online community translation involves self-organised communities with the goal of performing translation tasks collectively. In these communities economic factors are not significant, since the motivations of the community or the participants are non-economic in nature (Jiménez-Crespo 2017b). This scenario carries certain implications for quality, since, despite the motivations of self-organised communities to produce translations of quality as similar as possible to professional ones (Orrego-Carmona 2015), the absence of remuneration entails a different conceptualisation of output quality to communities with companies – and money – behind them.

---

[5]These are Read-Only Memory files, commonly used for emulation of outdated or incompatible software such as video or arcade games.

3   The Many Approaches to Crowdsourcing Translation Quality: Industry and Translation Studies Perspectives

The exploration of translation quality in crowdsourcing is not an easy task. While top-down professional approaches in TS and the language industry are guided by the aspiration to conform to quality standards, error typologies, QA models, and norms, collaborative scenarios are extremely open, creative, and dynamic, with a wide array of diverging approaches that defy categorisation or uniform analysis. According to Howe (2008), crowdsourcing is:

> [An] umbrella term for a highly varied group of approaches that share one obvious attribute in common: they all depend on some contribution from the crowd. But the nature of those contributions can differ tremendously.

The same can, in fact, be said of how different key players approach the evaluation of quality to guarantee 'good enough' levels of fitness for purpose; the nature of quality and the processes and workflows to evaluate it can be differently conceptualised across the board.

At the same time, translation quality has been evolving in parallel to the digital world that has multiplied the volume of content that audiences may want to access in their own language, as well as having accelerated the speed at which it is requested. According to Muzii (2013), it is not in fact quality that is under pressure, but translation. This has resulted in industry and academia finally acknowledging widely that quality, or, fitness for purpose, is a flexible notion to include the fulfilment of the needs of the users in an efficient and timely manner, whatever those needs might be (see Way, and Sect. 3.3 on 'acceptability' by Castilho et al. in this volume). This can thus encompass gisting translation in MT and high-quality human professional translation. In the words of Garcia (2015), quality now entails a continuum "with the enduring and critical at one extreme, and the ephemeral and inconsequential at the other". The impact of crowdsourcing on quality further accentuates that in the industry, traditional "one-size-fits-all approaches do not satisfy buyers and vendors of translation services anymore" (Görög 2014a). Therefore, the industry needs to develop "new ways of evaluating the quality of translated content" (Görög 2014b).

Similarly, TS scholars acknowledge that in certain situations, it is better to "provide some translations with available resources than none, even if quality is lower" (Drugan 2013) and that quality evaluation should "take into account the varying tolerance thresholds for quality that already exist in the professional sphere" (O'Brien 2012). House (1997) assumes the necessity of determining a priori these theoretical stances, and represents a firm defender of the need for sound theoretical principles in quality evaluation. In contrast, however, TS scholars have noted for over two decades that a certain set of evaluation criteria cannot be uniformly applied to all translation activities (Martínez Melis and Hurtado Albir 2001; Lommel in this volume). Quality theorists acknowledge this existing flexible approach, assuming that "different theoretical stances lead to [. . .] different ways of ensuring (prospectively) quality in the production of a translation" (House 2014).

Despite an understandable aversion to the notion of 'theory' in some industry circles, what House ultimately implies is the impact of the theoretical models, either explicit theoretical approaches or implicit and a- or pre-theoretical ones held by individuals or collectives, that influence the process through the way that certain basic constructs play a role in the process. These may be elements such as equivalence between source and target texts, and the intended audience, or notions such as usability or acceptability, the presence of errors or error thresholds, the role of client requests, and whether or not the translation is user-centred (Suojanen et al. 2015). Clearly, it is possible for empirical studies on crowdsourcing translation quality to proceed without defining what the relationship between the source and the target text is supposed to be. Nevertheless, an underlying theoretical stance is necessary for a deep critical analysis of the results. For example, in studies that have attempted to test crowdsourcing quality evaluation using monolingual MT post-editing (Hu et al. 2011), is an understanding the evolution of theoretical stances on equivalence necessary (cf. Pym 2012)? Probably not, but this does not preclude TS from critically analysing these studies in a perspective similar to that of professional approaches. After all, an underlying (a-)theoretical approach to the relationship between the source and target text exists, since analysing translation quality necessarily entails having, or building, a model of the relationship or equivalence that can (or should) exist between source and target texts.

Also, whether it is acknowledged or not, in certain cases, translation theories are present in supposedly novel approaches: the notion of quality in the MQM model (Koby et al. 2014; Lommel in this volume)[6] is a direct application of functionalist theories of translation, and it is clearly a direct application of Nord's (1997) "function plus loyalty" (to the audience and the client) model (see Sect. 2.1 of Castilho et al., this volume).

Three issues of particular interest in terms of the impact of translation crowdsourcing deserve a more detailed treatment: (i) the blind faith in the process or workflow-based approach to quality, (ii) the consolidation of the fitness for purpose approach, (iii) the sharing of the responsibility for the final quality of the translation.

3.1 The Consolidation of Process or Workflow-Based Approaches to Guarantee Quality

A great deal of research on quality in crowdsourcing is devoted to process- or workflow-based perspectives. Researchers have put forward proposals for translation crowdsourcing workflows (Exton et al. 2009; DePalma and Kelly 2011; Filip

---

[6]According to the working definition of quality for MQM, "a quality translation demonstrates the accuracy and fluency required for the audience and purpose and complies with all other specifications negotiated between the requester and provider, taking into account end-user needs" (Koby et al. 2014).

and Ó Conchúir 2011), as well as models that combine crowdsourcing with MT (i.e. Carson-Berndsen et al. 2009; Hu et al. 2011; Ambati et al. 2012; Mitchell et al. 2014; Mitchell 2015). The development of novel workflows has not only been the responsibility of researchers, but industry experts have also been extremely creative in their approaches to guaranteeing quality. The wide array of existing translation workflows has been addressed by several scholars at the University of Limerick (Morera-Mesa et al. 2012, 2014; Morera-Mesa 2014). They have provided contrastive descriptions of workflows that hold clues to the importance developers place on the design of distinctive crowdsourcing processes to achieve 'good enough' quality with available resources.

In these novel workflows, the dependence on skilled or trained professionals gives way to different methods to aggregate, validate, and evaluate the participation of crowd(s) of different nature and compositions. Their participation and goals can vary widely: in certain cases, the crowd can translate segments as 'feedback translations' to create corpora that train MT engines (Zaidan and Callison-Burch 2011); the quality of the translation is measured indirectly by the results of the MT systems developed and trained with these crowd-generated data. In other cases, participation can mean post-editing MT output either bilingually or monolingually (Hu et al. 2011). Yet in others, it can merely mean translating entire short texts from scratch in initiatives such as Kiva[7] or TED Open Translation Talks.[8] What is apparent is the intensive participation of developers, managers, and programmers that create, oversee, and structure new processes, and conceptualise and implement quality measurements according to their needs.

The issue here, as discussed by Castilho et al. elsewhere in this volume, is that quality approaches involve establishing procedures or workflows rather than defining what quality might mean. For over two decades, attempts have been made in the industry to standardise the evaluation of quality through metrics or models. The list of initiatives is long, from the novel MQM or the TAUS DQF (see Lommel in this volume for a description of their integration), international service standards such as the European EN-15038:2006, or classic industry ones such as the SJAE J2450, LISA QA, SICAL, etc. Normally all of them involve a procedural approach to translation quality. As previously mentioned, rather than defining translation quality per se, they tend to establish procedures to achieve quality as opposed to establishing what could be considered a 'quality' product or translated text. Basically, these approaches tend to govern procedures for achieving quality, rather than providing normative statements about what constitutes quality (Martínez Melis and Hurtado Albir 2001). They are generically process-oriented, rather than product-oriented (Wright 2006).

New crowdsourcing approaches also fail to define what translation quality means implicitly, or even if quality is one of their goals, assuming that processes and workflows set in place can help achieve the desired quality level to satisfy any

---

[7]https://www.kiva.org/

[8]https://www.ted.com/participate/translate

implicit needs. In some cases, quality is associated to content types given the focus on content prioritisation in the industry (O'Brien 2012). This happens, for example, in paid crowdsourcing models where different quality levels are associated to types of content, as well as the types of communities that can be used to achieve these levels. Such crowdsourcing companies are therefore not resorting to norms or standards to support their claims on quality, since high quality is not what they are offering. They are offering a customisable and selectable level of fitness for purpose. Companies such as Gengo,[9] Getlocalization,[10] Speaklike,[11] and Unbabel thus offer different quality tiers that are often described in relation to 'best-suited' content types. Speaklike, for instance, offers three types of translations, 'Basic', 'Marketing', and 'Specialised'. Basic translation is associated with social media, customer feedback, and support emails. Marketing is focused on website content, content marketing, or financial views, and specialised is offered for legal, medical, or other specialised content. In certain cases, each level may entail a different type of crowd, from bilinguals to vetted and/or 'certified' professional translators. The involvement of these different communities in the process is presented as the key to obtaining the required level of quality. In this shift, translation quality is not defined per se, but rather replaced by a scale of potential value or worth of different types of content, from trivial to highly important. Quality is thus associated to a preliminary analysis of the value of the source text and based on the agents its translation, rather than explicitly defined in terms of features of the target text (Jiménez-Crespo 2017a). Each type of translation is associated with a different type of process, with variables such as the composition of the crowd, and the presence or otherwise of revision. The fact that high translation quality can be secondary to other considerations, such as time, sentiment, speed, cost, value, or content type, can be identified in industry publications. For example, in discussing volunteer scenarios, Desilets and van de Meer (2011) argue that:

> Quality Control issues tend to resolve themselves, provided that enough of the "right" people can be enticed to participate and that you provide them with lightweight tools and processes by which they can spot and fix errors.

In this case, the issue would be that even when quality might not be that significant in some scenarios, the important aspect is to provide good enough tools and processes, that is, as long as an effective process is developed and managed by initiators, and volunteers are motivated, quality will deterministically be achieved. Of course, the 'right' people are never identified, nor are we told what the minimum number of people might be. This kind of belief shows a blind faith that a process-oriented or management-oriented approach when setting up the crowdsourcing task will lead to adequate quality, even when the notion of quality need not be defined.

---

[9]https://gengo.com/

[10]https://www.getlocalization.com/

[11]http://www.speaklike.com/

3.2   Consolidating the Fitness for Purpose

It can be argued that the varied and flexible nature of crowdsourcing practices requires a terminology shift as indicated by many prior scholars. Notions such as fitness for purpose emerge in both industry (Görög 2014a, b) and TS perspectives (Drugan 2013). Depending on the quality focus other similar terms such as 'acceptability' or 'adequacy'[12] would be better suited in this context (Jiménez-Crespo 2017a) given the complex interaction of user attitudes, business decisions (or lack thereof), content types, translation types, and the relative importance of the translated text.

The fitness for purpose models and the subsequent diversification of translation quality came about through MT and related dynamic scales of post-edited quality. MT approaches were instrumental in operationalising quality in terms of an equilibrium between a wide range of constraints and the potential needs of users. The change started with the widespread use of translation for gisting purposes.[13] In addition to gisting purposes, research on post-editing MT output is also associated with different quality levels, depending on the degree of human effort required to achieve a 'good enough' level of fitness for purpose. Allen (2003) identified different quality tiers of MT output: "no post-editing", "minor post-editing intended for gisting purposes", and "full post-editing". This is still reflected in the post-editing guidelines of TAUS (2010), which introduce two quality levels: "good enough" and "publishable quality". The first is defined as a translation that is comprehensible and accurate so that it conveys the meaning of the source text, but is not necessarily grammatically or stylistically perfect. This approach has been extended to professional approaches within TS. Gouadec (2010), for example, embraced a flexible paradigm and proposed different quality tiers depending on how much a translation is "fit for delivery or broadcast". He also proposed a 'fit for revision' grade, defined as a "translation that can be revised within a reasonable time at a reasonable cost" (ibid.). This is of interest since companies have started to also implement crowdsourcing in order to obtain translations at rates similar to dedicated MT systems that are then post-edited in-house.

Arguably, the dynamicity in crowdsourcing models relies on the fact that users or clients ultimately decide what a fit for purpose translation is. Evaluation can thus be achieved through user feedback as to whether the translation satisfied their implied needs (Mitchell et al. 2014; De Wille et al. 2015; Persaud and O'Brien 2017). In this change of paradigm, both industry participants and users implicitly conceptualise that the achievement of translation quality is a time, resource, and

---

[12]The notion of adequacy here is understood in functionalist terms (Nord 1997) to accept that translations can be more or less adequate for the purposes intended, and not the common use in MT to indicate that the translation is more or less coherent with the meaning of the source text (Papineni et al. 2002), also often used in recent standardisation efforts (i.e. Görög 2014a).

[13]Defined as a rough translation "to get some essential information about what is in the text and for a user to define whether to translate it in full or not to serve some specific purposes" (Chan 2014).

financially constrained process (Wright 2006; Jiménez-Crespo 2013). Therefore, fit for purpose models emerge as a "conscious attempt at using translation and revision resources intelligently" (Drugan 2013). Nevertheless, it has to be argued that in business and user-focused contexts employing the fit for purpose model, quality decisions are based on relatively uninformed translation clients and/or users based on the price and the value that they place on the translated text. Clients might not possess any knowledge of the difference between various types of quality that crowdsourcing providers offer; labels such as 'good enough', 'standard', 'ultra', 'basic', or 'specialised' might be as obscure to customers as the notion of 'translation quality' as a whole was previously.

The fitness for purpose model also implies that quality is fully conceptualised as a scalable commodity that can be requested on different degrees with associated price points (Jiménez-Crespo 2017a). These degrees are dependent on different variables such as the degree of specialisation, if any, of the crowd, and the value placed on the source text. In this context, translation quality can become secondary to other considerations, such as cost, speed or usability. In volunteer scenarios, quality is differently conceptualised when disassociated from economic pressures and market demands. Translations are here driven by user demand (Drugan 2013) and, in turn, initiators of translations and end users establish the 'expectancy norms' or the type of quality that might suit them depending on several factors, such as (i) their needs, (ii) the speed at which the translation is needed or (iii) the relative permanence or sentimental value of the translation (similarly to the notion of perishability described by Way in this volume). Bottom-up approaches also stress that in real life, the notion of quality is user- and context-dependent. That is, the clients' goals, the user(s), and the relationship between these elements and the situation of reception, among other factors, are ultimately what can help establish what an appropriate or adequate translation might be. Also, they establish whether the translation is 'good enough' for the purposes intended or how much effort or money anyone might be able and willing to invest to produce translations in any specific context and situation.

This leads to the next issue in relation to crowdsourcing and quality: if the gauge of quality follows a similar approach to other products or services on the market, such as a car or a house, who bears responsibility for the selection of the final translation quality and who defines, even in approximate terms, what each level of quality implies?

3.3   Who Is Responsible for Quality?

One of the most interesting aspects inherent in translation crowdsourcing is the expansion of responsibility in terms of translation quality. In classical approaches, the responsibility for translation quality fell squarely in the shoulders of both LSPs or institutions and qualified translators and revisers. On the one hand, institutions, companies, and LSPs could comply with national/international quality standards and they could establish or create quality assurance and quality control measures to control quality to the best possible degree. Standards such as the EN-15038 include the provision of having college-educated translators and revisers involved in the process as an assurance of quality. Involving specialised and skilled professionals is thus part of the responsibility of organisations to achieve high levels of quality. Thus, both the company, in involving qualified translators, and the translators themselves are responsible for producing quality. Producing quality is a skill that needs to be developed and delivered by professional translators and revisers. It is also characteristic of service provision by companies and LSPs. In addition to international standards, this paradigm appears in professional (Gouadec 2007), pedagogical (Kelly 2005), and cognitive approaches (Jääskeläinen 2016) to translation.

Crowdsourcing, with its diverse nature, expands the notion of responsibility for quality beyond LSPs, translation providers, and translators themselves. Since translations are often produced by non-professionals in collaborative environments, responsibility shifts towards other agents in the large network that intervenes in the process (Risku et al. 2016). Nevertheless, depending on the model, the brunt of responsibility is borne more by some agents than others. In certain cases, it is the responsibility of the workflow developer to achieve acceptable results taking into consideration the varied nature and quality of contributions. In others, responsibility can partly fall to community managers, such as those in Facebook or Twitter, who oversee the process and consequently are ultimately responsible for quality.

In paid crowdsourcing, there is a clear shift of responsibility from the translation provider towards the client or customer that has to decide which level of quality or fitness for purpose offered matches the value they place on the translation. Responsibility for quality is thus lifted to some extent from the provider and from participants in the crowd. Clients are directly presented with economic issues related to the different tiers of quality associated with diverse types of processes and crowds that might be involved in the process. OneHourTranslation,[14] for example, offer not only different tiers, such as general, expert, and exclusive, but also the possibility of including or excluding a revision service in the price. The translation processes recommended are also attached to the content requested and the company, in terms of quality, also offers different rates for translation than for translation plus proofreading. That is, not only does the customer need to select the correct type of process to achieve the quality requested, he/she also has to pay a higher rate if proofreading is requested. For example, in late 2016 expert translation was offered for 0.139 US cents per word while translation plus proofreading was 0.239 cents per word. Again, the company claims that they employ "only professional translators with rich translation experience" that are pre-screened to work for them. They also offer separate expertise groups in order to produce expert translations.

---

[14]https://www.onehourtranslation.com

4   The Blending of MT and Professional Paradigms: Of Practices and Blended Approaches

It can be argued that crowdsourcing approaches to quality range from those that attempt to replicate professional approaches to others mainly inspired by MT and computational linguistics. This section explores approaches pursued to test, evaluate, or produce quality in crowdsourcing initiatives, inspired by approaches along a continuum in which mainstream professional approaches appear at one end, and MT at the other. Figure 1 represents this continuum of crowdsourcing practices. The practices were identified through a comprehensive analysis of existing models, along with industry and scholarly publications, with the goal of identifying and describing new practices and approaches (Jiménez-Crespo 2017a). It should also be mentioned that, as described in previous sections, the evolution in crowdsourcing has led certain initiatives to replicate new crowdsourcing models that did not exist in professional contexts and to apply them using communities of 'professional' or 'expert' translators.

This should be understood as an open and dynamic cline in which hybrid practices can coexist. For example, even when Facebook users might propose translations and vote on preferred renditions, a language community manager might oversee the process and revise and approve the final translation, combining a global revision stage typical of professional approaches with the micro-task iterative voting approach (Dombek 2014).

4.1   Quality Practices Inspired by Professional Contexts

Traditional professional cycles, such as those described in the EN-15038 or other standards, require a minimum of a two-step process with an accredited translator and

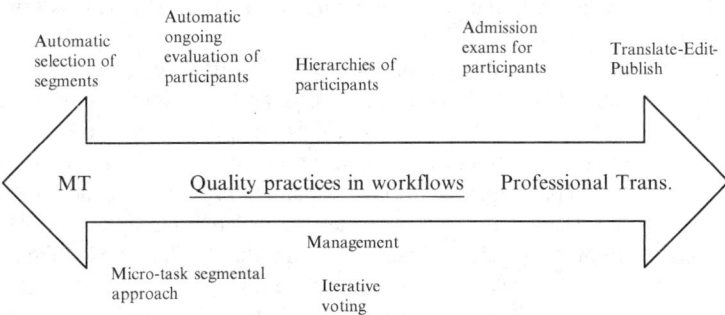

Fig. 1 Cline of similarity to difference in the development of translation crowdsourcing approaches to quality

a reviser using standardised metrics. The combination of management, translation, and revision is a common approach in professional circles (Gouadec 2007; Drugan 2013). This is paired with a priori established metrics to evaluate the quality of the product and using quality thresholds. Error-based metrics, or a combination of error-based and holistic evaluation are primarily used. Against this backdrop, certain non-professional collaborative workflows have developed practices by means of adopting existing professional approaches with variations to achieve the desired level of fitness for purpose. This section reviews quality practices identified in crowdsourcing practices inspired to a greater or lesser degree by professional contexts.

The first approach to achieve quality in crowdsourcing scenarios can be said to be typical of those initiatives that attempt to replicate the TEP models. This tends to appear primarily in non-profit scenarios such as Kiva or Translate America. It is common to replicate the 'waterfall' approach (Dunne and Dunne 2011), in which a text is assigned to a translator and, once the translation is completed, it is followed by revision and delivery. Normally, it is applied to texts that are short in length, such as microloan agreements or news reports. Since the responsibility for the production of quality falls to a greater degree on the individual processing the translation, participants are selected due to being 'qualified' or possessing the necessary skills in the eyes of the initiators. They correspond to what is known as a "closed model" (Mesipuu 2012), that is, a model in which participation is restricted to those selected in whichever fashion is deemed appropriate. These initiatives also include certain built-in hierarchies within the organisational structures to include revisers and managers that are perceived as possessing a higher degree of translation competence (Camara 2015). Revisers normally perform a revision and evaluation of the translation and they provide feedback to the original translator in order to improve future performance in a continuous quality loop. This not only benefits the overall quality of the process and product but also, given the volunteer context, improves the motivation of volunteers to continue participating, as stated in O'Brien and Schäler (2010). Hierarchies are thus an inherent part of these initiatives, with professional translators that volunteer performing revision or management roles, as in the Open Translation Initiative at TED Talks (Camara 2015). This is often also the case in non-profits such as Kiva.

The next approach inspired by professional models involves establishing certain gateways to be included in a limited community. This is also related to the above-mentioned 'closed model' (Mesipuu 2012). Such gatekeeping and community building is presented as a practice to guarantee quality, since there is a degree of control over who can participate in the crowdsourcing process. Whether the process is carried out in a TEP or an open micro-task crowdsourcing approach, there are restrictions set in place to select participants with a particular profile. This can be done through translation tests, for example, the most common practice instituted by LSPs to accept translators for in-house or freelance positions. This practice often recurs in non-profit organisations such as Kiva and Watching America, and it is always used in higher-paid crowdsourcing initiatives, such as those by GetLocalization, Speaklike, Steppes, and OneHourTranslation. Tests are often graded by language managers in paid crowdsourcing contexts or higher-status participants in fully voluntary settings. In most cases, the goal of this gatekeeping is to involve "as many skilled translators as possible" (DePalma and Kelly 2011). In some cases, the test is only required for proofreading or editing roles, e.g. for the translation into Chinese of the popular science website Gouker and its MOOC courses (Cao 2015).

In addition to testing, crowd selection and building communities with different profiles to tackle projects of different natures has emerged as an important practice in industry publications (i.e. DePalma and Kelly 2011; Desilets and Van de Meer 2011). It is always implemented in paid crowdsourcing circles, and it is also found in unpaid ones. This practice can even be found in open models in which gatekeeping filters are set in place. For example, in Translate Facebook[15] members have to be active for at least one month before being permitted to participate. This means that they have in principle to be acquainted with how Facebook works before participating in the crowdsourcing initiative. Changes to working languages are only allowed once a month. If a different language is selected to translate, the application flags the user and indicates that the language of translation is different from the language they are using. Other initiatives, nevertheless, do not have any time restrictions and in Twitter, users can participate immediately upon registering. In certain cases, communities can be open only to professional translators, such as the case of Translators Without Borders,[16] which requires four years of professional experience. In paid crowdsourcing models, companies offer different types of crowds, from bilinguals and general translators to specialists, or even allow the creation of a crowd of selected professionals to participate in the translation process, such as in the case of GetLocalization. Launchpad Rosetta[17] for open software localization, for example, allows users to set up projects with different types of contributions or permission policy, such as 'open', 'structured', 'restricted', or 'closed'. Anyone can collaborate in open projects. In the structured model, a member or a group of selected members can review and accept translation suggestions from the community. The restricted model is similar to the structured one, but languages without a management team are closed, while the closed-model-only participants assigned by the team can both translate and review/accept suggestions.

Control over participation does not stop with admission to the initiative; participants' performance can be continuously evaluated throughout their participation, either manually or automatically. While manual cases are those closer to professional translation, automatic cases are those related to MT and language automation. In manual cases, this can be accomplished by peer evaluation, such as the Unbabel or Stepes smartphone apps, in-house community managers, or higher-status participants. For example, the volunteer initiative to translate the *Economist* by ECOS into Chinese entails successfully translating seven articles in order to be fully accepted as a translator (Ray and Kelly 2011). In cases such as the bartering

---

[15] https://www.facebook.com/TranslateFacebookTeam/

[16] https://translatorswithoutborders.org/

[17] https://translations.launchpad.net/

platform Cucumis,[18] if translation performance in the review stage is consistently rated as superior, translators move to an 'expert' category. When this happens, their volunteer translations cost more 'translation points' in exchange. A similar approach has also been implemented in the Linqapp[19] platform.

An additional common practice is to create and/or apply workflows that incorporate traditional a priori quality assurance measures based on translation technologies. Initiatives can use off-the-shelf or custom-made platforms with built-in translation memories, termbases, the possibility of assigning roles in the process, and feedback loops, etc., such as Transifex,[20] Ackuna,[21] Trommons,[22] or MNH-TT.[23] In certain crowdsourcing initiatives, it is also common to establish shared resources such as glossaries, guidelines, norms, or discussion forums. The crowdsourcing initiatives in Facebook, Twitter, or Symantec[24] all include these resources. Facebook, for example, has gone through an evolution in this regard over the years; while the first versions of the crowdsourcing platform offered shared glossaries and iterative translate-vote processes, it now includes automatic term matches in segments to translate.

Role assignment, including management of the translation process, is also a key element to ensure quality (Dunne and Dunne 2011), and is also incorporated in crowdsourcing initiatives with certain variations. Aikawa et al. (2012), in discussing the Community Translation Framework by Microsoft, indicate that:

> One of the biggest concerns for crowdsourcing translation is the quality assurance of crowd-sourced translation. That is, how can we verify the quality of the edits or the translations coming from anonymous users? To address this concern, CTF allows a web owner to assign 'trusted' human translators the role of moderator and/or that of translator.

Crowdsourcing in social networking sites, for example, can involve language experts or community managers to oversee the crowdsourcing process from a macrostructural and professional perspective (DePalma and Kelly 2011). Their role involves the oversight of the process and the overall quality of the translation. In large initiatives, language managers appear online in all of the fully supported languages, while others are self-managed by the community. Many initiatives and platforms implicitly include the role of managers or language experts with different roles, such as Microsoft Collaborative Translation Framework (Aikawa et al. 2012) and most of the for- and non-profit platforms. In some instances, it is recommended that the expert become a company employee or, if that is not possible, a 'top contributor' as indicated in the TAUS Community evaluation guidelines (TAUS 2014).

---

[18]http://www.cucumis.org/translation_1_w/

[19]http://www.linqapp.com/

[20]https://www.transifex.com/

[21]https://ackuna.com/

[22]https://trommons.org/

[23]http://ecom.trans-aid.jp/

[24]https://www.symantec.com/

4.2 Approaches and Practices Inspired in MT and Language Automation

At the opposite end of the continuum, quality practices inspired by MT and language automation approaches have emerged. In general, the issue of translation quality in crowdsourcing is one of the most prolific areas of MT research. The number of publications and papers presented in conferences is extensive when compared with the relative lack of attention the issue has attracted in TS. Since the late 1990s, the intersection of crowdsourcing and MT has been explored as an alternative to both improve and train MT systems (Shimohata et al. 2001; Utiyama and Isahara 2003) and to post-edit the output in diverse ways. Google Translate[25] and Bing Translator[26] quickly allowed users to post-edit MT output, helping users to achieve the quality levels that they find acceptable, and also to continue to train their MT systems. New applications and widgets such as Google Website Translator[27] or Microsoft Collaborative Translation Framework (Tatsumi et al. 2012), also allow users to suggest "better translations" when the proposed renderings are not good enough for their purposes, putting post-editing even further into the hands of end users and focusing on their preferences. A complete review of MT approaches in crowdsourcing translation quality is outside the scope of this paper, and consequently, this section will only review practices observed in crowdsourcing workflows to maximise quality inspired by MT and language automation approaches.

The first practice related to MT is the extension of translation crowdsourcing to post-editing. In this approach, the final quality depends not only on the contribution of participants, but also on the quality of the MT output, and the final process of approval of segments prior to publication. Post-editing can be combined with either expert or peer selection of the post-edited segment, adding an additional layer of quality to the process. For example, the now discontinued case of Asia Online[28] translation of Wikipedia into Thai, in which their workflow combined automatic quality checking with professional human translators (Morera-Mesa 2014; Morera-Mesa et al. 2014). In this workflow three different participants post-edited the same MT segment. If any of the two participants' post-edited outputs matched, the segment was automatically selected and flagged for insertion in the target text. If the three renditions were different, then a 'professional' contributor was to select the best rendition. The quality approach did not end there, since the other two segments were fed into the MT engine for training purposes, with the hope of producing higher quality MT output in the future. The smartphone app Unbabel, for example,

---

[25] https://translate.google.com/

[26] https://www.bing.com/translator

[27] http://translate.google.com/manager/website/?hl=en

[28] More recently Omniscien Technologies (see https://omniscien.com/)

similarly incorporates post-editing of MT output that can subsequently be peer voted in order to assess its quality.

Another practice of interest to achieve quality in MT circles is to crowdsource and improve what is known as "feedback translations" (Volk and Harder 2007; O'Hagan 2013), using post-edited MT output that is later on used to feed the MT engines, in order to improve the quality of the output of MT engines. Zaidan and Callison-Burch (2011) attracted a great deal of interest with their paper on getting "professional quality from non-professionals" through crowdsourcing. In the paper, Zaidan and Callison-Burch (2011) state that "although many of the individual non-expert translators produce low-quality, disfluent translations, we show that it is possible to get high quality translations in aggregate by soliciting multiple translations, redundantly editing them, and then selecting the best of the bunch". The main focus was not on obtaining high quality from professional translators, but rather on using crowdsourcing as a tool to obtain translations to feed and improve MT engines (Zaidan and Callison-Burch 2011; Zbib et al. 2013; Gao et al. 2015; Yan et al. 2015). This entails a new model not explored in translation research, as it combines paid crowdsourced translation with volunteers using Amazon Mechanical Turk in the production of a translation that does not have humans or human communication as an objective, but rather MT engines. The notion of quality in this area refers not to the quality of the translations themselves, but rather to the quality of the output of the MT engine trained with these translated texts. This line of research has proven that crowdsourcing can produce, for the purposes of MT training, similar results to those from professional translations at one fifth of the cost (Zaidan and Callison-Burch 2011). This line of research focuses mainly on languages for which translation resources to create and train MT engines are scarce.

Language automation approaches also introduced the potential to evaluate automatically the quality of participants' performance or prior ability. For example, in the crowdsourcing management platform CrowdFlower,[29] automatic evaluation of performance can be introduced if requested. This platform can randomly insert multiple-choice questions during the crowdsourcing tasks in order to assess the potential reliability of participants. Similarly, MT approaches have also explored the ratings of translator contributors on Amazon Mechanical Turk in order to select and/or reject participants based on their worker ratings or past performance (i.e. Yan et al. 2015; Ehara et al. 2016). This selection of 'super-users' or establishment of user ratings also appears as a recommendation for general community evaluation by TAUS (2010).

One example of the impact of language automation and MT approaches is the introduction of iterative/redundancy voting mechanisms. Quality is achieved through the production of translation proposals that are subsequently voted. The translation renditions can be proposed either by the crowd, by experts or higher status participants or by MT engines. As Jiménez-Crespo (2015) indicates, user-based approaches are nothing new in translation studies. The works of Nida (1964)

---

[29]https://www.crowdflower.com/

and Nida and Taber (1969) are recognised as the first approach to translation quality that included reader responses as a basic component. This can be described as a response-oriented or behavioural approach to translation evaluation and is based on Nida's notion of "dynamic equivalence"; that is, that the manner in which the receptors of the translated texts respond to the translation must be equivalent to the manner in which the receptors of the source text respond to the source text (Nida 1964). One of the overall criteria to guarantee quality is the elicitation of the receiver's reaction to several translation alternatives or reading aloud the translation to several individuals before an audience. These two practical tests, even when the author's proposal does not explicitly include the source texts, would be the closest to current iterative mechanisms to guarantee quality.

Finally, another group of mechanisms are quality loops after the release of the test, including, among others, the 'many eyes' principle or 'Linus' law'. These a posteriori participatory mechanisms often take two forms, either the direct participation in open initiatives such as Wikipedia[30] or Amara,[31] where anyone can edit the translation in the future if left unfrozen, or in the form of discussion boards to report translation issues. Examples of this last practice are found in the Microsoft Language Portal or the Facebook forums for each locale version (Jiménez-Crespo 2015). In some platforms, such as Microsoft Collaborative Translation Framework, it is possible to authorise users to directly edit machine-translated webpages. The many eyes principle or 'Linus' law' was first formulated by Raymond (2001) in reference to open-source software development and is defined as situations in which "[g]iven a large enough beta-tester and co-developer base, almost every problem will be characterised quickly and the fix will be obvious to someone", or, as the author indicated less formally, "given enough eyeballs, all bugs are shallow". This open paradigm entails unrestricted community participation in the translation and editing process. It is assumed that broad crowd participation in a process with many people going over the same materials will identify and correct any existing flaw. Revision studies in Wikipedia have shown that this is often the case (McDonough-Dolmaya 2012). This can only work in systems that are totally open and in which it is possible to incorporate a step called 'freezing' of the translation, as is done in software development.

It is of interest that studies have explored whether crowdsourcing can be used for translation evaluation instead of using MT measures such as BLEU (Papineni et al. 2002) or other automatic measures. Goto et al. (2014) researched whether crowdsourcing quality evaluation of translation is feasible if compared to actual professionals. Their study focused on contrasting professionals or crowdsourcing participants to assess the quality of MT output in terms of an MT system comparison, providing a sentence score and translation scores. The results showed that when compared with professionals, crowdsourcing is as valid as professional translation for the evaluation of quality in comparing MT systems, but not necessarily in

---

[30]https://www.wikipedia.org/

[31]https://amara.org/en/

sentence or translation scores and sentence score evaluation. This implies that crowdsourcing MT output evaluation, at the sentence level, does not achieve the same result if volunteers are compared to professional translators. Nevertheless, comparing the quality of output of different MT engines can be crowdsourced to non-professionals. Other similar studies have also resorted to the crowd to compare MT system performance. Bowker and Buitrago (2016) studied the usefulness of MT in the translation of library websites, and the methodology involved users evaluating the performance of a statistical, a hybrid, and a rule-based system. The results of the study showed that the statistical MT system, Google Translate, produced the most acceptable results for the users.

5 Conclusions

This chapter has analysed the role of crowdsourcing in translation quality evaluation. It is clear that crowdsourcing has challenged industry experts on workflows, community visionaries, and MT researchers to achieve the highest possible level of fitness for purpose in a changing landscape. This new highly dynamic field has become an ideal breeding ground for innovations, introducing variations to basic elements in MT or professional approaches, as well as new ones, to achieve quality. As a whole, crowdsourcing approaches have further consolidated a move away from a static notion of quality, exploring approaches beyond top-down models in which error typologies, quality control, and quality management procedures are established a priori and applied across the board.

The chapter has critically analysed the theoretical implications for Translation Quality Assessment both for industry and for TS. It has also critically described practices observed in existing initiatives in order to guarantee the highest possible level of fitness for purpose or quality. As far as the impact of crowdsourcing to quality evaluation, it has been argued that three key issues are: the consolidation of the process-based understanding of quality that permeates the language industry, the push to further consolidate the fitness for purpose paradigm, and the sharing of responsibilities in terms of quality among the various participants in translation efforts.

Given the innovative and dynamic nature of crowdsourcing, it is likely that crowdsourcing will continue to impact conceptualisations of quality in translation. New models and workflows will emerge. Will new business models and workflows continue to exert an influence in the development of the language industry in terms of quality? It was initially thought that MT post-editing would quickly become the norm in the industry (i.e. Garcia 2010), but to date no more than 5% of the total volume of translation is produced using that model (Doherty 2016). Nevertheless, without any doubt MT approaches have helped to consolidate the fitness for purpose model, bringing clients and users into the quality equation. Similarly, the jury is still out on whether crowdsourcing initiatives, both volunteer and paid, will continue to provide high-quality translations with low costs and quick turnarounds with acceptable quality. As DePalma (2015) indicates when discussing crowdsourced mobile translation:

> It remains to be seen whether the price that seems attractive to bilinguals gains a significant uptake in commercial applications. If buyers are willing to pay what mobile users deem a worthy wage, no doubt there will be many years, conferences, and forums spent debating the merits.

To this it should be added that the jury is still out also on whether buyers and users will be willing to accept the level of quality that crowdsourcing models can provide in different situations. There is no doubt that massive scale cooperation initiatives such as those in social networking sites will continue to successfully produce high levels of quality that users will accept (Jiménez-Crespo 2013). The issue here will be whether the large number of variables at play in these scenarios, from differences in participation in language combinations, to interest in certain contexts, all the way to the inclusion or exclusion of certain types of context in crowdsourcing models such as legal or marketing, will make crowdsourcing appropriate only for certain domains, geographical areas, or textual genres in which fitness for purpose can be achieved. In a 2015 TAUS industry conference with representatives from some of the largest language industry players, Valli (2015) indicated that no company showed any interest in using crowdsourcing for translation purposes because "as a lesson learned from other companies, crowdsourcing requires significant efforts in terms of internal infrastructure to coordinate and manage the crowd". The lesson learnt here is that "crowdsourcing requires significant efforts" if high quality is the desired outcome. In the context of content prioritisation (O'Brien 2012), the answer to the question posed above might be found in the selection of content, language combination, and the desired level of fitness for purpose.

What is clear is that the varied nature of what can be understood in terms of fitness for purpose or acceptable/adequate translation will continue to evolve in parallel to the development of new initiatives, workflow models, audience expectations, and crowd participation. The blind faith in the power of workflow development to achieve adequate quality does not depend solely on developers and participants. For example, no matter how many developments emerge, it will be harder to find vetted communities to crowdsource texts from German to Norwegian than from English to Chinese. The variables, therefore, are many. Only time will tell how the interrelation of MT, crowdsourcing, paraprofessional translation, and high-quality professional translation will continue to intersect in order to achieve the highest possible fitness for purpose within whichever contextual limitations might emerge in each case. Nevertheless, what crowdsourcing will not help to elucidate is what the fuzzy notion of 'quality in translation' is, beyond statements that imply adherence to client instructions and user expectations, to the purpose of the translation coherence with the source text or the lack of errors. The debate, it seems, will continue to go on for decades.

References

Aikawa T, Yamamoto K, Isahara H (2012) The impact of crowdsourcing post-editing with the collaborative translation framework. In: Proceedings of JapTAL 2012: advances in natural language processing 7614, pp 1–10. Springer, Berlin. Available via: http://research.microsoft.com/pubs/172592/JapTal2012.pdf. Accessed 1 Oct 2016

Allen J (2003) Post-editing. In: Somers H (ed) Computers and translation: a translators guide. John Benjamins, Amsterdam, pp 297–317

Ambati V, Vogel S, Carbonell J (2012) Collaborative workflow for crowdsourcing translation. In: Proceedings of ACM 2012 conference on computer supported cooperative work, pp 1191–1194. Available via: https://www.cs.cmu.edu/~jgc/CollaborativeWorkflowforCrowdsourcingTranslationACMCoCSCW2012.pdf. Accessed 1 Oct 2016

Anastasiou D, Gupta R (2011) Comparison of crowdsourcing translation with machine translation. J Inf Sci 37(6):637–659

Arjona Reina L, Robles G, González-Barahona JM (2013) A preliminary analysis of localization in free software: how translations are performed. In: Petrinja E, Succi G, El Ioini N, Sillitti N (eds), Open source software: quality verification, pp 153–167, Springer, Heidelberg. https://doi.org/10.1007/978-3-642-38928-3_11

Bowker L, Buitrago J (2016) Investigating the usefulness of machine translation to newcomers in the public library. Trans Interpret 10(2):165–186

Brabham D (2013) Crowdsourcing. MIT Press, Cambridge, MA

Camara L (2015) Motivation for collaboration in TED open translation. Int J Web-Based Commun 11(2):210–229

Cao Y (2015) Crowdsourcing translation in contemporary China: an inspiring perspective of translation in the Web 2.0 age. Meta 60:316

Carson-Berndsen J, Somers H, Vogel C (2009) Integrated language technology as a part of next-generation localization. Localis Focus 81:53–66

Chan S-W (ed) (2014) Routledge encyclopedia of translation technology. Routledge, London

De Wille T, Exton C, Schäler R (2015) Multi-language communities, technology and perceived quality. Int Rep Socio-Inform 12:25–33

DePalma DA (2015) CSOFT swipes left for translation, right for the source to mobilize translation. Common Sense Advisory Publications. Available iva: http://www.commonsenseadvisory.com/Default.aspx?Contenttype=ArticleDetAD&tabID=63&Aid=36417&moduleId=390. Accessed Oct 10 2016

DePalma DA, Kelly N (2011) Project management for crowdsourced translation: how user-translated content projects work in real life. In: Dunne K, Dunne E (eds) Translation and localization project management: the art of the possible. John Benjamins, Amsterdam, pp 379–408

Deriemaeker J (2014) Power of the crowd: assessing crowd translation quality of tourist literature. Dissertation, Universiteit Ghent

Desilets A, van de Meer J (2011) Co-creating a repository of best-practices for collaborative translation. Linguistica Antverpiensia 10:11–27

Doherty S (2016) The impact of translation technologies on the process and product of translation. Int J Commun Stud 9:1–23

Dombek M (2014) A study into the motivations of internet users contributing to translation crowd-sourcing: the case of Polish Facebook user-translators. Dissertation, Dublin City University

Drugan J (2013) Quality in professional translation. Bloomsbury, London

Dunne K, Dunne E (eds) (2011) Translation and localization project management: the art of the possible. John Benjamins, Amsterdam

Ehara Y, Baba Y, Utiyama M, Sumita E (2016) Assessing translation ability through vocabulary ability assessment. In: Proceedings of the twenty-fifth international joint conference on artificial intelligence (IJCAI-16). Available via: https://pdfs.semanticscholar.org/47ea/223867dbe59f73f4f8ed1f429cfdb7abd68e.pdf. Accessed 10 Oct 2016

Estellés E, González F (2012) Towards an integrated crowdsourcing definition. J Inf Sci 38(2):189–200

Estellés E, Navarro-Giner R, González-Ladrón-de-Guevara F (2015) Crowdsourcing: definition and typology. In: Garrigos S, Gil P, Estellés M (eds) Advances in crowdsourcing. Springer, Heidelberg, pp 33–48

Exton C, Wasala A, Buckley J, Schäler R (2009) Micro crowdsourcing: a new model for software localization. Localis Focus 8(1):81–89

Fernandez Costales A (2011) Facing the challenges of the global era. Paper presented at Tralogy I, Le Centre national de la recherche scientifique, Paris, 3–4 March 2011. Available via: http://lodel.irevues.inist.fr/tralogy/index.php?id=120. Accessed 10 Dec 2017

Filip D, Ó Conchúir E (2011) An argument for business process management in localisation. Localis Focus 10:4–17

Gao M, Xu W, Callison-Burch C (2015) Cost optimization in crowdsourcing translation: low cost translations made even cheaper. In: Proceedings of the 2015 conference of the North American chapter of the Association for Computational Linguistics: Human Language Technologies (NAACL-HLT), pp 705–713

Garcia I (2010) Is machine translation ready yet? Target 22(1):7–21

Garcia I (2015) Cloud marketplaces: procurement of translators in the age of social media. JoSTrans 23:18–38. Available via: http://www.jostrans.org/issue23/art_garcia.pdf. Accessed 2 Oct 2016

Görög A (2014a) Quantification and comparative evaluation of quality: the TAUS dynamic quality framework. Revista Tradumàtica 12:443–454. Available via: http://revistes.uab.cat/Tradumàtica/article/view/n12-gorog2/pdf. Accessed 10 Oct 2016

Görög A (2014b) Translation and quality: editorial. Revista Tradumàtica 12:388–391. Available via: http://revistes.uab.cat/Tradumàtica/article/view/n12-gorog/pdf_2. Accessed 10 October 2016

Goto S, Lin D, Ishida T (2014) Crowdsourcing for evaluating Machine Translation quality. In: Proceedings of LREC 2014, Reykjavík, pp 3456–3463

Gouadec D (2007) Translation as a profession. John Benjamins, Amsterdam

Gouadec D (2010) Quality in translation. In: Gambier Y, van Doorslaer L (eds) Handbook of translation studies, p 270–275. John Benjamins, Amsterdam

House J (1997) Translation quality assessment: a model revisited. Gunter Narr, Tübingen

House J (2014) Translation quality assessment: past and present. Routledge, London

Howe J (2008) Crowdsourcing: why the power of the crowd is driving the future of business. Crown Publishing Group, New York

Hu C, Resnik P, Kronrod Y, Eidelman V, Buzek O, Bederson BB (2011) The value of monolingual crowdsourcing in a real-world translation scenario: simulation using Haitian creole emergency SMS messages. In: Proceedings of the sixth workshop on Statistical Machine Translation, Edinburgh, pp 399–404

Jääskeläinen R (2016) Quality and translation process research. In: Muñoz Martín R (ed) Reembedding translation process research. John Benjamins, Amsterdam, pp 89–106

Jiménez-Crespo MA (2013) Crowdsourcing, corpus use, and the search for translation naturalness: a comparable corpus study of Facebook and non-translated social networking sites. Trans Interpret 8:23–49

Jiménez-Crespo MA (2015) Translation quality, use and dissemination in an internet era: using single-translation and multi-translation parallel corpora to research translation quality on the web. JoSTrans 23:39–63

Jiménez-Crespo MA (2016) Testing explicitation in translation: triangulating corpus and experimental studies. Across Lang Cult 16(2):257–283

Jiménez-Crespo MA (2017a) Crowdsourcing and collaborative translations: expanding the limits of translation studies. John Benjamins, Amsterdam

Jiménez-Crespo MA (2017b) How much would you like to pay? Reframing and expanding the notion of translation quality through crowdsourcing and volunteer approaches. Perspectives 25(3):478–491

Jiménez-Crespo MA (2017c) Mobile apps and translation crowdsourcing: The next frontier in the evolution of translation. Revista Tradumática 14:75–84. Available via: http://revistes.uab.cat/ Tradumática/article/view/167/pdf_31. Accessed 10 December 2017

Kelly D (2005) A handbook for translator trainers. St Jerome, Manchester

Klaus C (2014) Translationsqualität und crowdsourced translation: Untertitlung und ihre Bewertung–am Beispiel des audiovisuellen Mediums TEDTalk. Frank & Timme GmbH, Berlin

Koby GS, Fields P, Hague D, Lommel A, Melby A (2014) Defining translation quality. Revista Tradumàtica 12:413–420. Available via: https://ddd.uab.cat/pub/Tradumática/ Tradumática_a2014n12/Tradumática_a2014n12p413.pdf. Accessed 10 Dec 2017

Koponen M, Salmi L (2015) On the correctness of machine translation: A machine translation post-editing task. JoSTrans 23:118–136. Available via: http://www.jostrans.org/issue23/ art_koponen.pdf. Accessed 30 October 2016

Lommel A, Burchardt A, Uszkoreit H (2014) Multidimensional Quality Metrics MQM: a framework for declaring and describing translation quality metrics. Revista Tradumática 12:455–463. Available via: http://revistes.uab.cat/Tradumática/article/view/n12-lommel-uzskoreit-burchardt/pdf. Accessed 2 Oct 2016

Martínez Melis N, Hurtado Albir A (2001) Assessment in translation studies: research needs. Meta 46(2):272–287

McDonough-Dolmaya J (2012) Analyzing the crowdsourcing model and its impact on public perceptions of translation. Translator 18(2):167–191

Mesipuu M (2012) Translation crowdsourcing and user-translator motivation at Facebook and Skype. Trans Space 1:33–53

Michalak K (2015) Online localization of Zooniverse citizen science projects - on the use of translation platforms as tools for translator education. Teach English Technol 3:61–72. Available via: http://yadda.icm.edu.pl/yadda/element/bwmeta1.element.desklight-32a1582e-2f8d-412c-80c6-d6d03086424d. Accessed 4 Oct 2016

Mitchell L (2015) Community post-editing of machine-translated user-generated content. Dissertation, Dublin City University

Mitchell L, O'Brien S, Roturier J (2014) Quality evaluation in community post-editing. Mach Transl 28(3):237–262

Morera-Mesa A (2014) Crowdsourced translation practices from the process flow perspective. Dissertation, University of Limerick

Morera-Mesa A, Aouad L, Collins JJ (2012) Assessing support for community workflows in localisation. Bus Process Manag Workshop Ser Lecture Note Bus Inf Process 99:195–206

Morera-Mesa A, Collins JJ, Filip D (2014) Selected crowdsourced translation practices. In: Proceedings of translating and the computer 35, London, 28–29 November 2013. Available via: http://www.mt-archive.info/10/Aslib-2013-Morera-Mesa.pdf. Accessed 2 Oct 2016

Muzii L (2013) Is quality under pressure? Or is translation? Paper presented at TMT conference 2013, The Hague, 27 September 2013

Nida E (1964) Towards a science of translation. Brill, Leiden

Nida E, Taber CR (1969) The theory and practice of translation. Brill, Leiden

Nord C (1997) Functionalist approaches explained. St. Jerome, Manchester

O'Brien S (2012) Towards a dynamic quality evaluation model for translation. JoSTrans 17:55–77. Available via: http://www.jostrans.org/issue17/art_obrien.pdf. Accessed 4 Oct 2016

O'Brien S, Schäler R (2010) Next generation translation and localization: users are taking charge. In: Proceedings from translating and the computer 32, London, 18–19 November 2010. Available via: http://doras.dcu.ie/16695/1/Paper_6.pdf. Accessed 10 Oct 2016

O'Hagan M (2013) The impact of new technologies on translation studies: a technological turn? In: Millán-Varela C, Bartrina F (eds) Routledge handbook of translation studies. Routledge, London, pp 503–518

Olohan M (2014) Why do you translate? Motivation to volunteer and TED translation. Perspect Stud Translatol 7(1):17–33

Orrego-Carmona D (2015) The reception of non-professional subtitling. Dissertation, University Rovira i Virgili

Papineni K, Roukos S, Ward T, Zhu W (2002) BLEU: a method for automatic evaluation of machine translation. In: Proceedings of the 40th annual meeting on Association for Computational Linguistics, Philadelphia, pp 311–318

Persaud A, O'Brien S (2017) Quality and acceptance of crowdsourced translation of web content. Int J Technol Hum Interact 13(1):100–115

Pym A (2012) On translator ethics: principles for mediation between cultures. John Benjamins, Amsterdam

Ray R, Kelly N (2011) Crowdsourced translation: best practices for implementation. Common Sense Advisory, Boston

Raymond ES (2001) The cathedral and the bazaar. O'Reilly and Associates, Sebastopol

Risku H, Rogl R, Pein-Weber C (2016) Mutual dependencies: centrality in translation networks. JoSTrans 25:232–253. Available via: http://www.jostrans.org/issue25/art_risku.pdf. Accessed 30 Oct 2016

Shimohata S, Kitamura M, Sukehiro T, Murata T (2001) Collaborative translation environment on the web. In: Proceedings from MT Summit VIII, Santiago de Compostela, pp 331–334

Siddique H (2011) Mob rule: Iceland crowdsources its next constitution. The Guardian, Thursday 9 June 2011. Available via: http://www.theguardian.com/world/2011/jun/09/iceland-crowdsourcing-constitution-facebook. Accessed 10 Oct 2016

Suojanen T, Koskinen K, Tuominen T (2015) User-centred translation. Routledge, London

Tatsumi M, Aikawa T, Yamamoto K, Isahara H (2012) How good is crowd post-editing: its potential and limitations. In: Proceedings of the tenth biennial conference of the Association for Machine Translation in the Americas, San Diego, 28 October – 1 November 2012

TAUS (2010) Post-editing guidelines. Available via: https://www.taus.net/academy/best-practices/postedit-best-practices/machine-translation-post-editing-guidelines. Accessed 10 Oct 2016

TAUS (2014) Community evaluation best practices. https://www.taus.net/academy/best-practices/evaluate-best-practices/community-evaluation-best-practices. Accessed 4 May 2018

Utiyama M, Isahara H (2003) Reliable measures for aligning Japanese-English news articles and sentences. In: Proceedings of the 41st annual meeting of the Association for Computational Linguistics, pp 72–79

Valli P (2015) Disrupt me not. Keynotes 2015 A review of the TAUS October Events, San Francisco, pp 46–54. Available via: https://www.taus.net/blog/disrupt-me-not. Accessed 4 Mar 2016

Volk M, Harder S (2007) Evaluating MT with translations or translators: what is the difference? In: Proceedings of MT Summit XI, Copenhagen, pp 499–506

Wright SE (2006) Language industry standards. In: Dunne K (ed) Perspectives on localization. John Benjamins, Amsterdam, pp 241–278

Yan J, Song Y, Li CT, Zhang M, Hu X (2015) Opportunities or risks to reduce labor in crowdsourcing translation? Characterizing cost versus quality via a pagerank-hits hybrid model. In: Proceedings of the twenty-fourth international joint conference on artificial intelligence, Buenos Aires, pp 1025–1032

Zaidan OF, Callison-Burch C (2011) Crowdsourcing translation: professional quality from non-professionals. In: Proceedings of the 49th annual meeting of the Association of Computational Linguistics, Portland, 19–24 June 2011, pp 1120–1129

Zbib R, Markiewicz G, Matsoukas S, Schwartz R, Makhoul J (2013) Systematic comparison of professional and crowdsourced reference translations for machine translation. In: Proceedings of the 2013 conference of the North American chapter of the Association for Computational Linguistics: Human Language Technologies, Atlanta, 9–14 June 2013, pp 612–616

On Education and Training in Translation Quality Assessment

4

Stephen Doherty, Joss Moorkens, Federico Gaspari, and Sheila Castilho

Abstract In this chapter, we argue that education and training in translation quality assessment (TQA) is being neglected for most, if not all, stakeholders of the translation process, from translators, post-editors, and reviewers to buyers and end-users of translation products and services. Within academia, there is a lack of education and training opportunities to equip translation students, even at postgraduate level, with the knowledge and skills required to understand and use TQA. This has immediate effects on their employability and long-term effects on professional practice. In discussing and building upon previous initiatives to tackle this issue, we provide a range of viewpoints and resources for the provision of such opportunities in collaborative and independent contexts across all modes and academic settings, focusing not just on TQA and machine translation training, but also on the use of assessment strategies in educational contexts that are directly relevant to those used in industry. In closing, we reiterate our argument for the importance of education and training in TQA, on the basis of all the contributions and perspectives presented in the volume.

Keywords Translation quality assessment · Principles to practice · Translation industry · Translation students · Translation teaching · Translation pedagogy

S. Doherty
School of Humanities and Languages, The University of New South Wales, Sydney, Australia
e-mail: s.doherty@unsw.edu.au

J. Moorkens
ADAPT Centre/School of Applied Language and Intercultural Studies, Dublin City University, Dublin, Ireland
e-mail: joss.moorkens@dcu.ie

F. Gaspari
ADAPT Centre/School of Computing, Dublin City University, Dublin, Ireland

University for Foreigners "Dante Alighieri" of Reggio Calabria, Reggio Calabria, Italy
e-mail: federico.gaspari@adaptcentre.ie

S. Castilho
ADAPT Centre/School of Computing, Dublin City University, Dublin, Ireland
e-mail: sheila.castilho@adaptcentre.ie

1 Introduction and Background

The advent of translation technologies has called for a more pragmatic approach to translation quality evaluation in both research and practice across the language services industry. In an increasingly competitive market where quality-focused translators come under intense pressure from clients to sustain quality standards while offering more attractive rates and faster turn-around times, models and tools to support translation quality assessment (TQA) are a necessity. The uptake of computer-assisted translation (CAT) tools, which have been widely shown to boost productivity, reduce turn-around time and enhance phraseological consistency (see, e.g. Granell Zafra 2006; Federico et al. 2012; Christensen and Schjoldager 2016; Moran et al. 2018), has proceeded in parallel with the gradual refinement of TQA models and tools (see O'Hagan 2013; Doherty 2016).

While the importance of adopting CAT tools is now a given, and there is a growing realisation of the potential of machine translation (MT) in the translation community at large, we feel that there is still a strong need to raise awareness and instil appreciation of the role of TQA. This is particularly important for translation educators, trainers, students, researchers, as well as professionals who are keen to keep their skillsets up-to-date to remain competitive on the market, e.g. by attending lifelong training programmes. In addressing the educational needs related to TQA, we consider both formal teaching contexts, typically as part of academic or vocational translator training programmes (such as degree programmes in translation studies or specialisation courses for language graduates) and more flexible and focused training opportunities in professional and industry-oriented settings, including tool-specific training for accreditation purposes, self-paced upskilling, online tutorials and webinars, etc. It is increasingly common, for example, to find ad-hoc training sessions and workshops specifically aimed at professionals within the programmes of industry-oriented conferences, and often translators associations expect that their members obtain certain qualifications or attend recognised training events on a regular basis (these may even be organised by the association as part of a professional development programme), to maintain full membership or retain their certified status.

In particular, most well-established translator training programmes at university level now include components focusing on the use of CAT tools and other translation technologies with their related skills, most notably MT and post-editing (PE), a development which, in our view, is certainly positive and responsive to industry needs. However, a cursory search of online translation programme descriptions and course syllabi available in English, as well as our own direct experience as educators in academia and in the industry, indicate that educators and their students are not yet sufficiently familiarised with TQA models and tools that are now commonplace in the industry. The focus of academic translation training programmes still appears to be firmly on theoretical frameworks that have only tenuous links with quality evaluation in real-world professional practice (see Castilho et al. this volume). While we recognise the value of more theoretically-oriented components in the training of well-rounded translators, we also advocate the importance of making room for the teaching of state-of-the-art quality evaluation metrics and tools that graduates are likely to encounter when they enter the translation marketplace.

In this respect, we believe that the role played by increasingly sophisticated evaluation procedures in professional translation is becoming even more important in today's technologised industry, which makes it essential for educators and students to be well-acquainted with the key principles and concepts in this area. This would ideally be achieved by embedding TQA knowledge and skills in curricula and syllabi, for example, by including recent literature in lecture content, by providing advanced workshops on TQA topics, by using industry-based marking criteria for translation assignments, by giving students clear guidelines for meeting expectations in industry contexts, and by introducing reproducible measures of quality that will then be familiar to graduates when they enter the language service industry. In the rest of this chapter, we substantiate these proposals with concrete examples and suggestions, with the purpose of encouraging the incorporation of TQA issues in a variety of formal academic educational contexts as well as more flexible industry-oriented training scenarios.

2 Translation Technology Education and Training

The importance of technology in translator education and training is well established and widely acknowledged, with several sources arguing for translation programmes to help students to become informed and critical users of the variety of technological tools they will encounter in their professional career (e.g. Pym 2003; Kenny 2007; EMT Expert Group 2009, 2017; Bowker and Marshman 2010; Doherty et al. 2012; Marshman and Bowker 2012; Doherty and Moorkens 2013; Doherty and Kenny 2014; Kenny and Doherty 2014). A general requirement for technical ability has consistently been a part of contemporary translation competence models for professionals and for university training for several years now (e.g. Beeby et al. 2009; EMT Expert Group 2009, 2017; Scarpa and Orlando 2017).

This is not to say that all university-trained translators are currently using the full range of translation technologies available to them. Indeed, we would never expect this to be the case, as different technologies may be more or less useful depending on a whole host of factors, including the area in which the translator is operating, the text type and the language pair in question, the file formats being used, and the quality levels expected, to name just a few. Rather, the wider field of translation has evolved and it behoves translation scholars and teachers to remain up to date, if not ahead of, such changes in their scholarship and teaching. The requirement to keep abreast of technological developments is arguably even more crucial for professional translators, who have to position themselves within rapidly changing markets as practitioners who may be asked to offer a diverse range of translation-related services including, for example, organising the language resources and terminological assets to be used via CAT tools in large multilingual translation and localisation projects, PE, diagnostic evaluation of MT systems, subtitling, etc., all of which depends, of course, on their clients, language pairs, fields of specialisation, etc. (Moorkens 2017).

Such an argument underlines why it is important to teach translation technology to the translators of today and tomorrow. An increasing number of publications are presenting detailed descriptions of how particular tools can be incorporated into a more narrowly-construed translation technology syllabus, or a more broadly-construed translation studies curriculum. For example, most of the papers in the *Journal of Translation Studies* 2010 special issue on teaching CAT (Chan 2010) fall into the former category, while work carried out under the banner of the Collection of Electronic Resources in Translation Technologies (CERTT; Bowker and Marshman 2010) at the University of Ottawa takes a broad, holistic view and attempts to create the conditions in which a range of technologies can be easily integrated into courses across the translation studies curriculum (Bowker and Marshman 2010; Marshman and Bowker 2012).

With a few notable exceptions such as Wältermann (1994), Kenny and Way (2001), Doherty et al. (2012), Kenny and Doherty (2014), and Sycz-Opoń and Gałuskina (2017), systematic studies on best practice to teach translation students about MT are difficult to find. Bowker and Marshman (2010, 204) mention, for example, that tutorials and exercises for the teaching of MT, exemplified by the rule-based system Reverso Pro, have been created as part of the CERTT project, but they do not give any further details. The other papers in Chan (2010) that mention MT say little if nothing about teaching MT. Flanagan and Christensen (2014) investigate how MA-level trainee translators interpret industry-focused PE guidelines designed to achieve publishable quality from raw MT output, and find that the trainees have difficulties interpreting them, primarily due to competency gaps, which leads to a set of proposals to address such shortcomings in academic training. Koponen (2015) notes students' variable post-editing speed and difficulty in following quality guidelines, but nonetheless views her teaching of PE as an important step in students' understanding of MT as a tool rather than a threat.

Pym's (2013) assertion that "there has actually been quite a lot of reflection on the ways MT and post-editing can be introduced into teaching practices" probably reflects more accurately the reality of the early 2000s than subsequent developments in translation pedagogy. Arguably, the heyday of reflection in the area was between 2001 and 2003, when the European Association for Machine Translation (EAMT) devoted some pioneering workshops to the teaching of MT (e.g. Forcada et al. 2001; EAMT/BCS 2002), and a workshop in 2003 devoted to teaching translation technologies at MT Summit IX (e.g. Forcada 2003; Knight 2003; Mitamura et al. 2003; Robichaud and L'Homme 2003; Vertan and von Hahn 2003; Way and Gough 2003).

Of particularly relevance here are the short papers by Knight (2003) and Way and Gough (2003). Way and Gough (2003) describe the development and assessment of a course in MT, focusing on RBMT and SMT, for undergraduate students in computational linguistics. Knight (2003) describes resources for introducing concepts of SMT, from which many researchers and lecturers have drawn, and remains valuable to this day. Since these workshops, however, teaching-oriented discussions on more recent approaches to MT, particularly hybrid and neural MT systems, have not yet emerged.

It is also true that for decades there was hardly any exchange between MT researchers and developers on the one hand, and professional translators and translation theorists on the other; this was mostly because translators have historically tended to see MT as a threat (England 1958), and (like translation theorists) the difficulties that MT faced in the days of rule-based systems were too banal from their point of view to take MT seriously (Taillefer 1992). Arguably, this scenario has since changed quite considerably. For a long time, the annual *Translating and the Computer* conference series (organised by ASLIB in London since 1978[1]) was arguably the only forum where these communities met, with some stimulating debate ensuing among kindred spirits discussing MT from different, but surprisingly complementary, perspectives, as reported by Kingscott (1990) from one such conference in the late 1980s. Following the advent of data-driven and machine-learning approaches that have made MT systems much more powerful and readily available for countless language pairs (including via free online MT services, see Gaspari and Hutchins 2007), today different commentators have different views on the degree of involvement that is desirable for translators in the development of SMT, in particular. These views range from the irenic (see Karamanis et al. 2011; Way and Hearne 2011) to the disruptive (e.g. Wiggins 2011). Even where translation scholars and teachers do engage with SMT, they can disagree on how much translators need to know about the technology: is it enough to use Google Translate? Enough to fix the output of MT systems with effective PE? Or enough to be able to build customised MT systems? In addition, depending on the future one predicts for the translation profession, different types of content would seem appropriate in the translation curriculum. In the somewhat deterministic picture presented by García (2011) and Pym (2013), translators are morphing into post-editors whose primary purpose will be to fix the output of MT systems.

Others, including Kenny and Doherty (2014), argue that translators who are able to remain abreast of technological developments will continue to be in demand and well placed in whatever form the language services industry takes in the future. We argue that confining their own professional profile to a narrowly-defined role undervalues the language expertise of translators. In addition, the recent trends of growing digital connectivity and communication are creating increasing needs to translate expanding numbers of texts and text types. These trends present opportunities for translators to take an advisory role, specifying the appropriate workflow for texts to be translated (Moorkens 2017), or assessing training data to be

---

[1] ASLING (the International Association for Advancement in Language Technology; https://www. asling.org) took over the organisation and management of the long-running *Translating and the Computer* conference series in 2014 and has been responsible for it since.

selected for MT system training and development, evaluating MT output, managing terminology, and refining workflows (O'Brien 2012); all of these roles benefit from a combination of skills involving, crucially, TQA.

3 TQA Models for Education and Training

Against this very dynamic background, there is a definite need for translation graduates to be familiar with a variety of TQA models and to have the skills to carry out TQA in a critical and efficient manner in a range of specific situations and contexts. Huertas Barros and Vine (2017) found that although over 53% of UK universities surveyed had recently updated their translation evaluation criteria, most do not believe that contemporary industry TQA is "relevant to an academic setting". The evaluation needs in industry and academia necessarily differ based on the pragmatic requirements of each scenario. For academics, it may involve testing a system or evaluating what sort of effort is required for a translator to work with a text type or a specific workflow. For industry, it may be to test the quality produced by a translator, or to assess the usefulness of translation leverage, also to measure productivity in terms of words processed per unit of time. The evaluation type and translation workflow are also likely to differ depending on the perishability of the content, as represented in Fig. 1 viz. broad categories of content types. Texts are considered perishable if they are for immediate consumption with little or no purpose thereafter, such as online travel reviews that are likely to slip into disuse as new reviews are added, social media posts or Internet fora messages concerning volatile information that are not locked to the top of a forum or thread; clearly, if this short-lived content requires translation into other languages, typically for quick multilingual dissemination, its quality is unlikely to be paramount or to warrant extensive evaluation (see also discussions of "fitness for purpose" in the chapters by Way and Jiménez-Crespo in this volume). Conversely, non-perishable texts (literary works and marketing copy being prime examples) are typically carefully crafted so as to possess aesthetic value and/or to clearly convey important, often durable, messages. These features must be accurately preserved in translation, thus requiring accordingly robust TQA procedures.

Since the advent of translation technology, and as computing power has grown, translation workflows have become more varied, complex, and technologised. This has necessitated a broader range of translation evaluation methods, suitable for the

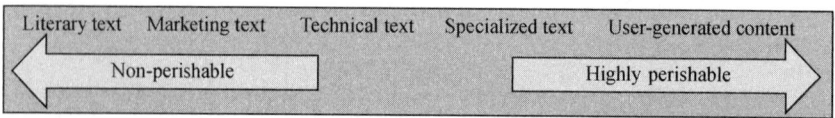

Fig. 1 Translated text perishability continuum

workflow, text type, or target audience. For researchers and language professionals, it is important to be aware of different types of evaluation to fit a particular project or workflow, and to consider whether a more innovative or agile approach could be used to replace another. We contend that TQA has become an essential component of vocational translator training for a range of roles, and is an advantage for translation graduates, some of whom begin their professional lives as freelance or in-house translators, but may then move to a translation management role at some point during their careers.[2]

Interestingly, in a large-scale survey that involved 438 language professionals, Gaspari et al. (2015) found that 35% ("largely freelance translators") had "no specific TQA processes in place". This can have a direct effect on freelance translators' earnings, as error typologies, for example, are usually applied to samples of translations, particularly those produced by less experienced translators, or those who have not built up a long-term trust relationship with their employer or client. If a translation is considered to be below a pre-defined threshold, it may be sent back to the translator for revision, with obvious consequences on the management of the relevant translation project and on the status of the professional concerned. There have been instances reported of translators being overlooked for subsequent jobs when translation sample scores fall below the employer's threshold (Koo and Kinds 2000). Only a handful of resources exist for training in contemporary TQA, i.e. those including CAT and MT. Doherty and Kenny (2014) describe the design of an SMT syllabus for postgraduate student translators with a focus on TQA using both human and automatic evaluation metrics, in order to enable the students to become critical users of the range of evaluation methods and metrics available to them; their investigation also reports the views of the students on this innovative syllabus devoted to teaching SMT with strong TQA elements, along with the students' self-assessment of their own learning. Depraetere and Vackier (2011) evaluate the use of an automatic QA tool (QA Distiller) as part of translation evaluation, which they find useful as a complement to human annotation, despite a high prevalence of false positives (incorrectly identified errors). Delizée (2011) also mentions the use of error typologies as part of summative assessment at the end of the Master's programme.

In Fig. 2, we propose a step-by-step guide to help educators and translators choose one of the various types of TQA compatible with their own translation scenario. The various TQA methods included in the figure are explained in more detail by Castilho et al. in this volume. In addition, Lommel (in this volume) explains the evolution of industry error typologies for human translation that often propose error types for language and formatting that may be considered minor, major, or critical errors, sometimes with a score appended. Typologies for automatic MT evaluation metrics are described in Popović (in this volume), and automatic QA checking tools are covered briefly by Castilho et al. (in this volume).

---

[2]This has been recognised, to an extent, in the updated European Master's in Translation Competence Framework 2017, which expects Master's programme graduates to be able to review translation according to standard or job-specific quality objectives, and to be able to implement process standards (such as ISO 17100).

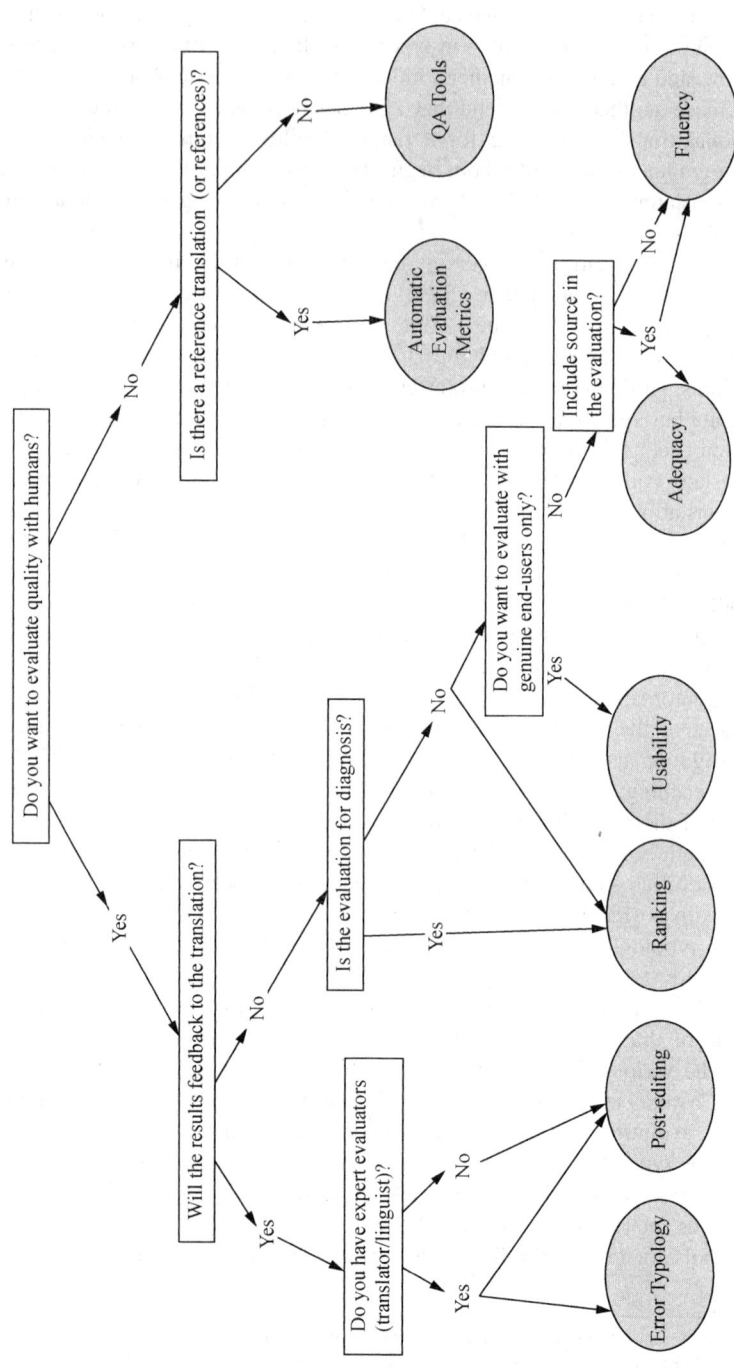

Fig. 2 TQA flowchart

4 The Next Steps for TQA in Education and Training

Education and training for human and machine TQA today stand out as largely overlooked, but essential, components of translators' skillsets, regardless of the role in which they seek to work. In this chapter we have discussed diverging viewpoints that range from arguments to include translation technologies and TQA in translation curricula to those who voice concerns that the role of the translator may be reduced and devalued in the face of such technologies.

Resources are of course a central consideration and limitation in both academic and industry settings. Performing TQA seriously costs time and money, and limited motivation to learn about and conduct TQA may also represent a stumbling block. We need to acknowledge that there are barriers to performing TQA and especially to performing it properly (Doherty 2017). In our view, education and training stakeholders should see TQA as a return on investment in terms of providing their students with an advantage in the graduate market and with the ability to change attitudes and inform clients in the future, to the long-term benefit of the profession. TQA can indeed be framed not only as a means to an end, as something that one must do because of external requirements, but also as an end in itself given its usefulness in a wide variety of applications including knowledge of the industry, translation skills, technology training, usage in performance review and progression, hiring, pricing, and improving linguistic abilities, etc. (see Doherty and Kenny 2014; Kenny and Doherty 2014; Gaspari et al. 2015).

In closing this chapter, we believe that the bottom line is that regardless of the debates on translation quality in academia, the industry will continue to have its own TQA metrics and models that will, in turn, evolve as the industry changes, largely dependent on market trends and technological developments. The challenge for lecturers and trainers is to understand the dynamics at play in the choice and use of these TQA metrics and models, so that their students can learn to appreciate their value while also being aware of their limitations and potential pitfalls. Equipped with this knowledge, human translators, especially university-educated ones, can enter the industry with confidence in their value in the face of developing technologies and increasing, some would say aggressive, automation, able to "recognise what they have learned and be able to articulate and evidence it to potential employers" (Higher Education Academy 2012). As such, dedicated and accessible educational resources on this topic are a useful addition to the field for researchers, scholars, student and professional translators and their educators alike.

Acknowledgments This work has been partly supported by the ADAPT Centre for Digital Content Technology which is funded under the SFI Research Centres Programme (Grant 13/RC/2106) and is co-funded under the European Regional Development Fund.

References

Beeby A, Fernández M, Fox O, Hurtado Albir A, Kozlova I, Kuznik A, Neunzig W, Rodríguez-Inés P, Romero L, Wimmer S, Hurtado Albir A (2009) Results of the validation of the PACTE translation competence model: acceptability and decision making. Across Lang Cult 10(2):207–230

Bowker L, Marshman E (2010) Towards a model of active and situated learning in the teaching of computer-aided translation: introducing the CERTT project. J Trans Stud 13(1/2):199–226

Chan S-W (ed) (2010) Journal of translation studies special issue: the teaching of computer-aided translation 13(1&2). The Chinese University of Hong Kong and The Chinese University Press, Hong Kong

Christensen TP, Schjoldager A (2016) Computer-aided translation tools: the uptake and use by Danish translation service providers. JoSTrans 25:89–105

Delizée A (2011) A global rating scale for the summative assessment of pragmatic translation at Master's level: an attempt to combine academic and professional criteria. In: Depraetere I (ed) Perspectives on translation quality. Walter de Gruyter, Berlin, pp 9–24

Depraetere I, Vackier T (2011) Comparing formal translation evaluation and meaning-oriented translation evaluation: or how QA tools can(not) help. In: Depraetere I (ed) Perspectives on translation quality. Walter de Gruyter, Berlin, pp 25–50

Doherty S (2016) The impact of translation technologies on the process and product of translation. Int J Commun 10:947–969

Doherty S (2017) Issues in human and automatic translation quality assessment. In: Kenny D (ed) Human issues in translation technology. Routledge, London, pp 131–148

Doherty S, Kenny D (2014) The design and evaluation of a statistical machine translation syllabus for translation students. Interpret TransTrain 8(2):295–315

Doherty S, Moorkens J (2013) Investigating the experience of translation technology labs: pedagogical implications. JoSTrans 19:22–136

Doherty S, Kenny D, Way A (2012) Taking statistical machine translation to the student translator. In: Proceedings of the tenth conference of the Association for Machine Translation in the Americas, San Diego. https://doi.org/10.13140/2.1.2883.0727

EAMT/BCS (2002) Proceedings of the BCS/EAMT workshop on Teaching Machine Translation. Organised by the European Association for Machine Translation in association with the British Computer Society Natural Language Translation Specialist Group. UMIST, Manchester, England, 14–15 November 2002. Available via: http://personalpages.manchester.ac.uk/staff/harold.somers/teachingMT/index.html. Accessed 12 May 2017

EMT Expert Group (2009) Competences for professional translators, experts in multilingual and multimedia communication. European Master's in Translation (EMT). Available via: https://ec.europa.eu/info/sites/info/files/emt_competences_translators_en.pdf. Accessed 5 Jan 2018

EMT Expert Group (2017) European Master's in Translation Competence Framework 2017. European Master's in Translation (EMT). Available via: https://ec.europa.eu/info/sites/info/files/emt_competence_fwk_2017_en_web.pdf. Accessed 9 Feb 2018

England M (1958) The end of translators? Linguist Rev 1958(1):26–27

Federico M, Cattelan A, Trombetti M (2012) Measuring user productivity in machine translation enhanced computer assisted translation. In: Proceedings of the tenth biennial conference of the Association for Machine Translation in the Americas (AMTA), San Diego, October 28–November 1 2012

Flanagan M, Christensen TP (2014) Testing post-editing guidelines: how translation trainees interpret them and how to tailor them for translator training purposes. Interpret Trans Train 8(2):257–275

Forcada M (2003) A 45-hour computers in translation course. In: Proceedings of Machine Translation Summit IX, New Orleans, USA, 23–27 September 2003, no page numbers

Forcada ML, Pérez-Ortiz JA, Lewis DR (2001) MT Summit VIII workshop on teaching Machine Translation. Santiago de Compostela. Available via: http://www.eamt.org/events/summitVIII/workshop-papers.html. Accessed 12 May 2017

García I (2011) Translating by post-editing: is it the way forward? Mach Transl 25(3):217–238

Gaspari F, Hutchins J (2007) Online and free! Ten years of online machine translation: origins, developments, current use and future prospects. In: Proceedings of Machine Translation Summit XI, Copenhagen, 10–14 September 2007, pp 199–206

Gaspari F, Almaghout H, Doherty S (2015) A survey of machine translation competences: insights for translation technology educators and practitioners. Perspect Stud Translatol 23(3):333–358

Granell Zafra J (2006) The adoption of computer-aided translation tools by freelance translators in the UK. Dissertation, Loughborough University

Higher Education Academy (2012) A marked improvement: transforming assessment in higher education. Higher Education Academy. Available via: https://www.heacademy.ac.uk/knowledge-hub/marked-improvement. Accessed 22 Mar 2018

Huertas Barros E, Vine J (2017) Current trends in MA translation courses in the UK: changing assessment practices on core translation modules. Interpret Trans Train 12(1):5–24

Karamanis N, Luz S, Doherty G (2011) Translation practice in the workplace: contextual analysis and implications for machine translation. Mach Transl 25(1):35–52

Kenny D (2007) Translation memories and parallel corpora: challenges for the translation trainer. In: Kenny D, Ryou K (eds) Across boundaries: international perspectives on translation. Cambridge Scholars Publishing, Newcastle-upon-Tyne, pp 192–208

Kenny D, Doherty S (2014) Statistical machine translation in the translation curriculum: overcoming obstacles and empowering translators. Interpret Trans Train 8(2):276–294

Kenny D, Way A (2001) Teaching machine translation and translation technology: a contrastive study. In: Proceedings of MT Summit VIII workshop on teaching translation, Santiago de Compostela, Spain, 18 September 2001, pp 13–17

Kingscott G (1990) Session 4: summary of the discussion. In: Proceedings of translating and the Computer 10: the translation environment 10 years on. 10–11 November 1988, London, pp 161–164

Knight K (2003) Teaching statistical machine translation. In: Proceedings of Machine Translation Summit IX, New Orleans, USA, 23–27 September 2003, no page numbers

Koo SL, Kinds H (2000) A quality-assurance model for language projects. In: Sprung RC (ed) Translating into success: cutting-edge strategies for going multilingual in a global age. John Benjamins, Amsterdam, pp 147–157

Koponen M (2015) How to teach machine translation post-editing? Experiences from a post-editing course. In: Proceedings of the 4th workshop on post-editing technology and practice, Miami, USA, 3 November, pp 2–15

Marshman E, Bowker L (2012) Translation technologies as seen through the eyes of educators and students: harmonizing views with the help of a centralized teaching and learning resource. In: Hubscher-Davidson S, Borodo M (eds) Global trends in translator and interpreter training. Bloomsbury, London, pp 69–95

Mitamura T, Nyberg E, Frederking R (2003) Teaching machine translation in a graduate language technologies program. In: Proceedings of Machine Translation Summit IX, New Orleans, USA, 23–27 September 2003, no page numbers

Moorkens J (2017) Under pressure: translation in times of austerity. Perspect Stud Trans Theory Pract 25(3):464–477

Moran J, Lewis D, Saam C (2018) Can user activity data in CAT tools help us measure and improve translator productivity? In: Corpas Pastor G, Durán-Muñoz I (eds) Trends in E-tools and resources for translators and interpreters. Brill, Leiden, pp 137–152

O'Brien S (2012) Translation as human-computer interaction. Transl Spaces 1:101–122

O'Hagan M (2013) The impact of new technologies on translation studies: a technological turn? In: Millán C, Bartrina F (eds) The Routledge handbook of translation studies. Routledge, Abingdon, pp 503–518

Pym A (2003) Redefining translation competence in an electronic age: in defence of a minimalist approach. Meta 48(4):481–497

Pym A (2013) Translation skill-sets in a machine-translation age. Meta 58(3):487–503

Robichaud B, L'Homme M-C (2003) Teaching the automation of the translation process to future translators. In: Proceedings of Machine Translation Summit IX, New Orleans, USA, 23–27 September 2003, no page numbers

Scarpa F, Orlando D (2017) What it takes to do it right: an integrative EMT-based model for legal translation competence. JoSTrans 27:21–42

Sycz-Opoń J, Gałuskina K (2017) Machine translation in the hands of trainee translators: an empirical study. Stud Log Gramm Rhetor 49(1):195–212

Taillefer L (1992) The history of the relationship between machine translation and the translator. In: Proceedings of the 33rd annual conference of the American Translators Association. Learned Information, Medford, pp 161–165

Vertan C, von Hahn W (2003) Specification and evaluation of machine translation toy systems: criteria for laboratory assignments. In: Proceedings of Machine Translation Summit IX, New Orleans, USA, 23–27 September 2003, no page numbers

Wältermann D (1994) Machine translation systems in a translation curriculum. In: Dollerup C, Lindegaard A (eds) Teaching translation and interpreting 2: insights, aims, visions. John Benjamins, Amsterdam, pp 309–317

Way A, Gough N (2003) Teaching and assessing empirical approaches to machine translation. In: Proceedings of Machine Translation Summit IX, New Orleans, USA, 23–27 September 2003, no page numbers

Way A, Hearne M (2011) On the role of translations in state-of-the-art statistical machine translation. Lang Linguist Compass 5(5):227–248

Wiggins D (2011) Blogpost to automated language translation group. Available via: http://www.linkedin.com/groups/Looks-like-licencebased-model-MT-148593. S.74453505?qid=579815d2-fdfd-46bb-ac04-3530d8808772andtrk=group_search_item_list-0-b-ttl. Accessed 12 May 2017

Part II
Developing Applications of Translation Quality Assessment

Metrics for Translation Quality Assessment: A Case for Standardising Error Typologies

5

Arle Lommel

Abstract Translation quality assessment (TQA) has suffered from a lack of standard methods. Starting in 2012, the Multidimensional Quality Metrics (MQM) and Dynamic Quality Framework (DQF) projects independently began to address the need for such shared methods. In 2014 these approaches were integrated, centring on a shared error typology (the "DQF/MQM Error Typology") that brought them together. This approach to quality evaluation provides a common vocabulary to describe and categorise translation errors and to create translation quality metrics that tie translation quality to specifications. This approach is currently (as of 2018) in the standardisation process at ASTM International and has seen significant uptake in industry, research, and academia. By bringing together disparate strands of quality assessment into a unified systematic framework, it offers a way to escape the inconsistency and subjectivity that have so far characterised TQA.

Keywords Translation quality assessment · Principles to practice · DQF · MQM · Translation errors · Translation metrics · Translation specifications · Standardisation

1 Introduction

This article provides an overview of three systems for translation quality assessment (TQA): (i) the Multidimensional Quality Metrics (MQM) framework,[1] developed by the author and colleagues at the German Research Centre for Artificial Intelligence (DFKI) in Berlin, Germany from 2012 through 2014 as part of the European Union-funded QTLaunchPad project; (ii) the TAUS Dynamic Quality Framework

---

[1] http://qt21.eu/mqm-definition/

A. Lommel
Common Sense Advisory (CSA Research), Indiana University, Bloomington, IN, USA

109

(DQF) Error Typology,[2] developed by the Amsterdam-based Translation Automation User Society (TAUS); and (iii) the harmonisation of the two, carried out as a collaborative effort by DFKI and TAUS within the EU-funded QT21 project in 2014 and 2015.

These projects had the common goal of improving the current state-of-the-art for TQA and to address the lack of best practice approaches in this area. Although MQM and DQF began separately and many perceived them as competing projects, they were successfully harmonised to create an emerging de facto standard for TQA, one that is now in the formal standardisation process at ASTM.

This chapter first provides a history of TQA in the translation and localisation industry, which developed along lines separate from those used in Translation Studies or machine translation (MT) research. It then describes the MQM framework in some detail before turning to the DQF Error Typology. It ends with a description of the harmonised error typology and closes with a description of plans for the future.[3]

2   Historical Background

As the translation industry emerged from a cottage industry in the late 1980s and shifted towards a technology-driven one serving global enterprises in the 1990s, it became evident that its ad hoc and subjective quality evaluation methods left much to be desired. At the time, best practice emphasised having a bilingual reviewer or a monolingual subject matter expert review translations and give an assessment. Such assessments were typically informal, in the sense that they did not use formal, predefined rubrics or tools for evaluation. As a result, actual practice varied from one translation provider to another and one reviewer to another, and this inconsistency was also a source of confusion for clients.

As an example of how subjective such review could be, consider the case of one US-based language service provider (LSP) that provided multiple languages for a large client that manufactured computer peripherals. In the mid-1990s it systematically sent its translations to third-parties for review. In one instance, the company had received a Korean-language translation of a manual from a trusted and reliable translator and sent it on to another linguist. This individual sent it back with a scathing review, in which he stated that the translation was unusable and would need to be completely redone from scratch.

After the company received this review, it took the unusual step of sending the translation to a second reviewer and asked him for his opinion and to confirm

---

[2]https://www.taus.net/knowledgebase/index.php?title=Error_typology

[3]Because most of this chapter is written from the perspective of the author, who was active in development of MQM and the MQM/DQF harmonisation effort – and who had previously led development of the LISA QA Model – much of the account contained here does not cite published sources. For details of MQM and DQF, please see the relevant online resources cited herein.

the judgement of the first reviewer. After examining the translation, the second reviewer explained that Korean has seven formality levels and that the translator had chosen one that was moderately formal, but the initial reviewer had wanted a more formal level. Due to how extensively Korean marks these levels at the grammatical level, changing levels would have required a complete rewrite of the translation. Fortunately for this LSP, the second review agreed with the translator and said that it could go as it was and that it was an excellent translation.

Unfortunately, such disagreements were a common occurrence and buyers of translation had little guidance in how to interpret such disagreements. Contributing to the problem was that feedback was often quite vague, consisting of a subjective impression couched in imprecise terms – "the style is off," "the translation is clumsy," "it needs to be reworked," etc. – that gave the translator little, if any, concrete feedback. As a result, many translators saw quality review steps as a way for unscrupulous clients to penalise them or renegotiate prices. At the same time, LSPs faced pressure from their clients to assure them that translations were adequate, and sometimes saw translator resistance to these methods as an evasion of responsibility.

2.1   Early Efforts Toward Systematic Quality Evaluation

One way that LSPs tried to improve the situation was by using translation "score-cards" for projects. These tools, typically in spreadsheet form, allowed reviewers to count numbers of errors to generate overall quality scores, usually represented as a percentage, with 100% indicating no errors. They usually included anywhere from 2 to 15 categories of errors. In some cases, reviewers simply counted errors for each category, but in others, they also assigned them weights – such as minor, major, and severe – that incurred different penalties.

Although these spreadsheets created the impression of objectivity, their categorisations remained ad hoc and varied from LSP to LSP. They also did not tie their counts to specific locations in the text. These characterisations resulted in two problems: (i) the scores were ultimately unverifiable because the only link to the text was in the mind of the reviewer; (ii) it was unclear if the scores they generated correlated with audience or customer requirements.

The first of these problems could be addressed in part if reviewers took copious notes or marked-up hard copies of the text, but these approaches were time-consuming and introduced manual steps into the review process. They did not create audit trails to ensure that required changes were made. For example, if a note said something like "awkward style, p.2, paragraph 3, second sentence," it would provide guidance for a reviser, but there was no way to mark the location digitally or confirm that appropriate steps were taken to address the issue.

The second problem was more severe. Ad hoc categorisations might work well in some cases, but not in others. Their application across heterogeneous content types resulted in an assessment method suitable for one text type being used for others with very different requirements. For example, if a scorecard that emphasised style were used for internal documentation aimed at service technicians, the translator might be unfairly penalised for failing to meet a certain level of style that was irrelevant to its audience. In addition, a text might receive exemplary marks on one scorecard and negative marks on another, calling into question the objective nature of the scores.

2.2   The Beginnings of Standardisation

The 1990s witnessed two systematic efforts to address the ad hoc nature of TQA:

- **SAE J2450**. This standard, from SAE International, developed a simple scorecard-style metric for automotive documentation. It featured six error types and two severity levels. GM reported that using it on a 5% sample of its texts enabled the company to simultaneously improve quality, time to market, and cost by substantial margins (Sirena 2004).
- **LISA QA Model**. Although never formally standardised, the LISA QA Model served as a de facto standard for quality assessment of software and documentation localisations after its release in the 1990s. It was developed within the auspices of the now-defunct Localization Industry Standards Association (LISA), which released it as a spreadsheet and later as stand-alone software. The Model featured 18 or 21 categories (there was a disagreement between its user interface and documentation) and three severity levels. It allowed customisation for two content types (documentation and software user interface) and included some issues specific to localisation into East Asian languages. A 2015 study found that the LISA QA Model remains the most common shared model for quality assessment in the translation industry, 4 years after its last commercial availability. However, most users modified it to some extent to meet their needs (Snow 2015).

Both efforts moved in the direction of shared metrics and promoted transparency across projects and translation providers. In theory, either of these allowed translation requesters to compare scores over time and to obtain them from various sources.

In practice, these approaches faced important limitations. First, low inter-annotator agreement (IAA) meant that reviewers were not interchangeable, particularly with regard to how severe they felt errors to be: Two reviewers, faced with the same error, might disagree as to how important it was, or even if was an error. Second, the effort to standardise error types only added to the problem that models that had been developed with specific scenarios or text types in mind might not be appropriate for different scenarios or text types. The frequency with which the LISA QA Model was modified shows that users felt the need to adapt it to their circumstances.

SAE J2450 explicitly addressed the problem of scope by stating up front that it was intended only for automotive service manuals and that other content types would require their own metrics. However, implementers were often not so careful or principled in their application of the model, and used it for other content types, including marketing materials. The LISA QA Model was developed with software documentation and UIs in mind, but its larger inventory of error types inadvertently encouraged the notion that it was a comprehensive translation quality metric.

By the late mid-2000s, the limitations of these models were increasingly evident and discussion began in LISA about a successor to the LISA QA Model that would address them. This effort resulted in internal documents and prototypes for a standard, tentatively called Globalization Metrics Exchange – Quality (GMX-Q) that was intended to be a companion to the existing LISA standard GMX-V (for the volume of translation) and the planned GMX-C (for representing the complexity of a source text). However, the closure of LISA in 2011 prevented the release of GMX-Q and only internal working drafts existed at that time.

Subsequent to the demise of LISA, two groups began active work on translation quality assessment: (i) the Translation Automation User Society (TAUS) developed its Dynamic Quality Framework (DQF), a collection of multiple approaches to the subject; (ii) the EU-funded QTLaunchPad project, led by the German Research Centre for Artificial intelligence (DFKI), took up the work carried out in GMX-V and developed an extensive translation error typology for use in detailed analysis of human and machine translation.[4]

The following sections provide an overview of MQM and the DQF error typologies and then I move on to describe the harmonised error typology based on them.

3   Overview of the Multidimensional Quality Metrics (MQM)

This section focuses on the MQM error typology. It covers the basics of the MQM and describes the approach and principles it adopts. As discussed above, MQM took up work and ideas previously developed by LISA's GMX-Q effort. In particular, it adopted the following principles:

- **A flexible catalogue of error types**. Rather than creating a list of issues that apply to all translation and content types, the MQM developers created a master vocabulary for describing translation errors. It is not intended that the list of types be applied in its entirety. Instead, adopters select issue types relevant to their needs and apply them. This principle means that MQM does not define a single metric, but rather a common vocabulary for declaring metrics. In this respect, it closely resembles the TermBase eXchange (TBX, ISO 30042:2008) standard, which provides an XML vocabulary to describe terminology databases.

---

[4]See Popović in this volume for a discussion of the application of MQM to MT.

- **Compatibility with existing specifications and tools**. Rather than attempting to create a categorisation from scratch, MQM examined existing specifications and tools to capture their approaches and harmonise them. The goal was to provide an easy path for tools to adopt MQM without changing their functionality more than necessary.
- **A hierarchical approach**. Not all assessment activities require the same degree of detail. For example, the project in which MQM was created detailed categories for types of grammatical errors, but most production evaluations would require only a single overall category for them. As a result, MQM has a tree-like structure in which categories have child types that can be used for greater specificity.
- **A specifications-based approach**. To address the problem of metrics that did not tie to requirements, and to be fair to translation providers, MQM strongly emphasises the use of documented translation specifications. Based on ASTM F2575 (ASTM 2014), specifications detail what is expected of the parties involved in translation production. Any assessment method should check only things that were actual requirements. For example, if specifications state that style is not important, reviewers should not penalise translations for problems with style.

3.1 MQM Harmonised Existing Approaches

Work on MQM started with a detailed comparison of nine existing error typologies and tools: the LISA QA Model, SAE J2450 and ISO CD 14080[5]; the error categories from SDL Trados Classic, ApSIC XBench, Okapi CheckMate, the XLIFF:doc specification, and Yamagata QA Distiller; and the grading rubric for ATA certification examinations. The number of issue types contained in these varied from 6 (SAE J2450) to 23 (Okapi CheckMate). In addition, the comparison considered the documentation of the original LISA QA Model, which enumerated sub-types of its basic list of issues, and raised the total to 65. The project harmonised the names of these issue types into a superset with 145 items (Table 1).

Of these 145 error types, only one was found in all of the examined metrics and tools (adherence to terminological guidelines) and only 23 were found in more than one. The most common error types were: Terminology/glossary adherence (9), Omission (8), Punctuation (6), Consistency (5), Grammar/syntax (5), Spelling (5), Mistranslation (4), and Style (4).

The MQM typology developed a superset of the tools it examined, with two exceptions, i.e. it omitted issue types related to project satisfaction from the LISA QA Model (1) and extremely detailed issues (2):

---

[5]This committee draft in ISO TC37 was subsequently withdrawn and bears no relationship to the current ISO 14080, a standard for management of greenhouse gases.

Tool name	Type	Number of issues
ApSIC XBench	Automatic checker	9
ATA Certification Exam	Grading exam for human translators	21
ISO CD 14080	Proposed standard for quality assessment	21
LISA QA Model	Quasi-standard and proprietary scorecard	21 (UI) 18 (doc. Top level) 65 (full doc.)
Okapi CheckMate	Automatic checker	23
SAE J2450	Standard	6
SDL TMS Classic	Human assessment tool in Trados suite	7
XLIFF:doc	Module in translation tool exchange format	11
Yamagata QA Distiller	Automatic checker	20
TOTAL		**145**

Table 1 Issue types in existing error typologies and tools

1. The LISA QA Model contained issue types related to overall project performance, such as adherence to deadlines, completeness of deliverables, compatibility of delivered software with external applications, and functional problems with localised software. Although these issues are very important, they were outside the scope of linguistic QA and were better addressed within the scope of ISO standards such as the ISO 9000 series or ISO 17100:2015. Accordingly, these were moved into a deprecated "compatibility" branch in MQM, with a caution that they should not be used.
2. In some instances, the tools examined had very fine-grained distinctions. For example, they had a combined total of 12 issues related to white-space within translation segments. In such cases, MQM adopted a more parsimonious approach and declared a single category, such as "whitespace," rather than try to capture all possible detail.

This effort and subsequent feedback within the QTLaunchPad project resulted in initial drafts of MQM that contained 104 issue types.[6] This number subsequently increased to 182 in the final version,[7] largely due to the inclusion of additional specific types of errors related to internationalisation that were not initially present. Here it must be re-emphasised that the creators of MQM never intended that any application would use all, or even most, of these categories. Instead, they were included to provide a way to systematically describe more task-appropriate metrics.

---

[6] See http://www.qt21.eu/mqm-definition/mqm-spec-2014-02-14.html#hierarchical_list for a full list.

[7] See http://www.qt21.eu/mqm-definition/issues-list-2015-05-27.html

3.2   Overall Structure of MQM

3.2.1   Hierarchy

MQM is highly hierarchical. The hierarchy of issue types extends up to four layers of increasing specificity, although most of the hierarchy stops at the second or third layer. Figure 1 illustrates this hierarchy: *Design* is a first-level issue type (also called a "dimension," as described in the next section), *Local formatting* a second-level issue type, *Font* a third-level, and *Bold/italic* is at the fourth level. Each layer of the hierarchy provides more specific instances of the parent. For example, *Bold/italic* is also an example of *Font*, *Local formatting*, and *Design*, and can be categorised at any of these levels, depending on whether a specific metric includes them or not.

It is important to note that children of an issue type are not comprehensive: they are not intended to enumerate all possible cases of the parent. For example, the issue type *Font* has three children: *Bold/italic*, *Single/double-width* (a reference to the width of character in East Asian Languages), and *Wrong size*. These encapsulate common issues with fonts, but if a reviewer found that a serif font had been used where a sans serif font was called for, there is no specific subtype for this and *Font* would be used.

As a general principle, MQM metrics should be as course-grained as possible while still serving their purpose. Fine-grained categories are often difficult to

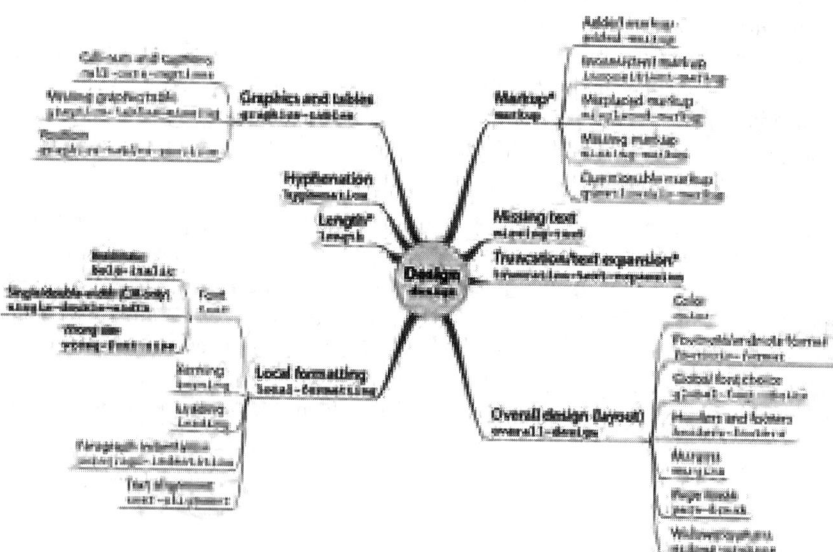

Fig. 1 Hierarchical structure in MQM (Source: http://www.qt21.eu/mqm-definition/issues-list. html. Note that this graphic includes two names for each issue. The top name is a human-readable name, which might be translated. The second is an ID for the issue, which remains constant and can serve as a valid identifier in XML and in most programming languages)

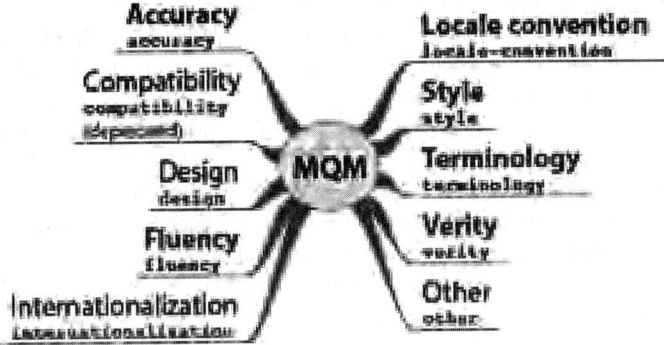

Fig. 2 Top-level "branches" or "dimensions" of MQM (Taken from http://www.qt21.eu/mqm-definition/issues-list-2015-05-27.html)

distinguish: testing in the QTLaunchPad project showed that annotators could often agree on a high-level category while remaining uncertain about lower-level ones. In cases of uncertainty, parent categories should be used because they represent the point of least uncertainty and their children also count as examples of their parents.

3.2.2 Dimensions

At the top level in the MQM hierarchy are eight primary "branches" or "dimensions" (Fig. 2).[8] They contain other issues.[9]

These branches are defined as follows:

- **Accuracy (18 issues)**. Issues related to the relationship of the meanings conveyed by the source and target content. It applies to cases where the propositional content of the source is incorrectly rendered in the target.
- **Design (33 issues)**. Issues related to the physical appearance of the content, e.g. formatting, desk-top publishing.
- **Fluency (39 issues)**. Issues related to the linguistic well-formedness of the content. These apply to *all* texts, regardless of whether they are translations or not.
- **Internationalisation (49 issues)**. Issues related to how well the content is prepared for localisation. These issues usually are detected through problems with the target content but indicate an engineering or design fault in the source.

---

[8]This total does not include the "Compatibility" branch, which is used only to represent project-related issues from the LISA QA Model, and "Other," which is used for anything that does not fit into other branches.

[9]The full hierarchy and list of issues is available at http://www.qt21.eu/mqm-definition/issues-list.html

- **Locale convention (14 issues).** These issues address whether correctly translated content is displayed correctly for the target locale. For example, dates are displayed in different formats depending on the locale, and using an incorrect one can lead to confusion.
- **Style (7 issues).** Issues related to the overall feel of a text or adherence to style guides.
- **Terminology (7 issues).** Issues related to the use of domain-specific terminology in the content. These are separated from general accuracy or fluency because localisation processes typically manage terminology separately.
- **Verity (7 issues).** Issues dealing with the relationship of the content to the world in which it exists.

Each of these branches can serve as an issue type on its own if no further specificity is needed. For example, an MQM metric that consisted of two issue types – e.g. *Accuracy* and *Fluency* – would be considered valid.

The last of the branches, *Verity*, is a novel contribution from MQM to the broader study of translation quality. It addresses cases in which a translation may be accurate and fluent and yet is not appropriate for the "world" or environment in which it is used. For example, consider a US English text about electrical systems that describes ground wires as *bare copper*. If this text were to be accurately translated as *bare Kupfer* into German, it would be problematic in Germany because ground wires there are covered in green and yellow-striped insulation. This problem is not directly with the translation itself, but rather in the relation between the text and the environment in which it will be used: If the translation were intended for German speakers in the US, *bare Kupfer* would be a correct and appropriate rendering of the text.

Verity errors frequently occur in legal or regulatory texts, which often require substantial adaptation to correctly refer to laws and regulations in the environment in which they occur. They also commonly occur even in technical documentation in cases where source texts may refer to call centers or service options that differ between locales. For example, if a text translated from German into Chinese contains only a phone number for a German support call center, even though a Chinese support number exists, it will convey inappropriate information to users.

3.2.3 Specifications

One difficulty in standardising translation quality assessment has been that most efforts are universalising. In other words, they try to set forth a set of criteria that *all* translations *should* follow, regardless of purpose or other requirements. By contrast, a *functionalist* or *Skopos*-oriented theory of translation emphasises that translations serve purposes and should be evaluated in terms of them (Nord 1997; see also Sect. 2.1 in Castilho et al., this volume). Without a knowledge of the intended purpose, an evaluator cannot say whether the translation fulfils it. This intended purpose is not always obvious from the source text because the target-language purpose may be dramatically different from that of the source-language. For example, a government body might intercept communication between two would-be terrorists who are trying to encourage each other. The translation of such a text should not aspire to be persuasive, but instead to convey nuance and detail relevant to the needs of an intelligence analyst who has to decide what action to undertake to prevent an attack.

MQM embraces a functionalist perspective at its core. For an MQM-based metric to be valid, it must measure how well a translation meets specifications. Accordingly, MQM metrics should be tied to a set of relevant specifications that follow ASTM F2575-14, which defines a standard set of 21 "parameters" that describe the information needed to complete a translation project (Fig. 3).

A. Linguistic work product parameters [1–13]

A.1. Source-content information [1–5]
1. textual characteristics
   a. source-language
   b. text type
   c. audience
   d. purpose
2. specialized language
   a. subject field
   b. terminology
3. volume
4. complexity
5. origin

A.2. Target content requirements [6–13]
6. target-language requirements
   a. target-language
   b. target-terminology
7. audience
8. purpose
9. content correspondence
10. register
11. format
12. style
   a. style guide
   b. style relevance
13. layout

B. Process tasks [14–15]
14. typical tasks
   a. preparation
   b. initial translation
   c. in-process quality assurance
15. additional tasks

C. Project Environment [16–18] and Relationships [19–21]
16. technology
17. reference materials
18. workplace requirements
19. permissions
   a. copyright
   b. recognition
   c. restrictions
20. submissions
   a. qualifications
   b. deliverables
   c. delivery method
   d. delivery deadline(s)
21. expectations
   a. compensation
   b. communication

Fig. 3 Translation project parameters defined in ASTM F2575:2014

To create an MQM metric, one determines which issue types are needed to check compliance with the specifications. During evaluation, if problems arise that the chosen issue types do not address, this typically indicates that the metric does not follow the specifications or that the specifications themselves were deficient and need to be revised.

Tying metrics to specifications helps ensure that evaluators do not try to fix issues they see that do not need to be fixed, or even make fixes that do the translation harm. This also enables requestors to tie feedback to requirements that translation providers had in advance, rather than providing feedback that seems to change the nature of the job after the fact.

Note that there is no expectation in MQM that new specifications and metrics will be created for every project. Such a practice would be wasteful and confusing. Instead, the intention is that implementers create specification templates and default metrics for different project types and reuse them to promote clarity and consistency.

3.2.4 Severities and Weights

When evaluating a translation, it is typically not enough to know how many errors are present. Evaluators also need to know (a) how severe they are and (b) how important the error type is for the task at hand. Severity and importance are distinct concepts in MQM.

Severity refers to the nature of the error itself and its effects on usability of the translation. The more severe an error is, the more likely it is to negatively affect the user in some fashion. Severity applies to individual errors, not to categories as a whole.

By default, MQM supports four severity levels:

1. **Critical**. Critical errors are those that by themselves render a project unfit for purpose. Even a single critical error would prevent a translation from fulfilling its purpose (e.g. by preventing the intended user from completing a task) and may have safety or legal implications. For example, if a translation of a text describing weight limits for an industrial centrifuge converts "2 pounds" into "2 kilograms" (instead of "0.9 kilograms"), it could result in destruction of the equipment or injury of its user, and is a critical error. These errors are especially problematic if the issue is not obvious in the translation.
2. **Major**. Major errors make the intended meaning of the text unclear in such a way that the intended user cannot recover the meaning from the text, but are unlikely to cause harm. They must be fixed before release, but if they were not they would not result in negative outcomes (other than possible annoyance for the user). For example, if a translation of an educational book about insects renders the Italian *ape* ('bee') as *monkey* in English because *ape* is a false friend, the intended meaning may not be recoverable from the text, but it is unlikely to result in negative outcomes.
3. **Minor**. Minor errors are those that do not impact usability. In most cases the intended user will correct them and move on, perhaps without even noticing

them. For example, if an English translation says "to who it may concern" instead of "to whom it may concern," no meaning is lost and many, perhaps a majority, of readers will not even notice the slight grammatical error. Because they do not affect usability, minor errors do not need to be fixed prior to distribution.

4. **Null**. The null level is used to mark changes that are not errors. For example, if the requestor decides to change a term after a translation is submitted, the reviewer could mark *Terminology* issues with this severity. No penalties are applied at this severity. It was added to MQM in 2014 to improve compatibility with the TAUS DQF.

Each severity level corresponds to penalty points that are used in scoring translations. The default penalties are 100 points (critical), 10 points (major), 1 point (minor), and 0 points (null). Previous metrics had tended to assign values much closer to each other (the LISA QA Model used values of 1, 5, and 10), but consultation with experts in evaluation indicated that these did not provide a distinction in value sufficient to guide evaluators. For those who wish to emulate older systems, the values assigned to each level can be adjusted, although doing so impedes comparison with scores generated using the default values.

By contrast, *importance* refers to the relative value assigned to different categories of errors, rather than to individual instances. For example, someone could say that style is not important for their technical documentation, meaning that even tremendously awkward style would not matter very much if the intended meaning comes across. On the other hand, such problems might be very important for their marketing materials, because those are selling a brand image where style is crucial. Importance is addressed through the use of *weights*.

Implementers assign weights to particular issue types. They indicate how important particular issues are and allow metrics to adjust how much they contribute to overall scores. The default weight in MQM is 1.0. Higher numbers indicate greater importance and lower ones indicating that issues are not as important. For example, if a content creator determines that terminology compliance is particularly important, it could assign a weight of 1.5 to *Terminology*, which would mean that all errors related to Terminology count 50% more than the default value. By contrast, if the creator determines that *Style* is not particularly important, it could assign a weight of 0.5, which indicates a 50% reduction in any penalties assigned to it.

Although weights had been a concept in earlier quality metrics (such as the LISA QA Model), they had generally not been implemented in software. As a result, few implementers currently use weights, but they do provide a mechanism to reflect relevant priorities within evaluation.

3.2.5   Scoring

One can use an MQM metric to evaluate a translation. If scoring is desired (rather than just identification of errors), the MQM definition suggests a default scoring model. To calculate a score, one takes each error, multiplies it by its severity value and its weight to generate penalty points. If default weights are used, a minor error is thus 1 penalty point, a major is 10, and a critical is 100. These points are then summed up to obtain the total. The score is then calculated per the following formula:

$$Score = 1 - \frac{Penalties}{WordCount}$$

The resulting score is typically presented as a percentage. As an example, if a translation has 500 words and the reviewer finds 3 minor errors and 2 major errors (23 penalty points), the score would be 95.4%. Note that negative scores are possible with this model if the penalty points exceed the number of words.

If it is desirable, scores can also be calculated for any issue type or branch within MQM by summing up the points for any issues it contains and applying the same formula. This ability allows implementers to understand what issue types contribute to quality problems and take remedial action. For example, if grammar and spelling errors pose a particular problem, an LSP or translation requester might add a requirement that the translation pass a grammar and spelling check before submission. On the other hand, if the translation receives low marks for terminology-related problems, that would suggest that the translators should receive training in terminology and apply tools to check and enforce proper terminology usage.

If implementers use scores to determine acceptance, they also need to set thresholds for what constitutes an acceptable translation. Thresholds should be set by applying the metric to translations the requesters found acceptable and some that they were unsatisfied with to find the score below which problems are evident. This value will vary between adopters of MQM and there is no universal threshold.

3.2.6 Holistic vs. Analytic Evaluation

Within translation evaluation, two general approaches apply: *holistic* and *analytic*. Holistic evaluation looks at the translation as a whole and attempts to evaluate its quality based on overall criteria. By contrast, analytic evaluation considers and analyses individual errors.

These two methods serve different purposes. Holistic evaluation is useful for obtaining a "big picture" image of a translation and quickly determining whether it meets specifications, but cannot provide detailed feedback on specific errors or suggest concrete remedial action. Analytic evaluation is good at identifying and documenting specific problems, but may not capture the overall impression. In addition, it is time-consuming and requires training for evaluators to apply consistently.

Because analytic quality evaluation is resource-intensive, MQM supports both types of evaluation. To use MQM for holistic evaluation, one must create a holistic metric that corresponds to an analytic one. In general, doing so requires the creator of the metric to select the high-level issues (typically the dimensions) that the analytic metric uses and ask evaluators to consider them for the entire text.

For example, if an analytic metric contains *Grammar*, *Spelling*, and *Typography* under *Fluency*, the corresponding holistic one would ask only about *Fluency*. Rating in such cases typically uses a Likert scale or similar rating mechanism, along the lines of the following:

> On a scale of 0 to 5, where zero indicates that the translation is completely unacceptable and 5 indicates that it is fully acceptable with no detectable problems, how *fluent* is the translation?

Asking these types of questions for each dimension allows the evaluator to form an overall image of how well the translation meets specifications without the need to mark all errors. If the holistic questions do not indicate problems, there is no need to conduct a detailed analytic evaluation except in cases where the consequences of undetected errors would be high. On the other hand, if the translation clearly fails the holistic evaluation, there is also no need to invest the time in a detailed analytic evaluation because the reviewer already knows it would not pass. In this case the reviewer would need to note a few examples of the problems to authenticate them and return the translation for rework.

Only in the case where it is unclear from the holistic evaluation whether the translation is acceptable per the specifications would a full analytic evaluation be advisable, although analytic spot-checking can help ensure that holistic evaluations accurately reflect requirements.

4 The DQF Error Typology

The TAUS DQF is a system developed by TAUS that addresses a variety of approaches to quality assessment, including those aimed specifically at MT, such as measuring post-editor productivity, adequacy/fluency evaluation, readability (see Castilho et al., this volume) and crowdsourced evaluation (see Jiménez-Crespo, this volume). The majority of DQF evaluation methods are out of the scope of this article, which focuses solely on the error typology.

Unlike MQM, which took existing metrics and attempted to harmonise them into one master categorisation, TAUS reached out to LSPs and buyers of translation to ask them for best practices in scorecard-style evaluation. They then used these to develop a simple error typology that was focused on the needs of its localisation-oriented members. Thus, rather than trying to address everything, the DQF Error Typology focused on solving a particularly important area.

The first release of the DQF Error Typology had six error types:

- **Accuracy**. Issues related to the transfer of meaning from source to target-language.
- **Linguistic**. Issues related to the language (rather than the meaning) of the target.

- **Terminology**. Issues related to the use of domain- or organisation-specific approved vocabulary.
- **Style**. Issues related to general or company-specific style.
- **Country Standards**. Issues related to adherence to locale-specific formatting guidelines (e.g. for numbers, addresses, or dates).
- **Layout**. Issues related to non-textual aspects of the content, such as links, formatting, length, and text truncation.

It also featured four additional categories that were used to mark issues that were not errors:

- **Query implementation**. Used to mark changes that needed to be made in response to questions to the content creator.
- **Client edit**. Edits requested by the client.
- **Repeat**. Used to mark cases where an error is repeated, but is done consistently, to avoid penalising the translator for each occurrence.
- **Kudos**. Adds a scoring bonus for something the reviewer feels the translator did well.

Each of the six primary issue types had a number of subtypes: these were initially broken out as their own issue types, but were instead eventually used as examples to explain the six types in question. The DQF Error Typology contained four severity levels, which were assigned numbers. These correspond roughly with the MQM severities.

The first release of the DQF Error Typology was as a scorecard in Excel format. It contained instructions for use and sheets where users could enter error counts for each of the categories with four severity levels to generate a score. This Excel sheet was comparable to what many LSPs used internally for their error-tracking activities.

5   Integrating MQM and DQF

In 2014 reviewers for the QTLaunchPad project pointed out that the development of MQM and DQF along separate tracks threatened to generate market confusion and delay adoption of improved quality practices. They recommended that any applications for future projects that involved translation quality should include integration of the two as a prerequisite for funding. Accordingly, the application for the follow-up project QT21, in which both TAUS and DFKI were partners, included a plan to integrate the two formats. Work began on this project in September 2014 and proceeded through the summer of 2015.

In this work, both formats underwent substantial changes, including the following:

- The dimensions of MQM were restructured to match DQF's top-level categories, meaning that implementers of the DQF error typology would not need to change

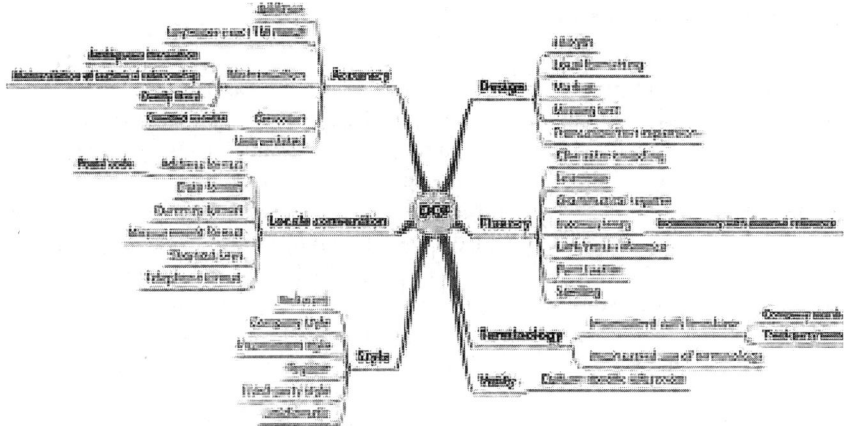

Fig. 4 DQF/MQM integrated error typology

their evaluation criteria. This resulted in the promotion of *Terminology* and *Style* to full dimensions (*Terminology* had previously been split between *Accuracy* and *Fluency*, and *Style* had been included in *Fluency*).

- MQM added a fourth severity level ("null") to match DQF's approach and to allow for issues to be marked without assigning penalties to them.
- DQF adopted the MQM issue names to become a subset of MQM.
- DQF expanded its catalogue of issues to include what had previously been examples so that they were tied to MQM issue types and could be used directly on their own.
- DQF added the *Internationalisation* and *Verity* dimensions to address these issues, which had previously been lumped with other issue types. This shift made the definitions of DQF issues more consistent and clear.

The resulting hierarchy, presented in Fig. 4, contains 50 issue types.

It is thus less than one-third the size of the full MQM hierarchy and is focused more tightly on those issues likely to concern industrial buyers of translation and localisation. As with the full MQM, it is not anticipated that adopters will use all the categories. Instead, they are available as needed. Individuals who had adopted the original DQF Error Typology need only to update the names of their categories (where they differ) to comply with MQM. In keeping with the MQM principle of using only as much detail as is needed and following TAUS' attempts to simplify TQA processes, the recommendation is to use the top-level categories unless there is a need to drill down to greater detail.

Since its release in 2015, the integrated DQF/MQM error typology has become the preferred method to implement MQM. Its smaller size makes it easier to use and grasp. Its inclusion in DQF has helped raise the profile of the MQM approach to TQA.

6   Status and Plans for the Future

Active development work on MQM was conducted at DFKI as part of two European Union-funded projects. With the completion of those projects, this work at DFKI ceased, but TAUS has continued to develop and promote DQF and the error typology, including pushing for its inclusion in translation tools.

The effort to develop MQM further has since been taken up within ASTM Committee F43,[10] which has decided to focus initial efforts exclusively on the DQF subset of MQM. It has the support of both DFKI and TAUS in this effort and has brought together a variety of industry, LSP, and governmental users to ensure widespread applicability. Committee F43 has agreed to keep the error typology free and open to the public, but will develop more detailed guidance that will be sold as a formal standard.

As of 2018, the integrated metric has seen considerable uptake and interest from industry. Trados, the most widely used computer-assisted translation tool, offered MQM starting in 2016. XTM Cloud, an online computer-assisted translation tool and translation management system, has implemented the full MQM typology in its error-checking module. Mozilla has adopted a custom MQM/DQF metric for its localisation needs and other companies such as eBay have publicly announced their adoption of the model. LSPs have moved to MQM, and several technology vendors have announced plans to add support for MQM in the future. DFKI continues to use MQM for research into MT quality.

Overall, the future is bright for MQM and DQF as the new standard approach to assessing translation quality. It provides a way to move past some of the problems of previous methods and to establish TQA on a systematic basis that ties it to the needs of users and to shared best practices that help promote transparency and consistency across applications.

Acknowledgements The author thanks the following individuals: Drs. Hans Uszkoreit and Aljoscha Burchardt (DFKI Berlin), who were integral in the development of MQM; Jaap van der Meer and Attila Görög (TAUS), for their development of DQF and contribution to the integrated MQM/DQF metric; Prof. Alan K. Melby (Brigham Young University Translation Research Group), who contributed greatly to MQM and introduced the notion of specifications. Any errors in this publication are the author's alone and do not reflect on the contributions of these individuals.

---

[10]ASTM International is a leading organisation in the development and delivery of voluntary consensus standards; its Committee F43 on Language Services and Products was formed in 2010 with the aim of enhancing the quality of language services and products.

References

ASTM (2014) ASTM F2575–14 standard guide for quality assurance in translation. ASTM International, West Conshohocken

Nord C (1997) Translating as a purposeful activity. St. Jerome, Manchester

Sirena D (2004) Mission impossible: improve quality, time and speed at the same time. Globalization Insider 13(2.2). Available via: http://www.translationdirectory.com/article387.htm. Accessed 1 Feb 2017

Snow T (2015) Establishing the viability of the multidimensional quality metrics framework. Dissertation, Brigham Young University. Available via: http://scholarsarchive.byu.edu/etd/5593/. Accessed 1 Feb 2017

Error Classification and Analysis for Machine Translation Quality Assessment

6

Maja Popović

Abstract This chapter presents an overview of different approaches and tasks related to classification and analysis of errors in machine translation (MT) output. Manual error classification is a resource- and time-intensive task which suffers from low inter-evaluator agreement, especially if a large number of error classes have to be distinguished. Automatic error analysis can overcome these deficiencies, but state-of-the-art tools are still not able to distinguish detailed error classes, and are prone to confusion between mistranslations, omissions, and additions. Despite these disadvantages, automatic tools can efficiently replace human evaluators both for estimating the distribution of error classes in a given translation output, as well as for comparing different translation outputs. They can also facilitate manual error classification by pre-annotation, since correcting or expanding existing error tags requires less time and effort than assigning error tags from scratch. Classification of post-editing operations is more convenient both for manual and for automatic processing, and also enables more reliable assessment of automatic tools. Apart from assigning error tags to incorrectly translated (groups of) words, error analysis can be performed by examining unmatched sequences of words, part-of-speech (POS) tags or other units, as well as by identifying language-related and linguistically-motivated issues. These linguistic categories can be then used to perform automatic evaluation specifically on these units, or to analyse their frequency and nature. Due to its complexity and variety, error analysis is an active field of research with many possible directions for development and innovation.

Keywords Translation quality assessment · Principles to practice · Automatic evaluation · Translation errors · Machine translation · Post-editing

M. Popović
Department of English and American Studies, Humboldt University of Berlin, Berlin, Germany
e-mail: maja.popovic@hu-berlin.de

1   Introduction

Evaluation of MT is an important but difficult task. How good is a given MT output?
Is it good enough for a particular task? These simple questions are not easy to answer
because there is no single correct translation of a text. If one sentence is translated
by several translators, or even by the same translator at different times, several
different translations could be produced. One way to evaluate MT is to present
the output to bilingual human evaluators who understand both source and target-
languages, in order to assign a quality score for a given task, e.g. from 1 (poor) to
5 (perfect). The criteria normally used are adequacy (i.e. meaning preservation),
fluency (i.e. grammaticality), overall quality (based on a combination of both),
as well as estimated cognitive post-editing effort. Comparing different MT of the
same source text can also be performed by ranking (Callison-Burch et al. 2007),
i.e. for each output sentence the evaluator should say if version A or version B is
better, without assigning any absolute score. Both approaches can also be performed
by monolingual evaluators who understand only the target-language, but a correct
reference translation should be available in this case.

The availability of reference translations also enables automatic evaluation,
normally using a script or program which produces a score based on the similarity
between the reference translation and the MT output. This score is usually produced
either as a percentage of matched n-grams[1] between the reference and the output
or as edit distance between them. Since automatic evaluation is significantly faster
and cheaper and also more consistent than human evaluation, a number of automatic
evaluation metrics (AEMs) have been investigated and used, e.g. BLEU (Papineni et
al. 2002) based on word n-gram precision, chrF (Popović 2015) based on character
n-gram F-score, METEOR (Banerjee and Lavie 2005) based on unigram precision,
recall and additional linguistic knowledge, or TER (Snover et al. 2006) based on
edit distance (see also Castilho et al. in this volume).

Whereas all of these overall scores and better-or-worse ranking decisions
represent very valuable information and help in the continuous improvement of
MT systems, MT researchers and developers often find it helpful to have additional
information about their systems. What are the most serious problems in a translation
system? What are the particular strengths and weaknesses of the system? Does a
particular modification improve some aspect of the system, although perhaps it does
not improve the overall score? Does a worse-ranked system outperform a higher-
ranked one in some aspect? Are some types of errors more difficult to post-edit than
others? A relationship between these questions and the overall quality scores is not
easy to find.

Therefore, error classification and analysis techniques have emerged, identifying
and classifying actual errors in a translated text in order to provide a better foundation for decisions about the task at hand, whether related to system development,
purchase, or use. Most often, the goal of error analysis is to obtain an error profile

---

[1]An n-gram is a sequence of N words in a text, so for example where N $=$ 3, this is a trigram: a
sequence of three words.

for a translation output, a distribution of errors over the defined error classes. Another application is comparison of different translation outputs, i.e. finding error distributions over different translations for each error class. Furthermore, more specific analyses can be carried out, such as relations between particular error types and user/post-editor preferences, the impact of different error types on different aspects of post-editing effort, and so forth.

Similarly to overall evaluation, error classification is by no means a straightforward task. It can be carried out manually, automatically, or using a combined method (semi-automatically). Different sources of information (in addition to the analysed translation output) can be used, such as source-language texts, reference translations or, recently, post-edited translations. Merely defining a suitable set of error classes (an error typology or taxonomy) is a challenging task in itself: which error types are of interest for the given task and how many details are needed? Once the error typology is defined, for a number of erroneous words there may be several possible error classes, and it is often difficult to determine the position of errors, i.e. to decide which exact words are erroneous.

Apart from classification and annotation of erroneous words, error analysis can be carried out by other means, e.g. by analysing words, POS, or other types of sequences which are not matched when comparing translation output with a reference. Another approach is the definition of linguistically-motivated categories in order to perform error analysis and/or automatic evaluation specifically on them.

For all these reasons which contribute to its complexity, error analysis is an active field of research. This chapter presents a variety of error analysis approaches and error typologies which have been used in the MT community, together with the associated advantages, disadvantages, and challenges. It should be noted that, despite the fact that the described approaches focus on analysis of MT output, the methods can also be used for evaluation of human translations (such as those produced by language learners, non-native speakers, non-experienced translators, and others).

2   Manual Error Classification and Error Typologies

The most obvious method for error analysis is to look into the translation output, mark each erroneous word, and assign a corresponding error tag to it. Apart from the analysed translation output, at least one correct text should be given to the annotator: either the original source text, or a reference translation, or both. The influence of different sources of information and different annotator profiles (bilingual vs. monolingual) has been investigated for assigning overall quality scores (Guzmán et al. 2015). Experiments on Spanish-to-English translation outputs showed that monolinguals are slower but more consistent than bilinguals, and that all annotators become slower and less consistent when exposed to additional information in the form of the source-language text. Therefore, the authors advise monolingual evaluators and the use of reference translations alone. For error classification, to the best of my knowledge, no similar study has been carried out to date.

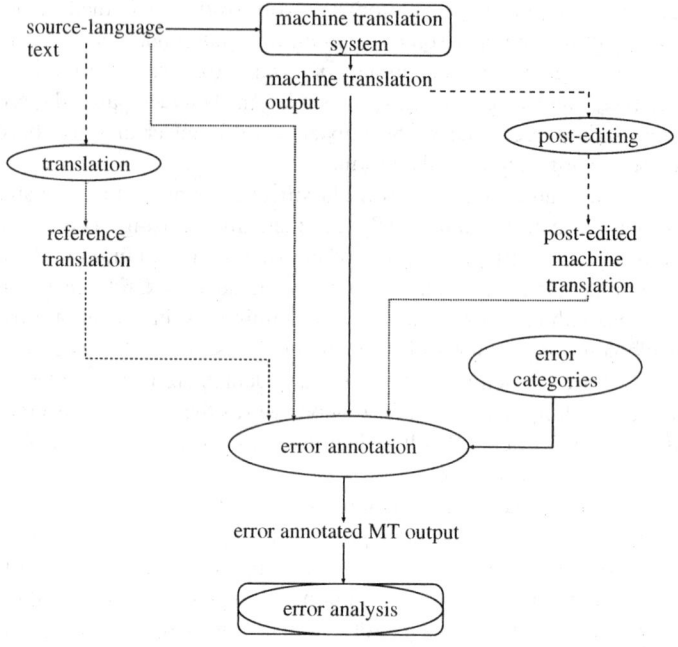

Fig. 1 General procedure of manual error annotation; the rectangle denotes automatic process, and the ellipse denotes manual process

In recent years, post-editing of MT output has become an increasingly common form of human-machine cooperation for translation. Therefore, we have seen more attention given to analysis of post-editing activity through the assignation of an error category to each performed post-edit operation. Usually, the analysis of post-edits is carried out in order to investigate relations between different error types and different aspects of post-editing effort, namely cognitive, temporal, and technical as defined in Krings (2001). For such an analysis, post-edited translation output is necessary as additional information whereas source-language text is optional.

The general process of manual error classification is illustrated in Fig. 1. For any task and approach, a set of error categories (i.e. an error typology or taxonomy) should be clearly defined beforehand. This itself is a demanding task for several reasons: the errors should reflect all advantages and disadvantages of the MT system, which are important for the task at hand as well as for the languages involved; more detailed errors are more informative but more difficult to distinguish; and the error types should cover both linguistic aspects as well as translation aspects. Although there is some work in progress in this direction, there are still no general rules for defining error categories, even on a broad level. The following subsection will present an overview of error typologies for manual classification used in the last decade (i.e. from the beginning until now) for different tasks, including analysis of post-editing process.

Level 1	Level 2	Level 3
Missing words	Content words	
	Filler words	
Word order	Word level	Local range
		Long range
	Phrase level	Local range
		Long range
Incorrect words	Sense	Wrong lexical choice
		Incorrect disambiguation
	Form	
	Extra words	
	Style	
	Idioms	
Unknown words	Unknown stem	
	Unseen forms	
Punctuation		

Table 1 Vilar et al. (2006) error categories

2.1 Overview of Error Typologies and Tasks

Vilar et al. (2006) report the first shift towards the use of explicit error classification and analysis. Error analysis of several Chinese-to-English, Spanish-to-English, and English-to-Spanish statistical MT (SMT) systems is carried out in order to identify the main problems with these systems. The proposed classification scheme presented in Table 1 has a hierarchical structure and is based on the error typology used for refinement of rule-based systems in Llitjós et al. (2005).

Since then, a number of error classification schemes have been used for distinct purposes. The same error scheme is used for error analysis of English-to-Czech MT by Bojar (2011).

Farrús et al. (2010) describe a simple error scheme containing five broad classes (as seen in Table 2) used for comparison of two SMT systems for the Spanish-Catalan language pair in both directions. The systems are also compared in terms of overall human scores, and it is observed that lexical and semantic errors have more influence on human evaluators' perception of quality than other categories. A similar error scheme is used in Comelles et al. (2012) as a basis for development of an AEM based on linguistic features.

Federico et al. (2014) use another similar typology containing a set of basic error classes (see Table 3) for analysing MT from English into Arabic, Chinese, and Russian. For each segment, the annotators marked both erroneous words, as well as assigning an overall quality score using the open-source tool MT-EQuAl[2] (Girardi et al. 2014). These annotations are used to investigate the impact of particular error types and their combinations to the overall quality score using mixed-effect

---

[2]http://www.mt4cat.org/software/mt-equal

| Morphological errors |
| Lexical errors |
| Orthographic errors |
| Syntactic errors |
| Semantic errors |

Table 2 Farrús et al. (2010) error categories

| Morphological errors |
| Lexical choice |
| Additions |
| Omissions |
| Casing and punctuation |
| Reordering errors |
| Too many errors |

Table 3 MT-EQuAl error categories (Federico et al. 2014)

models (Baayen et al. 2008). The largest correlation is observed for lexical errors and missing words. An additional and very interesting finding is that the human perception of quality does not necessarily depend on the frequency of a given error type; a sentence with a low overall score can easily contain fewer missing words and/or lexical errors than another sentence with a higher score.

A similar, basic typology (without "casing and punctuation" and "too many errors") was used by Castilho et al. (2017a) and Castilho et al. (2017b) to compare phrase-based SMT and neural MT outputs for a number of language pairs and genres/domains.

Kirchhoff et al. (2012) present another study which examines user preferences regarding different error classes. Different English-to-Spanish translations were annotated with error tags from a detailed typology shown in Table 4 and the overall quality of each translation is estimated by ranking. Then, conjoint analysis[3] is applied in order to find relations. The obtained results also showed that the frequency of a particular error type is not crucial; the least preferred (or most annoying) were word order and word sense errors, whereas the most frequent morphological errors were ranked as third-least preferred.

Stymne and Ahrenberg (2012), in the first work dealing with inter-annotator agreement for error classification, use a distinct but also detailed hierarchical error scheme presented in Table 5. In addition to inter-annotator agreement, the results for two English-to-Swedish MT systems (with and without compound processing) are presented. The error classes were assigned by two annotators, native Swedish speakers, using the BLAST tool for computer-aided manual error analysis (Stymne 2011). The annotation was carried out in two rounds, with and without guidelines.

---

[3] A "formal framework for preference elicitation", normally used for consumer studies in which participants rate or rank products based on a combination of attributes (Kirchhoff et al. 2012).

Level 1	Level 2
Missing words	Content words
	Function words
Extra words	Content words
	Function words
Word order	Local range
	Long range
Morphology	Verbal
	Nominal
Word sense error	
Punctuation	
Spelling	
Capitalisation	
Untranslated	Medical term
	Proper name
Pragmatics	
Diacritics	
Other	

Table 4 Kirchhoff et al. (2012) error categories

Level 1	Level 2
Error rates	Missing words
	Extra words
	Wrong word
	Word order
Linguistic	Orthography
	Semantics
	Syntax
GF	Grammatical words
	Function words
Form	Morphological categories
POS+	Part of speech
	Punctuation
FA	Fluency
	Adequacy
	Neither
	Both
Reo (cause of reordering)	
Index (position of an error)	
Other (other categories)	
Ser (seriousness of an error	

Table 5 Stymne and Ahrenberg (2012) error categories

For the detailed error schemes without guidelines, the rate of agreement reached roughly 25%, and guidelines increased this up to 40%. For simple typologies, agreements are in a range of between 65% (without guidelines) and 80% (guided). Aside from this, the authors report that the annotators often disagree regarding the exact positions of erroneous words. Their results also confirmed some findings reported in a study dealing with general inter-annotator agreement (Bayerl and Paul 2011), namely that the number of categories as well as the intensity/absence of training are very important factors.

The Multidimensional Quality Metric (MQM)[4] is used for another study about inter-annotator agreement (Lommel et al. 2014b, see also Lommel in this volume). The metric aims to provide a general mechanism for describing a family of related error categories which includes evaluation of human translations. The main idea is to have a large set of hierarchical error categories which allows selection of any subset appropriate for the task at hand. The metric is already being used for the evaluation and comparison of MT systems, for example by Lommel et al. (2014a) to compare rule-based and phrase-based systems for several language pairs and domains, and by Klubicka et al. (2017) to compare phrase-based and neural systems for English-to-Croatian.

Inter-annotator agreement is explored using a subset of MQM presented in Table 6 on a set of English-Spanish and English-German translation outputs in all directions generated by different MT systems. All outputs were annotated by several[5] professional translators using the open-source tool translate5.[6] The obtained results confirmed the main findings reported in Stymne and Ahrenberg (2012), based on:

(i)   the role of number of error categories,
(ii) the importance of annotator training, as well as
(iii) the importance of the exact positions of erroneous words as perceived by different annotators.

In addition, it is shown that "Mistranslation" and "Terminology" are very difficult to distinguish without very intensive training, and that the "Function words" category is generally rather unclear. The "Word Order" category exhibited a high level of general consistency, but there was also a high degree of positional disagreement.

Costa et al. (2015) use yet another hierarchical typology, presented in Table 7, slightly tailored for Romance languages to compare four different English-to-Portuguese translation systems. It is shown that lexical and semantic errors have most impact on sentence-level ranking. Furthermore, highly ranked sentences clearly exhibit a low number of grammatical errors, but the relationship between grammatical errors and poorly-ranked segments remained unclear. Apart from this, high inter-annotator agreement between two annotators is reported, which

---

[4]http://www.qt21.eu/mqm-definition/issues-list-2015-12-30.html

[5]three (de-en), four (es-en, en-es), or five (en-de)

[6]http://www.translate5.net/

Level 1	Level 2	Level 3	Level 4
Accuracy	Mistranslation		
	Terminology		
	Omission		
	Addition		
	Untranslated		
Fluency	Grammar	Morphology (form)	
		Part-of-speech Agreement Tense/mood/aspect Word order	
		Function words	Missing Extra Incorrect
	Register/style	Capitalisation	
	Spelling		
	Typography	Punctuation	
	Unintelligible		

Table 6 MQM error categories used for inter-annotator agreement

Level 1	Level 2	Level 3
Orthography	Punctuation	
	Capitalization	
	Spelling	
Lexis	Omission	
	Addition	
	Untranslated	
Grammar	Misselection	Word class
		Verbs
		Agreement
		Contraction
		Misordering
Semantic	Confusion of senses	
	Wrong choice	
	Collocational errors	
	Idioms	
Discourse	Style	
	Variety	
	Should not be translated	

Table 7 Costa et al. (2015) error categories

contradicts the results from former studies. The most probable factor is their removal of words with position disagreement from the calculations, which increased the agreement between the error types.

Level 1	Level 2
Noun phrase	Determiner
	Noun meaning
	Noun number
	Case
	Adjective
Verb phrase	Verb agreement
	Verb meaning
Preposition change	
Co-reference change	

Table 8 Blain et al. (2011) error (edit) categories

Level 1	Level 2	Level 3
Word form change		
Word change		
POS change		
Deleted (insertion)		
Added (omission)		
Order	Phrase level	Distance 1
		Distance ≥ 2
	Word level	Distance 1
		Distance ≥ 2

Table 9 Koponen (2012) error (edit) categories

2.1.1 Classification of Post-edit Operations

Blain et al. (2011) use the error scheme presented in Table 8 to analyse two post-edited English-to-French MT outputs from statistical and rule-based systems in the technical domain. After post-editing, the changes, defined as post-editing actions, were classified according to the given typology. Apart from the human classification, automatic classification based on TER (Snover et al. 2006) edit operations and linguistic rules was proposed. Both classification methods revealed that changes were mostly performed on noun meaning, indicating problems with terminology for both MT systems.

Koponen (2012) presents another type of edit operation analysis on English-to-Spanish MT from the news domain. The data set used contains human estimates of post-editing effort which do not necessarily correlate with the actual technical effort (i.e. the number of post-editing operations). In order to explore these differences, segments with high, medium, and low predicted effort were selected and edit operations were annotated according to the error scheme presented in Table 9. The results showed that reordering operations correlate with high predicted effort whereas morphological corrections correlate with low predicted effort. In addition, it is shown that segment length plays a significant role for predictions of post-editing effort regardless of the amount and type of operations that need to be performed, i.e. longer segments tend to be generally perceived as more difficult to post-edit.

Zaretskaya et al. (2016) use a variant of the MQM scheme for a similar analysis on English-to-German translation outputs where post-editing time and cognitive effort are measured for different types of edit operations. It is confirmed that for a number of error types these two aspects do not correlate, e.g. the estimated effort for reordering edits is high but the time is relatively short. Another important finding is that errors involving different types of multi-word expressions are associated with high cognitive and temporal effort.

2.2 Challenges and Possibilities for Facilitation

The previous section has shown that error classification has a large scope of distinct applications and can answer a number of questions that are important for the improvement and development of MT systems, as well as for better understanding of human evaluation criteria and the post-editing process. It has also shown that this useful task is rather time- and resource-intensive, and full of very challenging sub-tasks. Some of the particular challenges are discussed in this section.

Annotator's Profile Annotators can be fluent in both source and target-languages or only in the target-language, in which case a correct reference human translation is needed. To the best of my knowledge, differences between annotator profiles regarding error classification speed, consistency, and performance have not yet been investigated.

Consistency Regardless of the annotators' background, precise guidelines and intensive training are necessary in order to achieve sufficient inter-annotator agreement and to obtain reliable results. The training may have to be carried out in several phases in order to yield an acceptable classification performance. However, even in optimal scenarios, it is not possible to completely avoid certain inconsistencies. One problem is differing perception of the exact positions of erroneous words. This is especially problematic for word-order and phrase-order errors. Another problem is different perception of certain error classes in certain contexts, similar to the problem regarding several correct translations of the same sentence. This type of inconsistency is strongly related to the number and definition of the error categories.

Number of Error Classes More detailed error typologies usually provide better information about the errors, for example separating "morphological error" into "inflectional error", "derivational error", and "compositional error", or using an even deeper hierarchy, such as extending "verb inflection error" into "person", "tense", and "mood". In contrast, more error categories require more cognitive effort for the annotators and also lead to lower consistency and poor inter-annotator agreement. Nevertheless, not only the number, but also the exact definition of error categories is very important. For example, even a simple distinction between adequacy and fluency can be difficult because of certain types of grammatical errors. Usually, all grammatical errors are considered as fluency errors, i.e. they are considered not to have anything to do with the source-language and meaning preservation. However, a number of these errors actually occur due to the properties of the source-language and its differences with the target-language, such as incorrect, missing, or added prepositions, conjunctions, and determiners. Therefore, the exact definition of each error class also plays a significant role in the difficulty of the classification task and reliability of the obtained results.

Definition of Error Classes This mainly depends on the task, but can also depend on the language pair(s). For example, if the texts are drawn from a specific domain, "terminology error" is a very important class, whereas for general domain texts it is not. Similarly, if a Romance language is involved, "verb inflection error" is usually used. Generally, some error classes are more problematic for annotators than others. Whereas an "inflection error" usually does not pose problems, its subcategory "agreement error" often requires high cognitive effort in order to be distinguished from general inflection. Disambiguation between "mistranslation" and its subclass "terminology error" has also been found to be rather difficult without intensive training.

Sometimes an error definition is appropriate for one task and language pair, but becomes insufficiently precise when ported to another language or task. For example, "POS error" is equivalent to "derivational morphology error" for English, but not for German where a large portion of derivations consist of adding different prefixes to verbs. Thus, if a German verb prefix is incorrect, this cannot be tagged as "POS error".

The following lines of work can help with overcoming some of the described obstacles and facilitate the general process:

(i) unification and generalisation of error typologies,
(ii) annotation of post-edited operations instead of raw translation outputs, as well as
(iii) automation of (a part of) the error classification process.

Unification and Generalisation of Error Typologies Establishing a general error typology which can easily be adapted to different tasks and language pairs could significantly reduce effort and inconsistencies related to the definition of error typology and particular classes. Current work in this direction consists of developing the MQM metric described in Sect. 2.1 (see Lommel, this volume), which offers a very large detailed error set containing several subsets. The idea is to use this set as a starting point and select a desired subset appropriate for the task at hand. A further advantage here would be consolidation with human translation evaluation.

Generalisation can also be achieved in other ways, for example, by using a generalised small set of broad error classes as a starting point and enabling its expansion in distinct directions and depths depending on the task/language pair/domain. For example, it can be observed that certain types of broad error classes are present in one way or another in all typologies described in the previous section: lexical errors, morphological errors, syntactic errors, semantic errors, and

Level 1	Level 2	Level 3
Lexis	Mistranslation	Terminology
	Addition	
	Omission	
	Untranslated	
	Should not be translated	
Morphology	Inflection	Tense, number, person
		Case, number, gender
	Derivation	Part of speech
		Verb aspect
	Composition	
Syntax	Word order	Range
	Phrase order	Range
Semantic	Multi-word expressions	
	Collocations	
	Disambiguation	
Orthography	Capitalisation	
	Punctuation	
	Spelling	
Too many errors		

Table 10 A possible general error typology which starts from broad classes and enables various possibilities for expansion

orthographic errors. A possible general typology on this basis is presented in Table 10, together with a set of suggested expansions. It should be noted that the category "too many errors" should be used carefully: it can be very useful for very low quality segments where errors are really difficult to classify, but on the other hand, backing off to this class should not be overused.

Annotating Post-edit Operations Post-editing and error classification are usually observed and carried out as two separate tasks. Error classification has been carried out on post-editing operations mainly in order to better understand different aspects of the post-editing process, but rarely to analyse properties of an MT system. However, the two tasks are actually highly related; post-editing can be viewed as implicit error annotation, since each edit operation is actually a correction of a translation error. Therefore, merging these two tasks can give better insight into the nature of errors. In addition, it can facilitate the annotation process (whatever is changed should be annotated) and improve inter-annotator agreement by reducing error position inconsistencies.

Automatic Error Classification An obvious method for reducing efforts of manual error classification is automation of the process. The advantages and disadvantages are similar to those of automatic evaluation metrics, i.e. faster, cheaper and more consistent, but also less precise, prone to assignment of incorrect error tags, and strongly dependent on a given reference translation. A detailed overview of automatic error classification is provided in the next section.

3   Automatic Error Classification

As mentioned in the previous section, automatic methods for error classification emerged due to resource – and time – intensity, as well as the inconsistency of the manual process. The motivation is the same as for AEMs, namely use a program to compare the translation output with a reference translation. The goal, however, is not to produce a single overall score, but to estimate the amount of different error types.

One of the first steps in this direction (Popović et al. 2006) proposes automatic estimation of reordering and inflectional errors based on Word Error Rate (WER) and Position-independent Word Error Rate (PER) differences. WER, i.e. word level Levenshtein distance (Levenshtein 1966), requires exactly the same order of words in hypothesis and reference segments. PER, on the other hand, neglects word order completely and measures only the difference in the count of words occurring in hypothesis and reference segments. For both metrics, the resulting number of errors is divided by the number of words in the reference. The main idea is that the reordering errors are reflected in the difference between WER and PER, and the inflectional errors are correlated with the difference between PER of original words and PER of lemmas. More detailed analysis of Spanish verb inflections based on the same approach is described in Popović and Ney (2006).

Estimating the amount of inflectional errors and omissions by identification of actual erroneous words contributing to WER and PER is described in Popović and Ney (2007). Further work in this direction resulted in a complete automatic classification scheme (Popović and Ney 2011), which covers a large portion of broad error classes used in human error analysis. These are:

- inflectional errors,
- reordering errors,
- missing words (omissions),
- extra words (additions), and
- lexical errors (mistranslations).

The word-level alignment between the translation output and the reference translation is based on WER, and precision and recall are used as additional information for classification of erroneous words. The transition from PER to precision and recall emerged from the inability of the standard efficient algorithms for PER to give precise information about contributing words. Therefore alternative PER-based metrics were introduced – HPER, RPER, and FPER – which basically correspond to the precision, recall and F-score. The open-source tool Hjerson[7] (Popović 2011) is based on this scheme. The original version of the tool required lemmas in addition to the original word forms in order to distinguish inflectional errors. The extended version (Hjerson+ as described in Popović et al. 2015) enables back-off to the first four characters of the word if the lemmas are not available.

---

[7]https://github.com/cidermole/hjerson

Another automatic error classification tool with a similar but slightly larger set of error classes is Addicter[8] (Fishel et al. 2011; Zeman et al. 2011). In addition to the previously described five Hjerson error classes, the tool allows detection of untranslated words as well as a variable span of reordering errors (short and long range). The word-level alignment is based on a first-order Markov dependency model, similar to bilingual Hidden Markov Model (HMM)-based word alignment used for MT (Vogel et al. 1996). It stimulates adjacent words to be aligned similarly, which results in a preference towards aligning longer phrases. The tool also accepts external alignments (from GIZA++ (Och and Ney 2003), METEOR, etc.). Lemmas are also required for distinguishing inflectional errors from lexical errors.

Similarly to AEMs, automatic error classification also suffers from relying on just one of many viable reference translations. Therefore both tools accept multiple references: for each segment, Hjerson chooses the reference with minimal WER, and Addicter chooses the reference with the minimal total number of errors. The general procedure for automatic error classification is presented in Fig. 2.

Both tools were tested by comparing the results with those obtained by manual error classification and exhibited sufficiently high correlations to be able to replace human annotators for a number of tasks. The details of automatic error-classification assessment process will be described in the next section.

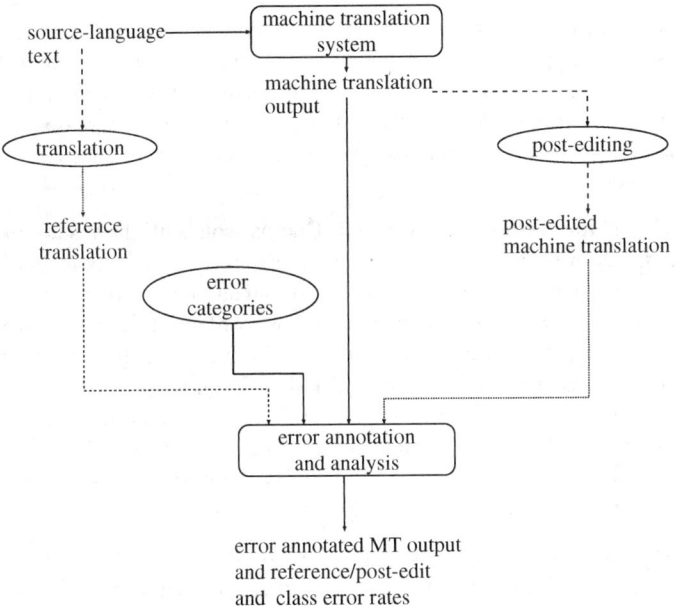

Fig. 2 Procedure of automatic error classification; the rectangle denotes automatic process, and the ellipse denotes manual process

---

[8]https://wiki.ufal.ms.mff.cuni.cz/user:zeman:addicter

3.1 Evaluation of Automatic Error Classification

In principle, evaluation of automatic error classification consists of comparing results with the results of manual classification for the following three aspects:

1. Distribution of different error classes within a translation output,
2. Distribution of an error class across different translation outputs,
3. Detecting actual erroneous words and assigning a correct error tag.

For the first two aspects, Spearman and Pearson correlation coefficients between manual and automatic scores are calculated. For the third aspect, for each error class, precision and recall are calculated together with the percentage of confusions with each of the remaining classes.

Assessment of Hjerson and Addicter Both automatic evaluation tools, especially Hjerson, exhibit high correlations for the first as well as for the second aspect, and they are already being used for obtaining error profiles or comparisons of MT systems as well as for some other analyses. As for the third aspect, high recall has been reached for all error classes. Nevertheless, precision scores are rather low, mainly because the number of automatically-detected errors is generally much higher due to the usage of one reference translation; many detected errors are not real errors but just correct variations.

Another disadvantage is the high degree of confusion between lexical errors, omissions, and additions. This distinction, however, is often problematic even for human annotators. Another similarity to manual classification is frequent disagreement regarding position of reordering errors, which decreases both inter-annotator agreement for the manual process as well as precision and recall for automatic tools.

Drawbacks of the Assessment Method Comparison with the results of manual error classification is the most natural way to assess automatic tools, but it should be taken into account that the exact process of manual annotation can influence the results. First of all, the information which was available to the annotators plays an important role; if the reference translation is available, the results of human and automatic classification will be closer than if only the source text is used. Furthermore, if only the reference translation is used, without the source text, the results will be even closer. The annotation guidelines are also important; if the annotators were told to pay specific attention to the reference, the results will be closer than if the reference was used only for orientation.

Another important factor is the fact that the vast majority of manual error-classification tasks have not been carried out for the sake of evaluation of an automatic tool; for a small number of tasks when that was the case, the results are closer. Furthermore, since there is no general error typology for manual error classification, exact mapping to a narrower automatic error typology also differs from task to task. Due to all these factors, the automatic tools available so far had to be evaluated on rather heterogeneous data. These annotated texts were eventually collected, partially homogenised and published as the Terra corpus[9] (Fishel et al. 2012), and despite the described disadvantages, represent a valuable corpus for further development of automatic error-classification tools.

Evaluating on Post-edited Data Recently, the Hjerson tool has been applied for automatic analysis of post-editing operations, such as exploring relations between different error (or edit) classes and different aspects of post-editing effort (cognitive, temporal, and technical; Popović et al. 2014). The results confirmed the main findings of Koponen (2012), and showed that sentence length, in addition to cognitive effort, strongly influences temporal effort. It is also shown that technical effort for all edit classes strongly correlates with estimated cognitive effort regardless of temporal effort. In the experiments, it is observed that automatic error classification produces more reliable results when post-edited MT output is used as a reference translation. Therefore, systematic experiments have been carried out in this direction and the details are presented in the next section.

3.2 Semi-automatic Classification of Post-edit Operations

As mentioned in Sect. 2.2, post-editing and error classification are closely related tasks since post-editing can be viewed as implicit error annotation. Therefore, classification of post-editing operations can not only facilitate manual error classification, but also enable more reliable automatic error classification. In addition, it can also provide more reliable assessment of automatic tools and give a better insight into possibilities for their improvement.

These premises are thoroughly investigated by Popović and Arcan (2016). In their study, a set of around 2800 segments containing different language pairs were post-edited, annotated, and analysed, thus creating a publicly available resource.[10] The texts are first post-edited, then the error annotation is performed in two stages in order to facilitate the manual part: the first stage consists of automatic pre-annotation by Hjerson, and the second stage consists of correcting or expanding Hjerson error classes by human annotators. In addition to the five Hjerson classes, three additional error classes were introduced based on findings in the data:

(i) contraction errors, including any merging of words, mainly compounds,
(ii) derivational morphology errors, and
(iii) untranslated words.

---

[9] http://terra.cl.uzh.ch/terra-corpus-collection.html

[10] http://nlp.insight-centre.org/research/resources/pe2rr/

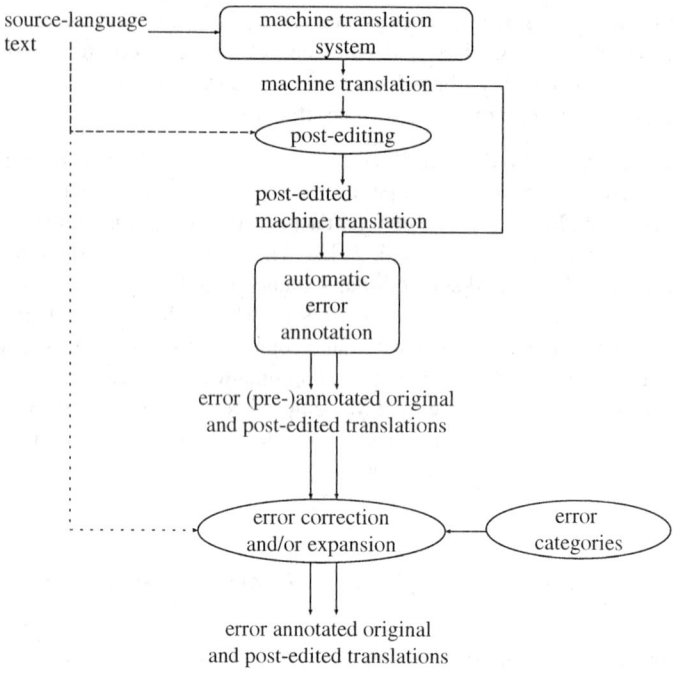

Fig. 3 Procedure of manual error annotation of post-edit operations using automatic pre-annotation; the rectangle denotes automatic process, the ellipse denotes manual process

In addition, multiple error tags are assigned when necessary, mainly for reordering errors which are also incorrectly translated in some way. The general procedure for such error annotation is presented in Fig. 3. Rectangular processes were carried out automatically and elliptical processes manually.

When the Hjerson tool was tested on this corpus and results compared to the previous assessment, the correlations for error distributions remained high, and precision improved significantly. Recall either improved or remained unchanged. This confirmed the hypothesis that annotated post-editing operations are more suitable for assessment and development of an automatic error-classification tool. As for Hjerson itself, despite a large improvement in precision, a significant (albeit smaller) amount of confusion between lexical errors, omissions, and additions still remains. Therefore, addressing this problem should be one of the first steps for its improvement.

Taking into account the described findings regarding confusions between lexical errors, omissions and additions, Bentivogli et al. (2016) and Toral and Sánchez-Cartagena (2017) used automatic classification for three broad error types for comparing phrase-based and neural MT outputs: morphological errors, reordering errors and lexical errors, which also comprise additions and omissions.

4 Other Methods for Error Analysis

Apart from explicit and implicit error classification through assignment of tags to erroneous/edited words, other approaches also enable better understanding of the advantages and problems of MT systems, such as identification and analysis of unmatched patterns, as well as checking and evaluating specific linguistic features.

4.1 Analysis of (Un)matched Sequences

The basis for such analysis is automatic comparison of the translation output with a reference translation and detecting either "recall" mismatches, i.e. sequences in the reference segment that are not present in the output segment, or "precision" mismatches, i.e. sequences in the translation output segment that are not present in the reference. Further analysis of these patterns can be carried out either automatically or manually.

Automatic analysis of POS sequences in translation output is proposed by Lopez and Resnik (2005) in order to see how well a translation system is capable of capturing systematic reordering patterns. Recall is calculated for every POS sequence in a translation output, and the patterns with a low recall score are considered as problematic.

The publicly available evaluation tool rgbF (Popović 2012) which calculates n-gram precision, recall, and F-score also enables detecting unmatched n-grams for arbitrary units: words, POS tags, lemmas, morphemes, etc. The tool provides a list of unmatched n-grams, both in the translation output (precision) as well as in the reference translation (recall). Further analysis is left to the user, depending on the task and goals.

Another open-source tool MT-ComparEval[11] (Klejch et al. 2015), for comparing and evaluating different MT systems by several measures, also offers n-gram matching. The tool identifies both unmatched as well as confirmed n-grams (those appearing both in the translation output as well as in the reference segment). When comparing two translation outputs, the tool provides information about improving n-grams (i.e. confirmed n-grams occurring in only one of the outputs), as well as worsening n-grams (i.e. unmatched n-grams occurring in only one of the outputs).

---

[11] https://github.com/choko/MT-ComparEval

4.2 Evaluating Specific Linguistic Phenomena – Linguistic Check-Points

Another approach for error analysis is to define specific linguistic units, such as a noun phrase, an ambiguous word, or a verb-object collocation, and perform evaluation specifically on them. The general method is to divide each segment into a collection of sub-units which can be classified into linguistic categories and evaluated separately.

First, a linguistic check-point database has to be created from a parallel bilingual text. Both source- and target-language sentences have to be parsed and then linguistic units for each of the defined linguistic categories have to be identified in the parsed sentences. Linguistic units on the target side are directly used as reference translations whereas those on the source side have to be mapped into the target-language. This mapping can be carried out by automatic or manual word alignment and/or other knowledge resources, such as dictionaries or manually-defined rules. Extracted linguistic units and their reference translations represent the linguistic check-point database.

Once a database is available, the evaluation is performed in the following way:

- source sentences containing the desired linguistic categories are selected and translated by an MT system;
- for each check-point, the percentage of matched reference n-grams (i.e. recall) is calculated;
- the total score for the given linguistic category is obtained by summing up the scores of all detected check-points.

Zhou et al. (2008) first proposed this approach to analyse problems in English-Chinese MT output using the Woodpecker tool (Wang et al. 2014). Toral et al. (2012) developed the DELiC4MT tool,[12] which builds on the concept introduced by Woodpecker and overcomes two of its limitations:

(i) DELiC4MT is language-independent, while Woodpecker is designed for English-Chinese, and adaptation to other language pairs is not straightforward,
(ii) DELiC4MT's licence allows anyone to work on it and release modifications, while Woodpecker's licence (MSR-LA) is quite restrictive in this regard.

The general procedure for this type of evaluation is shown in Fig. 4. Similar to the standard error-classification task where the error typology has to be defined, one of the important steps for the linguistic check-point approach is the definition of linguistic categories. Such a linguistic typology is, in principle, an inventory of linguistic phenomena of the source-language that can present problems due to, for example, inherent ambiguity, or for translation into a specific target-language, for instance because of syntactic divergence between the two languages involved in

---

[12]http://www.computing.dcu.ie/~atoral/delic4mt/

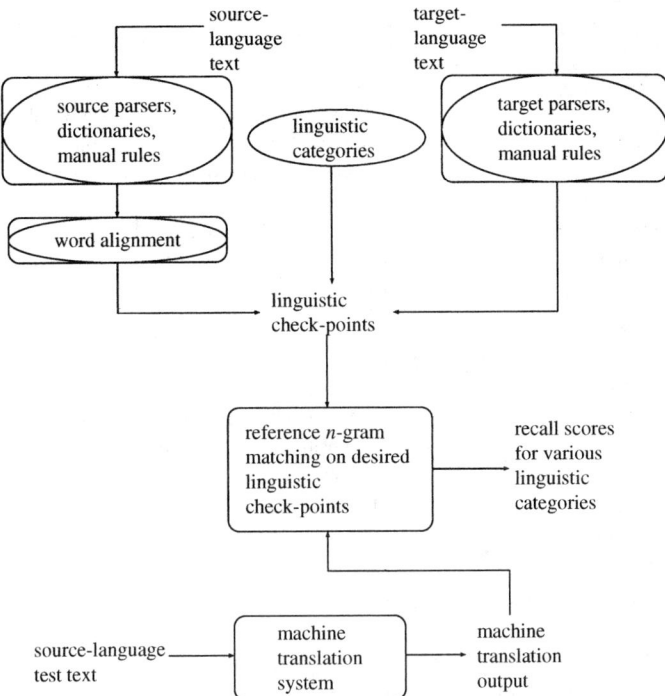

Fig. 4 Procedure of evaluation on linguistic check-points; the rectangle denotes automatic process, and the ellipse denotes manual process

the translation process. The level of detail and the specific linguistic phenomena included in the typology can vary, depending on what the developers and/or the end-users want to investigate as part of the diagnostic evaluation and on the number of aspects that they are interested in.

The Woodpecker linguistic typology is presented in Table 11. It is based on rich linguistic knowledge from various resources and includes important language phenomena on different linguistic levels in both English and Chinese. Different categories are defined by means of different information sources: some by POS tags, others by dependency tags, others by the use of a dictionary, and some of them, especially those on the sentence level, by manual rules. For DELiCM4T, on the other hand, there is no predefined linguistic typology – the tool enables user-defined language-independent specifications, which are then extracted from texts automatically by Kybots (Knowledge-Yielding Robots) which use a collection of profiles that represent patterns of information of interest (Vossen et al. 2010).

Apart from linguistic check-point evaluation, similar linguistic typologies have been explored for other types of evaluation, which are described in detail in the following section.

	Word level	Phrase level	Sentence level
English	Noun	Noun phrase	Time clause
	Verb	Verb phrase	Reason clause
	Adjective	Adjectival phrase	Conditional clause
	Adverb	Adverb phrase	Result clause
	Preposition	Prepositional phrase	Purpose clause
	Pronoun		
	Modal verb		
	Plural		
	Ambiguous word		
	Possessive pronoun		
	Comparative and superlative		
Chinese	Noun	Subject-predicate phrase	Ba sentence
	Verb	Predicate-object phrase	Bei sentence (passive)
	Adjective	Preposition-object phrase	Shi sentence
	Adverb	Measure phrase	You sentence
	Pronoun	Location phrase	Compound sentence
	Preposition		
	Quantifier		
	Ambiguous word		
	Idiom		
	New word		
	Overlapping word		
	Collocation		

Table 11 Zhou et al. (2008) linguistic categories

4.3 Identifying and Analysing Language-Related Issues

Identifying patterns that are causing translation problems due to the characteristics of the involved languages and differences between them can be used not only for linguistic check-point evaluation, but also for analysis of MT systems that goes beyond the standard error classification. For example, phrase-based SMT systems tend to have problems with long-range dependencies involving German verbs. Actual errors that emerged in affected sentences were not only the reordering errors of English verbs, but also missing verbs, as well as mistranslations of other parts of the sentence. The standard error categories for these segments would be "(verb) reordering error", "missing verb", and "mistranslation", and the language-related issue would be "the German verb structure".

Popović and Arcan (2015) present an identification of such patterns for SMT between Slovenian and Serbian on one side and English or German on the other. The analysis is carried out semi-automatically, namely by manual inspection of texts automatically annotated by Hjerson. Definition of issues is based both on general linguistic knowledge, as well as on phenomena related to the (machine)

Languages	Issues
General	Phrase structure and boundaries
	Literal translations
	Structures involving auxiliary verbs
	Structures involving modal verbs
	Prepositions
	Negation
English	Noun (+adjective) collocations
German, south Slavic	Noun-verb disambiguation
	Inflections (case, gender, number, person, tense)
German	Compositional morphology
South Slavic	Articles

Table 12 Some of the most prominent language-related issues found in the PE2rr corpus

translation process. Some of the identified issues are common for all translation directions, whereas some of them depend on the language pair and/or on the translation direction. The PE2rr corpus (Popović and Arcan 2016) described in Sect. 3.2 is partly annotated with these types of issues, and the most frequent ones across different language pairs are shown in Table 12. The same approach is used for analysing issues related to translation between closely-related South Slavic languages (Popović et al. 2016), and for comparison of problematic patterns for phrase-based and neural German-English MT systems (Popović 2017).

Comelles et al. (2016) present a similar study dealing with identification and classification of relevant linguistic features based on general linguistic knowledge as well as on phenomena occurring in a given corpus. The basic typology from Farrús et al. (2010) was extended, as shown in Table 13, and used for development of a linguistically-motivated AEM called VERTa (Comelles et al. 2012), which enables the use of different combinations of the described linguistic features.

Recently, another approach for analysis of language-related phenomena emerged, namely the creation of test sets targeted to specific phenomena. The main advantage over the previously-described approach, which uses "real" data, is the controlled distribution and frequency of desired phenomena.

Guillou and Hardmeier (2016) developed the test suite PROTEST, specifically designed for evaluation of pronoun translation from English to French. The annotation and selection of English source segments is carried out manually, and the evaluation is done manually only for those pronouns which are not found in the reference French translation; an automatic evaluation script is available to discard pronouns that are present in the reference.

Burchardt et al. (2017) developed a corpus containing a larger set of linguistic phenomena for the German-English language pair which was used for comparing three approaches for building MT systems: rule-based, phrase-based, and neural network-based. The selection of language-related phenomena is based on linguistic knowledge, the corpus is created manually, and the translation quality is reported as percentage of correctly-translated instances. A similar strategy is proposed in

Orthography	Capitalisation
	Punctuation
	Date, time, money
Lexical error	Multi-word expressions
	Acronyms and abbreviations
	Untranslated source words
	Omissions
	Proper nouns
Morphology	Inflectional
	Derivational
	Compounding
	Morpho-syntax
Syntax	Syntactic structure
	Word order
	Prepositions
	Relative clauses
	Ungrammatical chunks
Semantics	Lexical semantic relations (synonymy, homonymy, etc.)
	Sentence semantics

Table 13 Comelles et al. (2016) linguistic categories

Isabelle et al. (2017): An English-to-French test corpus of about 100 sentences is created, which contains short examples of several morpho-syntactic phenomena, motivated both by linguistic knowledge as well as experience with issues for phrase-based MT.

Burlot and Yvon (2017) evaluate morphological variations in the target-languages for translation from English to Czech and Latvian. Each segment contains a structure which is expressed syntactically in English but morphologically in the target-language. This work reports the first steps towards automation of the process, using language-model probabilities for the extraction of desired segments (Fig. 5).

4.4 Challenges

After a long hiatus, identification of language-related issues for MT has re-emerged relatively recently and recent works in progress are in the preliminary stages. Therefore, the following important aspects have to be taken into account for further work and development of this evaluation approach:

Definition The decision as to which particular phenomena to concentrate on is far from trivial. The issues have to be linguistically-motivated so that they can reflect

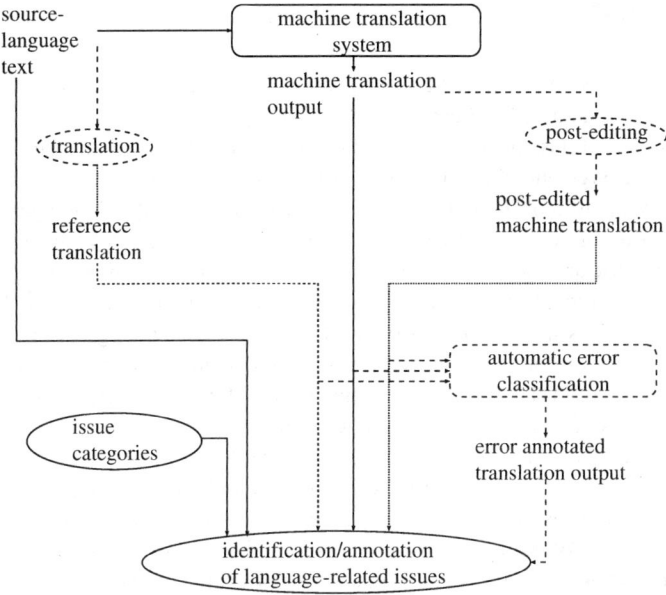

Fig. 5 Identification of language-related issues; the rectangle denotes automatic process, and the ellipse denotes manual process

the (in)ability of an MT system to translate specific linguistic phenomena. However, they should not only contain traditional linguistic categories but also categories which are related to the translation process.

Generalisation The issues should be clearly defined and widely accepted so that the results can be easily understood and shared. Similarly to error-typology generalisation, the optimal way would be to establish a broad class of issues which can easily be expanded in different directions appropriate for the languages involved and task at hand.

Relation to Error Categories Although some of the issues defined so far directly correspond to some typical error categories, such as "inflectional error", for a number of issues such a relationship is hard to find. Finding correspondences between the two types of categories can be useful for both tasks.

Automation Analogously to MT evaluation and error classification, automation of issue identification would be beneficial in order to speed up the process and increase consistency. Some of the issues can already be detected automatically but there are a number of directions for future work.

5 Summary

This chapter presents an overview of different approaches and tasks related to the classification and analysis of errors in MT output.

Manual error classification can provide more detail as human annotators can distinguish a larger number of error classes than state-of-the-art automatic tools, but it is a very difficult task for several reasons. The main disadvantages are high costs in terms of time and money, as well as low consistency, especially if the error categories are numerous and complex. In addition, defining an appropriate error typology represents a challenging task itself. Ongoing work (see Lommel, this volume) aims at generalisation by offering a large typology from which an appropriate sub-set could be selected for the task at hand. Generalisation could also start from a set of broad classes and enable different ways and depths of expansion according to the language (pair) and the goal of the evaluation.

Automatic error analysis is faster, cheaper, and more consistent, yet state-of-the-art tools are still not able to provide many details. In addition, existing tools are prone to confusion between certain error classes, although some of these distinctions are not easy even for human evaluators. Despite these drawbacks, automatic classification tools can replace human evaluators both for obtaining an error profile (distribution of error classes) for a given translation output, as well as for comparing different translation outputs. Apart from this, they can facilitate manual error classification by introducing a pre-annotation step; correcting or expanding existing error tags requires less effort and time than assigning error tags to an unannotated text from scratch.

Classification of post-editing operations both by human evaluators as well as by automatic tools is normally used for analysing the post-editing process, and rarely for analysis of translation errors. However, the edit-classification results are more reliable than error classification of raw translation output since the two tasks are actually closely related; post-editing is actually error correction, and therefore can be viewed as implicit error annotation. In addition, annotated post-editing operations are more appropriate for the assessment of automatic classification tools. Of course, post-editing is a resource-intensive task that has to be performed by qualified translators, but taking into account that some kind of human processing is always needed, post-editing certainly represents a good option.

Apart from the typical error classification carried out by assigning error tags to incorrectly translated (groups of) words, other approaches have been used as well. One method is analysis of unmatched sequences of words, POS tags, or other units, such as the sequences which do not appear both in the translation output and in the reference translation. Another approach aims to identify language-related and linguistically-motivated issues in order to automatically evaluate them specifically. Such issues have also been used for analysing their frequency and nature in order to better understand the language-related phenomena that are difficult for an MT system to handle.

Due to its complexity and variety, error analysis is an active field of research with many possible directions for development and innovation. Regarding details about any particular approach or task, all relevant references are given for further reading.

References

Baayen HR, Davidson DJ, Bates DM (2008) Mixed-effects modeling with crossed random effects for subjects and items. J Mem Lang 59(4):390–412

Banerjee S, Lavie A (2005) METEOR: an automatic metric for MT evaluation with improved correlation with human judgements. In: Proceedings of the ACL 05 Workshop on intrinsic and extrinsic evaluation measures for machine translation and/or summarization, Ann Arbor, pp 65–72

Bayerl PS, Paul KI (2011) what determines inter-coder agreement in manual annotations? A meta-analytic investigation. Comput Linguist 37(4):699–725

Bentivogli L, Bisazza A, Cettolo M, Federico Ml (2016) Neural versus phrase-based machine translation quality: a case study. In: Proceedings of the 2016 conference on Empirical Methods in Natural Language Processing (EMNLP2016), Austin, pp 257–267

Blain F, Senellart J, Schwenk H, Plitt M, Roturier J (2011) Qualitative analysis of post-editing for high quality machine translation. In: Machine Translation Summit XIII, Xiamen

Bojar O (2011) Analyzing error types in English-Czech machine translation. Prague Bull Math Linguist 95:63–76

Burchardt A, Macketanz V, Dehdari J, Heigold G, Peter JT, Williams P (2017) A linguistic evaluation of rule-based, phrase-based, and neural MT engines. Prague Bull Math Linguist 108(1):159–170

Burlot F, Yvon F (2017) Evaluating the morphological competence of machine translation systems. In: Proceedings of the 2nd conference on Statistical Machine Translation (WMT 2017), Copenhagen, pp 43–55

Callison-Burch C, Fordyce C, Koehn P, Monz C, Schroeder J (2007) (Meta-)evaluation of machine translation. In: Proceedings of the 2nd workshop on Statistical Machine Translation (WMT 2007), Prague, pp 136–158

Castilho S, Moorkens J, Gaspari F, Calixto I, Tinsley J, Way A (2017a) Is neural machine translation the new state of the art? Prague Bull Math Linguist 108(1):109–120

Castilho S, Moorkens J, Gaspari F, Sennrich R, Sosoni V, Georgakopoulou P, Lohar P, Way A, Barone AVM, Gialama M (2017b) A comparative quality evaluation of PBSMT and NMT using professional translators. In: Proceedings of MT Summit XVI, Nagoya, pp 116–131

Comelles E, Atserias J, Arranz V, Castellón I (2012) VERTa: linguistic features in MT evaluation. In: Proceedings of the 8th international conference on Language Resources and Evaluation (LREC 2012), Istanbul

Comelles E, Arranz V, Castellón I (2016) Guiding automatic MT evaluation by means of linguistic features. Digital Scholarship in the Humanities

Costa A, Ling W, Luís T, Correia R, Coheur L (2015) A linguistically motivated taxonomy for machine translation error analysis. Mach Transl 29(2):127–161

Farrús M, Costa-Jussà MR, Mariño JB, Fonollosa JAR (2010) Linguistic-based evaluation criteria to identify statistical machine translation errors. In: Proceedings of the 14th annual conference of the European Association for Machine Translation (EAMT 2010), Saint-Raphael, pp 167–173

Federico M, Negri M, Bentivogli L, Turchi M (2014) Assessing the impact of translation errors on machine translation quality with mixed-effects models. In: Proceedings of the 2014 conference on Empirical Methods in Natural Language Processing (EMNLP 2014), Doha, pp 1643–1653

Fishel M, Bojar O, Zeman D, Berka J (2011) Automatic translation error analysis, Pilsen, pp 72–79

Fishel M, Bojar O, Popović M (2012) Terra: a collection of translation error-annotated corpora. In: Proceedings of the 8th international conference on Language Resources and Evaluation (LREC-12), Istanbul, pp 7–14

Girardi C, Bentivogli L, Farajian MA, Federico M (2014) MT-EQuAl: a toolkit for human assessment of machine translation output. In: 25th international conference on Computational Linguistics (CoLing), System Demonstrations, Dublin, pp 120–123

Guillou L, Hardmeier C (2016) PROTEST: a test suite for evaluating pronouns in machine translation. In: Proceedings of the tenth international conference on Language Resources and Evaluation (LREC 2016), Portoroz

Guzmán F, Abdelali A, Temnikova I, Sajjad H, Vogel S (2015) How do humans evaluate machine translation. In: Proceedings of the 10th workshop on Statistical Machine Translation (WMT 2015), Lisbon, pp 457–466

Isabelle P, Cherry C, Foster G (2017) A challenge set approach to evaluating machine translation. In: Proceedings of the 2017 conference on Empirical Methods in Natural Language Processing (EMNLP 2017), Copenhagen, pp 2476–2486

Kirchhoff K, Capurro D, Turner A (2012) Evaluating user preferences in machine translation using conjoint analysis. In: Proceedings of the 6th conference of European Association for Machine Translation (EAMT-12), Trento, pp 119–126

Klejch O, Avramidis E, Burchardt A, Popel M (2015) MT-ComparEval: graphical evaluation interface for machine translation development. Prague Bull Math Linguist 104:63–74

Klubicka F, Toral A, Sánchez-Cartagena VM (2017) Fine-grained human evaluation of neural versus phrase-based machine translation. Prague Bull Math Linguist 108(1):121–132

Koponen M (2012) Comparing human perceptions of post-editing effort with post-editing operations. In: Proceedings of the seventh workshop on Statistical Machine Translation, Montreal, pp 181–190

Krings HP (2001) Repairing texts: empirical investigations of machine translation post-editing processes. Kent State University Press, Kent

Levenshtein VI (1966) Binary codes capable of correcting deletions, insertions and reversals. Sov Phys Dokl 10(8):707–710

Llitjós AF, Carbonell JG, Lavie A (2005) A framework for interactive and automatic refinement of transfer-based machine translation. In: Proceedings of the 10th conference of European Association for Machine Translation (EAMT2005), Budapest, pp 87–96

Lommel A, Burchardt A, Popović M, Harris K, Avramidis E, Uszkoreit H (2014a) Using a new analytic measure for the annotation and analysis of MT errors on real data. In: Proceedings of the 17th annual conference of the European Association for Machine Translation (EAMT 2014), pp 165–172

Lommel A, Popović M, Burchardt A (2014b) Assessing inter-annotator agreement for translation error annotation. In: Proceedings of MTE workshop on automatic and manual metrics for operational translation evaluation, LREC 2014, Reykjavík

Lopez A, Resnik P (2005) Pattern visualization for machine translation output. In: Proceedings of HLT/EMNLP on interactive demonstrations, Vancouver, pp 12–13

Och FJ, Ney H (2003) A systematic comparison of various statistical alignment models. Comput Linguist 29(1):19–51

Papineni K, Roukos S, Ward T, Zhu WJ (2002) BLEU: a method for automatic evaluation of machine translation. In: Proceedings of the 40th annual meeting of the Association for Computational Linguistics (ACL 2002), Philadelphia, pp 311–318

Popović M (2011) Hjerson: an open source tool for automatic error classification of machine translation output. Prague Bull Math Linguist 96:59–68

Popović M (2012) RgbF: an open source tool for n-gram based automatic evaluation of machine translation output. Prague Bull Math Linguist 98:99–108

Popović M (2015) ChrF: character n-gram F-score for automatic MT evaluation. In: Proceedings of the tenth workshop on Statistical Machine Translation (WMT2015), Lisbon, pp 392–395

Popović M (2017) Comparing language related issues for NMT and PBMT between German and English. Prague Bull Math Linguist 108(1):209–220

Popović M, Arcan M (2015) Identifying main obstacles for statistical machine translation of morphologically rich South Slavic languages. In: The 18th annual conference of the European Association for Machine Translation (EAMT 2015), Antalya, pp 97–104

Popović M, Arcan M (2016) PE2rr corpus: manual error annotation of automatically pre-annotated MT post-edits. In: Proceedings of the tenth international conference on Language Resources and Evaluation (LREC 2016)

Popović M, Ney H (2006) Error analysis of verb inflections in Spanish translation output. In: Proceedings of the TC-Star workshop on speech-to-speech translation, Barcelona, pp 99–103

Popović M, Ney H (2007) Word error rates: decomposition over POS classes and applications for error analysis. In: Proceedings of the 2nd workshop on Statistical Machine Translation (WMT 2007), Prague, pp 48–55

Popović M, Ney H (2011) Towards automatic error analysis of machine translation output. Comput Linguist 37(4):657–688

Popović M, de Gispert A, Gupta D, Lambert P, Ney H, Mariño JB, Federico M, Banchs R (2006) Morpho-syntactic information for automatic error analysis of statistical machine translation output. In: Proceedings on the 1st workshop on Statistical Machine Translation, New York, pp 1–6

Popović M, Lommel A, Burchardt A, Avramidis E, Uszkoreit H (2014) Relations between different types of post-editing operations, cognitive effort and temporal effort. In: Proceedings of the 7th annual conference of the European Association for Machine Translation (EAMT 2014), pp 191–198

Popović M, Arcan M, Avramidis E, Burchardt A, Lommel A (2015) Poor man's lemmatisation for automatic error classification. In: The 18th annual conference of the European Association for Machine Translation (EAMT 2015), pp 105–112

Popović M, Arcan M, Klubicka F (2016) Language related issues for machine translation between closely related South Slavic languages. In: Proceedings of the third workshop on NLP for Similar Languages, Varieties and Dialects (VarDial 2016), Osaka, pp 43–52

Snover M, Dorr B, Schwartz R, Micciulla L, Makhoul J (2006) A study of translation edit rate with targeted human annotation. In: Proceedings of AMTA 2006, the 7th conference of the Association for Machine Translation in the Americas, Cambridge, pp 223–231

Stymne S (2011) Blast: a tool for error analysis of machine translation output. In: Proceedings of the 49th annual meeting of the Association for Computational Linguistics – Human Language Technologies (HLT 2011): Systems Demonstrations, Portland, pp 56–61

Stymne S, Ahrenberg L (2012) On the practice of error analysis for machine translation evaluation. In: Proceedings of the 8th international conference on Language Resources and Evaluation (LREC 2012), Istanbul

Toral A, Sánchez-Cartagena VM (2017) A multifaceted evaluation of neural versus statistical machine translation for 9 language directions. In: Proceedings of the 15th conference of the European chapter of the Association for Computational Linguistics (EACL 2017), Valencia

Toral A, Naskar SK, Gaspari F, Groves D (2012) DELiC4MT: a tool for diagnostic MT evaluation over user-defined linguistic phenomena. Prague Bull Math Linguist 98:121–132

Vilar D, Xu J, D'Haro LF, Ney H (2006) Error analysis of statistical machine translation output. In: Proceedings of 5th international conference on Language Resources and Evaluation (LREC 2006), Genoa, pp 697–702

Vogel S, Ney H, Tillmann C (1996) HMM-based word alignment in statistical translation. In: Proceedings of the 16nd international conference on Computational Linguistics (CoLing 1996), Copenhagen, Denmark, pp 836–841

Vossen P, Rigau G, Agirre E, Soroa A, Monachini M, Bartolini R (2010) KYOTO: an open platform for mining facts. In: Proceedings of the 6th workshop on Ontologies and Lexical Resources (Ontolex 2010), Beijing, pp 1–10

Wang B, Zhou M, Liu S, Li M, Zhang D (2014) Woodpecker: an automatic methodology for machine translation diagnosis with rich linguistic knowledge. J Inf Sci Eng 30(5):1407–1424

Zaretskaya A, Vela M, Pastor GC, Seghiri M (2016) Measuring post-editing time and effort for different types of machine translation errors. New Voice Trans Stud 15:63–92

Zeman D, Fishel M, Berka J, Bojar O (2011) Addicter: what is wrong with my translations? Prague Bull Math Linguist 96:79–88

Zhou M, Wang B, Liu S, Li M, Zhang D, Zhao T (2008) Diagnostic Evaluation of machine translation systems using automatically constructed linguistic check-points. In: Proceedings of the 22nd international conference on Computational Linguistics (CoLing 2008), Manchester, pp 1121–1128

Quality Expectations of Machine Translation

7

Andy Way

Abstract Machine Translation (MT) is being deployed for a range of use-cases by millions of people on a daily basis. There should, therefore, be no doubt as to the utility of MT. However, not everyone is convinced that MT can be useful, especially as a productivity enhancer for human translators. In this chapter, I address this issue, describing how MT is currently deployed, how its output is evaluated and how this could be enhanced, especially as MT quality itself improves. Central to these issues is the acceptance that there is no longer a single 'gold standard' measure of quality, such that the situation in which MT is deployed needs to be borne in mind, especially with respect to the expected 'shelf-life' of the translation itself.

Keywords Translation quality assessment · Translation metrics · Neural machine translation · Translator productivity · Translation users

1 Machine Translation Today

Machine Translation (MT) is being deployed for a range of use-cases by millions of people on a daily basis. I will examine the reasons for this later in this chapter, but one inference is very clear: those people using MT in those use-cases *must* already be satisfied with the level of quality emanating from the MT systems they are deploying, otherwise they would stop using them.

That is not the same thing at all as saying that MT quality is perfect, far from it. The many companies and academic researchers who develop and deploy MT engines today continue to strive to improve the quality of the translations produced. This too is an implicit acceptance of the fact that the level of quality is sub-optimal – for some use-cases at least – and can be improved.

A. Way
ADAPT Centre/School of Computing, Dublin City University, Dublin, Ireland
e-mail: andy.way@adaptcentre.ie

If MT system output is good enough for some areas of application, yet at the same time system developers are trying hard to improve the level of translations produced by their engines, then translation quality – whether produced by a machine or by a human – needs to be *measurable*.

Note that this applies also to translators who complain that MT quality is too poor to be used in their workflows; in order to decide that with some certainty – rather than rejecting MT out-of-hand merely as a knee-jerk reaction to the onset of this new technology – the impact of MT on translators' work needs to be measurable.

In Way (2013), I appealed to two concepts, which are revisited here, namely:

1. Fitness for purpose of translations,[1] and
2. Perishability of content.

In that work, I noted that:

> the degree of human involvement required – or warranted – in a particular translation scenario will depend on the purpose, value and shelf-life of the content. More specifically, we assert that in all cases, the degree of post-editing or human input should be clearly correlated with the content lifespan.

In that paper, I also put forward the view that if there ever truly was a single notion of quality as regards translation – namely 'perfect' human translation – then this needs to be abandoned forthwith; the range of situations in which MT is being deployed nowadays includes many where there simply is no place for human intervention, either in terms of speed, or cost, or both.

In the remainder of this chapter, I will attempt to place MT in its proper place as we approach 2020. This involves examining the use-cases in which MT is deployed today, and how MT quality is measured. I will demonstrate how the construction of MT systems is changing, and describe ways in which MT evaluation needs to change. At all times, I will bear in mind the two constructs above as being of utmost importance when thinking about these issues: how will the translation be used, and for how long will we need to consult that translation?

2   Machine Translation Use Today

There are many estimates as to how much the translation industry is worth today, and how much it will expand over the coming years. For example, the size of the overall global language industry in 2015 was estimated at $38 billion, with estimates of up to $46 billion by 2016.[2] Thought leaders in this space have even begun to estimate

---

[1] This concept is also applied to crowdsourced translation by Jiménez-Crespo in this volume.
[2] https://www.gala-global.org/industry/industry-facts-and-data

the worth of the MT sector itself; in August 2014, TAUS stated that the MT industry was worth $250M.[3]

This was a significant announcement for a number of reasons. First and foremost, it recognised that MT was *already* being used successfully for a number of use-cases; secondly, it noted that while this estimate might be seen to be on the low side, for MT companies even a small slice of $250M was not to be sniffed at;[4] and thirdly, it pointed out that MT technology is a key enabler and a force multiplier for new services, with innovative companies in IT and other sectors converging MT technology in new applications and products or using MT to enhance their existing products.

As we have pointed out before (Penkale and Way 2013; Way 2013), some translators like to pour scorn on the capability of MT, but by any measure, there is no real doubt that MT is being used at scale on a global basis every day. Back in 2012, Franz Och, who headed up the Google Translate team at that time, stated that:

> Today we have more than 200 million monthly active users on translate.google.com. In a given day we translate roughly as much text as you'd find in 1 million books. To put it another way: what all the professional human translators in the world produce in a year, our system translates in roughly a single day.[5]

At a rough estimate, in 2012 Google was translating around 75 billion words per day. At the Google I/O event in May 2016,[6] Google stated that the average daily volume is about 143 billion words a day across 100 language combinations (see Fig. 1), meaning that their translation volume has more or less doubled in just 4 years.

While Google translates by far the most words per day, other players also service huge amounts of translation requests. In March 2016, Joaquin Quiñonero Candela, Director of Engineering for Applied Machine Learning at Facebook, spoke about the amount of translation requests provided by his company today.[7] As shown in Fig. 2, with 2 billion translations being provided on a daily basis, and almost 1 billion users seeing these translations each month, the numbers are truly staggering.

If all the translation requests that Bing Translator[8] and other online systems respond to on a daily basis are added in, this is a clear demonstration of the utility of online MT across a wide range of use-cases and language pairs to millions of distinct users.

Many other companies either produce generic MT toolkits available for purchase, or build customised engines that enable their clients to improve productivity, allow

---

[3]https://www.taus.net/think-tank/news/press-release/size-machine-translation-market-is-250-million-taus-publishes-new-market-report

[4]Technavio estimate that the MT market will grow at a CAGR rate of 23.53% during 2015–19 (http://www.slideshare.net/technavio/global-machine-translation-market-20152019)

[5]https://googleblog.blogspot.ie/2012/04/breaking-down-language-barriersix-years.html

[6]https://events.google.com/io2016/

[7]https://www.quora.com/Is-Facebooks-machine-translation-MT-based-on-principles-common-to-other-statistical-MT-systems-or-is-it-somehow-different

[8]https://www.bing.com/translator

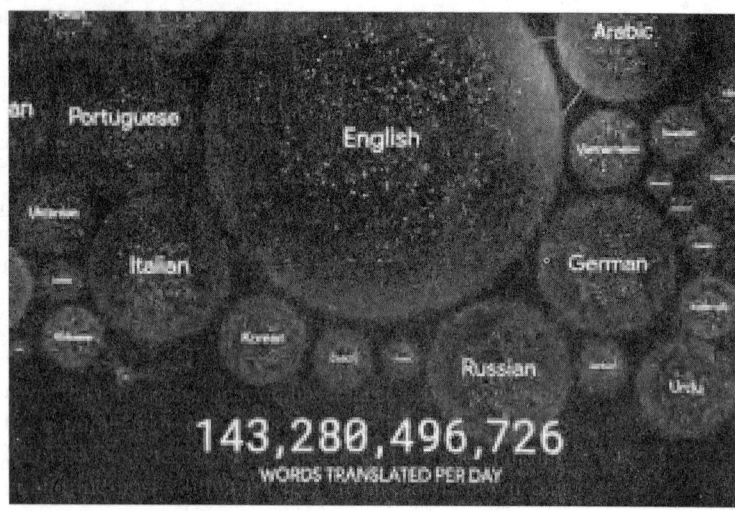

Fig. 1 Daily translation usage in Google Translate (May 2016)

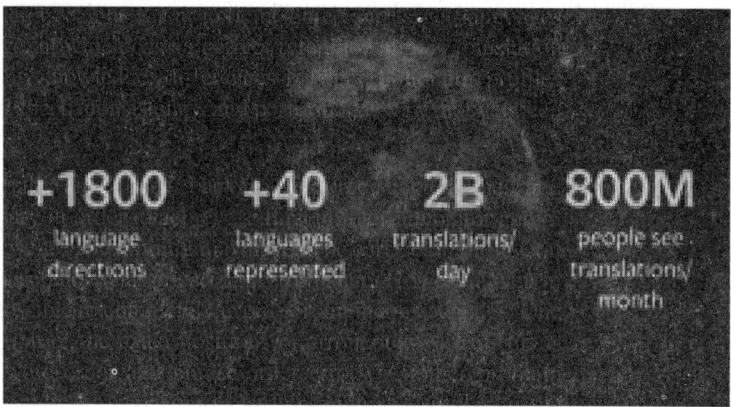

Fig. 2 Translation usage in Facebook (May 2016)

users to translate content previously not feasible due to time or cost constraints, and reduce time to market (see Way (2013) for a list of successful use-cases for MT).

Of course, there are other types of MT supplier too. One of these is KantanMT,[9] which like the Microsoft Translator Hub[10] allows users to upload their own translation assets and quickly build Statistical MT (SMT) systems with good translation performance in just a few hours. KantanMT have produced some impressive figures

---

[9]https://www.kantanmt.com/

[10]https://www.microsoft.com/en-us/translator/hub.aspx

of their own in this space. Managing over 80 billion words of user-supplied MT engine training data, their platform currently performs 650 million translations each year.

Scale and robustness are one thing, but of course users care about quality too. Microsoft note on their webpage (see footnote 8) that "given the appropriate type and amount of training data it is not uncommon to expect gains between 5 and 10, even 15 in some instances, BLEU points on translation quality by using the Hub".[11]

This brings me to the main thrust of this chapter, namely how MT is evaluated, both in academic research labs and in industry, what is wrong with those methods, whether they are equally applicable to all MT system types, and how the myriad ways in which MT is being/will be deployed might affect the notion of utility in the future.

3   Machine Translation Evaluation Today

Of course, it is one thing building an MT system; it's another thing entirely knowing whether the quality produced is any good. In this section, I describe how MT quality has been measured over the years, focusing in particular on human and automatic evaluation, as well as task-based evaluation.

3.1   Human Evaluation

Human evaluation of MT quality goes back many years. There are different types of human evaluation of MT, including (Humphreys et al. 1991):[12]

- *Typological evaluation*, which addresses which translational phenomena can be handled by a particular MT system;

---

[11] In its original exposition in Papineni et al. (2002), the BLEU ("Bilingual Evaluation Understudy") score for a document was a figure between 0 and 1, the higher the better indicator of the quality of the MT system being evaluated. Here, and more commonly used nowadays in the field, this score is multiplied by 100 so that 'BLEU points' can be used to indicate progress compared to some benchmark.

[12] We omit a lengthy discussion here on 'round trip' translation as an evaluation method (but cf. footnote 25), as it has been demonstrated by Somers (2005) to be an untrusted means of MT evaluation. In Way (2013), I note that in order to show that MT is error-prone, "sites like Translation Party (http://www.translationparty.com/) have been set up to demonstrate that continuous use of 'back translation' – that is, start with (say) an English sentence, translate it into (say) French, translate that output back into English, *ad nauseum* – ends up with a string that differs markedly from that which you started out with". I quickly show that such websites have the opposite effect, and observe that "It's easy to show MT to be useless; it's just as easy to show it to be useful, but some people don't want to".

- *Declarative evaluation*, which addresses how an MT system performs relative to various dimensions of translation quality;
- *Operational evaluation*, which establishes how effective an MT system is likely to be (in terms of cost) as part of a given translation process.

Typological evaluations were conducted by MT system developers to ensure that their engines were continuing to improve over time. These were typically carried out with reference to a test suite of examples (King and Falkedal 1990; Arnold et al. 1993; Balkan et al. 1994). In particular, test suites need to be designed to ensure wide coverage of the source language as well as test certain key translational phenomena. King and Falkedal (1990) note that if this is to be done properly, "this assumes the availability of someone with at least a knowledge of the languages concerned, of linguistics and preferably some experience of machine translation". They quickly lament that this is rarely the case in practice.

One of the earliest, most well-known instances of a declarative (or "static") evaluation was the ALPAC report (Pierce et al. 1966). Translation quality was measured along two dimensions: (i) *fidelity* (or "informativeness"), the extent to which a translated text contains the same information as the source text; and (ii) *intelligibility*, the extent to which the output sentence is a well-formed example of the target language. In their study, a group of 18 English monolinguals and 18 English native speakers with a "high degree of competence in the comprehension of scientific Russian" were asked to evaluate 3 human and 3 machine translations on 9- and 10-point scales for the dimensions of intelligibility and informativeness, respectively.

In subsequent similar evaluations (e.g. Balkan et al. 1991), more coarse-grained scales (with 1–4 or 1–5 rather than a 10-point scale) are typically used, as it is difficult for humans to discriminate with confidence using such a fine-grained scale. Note too that using fewer decision points tends to ensure greater inter-rater scoring consistency. In addition, terms such as "accuracy" (or "adequacy") and "fluency" are more likely to be seen as replacements for the terminology introduced by Pierce et al. (1966).

Arnold et al. (1994) observe that "accuracy testing follows intelligibility rating", but clearly the two evaluations are related; if a particular output string is deemed to be unintelligible (or disfluent), it is arguable whether there is any point in performing an accuracy test. When comparing the two tasks, Arnold et al. (*ibid.*) note that "accuracy scores are much less interesting than intelligibility scores … because accuracy scores are often closely related to the intelligibility scores; high intelligibility normally means high accuracy".[13] Until quite recently, it would have been rare indeed for an MT system to output a well-formed target translation that bore no resemblance to the input string, but as I note in Way (2018):

> [Neural] MT output can be deceptively fluent; sometimes perfect target-language sentences are output, and less thorough translators and proofreaders may be seduced into accepting such translations, despite the fact that such translations may not be an actual translation of the source sentence at hand at all!

---

[13] Indeed, the results from the ALPAC evaluation demonstrated there to be considerable correlation between intelligibility and fidelity.

Whatever terms are used, outputting numbers on scales as an assessment of quality gives the user little idea about the actual amount of effort it would take for the MT output to be post-edited into the final translation. Accordingly, operational evaluations were designed to take other factors into account, not just the quality of the MT output itself.

Vasconcellos (1989) details one of the first studies comparing post-edited MT against human translation *per se*. While the findings were positive as far as MT usage at the Pan-American Health Organisation was concerned in terms of quality and speed, it did not attempt to measure the overall cost.

Humphreys et al. (1991) were one of the first to detail the contents of such an operational evaluation, addressing questions such as translator selection, quality required, how quality is to be assessed (e.g. scores according to scales, or ranking), speed improvements over time, type of data to be used, dictionary usage etc. In closing, they note that "an adequate model of operational evaluation requires very substantial input (in terms of subject numbers and subject and experimenter time)".

In concluding this section, it is worth pointing out that this remains a problem for the industry as a whole, with no clearly defined process as to whether MT should or should not be introduced into a company's translation workflow. Companies often overlook how disruptive a technology MT actually is: it impacts not just technically trained staff, but also project managers, sales and marketing, the training team, finance employees, and of course post-editors and quality reviewers. All of this should be taken on board beforehand if the correct decision is to be taken with full knowledge of the expected return on investment, but in practice it rarely is.

3.2   Automatic Evaluation

Despite its obvious benefits, human evaluation is slow, expensive and inconsistent. Metrics such as Word Error Rate (WER: Levenshtein 1966), and Position-Independent Word Error Rate (PER: Tillmann et al. 1997) had been used for some time to measure the effectiveness of automatic speech recognition (ASR). These methods simply examine how many of the target words are correct (PER) and in the right position (WER) compared to some human reference. This is fine for ASR, which is a monolingual task. These metrics have been used for MT evaluation, but of course, the effectiveness of the translation needs to be measured not just as an example target string ("fluency", in human terms), but also with respect to its being an accurate translation of the source ("adequacy"). For an overview of automatic MT evaluation metrics, see Castilho et al. in this volume.

3.2.1   Inherent Problems with Automatic Evaluation Metrics

Nonetheless, when new metrics came in at the start of the century designed specifically for MT evaluation, they ignored the source sentence altogether. BLEU and NIST (Doddington 2002) both came on the scene at around the same time, and used different (but related) ways to compute the similarity between a human supplied 'gold standard' reference and the MT output string based (largely) on n-gram co-occurrence, i.e. how often words and phrases (up to length 4) occur both in the human reference and the MT output string.

As well as ignoring the source sentence altogether, a further problem for these evaluation metrics is that while they do function (better) with multiple human-supplied references (e.g. NIST MT-06 English-to-Chinese and English-to-Arabic tasks, which "had four independently generated high quality translations that were produced by professional translation companies"),[14] most of the time only a single reference is supplied; traditionally MT system developers hold out sections of the parallel training data – a (large) collection of source sentences and their translations, such as appears in a Translation Memory (TM: Heyn 1998) – to act as development (to optimally tune the system parameters)[15] and test sets.

There are a number of problems with this. One is that, as He and Way (2009a) demonstrated, Minimum Error Rate Training (Och 2003) – the tool most used for parameter tuning in SMT – is sub-optimal despite being tuned on translation-quality measures such as (document-level) BLEU.[16] More specifically, we showed that tuning on a particular objective measure (on the development set) cannot be guaranteed to deliver the optimal score on the test set, i.e. in order to deliver (say) the best BLEU score in testing, one might be better off tuning on (say) METEOR (Banerjee and Lavie 2005) rather than BLEU itself, as might be expected.

More importantly, as any pair of translators will tell you, there is no such thing as *the* correct translation. In a discussion regarding translator resistance towards MT in Way (2012), I summoned Bellos' (2011) observation that translators are often less than complimentary regarding each other's translations; specifically, he states that "translation commentators lead the field in throwing most of its work in the direction of the garbage dump", and soon thereafter that "it seems implausible that anyone would ever make such a statement about any other human skill or trade". Note that this can be observed in practice, too; when translators are asked to post-edit MT, they often make unnecessary changes, as while the MT output might have been acceptable to some, 'it's not quite how they would have said it themselves'. Note too the place of proofreaders in the human translation cycle, who alongside fixing errors made by the original translator, may be incentivised to make unnecessary changes to continue to justify their own positions in the workflow. In this regard, de Almeida (2013) observes that for both English-to-French and English-to-Spanish, 'essential' changes (language errors and mistranslations) comprise only about half

---

[14]http://www.itl.nist.gov/iad/mig/tests/mt/2006/doc/mt06eval_official_results.html

[15]Minimally, in an SMT system these would be the "translation model" inferred from the parallel data, which essentially suggests which target-language words and phrases might best be used to try to create a translation of the source string; and the "language model" inferred from large collections of monolingual data, and used to try to create the most likely target-language ordering of those suggested target words and phrases.

[16]See Sect. 3.2.2 for discussion of document-level versus sentence-level MT evaluation.

of the overall edits made to documents, with the others concerning lexical choice, adding extra words, reordering, and even changing punctuation.

Finally, here, as I noted in Way (2013), "MT developers are forced to (wrongly) assume human translations to be perfect when conducting automatic MT evaluation". As Penkale and Way (2013) observe, some translators still argue that there is only one level of quality – 'perfect' human translation – despite the myriad of use-cases available today, many of which omit a human in the loop entirely. Even with proofreaders in the fully managed translation, editing, and proofreading cycle, mistakes do occur, and sometimes these wrong human translations are precisely those against which the output from MT systems is compared.

3.2.2 Problems with Automatic Evaluation Use

A further problem with the use of such metrics in practice is that BLEU is often used at the sentence level, either by system developers against a common test set to track system improvement over time, or in ranking tasks with human evaluators to try to seek insight into which translation produced by different systems might be 'better'. Of course, this is not the fault of the designers of the automatic evaluation metrics, which were designed to work at the document level. As a consequence, several variants of BLEU have been designed and can be used for that purpose (e.g. Lin and Och 2004; Liang et al. 2006).

Note too that He and Way (2009a, b) demonstrate that certain automatic metrics prefer shorter/longer translations. METEOR prefers longer outputs than the reference translations owing to the different chunk penalties assigned to different languages.[17] He and Way demonstrate clearly that by imposing a static chunk penalty when tuning with METEOR gives better translation results when measured by BLEU, Translation Edit Rate (TER: Snover et al. 2006) and METEOR.

TER, in contrast, prefers shorter sentences to be generated by MT. As it is an error metric, the more words generated by an MT system, the larger the number of insertions, deletions and substitutions which will typically be required to transform the MT hypothesis into the reference sentence. He and Way (2009a) note that this is "less likely to harm in MT evaluation, unless a system is developed specifically to game the metric. However, if such knowledge is made use of in tuning, the system will be *tuned* to take advantage of this preference, and will tend to output overly succinct sentences" (original emphasis).

---

[17]METEOR rewards MT output composed of fewer chunks. Output containing bigram (or longer) matches compared to the reference translation is penalised less than that comprising unigram matches only.

3.2.3   Does Automatic Evaluation Corroborate Human Evaluation?

If automatic evaluation metrics are to be of any use as arbiters of translation quality, then the predictions they make should correlate with human judgement, assuming humans can be trusted to evaluate MT output in a consistent fashion.

Since its introduction over 15 years ago, BLEU has been by some distance the most reported metric in papers involving MT experiments. While early studies (Doddington 2002; Coughlin 2003) demonstrated its correlation with human judgements of translation under certain circumstances, it has been widely accepted for some time now that BLEU has many limitations.[18]

Callison-Burch et al. (2006) explain that BLEU places no explicit constraints on the order in which matching n-grams occur, in order to permit variation in word choice in MT outputs. In the multiple reference scenario, matches can be extracted in a huge number of different ways, so that millions of variants all receive the same BLEU score for any particular translation hypothesis. They argue that "because the number of translations that score the same is so large, it is unlikely that all of them will be judged to be identical in quality by human annotators". By extension, they note that translations with higher BLEU scores might be deemed worse by human judges.

Hovy and Ravichandran (2003) give a nice example to illustrate this point. Let us assume the reference translation to be (1):

1. The President frequently makes his vacation in Crawford Texas .
2. George Bush often takes a holiday in Crawford Texas .
3. holiday often Bush a takes George in Crawford Texas .

If the two MT hypotheses in (2) and (3) were produced, then they would receive exactly the same BLEU score! Why? Firstly, both (2) and (3) are the same length, so the brevity penalty[19] plays no role here. They both share the 4-gram "in Crawford Texas .", the trigrams "in Crawford Texas" and "Crawford Texas .", the bigrams "in Crawford", "Crawford Texas", and "Texas .", and the unigrams "in", "Crawford", "Texas", and ".". All the other words in (2) and (3) are treated by BLEU as non-matches; there is no benefit gained by the fact that we know – at least in 2003! – the phrase "George Bush often takes a holiday" is synonymous with "The President frequently makes his vacation" in (1). As Babych and Hartley (2004) pointed out, BLEU weights all items in the reference sentence equally, so the fact that for the most part (3) is word salad makes no difference to its overall BLEU score.

Note too that BLEU pays no attention to semantic errors either. This is easily demonstrated with the (somewhat artificial) example in (4):

4. George rhododendron often takes a holiday in Crawford Texas .

---

[18]Nonetheless, more recent papers (Agarwal and Lavie 2008; Farrús et al. 2012) have also demonstrated that BLEU correlates extremely well with human judgement of translation quality.

[19]This was introduced to prevent systems from outputting very short target-language strings (such as "the") but nonetheless obtaining a high score. Accordingly, the shorter the translation compared to the reference translation, the more punitive the brevity penalty.

That is, assuming (again) the reference translation to be (1), the BLEU score for (2) and (4) would again be identical; despite the fact that rhododendron is a type of bush, it is clearly an inferior translation compared to (2). To BLEU, both "Bush" (in (2)) and "rhododendron" (in (4)) are simply words that do not occur in the reference (1), so are treated exactly the same.

As a result of these sorts of problems, diagnostic MT evaluation emerged as a sub-field in its own right, as a means of capturing more precisely the types of errors made by various systems.[20] Vilar et al. (2006) observe that "a relationship between [automatic] error measures and the actual errors found in the translations is ... not easy to find". Accordingly, they produced a human error analysis and error-classification scheme which extends the error typology presented in Llitjós et al. (2005), as a means of focusing research effort. Popović and Ney (2011) present the first steps towards a framework for automatic analysis and classification of errors, while Naskar et al. (2011) produced the DELiC4MT system, which identified user-specified fine-grained classes of translation errors based on the linguistic shortcomings of the particular MT system. This is of interest to users to gain insights into the linguistic strengths and weaknesses of the MT system, but also allows the MT system developers to try to correct these errors and improve translation performance.

Returning to the merits of the automatic MT metrics *per se*, Callison-Burch et al. (2006) go on to explain why human rankings of translation systems do not tally with automatic rankings computed via the BLEU score. Firstly, as I pointed out at the beginning of Sect. 3.2.1, humans are asked to evaluate fluency without recourse to the source sentence; while this can of course be done as a monolingual task, in reality a human would surely calculate fluency and adequacy at the same time. Secondly, the authors demonstrate an inherent bias in BLEU (and similar metrics) against systems (such as rule-based systems) which do not have at their core a component founded on n-gram statistics.[21]

Callison-Burch et al. (2008) show that BLEU has a lower correlation with human judgement than metrics which take into account linguistic resources (such as part-of-speech tags) and better matching strategies, e.g. METEOR computes word matching based on stemming and WordNet synonymy (Miller et al. 1990).

A recent paper by Smith et al. (2016) serves to remind us of the fallibility of BLEU. They note that it "can be 'cheated': very bad translations can get high BLEU scores", although they do accept that their experiments "used BLEU in a very different fashion from that for which it was designed" (*op cit.*).

In the interim, partly because the community knows that better evaluation measures are needed, many other types of MT metrics have been developed which exploit deeper features such as paraphrases (Zhou et al. 2006), or syntax (Liu and Gildea 2005; Owczarzak et al. 2007), as well as metrics that try to exploit machine-

---

[20] See Popović (this volume) for a discussion of the evolution of diagnostic MT error typologies.

[21] 'Phrases' in phrase-based SMT refer only to n-gram sequences, i.e. contiguous sequences of surface words, not to the linguistic "constituent" sense of the word.

learning techniques (Albrecht and Hwa 2007; Ye et al. 2007; He and Way 2009c). The Rank-based Intuitive Bilingual Evaluation Score (RIBES: Isozaki et al. 2010) was developed especially to take reordering into account between languages with very different word orders, and has been demonstrated to have high correlation with human evaluations of MT systems.

Nonetheless, none of these metrics are widely used. Despite the well-known problems with BLEU, and the availability of many other – arguably better – metrics, MT system developers have continued to use it in the intervening 10 years as the primary measure of translation quality, in academic circles especially.

3.3 Task-Based Evaluation

When evaluation of MT systems started to be taken seriously in the 1990s, some of the early papers on the topic (e.g. Doyon et al. 1999) noted that the aims which the technology was expected to be used for had to be known in advance. Of course, some objectives could be more tolerant of MT errors than others.

Taking this on board, more and more evaluations have taken place in the interim with the specific task in mind (e.g. Thomas (1999) for spoken-language MT; or Voss and Tate (2006) for information extraction). Indeed, WMT evaluations[22] regularly include specific tasks nowadays, including medical translation (e.g. Zhang et al. 2014), automatic post-editing (e.g. Chatterjee et al. 2015) and MT for the IT domain (e.g. Cuong et al. 2016). I take this as evidence that the community as a whole is well aware of the fact that when evaluating MT quality, the actual use-case and utility of the translations therein need to be borne in mind.

4 The Changing Nature of MT System Design

When MT evaluation began in earnest, most systems were rule-based (RBMT). Since then, of course, we have seen the advent of SMT, and the rise of automatic MT evaluation metrics, as described in the previous section. When these came in, many people noted that as they were largely n-gram-based, there was an implicit bias against RBMT, the output of which was demonstrated to be considerably better in human evaluations (e.g. Riezler and Maxwell 2005; Farrús et al. 2012; Lewis and Quirk 2013).[23]

---

[22]The Workshop (now Conference) on Machine Translation runs annual competitive MT system evaluations for a range of tasks. See http://www.statmt.org/wmt17/ for the latest in the series.

[23]Over the past 10 years or so, SMT system developers have been incorporating more and more linguistic features. It is interesting to ponder whether BLEU (and similar metrics) disadvantages such linguistically enhanced systems compared to 'pure' SMT engines, in much the same way as RBMT output was penalised compared to pure n-gram-based systems.

More recently, Neural MT (NMT, e.g. Sennrich et al. 2016a) has been demonstrated to be very competitive compared to state-of-the-art SMT models, albeit to date for a limited number of language pairs and document types. On average, improvements over Phrase-Based SMT (PBSMT, cf. Koehn et al. 2003, 2007) were of the order of two BLEU points. Indeed, most evaluation of NMT was conducted in terms of automatic MT metrics until Jean et al. (2015) set a manual ranking evaluation with non-professional annotators.

As a result of this good performance, Bentivogli et al. (2016) undertook an in-depth (diagnostic) human evaluation to try to understand exactly where these improvements in terms of automatic metrics actually came from. In particular, they leveraged high-quality post-edits performed by professional translators on 600 output sentences from both PBSMT and NMT systems for English-to-German translation of TED talks. The NMT system of Luong and Manning (2015) was compared against a standard PBSMT system (Ha et al. 2015), a hierarchical SMT system (Jehl et al. 2015) and a system combining PBSMT and syntax-based SMT (Huck and Birch 2015). HTER – essentially, TER with a human-in-the-loop (Snover et al. 2006) – and multi-reference TER was used, and results showed that NMT outperformed the other approaches in all metrics at a statistical significance level of $p = 0.01$.

From a linguistic point of view, NMT was seen to produce significantly fewer morphological errors (–19%), lexical errors (–17%), and substantially fewer word order errors (–50%) than its closest statistical competitor. With respect to word order, NMT demonstrated a 70% reduction in the incorrect placement of verbs, and an almost 50% reduction for erroneous noun placement. With respect to overall post-editing effort, NMT generated outputs that required about a quarter fewer edits compared to the best PBSMT system.

However, while the body of evidence in favour of NMT continues to grow, it is unclear that NMT is in a position to replace SMT entirely just yet. For example, Bentivogli et al. (2016) found that NMT degrades with sentence length for transcribed speeches. While NMT outperformed SMT for subsets of all lengths in their dataset, the gap became smaller as sentence-length increased. Our own in-house tests have shown that for small amounts of good quality training data, NMT cannot outperform PBSMT systems. Note too that NMT currently takes much more time to train, and translation speed is slower compared to PBSMT.

Nonetheless, the translational improvements discovered by Bentivogli et al. (2016) lead me to think that n-gram-based metrics such as BLEU are insufficient to truly demonstrate the benefits of NMT over PBSMT. This is especially the case as character-based models (Chung et al. 2016) – or combinations of word- and character-based models (e.g. Luong and Manning 2016) – become more prevalent, in which case evaluation metrics such as ChrF (Popović 2015) which operate at the character level become more appropriate.

In practice, a 2-point improvement in BLEU score which was typically seen in WMT-2016 would be far too small to be noticed in a real industrial translation task. If word order is drastically improved, and fewer morphological and lexical errors are being made in NMT, one would expect to see a *huge* improvement in terms of automatic evaluation metrics, rather than a relatively modest – albeit statistically significant – one.[24] If NMT does become the new state-of-the-art as the field expects, one can anticipate that further new evaluation metrics tuned more precisely to this paradigm will appear sooner rather than later.[25]

5   A View on Future Deployment of MT, and Its Impact on Translation Evaluation

I began this chapter by emphasising that MT needs to be evaluated in the context of the use-case for which it is intended. Despite the ever-increasing range of use-cases that are springing up, one can predict with confidence that for many use-cases, MT output will continue to require post-editing by expert human translators.

Clearly, human translators have for some time now been using Translation Memory (TM) systems to good effect. TM systems work as follows (Moorkens and Way 2016):

> TM systems search the source side of a set of translation pairs for the closest-matching instances above some pre-determined threshold imposed by the translator (so-called 'fuzzy matches'; Sikes (2007)). A ranked list of the said translation pairs is then presented to the translator with user-friendly colour-coding to help the user decide which parts are useful in the composition of the target translation, and which should be ignored and discarded.

Accordingly, translators have been accustomed to using fuzzy match score as a predictor of translation quality. What is more, translators can configure fuzzy match thresholds – a balance between precision and recall – themselves, so they remain in control of the translation process. In real translation pipelines, MT usually kicks in for matches below the fuzzy match threshold set by the user, despite the fact that many researchers (e.g. Simard and Isabelle 2009; Moorkens and Way 2016) have demonstrated that translator performance can be harmed by the imposition of such arbitrary cut-offs; MT can be better than TM above the fuzzy match threshold, while TM may have more utility than MT below it.

Nonetheless, recognising that translators will remain a large cohort of MT users compels MT developers to begin to output translations from their MT systems

---

[24]Note, however, that the NMT system of Luong and Manning (2015) was more than 5 BLEU points better than a range of SMT systems for English to German. This sort of difference in BLEU score is more like what we might expect given the huge improvements in quality noted by Bentivogli et al. (2016) in their study. In this regard, both Shterionov et al. (2018) and Way (2018) note that BLEU may be under-reporting the difference in quality seen when using NMT systems, with the former attempting to measure the level of under-reporting using a set of novel metrics.

[25]Without further comment, we merely note here that the 'round trip' (or 'back') translation discredited by Somers (2005) – cf. footnote 12 – has been demonstrated to be very useful in NMT as a means of generating additional 'synthetic' parallel training material (e.g. Sennrich et al. 2016b).

with an accompanying estimation of quality that makes sense to translators;[26] while BLEU score is undoubtedly of use to MT developers, outputting a target sentence with a BLEU score of (say) 0.435 is pretty meaningless to a translator. The automatic MT metric that is most appealing in this regard is TER, as it is indicative of the amount of post-editing (in terms of substitutions, insertions and deletions) required to produce a good quality target-language sentence from the MT output. In a few cases, where MT is integrated with TM, MT matches are output as 'just another match', with MT matches used to reinforce TM fuzzy matching (Hofmann 2015).

Translators are used to being paid different rates depending on the level of fuzzy match suggested by the TM system for each input string. With that in mind, another area where MT can work to the benefit of the translation community is in promoting fuzzy matches to the next highest level (Biçici and Dymetman 2008). Moorkens and Way (2016) also observe that translators are used to not receiving help from TM for all input sentences, so that "MT developers have allowed the soft underbellies of their engines to be exposed 'warts and all' to translators, as MT outputs are typically provided for every source segment". In order to prevent this, they suggest that better system-internal confidence measures are needed so that translators can learn to trust the MT output they are confronted with.

Finally, despite the fact that more and more use-cases are emerging where MT can be useful, and regardless of whether PBSMT or NMT systems prevail, we can expect TM technology to remain as an essential tool in the translator's armoury. Many researchers have demonstrated how the two technologies can co-exist to good effect, either via system recommendation (He et al. 2010a, b) or by using fragments from TM in SMT (e.g. Koehn and Senellart 2010; Ma et al. 2011; Wang et al. 2013; Li et al. 2014). Whatever the individual set-up preferred by translators, candidate translation outputs have to come with a readily intelligible indicator of quality, lest their decision-making process be cognitively overloaded such that rather than being a translation aid, such tools turn out to actually be an impediment to improved translation throughput.

6 Final Remarks

This chapter has addressed the notion of what level of quality can be expected from MT. MT is not going away; year on year, its usage is increasing exponentially, which is a clear indication that MT quality is continually improving. Accordingly, those translators who remain opposed to the improvements that can be brought about by MT are only hurting themselves.

---

[26]The subfield of quality estimation (see Specia and Shah in this volume) attempts to predict whether a new source string will result in a good or bad translation. This is different from MT evaluation, where we have a reference translation to compare the MT hypothesis against *post hoc*.

At the same time, although MT quality is getting better all the time, for this to be truly impactful in industry, we will need to see a quantum leap in terms of improved output as measured by traditional automatic evaluation metrics, or where quality of newer systems is better reflected by more suitable novel metrics. While incremental improvements are to be welcomed, there are many more pressing concerns for industry, including better terminology integration, improvements in post-editing environments, and indeed novel pricing models.

Furthermore, there are use-cases emerging where there is no role for the human translator/post-editor, and where translation quality can only be interpreted in terms of fitness for purpose of the translation outputs. Nonetheless, many use-cases will continue to require humans to post-edit the translations output by MT systems. Accordingly, it behoves the entire MT developer community to deliver MT output with a score that is meaningful to human post-editors, so that they can immediately decide whether it is either quicker to post-edit the MT suggestion, or to translate the source string from scratch by hand.

The MT developer community continues to use automatic metrics most suited to evaluating MT output emanating from word- and phrase-based systems. In much the same way as metrics like BLEU were not suited to output coming from grammar-based systems, in this chapter, I hypothesise that they are not discriminative enough to accurately reflect the translation quality of (largely) character-based NMT systems. Accordingly, despite the fact that they are expensive to set up and slow to analyse the results, human evaluation of MT output remains crucial if system developers are to improve their systems still further.

Acknowledgments This work has been supported by the ADAPT Centre for Digital Content Technology which is funded under the SFI Research Centres Programme (Grant 13/RC/2106) and is co-funded under the European Regional Development Fund.

References

Agarwal A, Lavie A (2008) METEOR, M-BLEU and M-TER: evaluation metrics for high-correlation with human rankings of machine translation output. In: Proceedings of the third workshop on Statistical Machine Translation, Columbus, pp 115–118

Albrecht J, Hwa R (2007) Regression for sentence-level MT evaluation with pseudo references. In: Proceedings of the 45th annual meeting of the Association of Computational Linguistics, Prague, pp 296–303

Arnold D, Moffat D, Sadler L, Way A (1993) Automatic generation of test suites. Mach Transl 8:29–38

Arnold D, Balkan L, Meijer S, Humphreys L, Sadler L (1994) Machine translation: an introductory guide. Blackwells-NCC, London

Babych B, Hartley A (2004) Extending the BLEU MT evaluation method with frequency weightings. In: Proceedings of ACL 2004: 42nd annual meeting of the Association for Computational Linguistics, Barcelona, pp 621–628

Balkan L, Jäschke M, Humphreys L, Meijer S, Way A (1991) Declarative evaluation of an MT system: practical experiences. In: Proceedings of the evaluators' forum, Les Rasses, Vaud, pp 85–97

Balkan L, Arnold D, Meijer S (1994) Test suites for natural language processing. In: Proceedings of translating and the computer 16, London, pp 51–58

Banerjee S, Lavie A (2005) METEOR: an automatic metric for MT evaluation with improved correlation with human judgments. In: Proceedings of ACL 2005, Proceedings of the workshop on intrinsic and extrinsic evaluation measures for MT and/or summarization at the 43rd annual meeting of the Association for Computational Linguistics, Ann Arbor, pp 65–72

Bellos D (2011) Is that a fish in your ear: translation and the meaning of everything. Particular Books, London

Bentivogli L, Bisazza A, Cettolo M, Federico M (2016) Neural versus phrase-based machine translation quality: a case study. In: Proceedings of the 2016 conference on empirical methods in natural language processing, Austin, pp 257–267

Biçici E, Dymetman M (2008) Dynamic translation memory: using statistical machine translation to improve translation memory fuzzy matches. In: Proceedings of the 9th international conference on computational linguistics and intelligent text processing, Haifa, pp 454–465

Callison-Burch C, Osborne M, Koehn P (2006) Re-evaluating the role of BLEU in machine translation research. In: Proceedings of EACL 2006, 11th conference of the European chapter of the Association for Computational Linguistics, Trento, pp 249–256

Callison-Burch C, Fordyce C, Koehn P, Monz C, Schroeder J (2008) Further meta-evaluation of machine translation. In: Proceedings of the third workshop on Statistical Machine Translation, Columbus, pp 70–106

Chatterjee R, Turchi M, Negri M (2015) The FBK participation in the WMT15 automatic post-editing shared task. In: Proceedings of the tenth workshop on Statistical Machine Translation, Lisbon, pp 210–215

Chung J, Cho K, Bengio Y (2016) A character-level decoder without explicit segmentation for neural machine translation. In: Proceedings of the 54th annual meeting of the Association for Computational Linguistics, vol 1: Long Papers. Berlin, pp 1693–1703

Coughlin D (2003) Correlating automated and human assessments of machine translation quality. In: Proceedings of MT Summit IX, New Orleans, pp 63–70

Cuong H, Frank S, Sima'an K (2016) ILLC-UvA adaptation system (Scorpio) at WMT'16 IT-DOMAIN Task. In: Proceedings of the first conference on Machine Translation, Berlin, pp 423–427

de Almeida G (2013) Translating the post-editor: an investigation of post-editing changes and correlations with professional experience across two Romance languages. Dissertation, Dublin City University

Doddington G (2002) Automatic evaluation of machine translation quality using n-gram co-occurrence statistics. In: Proceedings of HLT 2002: human language technology conference, San Diego, pp 138–145

Doyon J, White J, Taylor K (1999) Task-based evaluation for machine translation. In: Proceedings of MT Summit VII "MT in the Great Translation Era", Singapore, pp 574–578

Farrús M, Costa-Jussà M, Popović M (2012) Study and correlation analysis of linguistic, perceptual and automatic machine translation evaluations. J Am Soc Inf Sci Technol 63(1):174–184

Font Llitjós A, Carbonell J, Lavie A (2005) A framework for interactive and automatic refinement of transfer-based machine translation. In: 10th EAMT conference "Practical applications of machine translation", Budapest, pp 87–96

Ha T-L, Niehues J, Cho E, Mediani M, Waibel A (2015) The KIT translation systems for IWSLT 2015. In: Proceedings of international workshop on spoken language translation, Da Nang, pp 62–69

He Y, Way A (2009a) Improving the objective function in minimum error rate training. In: Proceedings of Machine Translation Summit XII, Ottawa, pp 238–245

He Y, Way A (2009b) Metric and reference factors in minimum error rate training. Mach Transl 24(1):27–38

He Y, Way A (2009c) Learning labelled dependencies in machine translation evaluation. In: Proceedings of EAMT-09, the 13th annual meeting of the European Association for Machine Translation, Barcelona, pp 44–51

He Y, Ma Y, van Genabith J, Way A (2010a) Bridging SMT and TM with translation recommendation. In: Proceedings of the 48th annual meeting of the Association for Computational Linguistics, Uppsala, pp 622–630

He Y, Ma Y, Way A, van Genabith J (2010b) Integrating n-best SMT outputs into a TM system. In: Proceedings of the 23rd international conference on computational linguistics, Beijing, pp 374–382

Heyn M (1998) Translation memories – insights & prospects. In: Bowker L, Cronin M, Kenny D, Pearson J (eds) Unity in diversity? Current trends in translation studies. St Jerome, Manchester, pp 123–136

Hofmann N (2015) MT-enhanced fuzzy matching with Transit NXT and STAR Moses. EAMT-2015: Proceedings of the eighteenth annual conference of the European Association for Machine Translation, Antalya, p 215

Hovy Y, Ravichandran D (2003) Holy and unholy grails. Panel discussion at MT Summit IX, New Orleans. Available from http://www.mt-archive.info/MTS-2003-Hovy-1.pdf. Accessed 12 Nov 2017

Huck M, Birch A (2015) The Edinburgh machine translation systems for IWSLT 2015. In: Proceedings of the international workshop on spoken language translation, Da Nang, pp 31–38

Humphreys L, Jäschke M, Way A, Balkan L, Meyer S (1991) Operational evaluation of MT, draft research proposal. Working papers in language processing 22, University of Essex

Isozaki H, Hirao T, Duh K, Sudoh K, Tsukada H (2010) Automatic evaluation of translation quality for distant language pairs. In: Proceedings of the 2010 conference on empirical methods in natural language processing, Cambridge, pp 944–952

Jean S, Firat O, Cho K, Memisevic R, Bengio Y (2015) Montreal neural machine translation systems for WMT15. In: Proceedings of the tenth workshop on Statistical Machine Translation, Lisbon, pp 134–140

Jehl L, Simianer P, Hitschler J, Riezler S (2015) The Heidelberg University English-German translation system for IWSLT 2015. In: Proceedings of the international workshop on spoken language translation, Da Nang, pp 45–49

King M, Falkedal K (1990) Using test suites in evaluation of MT systems. In: Proceedings of COLING-90, Papers presented to the 13th international conference on computational linguistics, vol 2, Helsinki, pp 211–216

Koehn P, Senellart J (2010) Convergence of translation memory and statistical machine translation. In: Proceedings of AMTA workshop on MT Research and the Translation Industry, Denver, pp 21–31

Koehn P, Och F, Marcu D (2003) Statistical phrase-based translation. In: Proceedings of HLT-NAACL 2003: conference combining Human Language Technology conference series and the North American chapter of the Association for Computational Linguistics conference series, Edmonton, pp 48–54

Koehn P, Hoang H, Birch A, Callison-Burch C, Federico M, Bertoldi N, Cowan B, Shen W, Moran C, Zens R, Dyer C, Bojar O, Constantin A, Herbst E (2007) Moses: open source toolkit for statistical machine translation. In: Proceedings of the 45th annual meeting of the Association of Computational Linguistics, Prague, pp 177–180

Levenshtein V (1966) Binary codes capable of correcting deletions, insertions, and reversals. Sov Phys Dokl 10:707–710

Lewis W, Quirk C (2013) Controlled ascent: imbuing statistical MT with linguistic knowledge. In: Proceedings of the second workshop on Hybrid Approaches to Translation, Sofia, pp 51–66

Li L, Way A, Liu Q (2014) A discriminative framework of integrating translation memory features into SMT. In: Proceedings of the 11th conference of the Association for Machine Translation in the Americas, vol 1: MT Researchers Track, Vancouver, pp 249–260

Liang P, Bouchard-Côté A, Klein D, Taskar B (2006) An end-to-end discriminative approach to machine translation. In: Proceedings of the 21st international conference on computational linguistics and 44th annual meeting of the Association for Computational Linguistics, Sydney, pp 761–768

Lin C-Y, Och F (2004) ORANGE: a Method for evaluating automatic evaluation metrics for machine translation. In: COLING 2004: Proceedings of the 20th international conference on Computational Linguistics, Geneva, pp 501–507

Liu D, Gildea D (2005) Syntactic features for evaluation of machine translation. In: Proceedings of the ACL workshop on intrinsic and extrinsic evaluation measures for machine translation and/or summarization, Ann Arbor, pp 25–32

Luong M-T, Manning C (2015) Stanford neural machine translation systems for spoken language domains. In: Proceedings of the international workshop on spoken language translation, Da Nang, pp 76–79

Luong M-T, Manning C (2016) Achieving open vocabulary neural machine translation with hybrid word-character models. In: Proceedings of the 54th annual meeting of the Association for Computational Linguistics, vol 1: Long Papers, Berlin, pp 1054–1063

Ma Y, He Y, Way A, van Genabith J (2011) Consistent translation using discriminative learning – a translation memory-inspired approach. In: Proceedings of the 49th annual meeting of the Association for Computational Linguistics: Human Language Technologies, Portland, pp 1239–1248

Miller G, Beckwith R, Fellbaum C, Gross D, Miller K (1990) Introduction to WordNet: an on-line lexical database. Int J Lexicogr 3(4):235–244

Moorkens J, Way A (2016) Comparing translator acceptability of TM and SMT outputs. Balt J Mod Comput 4(2):141–151

Naskar S, Toral A, Gaspari F, Way A (2011) Framework for diagnostic evaluation of MT based on linguistic checkpoints. In: Proceedings of Machine Translation Summit XIII, Xiamen, pp 529–536

Och F (2003) Minimum error rate training in statistical machine translation. In: ACL 2003, 41st annual meeting of the Association for Computational Linguistics, Sapporo, pp 160–167

Owczarzak K, van Genabith J, Way A (2007) Labelled dependencies in machine translation evaluation. In: Proceedings of the second workshop on Statistical Machine Translation, Prague, pp 104–111

Papineni K, Roukos S, Ward T, Zhu W-J (2002) BLEU: a method for automatic evaluation of machine translation. In: ACL-2002: 40th annual meeting of the Association for Computational Linguistics, Philadelphia, pp 311–318

Penkale S, Way A (2013) Tailor-made quality-controlled translation. In: Proceedings of translating and the computer 35, London, 7 pages

Pierce J, Carroll J, Hamp E, Hays D, Hockett C, Oettinger A, Perlis A (1966) Language and machines – computers in translation and linguistics. ALPAC report, National Academy of Sciences, Washington, DC

Popović M (2015) ChrF: character n-gram F-score for automatic MT evaluation. In: Proceedings of the tenth workshop on Statistical Machine Translation, Lisbon, pp 392–395

Popović M, Ney H (2011) Towards automatic error analysis of machine translation output. Comput Linguist 37(4):657–688

Riezler S, Maxwell J (2005) On some pitfalls in automatic evaluation and significance testing for MT. In: Proceedings of the ACL workshop on intrinsic and extrinsic evaluation measures for machine translation and/or summarization, Ann Arbor, pp 57–64

Sennrich R, Haddow B, Birch A (2016a) Edinburgh neural machine translation systems for WMT 16. In: Proceedings of the first conference on Machine Translation, Berlin, pp 371–376

Sennrich R, Haddow B, Birch A (2016b) Improving neural machine translation models with monolingual data. In: Proceedings of the 54th annual meeting of the Association for Computational Linguistics, vol 1, Berlin, pp 86–96

Shterionov D, Nagle P, Casanellas L, Superbo R, O'Dowd T, Way A (2018) Human vs automatic quality evaluation of NMT and PBSMT. Mach Transl 32(3–4.) (in press)

Sikes R (2007) Fuzzy matching in theory and practice. Multilingual 18(6):39–43

Simard M, Isabelle P (2009) Phrase-based machine translation in a computer-assisted translation environment. In: Proceedings of the twelfth Machine Translation Summit (MT Summit XII), Ottawa, pp 120–127

Smith A, Hardmeier C, Tiedemann J (2016) Climbing mount BLEU: the strange world of reachable high-BLEU translations. Balt J Mod Comput 4(2):269–281

Snover M, Dorr B, Schwartz R, Micciulla L, Makhoul J (2006) A study of translation edit rate with targeted human annotation. In: Proceedings of AMTA 2006, the 7th conference of the Association for Machine Translation in the Americas, Cambridge, pp 223–231

Somers H (2005) Round-trip translation: what is it good for? In: Proceedings of the Australasian Language Technology workshop 2005 (ALTW 2005), Sydney, pp 71–77

Thomas K (1999) Designing a task-based evaluation methodology for a spoken machine translation system. In: Proceedings of 37th annual meeting of the Association for Computational Linguistics, College Park, pp 569–572

Tillmann C, Vogel S, Ney H, Sawaf H, Zubiaga A (1997) Accelerated DP-based search for statistical translation. In: Proceedings of the 5th European conference on Speech Communication and Technology (EuroSpeech '97), Rhodes, pp 2667–2670

Vasconcellos M (1989) MT utilization at the Pan American Health Organization. In: IFTT'89: harmonizing human beings and computers in translation. International Forum for Translation Technology, Oiso, pp 56–58

Vilar D, Xu J, D'Haro L, Ney H (2006) Error analysis of statistical machine translation output. In: Proceedings of the fifth international conference on Language Resources and Evaluation (LREC), Pisa, pp 697–702

Voss C, Tate C (2006) Task-based evaluation of machine translation (MT) engines: measuring how well people extract who, when, where-type elements in MT output. In: EAMT-2006: 11th annual conference of the European Association for Machine Translation, Proceedings, Oslo, pp 203–212

Wang K, Zong C, Su K-Y (2013) Integrating translation memory into phrase-based machine translation during decoding. In: Proceedings of the 51st annual meeting of the Association for Computational Linguistics, vol1, Sofia, pp 11–21

Way A (2012) Is that a fish in your ear: translation and the meaning of everything – David Bellos, book review. Mach Transl 26(3):255–269

Way A (2013) Traditional and emerging use-cases for machine translation. In: Proceedings of translating and the computer 35, London

Way A (2018) Machine translation: where are we at today? In: Angelone E, Massey G, Ehrensberger-Dow M (eds) The Bloomsbury companion to language industry studies. Bloomsbury, London. (in press)

Ye Y, Zhou M, Lin C-Y (2007) Sentence level machine translation evaluation as a ranking. In: Proceedings of the second workshop on Statistical Machine Translation, Prague, pp 240–247

Zhang J, Wu X, Calixto I, Hosseinzadeh Vahid A, Zhang X, Way A, Liu Q (2014) Experiments in medical translation shared task at WMT 2014. In: Proceedings of WMT 2014: the ninth workshop on Statistical Machine Translation, Baltimore, pp 260–265

Zhou L, Lin C-Y, Munteanu D, Hovy E (2006) Paraeval: using paraphrases to evaluate summaries automatically. In: Proceedings of the Human Language Technology conference of the NAACL, main conference, New York City, pp 447–454

Assessing Quality in Human- and Machine-Generated Subtitles and Captions

8

Stephen Doherty and Jan-Louis Kruger

Abstract The depth, breadth, and complexity of audiovisual translation (AVT) are growing at a rapid rate. AVT is becoming increasingly merged with language technologies, including computer-assisted translation tools, machine translation, automated subtitling and captioning software, and automatic speech recognition systems. An essential component in this exciting and challenging technological development of current and future applications of AVT is the definition and assessment of quality in a way that is transparent, reliable, consistent, meaningful to all stakeholders, and readily applicable to the growing diversity of AVT. This chapter first provides a critical overview of current and future issues in the assessment of quality in human and machine-generated subtitling and captioning. It builds upon a range of contemporary industry sources and moves into cutting-edge research on the processing and reception of AVT products across a variety of media and languages. We then move to discuss the impact of new media and technologies on best practice, policy, and research. Lastly, we identify numerous challenges and potential solutions for all stakeholders in order to encourage dialogue between disciplines with the aim of articulating and answering questions of quality in AVT in an evolving technological landscape.

Keywords Translation quality assessment · Principles to practice · Audiovisual translation · Cognition · Multimodality · New media · Eye-tracking · AVT · Reception studies

S. Doherty
School of Humanities and Languages, The University of New South Wales, Sydney, Australia
e-mail: s.doherty@unsw.edu.au

J.-L. Kruger
Department of Linguistics, Macquarie University, Sydney, Australia

North-West University, Vanderbijlpark, South Africa
e-mail: janlouis.kruger@mq.edu.au

1 Background

Audiovisual translation (AVT) spans all forms of multimodal communication including intralingual (also called same-language subtitling or captioning) and interlingual subtitling in traditional and new media, as well as dubbing and audio description (discussions of terminology can be found in Díaz Cintas 2013 and Sasamoto and Doherty 2016). For the purposes of clarity, we will use the term "captioning" to refer to intralingual subtitling, and "subtitling" to refer to interlingual (or translation) subtitling. This chapter limits its focus to subtitling and captioning and does not include dubbing and audio description in its remit, although some of the content may be relevant to these other areas of AVT. AVT typically places great emphasis on functional approaches to intralingual and interlingual translation where the audience is a critical element in the choice of strategies employed by the subtitler. As such, a concerted effort is made to understand as much as possible about the audience needs and expectations (e.g. hearing, deaf and hard-of-hearing audiences, and first and second language viewers), the context in which viewing is taking place (e.g. entertainment, education, and public service), as well as the medium through which the multimodal information is being transferred (e.g. cinema, television, tablet, and smart phone).

Inherent in all aspects of AVT is its multimodal nature, where each video can contain a complex interaction of different modes of information, audio and visual, in verbal and non-verbal dimensions. Subtitlers often make use of semiotics (see Gambier 2013) to navigate this rich multimodal information in order to render the original meaning in the source-language accurately in the target-language in line with unforgiving spatial and temporal constraints (see Díaz Cintas 2013).

While the field of AVT has developed substantially over the past two decades with a more recent emphasis on empirical research and reception studies (see Perego 2016; Doherty and Kruger 2018), the interaction of AVT and language technology has received relatively less attention arguably due to a lack of interface between the two fields of research. The development of language technologies over the same period of time has led to a plethora of new tools and methods for linguistics, used by translators, subtitlers, and researchers who study these processes and products (see Doherty 2016). A widespread technological turn (O'Hagan 2013) in Translation Studies has also led to new questions arising in terms of translation quality assessment (TQA) in both traditional and new translation workflows (see Castilho et al. in this volume).

AVT has not been exempted from these technological developments with a wave of new tools becoming available, including manual, semi- and fully-automated subtitling and captioning software, speech-to-text systems, and machine translation (MT). The interest in and applications of AVT have experienced a boom where traditional usage of subtitles for foreign movies and for the deaf and hard-of-hearing has been supplemented by new usage scenarios for language education, literacy, language learning, accessibility, clinical applications, and specialised and general education. Indeed, the increasing visibility of AVT in language technology is also becoming apparent with recent additions of multimodal language processing and translation tasks in natural language processing groups, including the Association of Computational Linguistics[1] (ACL), and the increasing availability of corpora of subtitles and multimodal datasets for a variety of research aims and practical applications.

While these new tools and systems offer many advantages to all stakeholders in AVT, their current and future impact remains unclear and a growing number of questions of quality remain unanswered. At a time in AVT when the focus is shifting from quantity to quality (Romero-Fresco 2016), these questions now include:

- *How can quality be measured in intra- and interlingual human and machine-generated subtitling and captioning?*
- *How do language technologies impact upon the quality of the AVT process and its products?*
- *How can quality be maintained for a diverse range of stakeholders with concurrent and overlapping general and specific accessibility needs?*
- *How can stakeholders ensure that quality is at the centre of technological developments in AVT rather than a secondary concern?*

In order to create a dialogue between stakeholders in language technology and AVT and to begin articulating an attempt to answer such questions, this chapter aims to provide a comprehensive description of the current approaches to quality and its assessment in AVT in the contexts of research, education, and industry. We first present the guiding principles of quality in AVT and show how they inform industry standards across the globe at local, regional, national, and international levels. Drawing upon empirical studies of the reception and processing of audiovisual texts, we then examine how research findings are changing our understanding of how such texts are processed by diverse audiences. Finally, we discuss how the impact of new technologies and the growing diversity of new media are challenging the traditional concept of quality in audiovisual translation where we identify areas in which quality is at risk. We conclude by arguing for increased awareness and education in language technologies in AVT in order to overcome current and future challenges in these converging fields, so that evidence-based interdisciplinary approaches increase the likelihood of higher quality AVT for all.

2 Guiding Principles for Quality in AVT

Each form of AVT brings its own considerations for quality and its assessment. A central part of this is the linguistic information at the core of the audiovisual text. We therefore build upon the relevant discussions of the theoretical and practical dimensions of TQA provided in this volume in order to achieve the above aim and

---

[1] http://www.statmt.org/wmt16/multimodal-task.html

dedicate this chapter to the TQA dimensions specific to AVT against a changing technological backdrop.

Unique to AVT are the spatial and temporal restrictions inherent in subtitling and captioning which often force the usage of indirect translation techniques (especially condensation, reformulation, and omission of linguistic elements), in order to achieve the functional purpose, e.g. comprehension, education, and entertainment. These restrictions therefore severely limit the usage of translation choices and result in a general preference for approaches to translation quality that champion functionalism and pragmatic equivalence. As a result, quality assessment in AVT is carried out in a diverse range of contexts, including in-house at the broadcaster, within an LSP, and by a freelancer. This leads to a variety of requirements for assessing quality in individual and ongoing projects (e.g. for a TV series) as well as once-off assessments (e.g. for a feature film or video game). As projects, client requirements, and genres vary substantially, these parameters are typically taken into account as their impact on expectations is significant.

Unlike traditional TQA models and metrics, assessment in AVT is largely based on prescriptive industry guidelines that vary by organisation, medium, region, language, and country. While rubrics and error-based models are not commonplace, the majority of LSPs that include subtitling and captioning services in their offerings report that they have their own way of assessing quality. Further to this, LSPs claim to assess quality "always and systematically", and report that current assessment standards and methods should be improved (Gaspari et al. 2015).

The critical need for AVT-specific requirements for TQA has led to several *de facto* industry standards being established in recent years, particularly those written by and for public broadcasters in their respective countries. As demand for subtitling and captioning is continuing to grow, there has been an increasing focus on quality assurance from consumer and regulatory groups (Mikul 2014). While no international standard (such as an ISO standard from the International Organization for Standardization) has yet been established, these industry guides form the backbone of TQA in a wide range of AVT contexts. This is coupled with national standards and quotes being adopted in a growing number of countries. Table 1 provides examples of some of the existing major industry documentation that pertains to quality standards. Recent comprehensive reviews, summary reports, and guidelines can also be found in Kubitschke et al. (2013), Díaz-Cintas and Remael (2014), and Mikul (2014).

While several guidelines have been developed in order to measure quality, such a process is invariably problematic given the complexity of AVT compared to traditional, static text, and the need to quantify dimensions that are inherently qualitative. Commonalities among the above models can be found under the general parameters of accuracy, presentation, and timing.

Organisation	Year	Country
Australian Communications and Media Authority (ACMA)	2013	Australia
Consortium of public broadcasters: Arbeitsgemeinschaft der öffentlich-rechtlichen Rundfunkanstalten der Bundesrepublik Deutschland (ARD), Österreichischer Rundfunk (ORF), Schweizer Radio und Fernsehen (SRF) and Zweites Deutsches Fernsehen (ZDF)	2016	Austria, Germany, and Switzerland
Canadian Radio-television and Communications Commission (CRTC)	2012	Canada
Canadian Association of Broadcasters (CAB)	2012	Canada
Conseil supérieur de l'audiovisuel (CSA)	2011	France
La Asociación Española de Normalización y Certificación (AENOR)	2012	Spain
Office of Communications (Ofcom)	2017	United Kingdom
British Broadcasting Corporation (BBC)	2016	United Kingdom
Federal Communications Commission (FCC)	2014	United States of America

Table 1 Examples of existing major industry documentation pertaining to subtitling and captioning quality

2.1 Accuracy

While the concept of accuracy is used to indicate equivalence between source and target texts in the context of translation studies and translation technology, its meaning in AVT refers to the correctness of the rendition of spoken utterances, e.g. dialogue and their translation. In other words, it measures the correspondence between the words uttered in the auditory mode and the words appearing on screen (between auditory and written modes), rather than between text written in a source and target-language (within the written mode). Depending on the context, subtitles and captions may be verbatim, in which case the aim is to achieve the highest accuracy rate possible. However, most subtitles and captions require minor and even major reduction strategies including reformulation, condensing, adaptation, and omission in line with the priority of the linguistic information (e.g. up to 30% described by Díaz-Cintas and Remael 2014). To complicate matters further, accuracy also refers to the performance of automatic speech recognition (ASR) and speech-to-text systems that are now becoming more commonplace in AVT contexts. In that context, accuracy is measured in terms of elements such as omissions and transcription errors and is often expressed as a value (see Sect. 2.4).

2.2 Presentation

Presentation concerns the appropriate usage of fonts, colours, and positioning of subtitles and captions. Legible fonts should be used consistently and in sentence case. A limited range of colours is advised and typically used to indicate different speakers. Most subtitles and captions are in white text on a black background to increase legibility. Other recommended colours include yellow, green, and light blue. Combinations of red and green and vibrant colours and hues should be avoided.

Static 'blocks' of subtitles are preferred to scrolling subtitles as the former are deemed to be the best approach to provide accurate, legible, and well-synchronised subtitles and captions. The subtitles should start and end at logical points in the utterance. Subtitles should also be split, as necessary, at a logical point within the utterance typically at the end of a clause, phrase or noun or verb phrase (Karamitroglou 1998). A maximum of two lines should be used for a subtitle with approximately 32 to 39 characters per line, including all punctuation, for Latin-based languages, 12 to 16 for Asian languages, and approximately 35 for Cyrillic and Arabic script.

2.3 Timing

Subtitles and captions should be presented for a sufficient time for the intended viewer to read them while simultaneously processing the other multimodal information on screen. Subtitles and captions should appear and disappear in line with the utterance as viewers make use of visual cues, including lips and faces, for the respective speaker on screen, if present. In order to avoid miscomprehension and confusion, subtitles and captions should not appear before the utterance is made nor stay on screen long after it has been completed. Extra time can be added for unfamiliar and technical words, changes between speakers, numerical figures, shot changes, and slow speech.

Synchronisation with dialogue should be achieved as far as possible with the delay in live presentations not exceeding 3 s. If synchronisation is not possible in an individual subtitle, it should not be out of sync for more than one second to minimise the impact of the desynchronisation and allow for the next subtitles to return to synchronisation.

Presentation rates are expressed in words per minutes or characters per seconds. For general audiences, rates of up to 140–180 words per minute (wpm) are recommended, with slower rates for multiple speakers, accessibility purposes, and young audiences. The so-called "six-second rule" (Díaz Cintas 2013) is typically used, whereby two full lines of around 35 characters can be read in 6 s by the average TV viewer. Díaz Cintas (2013) notes that rates of 160 wpm are standard for TV, while DVDs and new media can extend to 180 wpm. In reality, though, many online providers and broadcasters are pushing for higher rates to allow them to present verbatim transcripts which reduces the need for editing.

2.4 Error-Based Metrics

In addition to the above guidelines, several error-based metrics and models that are conceptually similar to traditional TQA have also been developed to classify and quantify errors in subtitling and captioning, including the Word Error Rate (Dumouchel et al. 2011), Weighted Word Error Rate (Apone et al. 2011) and the Net Error Rate (NER) Model (Romero-Fresco and Pérez 2015). An interesting link is emerging here between AVT metrics and the automatic evaluation metrics used in MT evaluation, a point to which we will return later. These metrics count the number of errors and error types in order to identify how accurate the subtitling or caption is based on the spoken utterance. Unnecessary additions, omissions and distortions result in penalties thereby reducing the level of reported accuracy.

Mikul (2014) argues however that such metrics and models do not take into account the diversity of error types in AVT and that a one-size-fits-all approach is too restrictive and would be impractical and expensive for all stakeholders while not necessarily achieving higher levels of quality from the perspective of the end user. Given the traditional parameters used in AVT, as described in the sub-sections above, it appears that the gap between the two approaches needs to be addressed. An argument similar to that of human versus machine-based TQA metrics in static text workflows should be followed.

These latest additions to AVT quality assessment stem from a recent surge in empirical research into AVT which aims to establish an evidence base to influence best practice and policy in addition to the convergence of AVT and language technologies more generally, including automated subtitling and captioning, ASR, speech-to-text systems, and novel multimodal input methods. Research findings into the effects of errors on language processing in static text are also beginning to inform research and practice in AVT where dynamic texts pose unique challenges (see, for example, Kruger and Steyn 2014) and the treatment of errors should take this into consideration. This body of research uses quantitative, qualitative, and mixed-methods approaches to explore the processing of subtitles and captions and the reception of AVT products in diverse groups and platforms.

3 Insights from AVT Research

A major focal point of AVT research has been on the examination of the cognitive and affective processing of AVT products using a growing number of interdisciplinary research methods. By understanding more about how diverse audiences process and receive AVT products, the discussion and measurement of quality can be more robust and more directly based on viewers, or as Perego (2016) argues: "the quality of a translated product hinges on the awareness of the audience's cognitive and evaluative response to the product itself".

AVT researchers employ a variety of offline and online research methods including surveys, questionnaires, eye-tracking, and electroencephalography (EEG), which are often combined in order to reap the benefits of each method while overcoming its specific limitations. As such, the use of mixed-methods research has become commonplace, as confirmed in a recent large-scale review by Doherty and Kruger (2018). Measures derived from these methods are typically in the form of pre- and post-task self-reported measures (e.g. viewing behaviours, beliefs, and attitudes), online and post-task performance measures (e.g. comprehension, recall, retention of content), and direct online measures of physiological activity tied to more complex constructs (e.g. cognitive load). We will now focus on three avenues of research that directly link to quality as they provide unprecedented insight into how AVT products are processed and received by viewers: visual attention in processing subtitles and captions, cognitive load, and psychological immersion.

3.1 Visual Attention in Processing Subtitles and Captions

Subtitled and captioned media present viewers with a dynamic, audiovisual text that makes complex demands on their cognitive capacity. Viewers have to process both auditory and visual sources of information simultaneously, and these sources could contain both verbal and nonverbal information. Unlike the processing of scenes in real life, which tends to be a continuous process, viewers of subtitled and captioned media have to further interpret a range of audiovisual information that requires them to conduct both deductive and inductive reasoning. The visual aspect of the audiovisual stimuli in subtitles was the primary interest of early 'researchers in this field as they sought to uncover what viewers were looking at when watching subtitled and captioned media and why.

While multimodal processing of audiovisual information is commonplace in everyday communication (see Smith et al. 2017), viewers' cognitive resources may face an even greater demand when subtitles or captions are added to this process, as the viewer has to process all of the information already being presented in addition to the subtitles or captions at the bottom of the screen. In order to follow the speech, the viewer therefore has to engage in a continuous and dynamic strategic reading activity while processing the auditory information in the soundtrack as well as the image, i.e. the reader has to engage in multimodal processing.

In determining what viewers were looking at, the construction of visual attention was borrowed from the cognitive and psychological sciences where it had already been widely developed. Visual attention refers to "the cognitive operations that allow us to efficiently deal with this capacity problem by selecting relevant information and by filtering out irrelevant information" (McMains and Kastner 2009). Visual attention is considered as both top-down and bottom-up: top-down processing as viewers can actively decide to allocate their visual attention to a given stimulus at a given time, and bottom-up as a stimulus can attract our visual attention in an involuntary way due to its traits, e.g. movement, luminosity, colour, position, etc. The allocation of visual attention during subtitle and caption processing is a combination of these two processes and this distinction has implications for research design due to the rich, multimodal and dynamic nature of subtitled and captioned media.

Visual attention is of obvious interest in AVT research as it allows researchers to directly observe where viewers of subtitled and captioned media are allocating their visual attention, e.g. by using fixation count and related measures, and how they are distributing and switching their attention between the subtitles and captions and the other elements on the screen. Central to discussions of visual attention is the *Eye-Mind Hypothesis* (Just and Carpenter 1980), a foundational aspect of eye-tracking which asserts that there is a close relationship between what the eyes are fixating upon and what the mind is engaged with, or what the brain is processing, in that "there is no appreciable lag between what is fixated and what is processed".

Our perceptual span while reading is limited to approximately 7–8 characters to the right of a fixation (where the eye remains relatively still to focus on in a small area to extract information) and 2–3 characters to the left of the fixation in Indo-European languages, and does not allow us to extract meaningful information from text on the line above or below the word we are reading (e.g. Pollatsek et al. 1993). Given that much of the reading process is an automatic cognitive process (see Gunter and Friederici 1999; Rossi et al. 2006), and that the depth of processing during reading is shallow by default (see Bentin et al. 1993), a limited amount of information can be obtained during each fixation, where contextual facts such as word frequency and contextual predictability can also come into play to increase or even decrease the quantity and quality of this information (see Staub and Rayner 2007).

Similarly, empirical research on subtitling and captioning has understandably focused on examining their processing and reception by diverse audiences as part of a rich multimodal experience that spans various genres and formats (see Doherty and Kruger 2018). Seeking to explore this multimodal processing of subtitles and captions, eye-tracking in this field of research originated in the 1980s and 1990s through the work of d'Ydewalle and colleagues (e.g. d'Ydewalle et al. 1985, 1991). This work has provided the basis for a growing number of eye-tracking studies of subtitle and caption processing and the resultant effects on the reading and viewing process. It has shown us that subtitles and captions are readily attended to by diverse viewer groups; that, like the reading process, the cognitive processing of subtitles and captions can be automated and employed easily with a low cognitive cost; and that viewers of subtitled media have the ability to process subtitles and captions in an efficient manner and take in the salient elements of the visuals simultaneously (see Perego et al. 2010; Fox 2016).

Other studies have moved from the processing of subtitles and captions as a whole, to the processing of their components in order to determine the most effective way to present subtitles and captions to viewers. D'Ydewalle and De Bruycker (2007) examined the differences between one-line and two-line subtitles and concluded that two-line subtitles are more likely to be processed in full as they are deemed to contain essential information that cannot be found elsewhere on the screen. It has also been reported that the segmentation of subtitles has a significant impact on reading speed and comprehension (see Rajendran et al. 2013), with initial efforts being made to automate, using computational algorithms, the segmentation of subtitles (e.g. Álvarez et al. 2017). Lastly, the computational processing of verbatim and edited (condensed and reformulated) subtitles and captions has also been explored using empirical methods with differences in reading behaviour being reported but with no apparent benefits to edited subtitles (Szarkowska et al. 2016).

Understanding how viewers process subtitles and captions has considerable implications for quality assessment in AVT. Findings in this avenue of research have shown us that viewers are generally able to process subtitles and captions in an efficient manner, much like reading, and that how the subtitles and captions are presented plays a significant role in the viewer's processing and reception. These findings somewhat confirm the validity of the industry standards reviewed in the previous section. They also shed light onto how limited the visual attention of viewers can be and how easily it can be disrupted in multimodal contexts, a factor that has not yet been touched upon by quality standards given the granularity required and the infancy of rigorous empirical research in AVT research compared to more established disciplines in psychology and cognitive science.

3.2 Cognitive Load and Immersion in Subtitled and Captioned Media

Building upon the directly observable phenomenon of visual attention, Cognitive Load Theory (Plass et al. 2010) is a theoretical construct that originated in the psychological sciences and posits a limited working memory and processing capacity in the human cognitive system. This theoretical framework has been applied to AVT research given its direct application to the exploration of the multimodal processing of subtitled and captioned media. This theoretical framework brings a well-established inventory of media design principles that have been shown to ease the cognitive processing of multimodal information and reduce problems in processing due to overload and redundancy, including consistent findings for text presentation, timing, and positioning (see Kalyuga 2012).

As it is a theoretical construct, cognitive load can only be indirectly assessed using eye-tracking and/or EEG with or without self-report and task performance measures due to its multidimensionality. Based on Mayer and Moreno (2003), this multidimensionality can be formalised and applied to AVT as follows:

1. intrinsic load (inherent to the viewer and the task);
2. extraneous load (aspects of the viewer experience that impose cognitive effort);
3. germane load (the level of cognitive activity that is required for successful viewing to take place).

As such, the main application of Cognitive Load Theory in subtitling and captioning research should be to determine and reduce the extraneous load in order to avoid cognitive overload for the viewer, thereby optimising the cognitive capacity to be assigned to germane load, thus ensuring the viewer can become immersed in the multimodal experience. While research in subtitling and captioning has widely used the construct of cognitive load, it has yet to fully incorporate the multidimensionality of cognitive load that has since developed in the cognitive and psychological sciences. Kruger and Doherty (2016) provide a discussion of the applications of Cognitive Load Theory in subtitling research and outline methodologies that can capture its multidimensionality and overcome limitations of current eye-tracking methods in AVT research.

Recent work on using Cognitive Load Theory in AVT has begun to compare the cognitive processing demands of unsubtitled film, film with traditional subtitles, and film with dynamic subtitles to establish a more optimal placement and aesthetic characteristics of subtitles to optimise the viewer's cognitive load (see Kruger et al. 2018). Their findings show that the manipulation and placement of the position of subtitles, termed integrated titles by the authors, can reduce cognitive load. This placement is determined using eye-tracking data to calculate the most effective way to reduce spatial and temporal distance between the subtitle and its surrounding audiovisual elements, thus enabling the viewer to integrate the multimodal information with greater ease than the traditional subtitle placement at the bottom of the screen.

The link between cognitive load and quality is yet to be fully articulated. Depending on the nature of the task at hand, cognitive load may reflect different and even confounding effects. Errors in subtitles and captions are likely to lead to increased cognitive load as the viewer must overcome the error in order to comprehend and integrate the presented information. Cognitive load also has compelling links to cognitive-affective responses, including enjoyment and immersion. However, further empirical investigations of cognitive load in subtitled and captioned media will enable the creation of an AVT-specific evidence base that can better inform all stakeholders about how cognitive load can be optimised for diverse viewers in a variety of scenarios, including education and entertainment.

Similar to cognitive load, the construct of psychological immersion is also a theoretical construct that is becoming an attractive avenue of research for AVT as it can potentially contribute to the measurement and optimisation of viewers' immersion in and enjoyment of subtitled and captioned media. Such insights would also have direct implications for defining and assessing quality in AVT if factors can be identified that increase or decrease the viewer's immersion in terms of subtitles and captions. Immersion is an umbrella term for a number of terms used in media psychology and computer science to refer to the experience of a viewer or reader of becoming lost in a fictional reality. According to Nilsson et al. (2016), immersion "has come to stand for a multitude of different types of experiences and it is oftentimes used more or less interchangeably with concepts such as *presence*, *involvement*, and *engagement*." Indeed, the term also includes the concepts of transportation and character identification (see Green et al. 2004; Tal-Or and Cohen 2010), presence flow and enjoyment (Wissmath et al. 2009) as well as perceived realism (Cho et al. 2014).

Due to the immersive nature of film, it is understandable that reception research in AVT has started to turn towards this concept in recent years. In a comparison between subtitling and dubbing across genres, Wissmath et al. (2009) report no significant differences in immersion, as measured using post-task self-reports of presence, transportation, flow, and enjoyment. They note that all measures of immersion are correlated, with transportation being the most strongly related to enjoyment.

Further to this, Kruger et al. (2016) and Kruger et al. (2017a, b) use a range of measures, including self-report, eye-tracking, and EEG to find that subtitles make film more immersive to viewers with English as a second language who watch a film in English with English subtitles. They also report that with viewers who do not necessarily need the subtitles to access the dialogue, e.g. same-language subtitles for a general audience speaking that language, there are no negative effects to immersion. These studies also find the measure of transportation to be the most consistent and reliable offline measure of immersion. Lastly, Kruger and Doherty (2016) and Kruger et al. (2017a, b) show how a similar mixed-methods approach can be used in educational video to measure cognitive load and immersion. They report that students studying through their first or second language can benefit from subtitled educational content and claim that, with sufficient technical resources, future educational content can adapt to students' needs in real-time owing to the high temporary resolution of the online measures of eye-tracking and EEG, if these measures can be further refined for usage in AVT applications. These early explorations of immersion in subtitled and captioned media may provide more fruitful empirical evidence that will be directly linked to future discussions and assessments of quality in AVT given the compelling link between them.

4   New Media, New Technologies and New Challenges

With the rapid growth in new media in recent years, e.g. websites, streaming video, video games, social media, and online education, and the establishment of video at the centrality of this development, AVT applications have become more popular and accessible for a wide variety of purposes that go beyond traditional media and AVT contexts. This growth goes hand in hand with the expectation of content being available simultaneously in numerous languages and territories, also known as the 'sim-ship' model, and that content should be accessible to diverse audiences including non-native speakers of a language and the deaf and hard-of-hearing. A range of new language technologies have emerged to enable and indeed elicit this growth, including computer-assisted translation (CAT) tools, MT, and ASR, alongside (and often in combination with) crowdsourcing of subtitles. While these developments bring unprecedented opportunities for all stakeholders, from content creators, to LSPs, and viewers, they also bring new challenges to AVT practitioners, AVT companies, and researchers in terms of quality management and expectations.

CAT tools have typically not been used in media translation, including AVT, given the genres and text types dealt with in this area of translation. Texts, including audiovisual texts, tend to require indirect translation techniques that require subtitlers to adopt a functionalist approach to achieve pragmatic equivalence in order to elicit the desired effect, e.g. humour. The multimodality of such texts also limits the usage of CAT tools given the static, window-based approach that these tools have traditionally afforded. Recent developments in MT and CAT tools, however, have enabled a more multimodal and dynamic perspective of texts that has increased the usability and relevance of these tools for AVT purposes (e.g. Ortiz-Boix and Matamala 2017). Indeed, it is now commonplace for subtitling software to be used in tandem with a CAT tool in order to reap its benefits of productivity, consistency, and interoperability across projects and languages. This has, in turn, led to an increasing available of datasets of subtitles and captions that can be shared publicly and privately via the Internet. Websites such as www.opensubtitles.org provide stakeholders access to thousands of subtitle files in over 50 languages across all domains as part of a global shift towards fan-based subtitling (see O'Hagan 2009). Researchers in language technology have also made use of such invaluable datasets for projects across a wide range of language technology applications, including MT. OPUS, for example, now holds a wealth of multilingual subtitle corpora, including OpenSubtitles2016 which contains 2.60G sentences in 65 languages (Lison and Tiedemann 2016). As a result of this increased availability of data and wider technological developments, MT systems have also begun to show significant improvements in output quality when dealing with audiovisual texts.

In attempting to deal with the explosion of digital content that requires subtitles and captions, ASR systems have emerged with some demonstrating an acceptable level of accuracy (see Romero-Fresco and Pérez 2015). Automated subtitles are created by the ASR system by automatically transcribing dialogue into text in both pre-recorded and live applications. In pre-recorded scenarios, such as YouTube videos, the text transcription is then synchronised with the video using timing information derived from the audio embedded in the video (see Wald and Bain 2008). In live applications, the transcription happens in real time and relies solely on the speech without any external timing information (see Romero-Fresco and Pérez 2015), further considerations have to be made as a result (see Romero-Fresco 2016).

While this approach has become the default approach to subtitling and caption in the absence of an alternative, many issues remain in terms of accuracy, presentation, and timing, particularly in the accuracy of the transcription in the presence of noise, multiple speakers, and irregular speech, and in terms of presentation rate and segmentation. In order for automated subtitling or captioning to reach the level of professional quality (and indeed usability), these issues will need to be appropriately addressed. It seems, however, that such systems have become the *de facto* standard for most public and commercial new media services including YouTube.

YouTube's automated subtitling or captioning software is an excellent example of the quality possible with current publically-available systems. It is based on ASR technology provided by Google (Harrenstien 2009) with reported accuracy rates of only 80% (Blake 2015, Lockrey 2015) well below the accepted threshold for other ASR systems of 98% (Romero-Fresco 2016). The deployment of the software comes with options for manual settings to allow users to upload their own subtitles and captions, make use of auto-timing functions with manual intervention, and with iterative development so that the system quality itself can improve over time (Harrenstien 2009). Further improvements can be made to the system in terms of training the software to the speaker's voice (Wald and Bain 2008), reducing noise and unnatural speech (Jurafsky and Martin 2009), and by using pre-recorded scripts and post-editing.

YouTube also encourages its content creators to profile their viewer base to determine the requirements of their existing audience. Their guidelines encourage content creators to provide subtitles and captions in order to increase access to viewers in other language communities and for accessibility purposes.[2] The service then provides several options including uploading one's own subtitle and caption files, outsourcing the work to the YouTube community, and making use of its automated captioning software. There are no technical guidelines provided in terms of standards or quality. General tips are provided for using automated captioning, including using high-quality sound and being mindful of overlapping speakers.[3]

Figure 1 provides an example of a popular YouTuber who, in this case, makes use of the automated captioning software. It shows how the captions do not adhere to the standards described in the previous sections, including punctuation, segmentation, line breaking, indicating a change of speaker, and usage of static block subtitles. Issues in accuracy are indicated in the use of greyed-out words, e.g. "clover" in this figure, to indicate to the viewer that the confidence of accuracy for an individual word is not high.

It is not only the technologies used in AVT that are changing, but also the content to be subtitled and captioned. A significant amount of video found in new media appears in social media, e.g. YouTube, and in video games and gaming apps. Mangiron (2013) reports that the latter do not adhere to the traditional AVT standards as described in Sect. 2. Mangiron reports that the number of characters per line can go as high as 70 with the usage of three or more lines also common. As such, Mangiron argues that video games cannot be considered appropriate for accessibility as they do not conform to known needs for the deaf and hard-of-hearing and users playing through their foreign language. Further issues are identified in the absence of captioning for sounds and the usage of verbatim captioning methods. Mangiron then shows how the interactivity of new media, and video games in particular, is severely curtailed due to the lack of appropriate accessibility in subtitling and captioning required for such a medium, e.g. players need to perform specific actions in the game in order to progress but may not have understood what is required due to the above issues.

---

[2]http://creatoracademy.youtube.com/page/lesson/captions

[3]http://support.google.com/youtube/answer/6373554

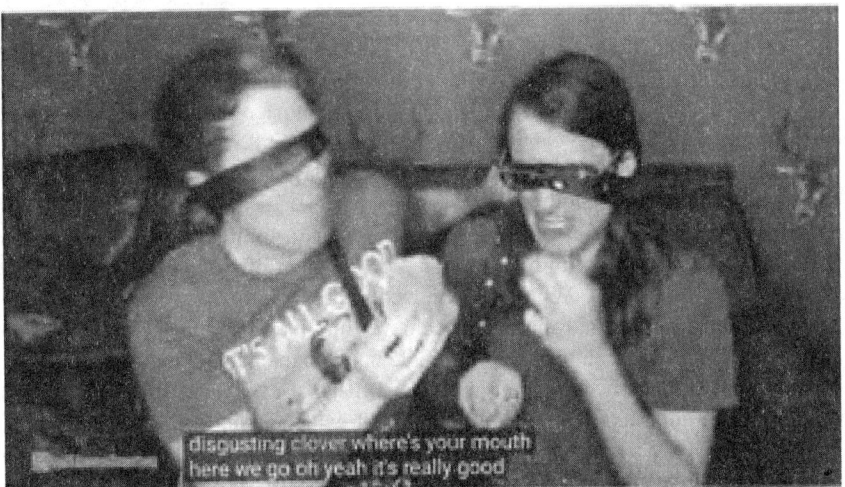

Fig. 1 Example of YouTube's automated captioning on a popular channel (Dawson 2015)

Mangiron (2016) later provides empirical evidence to support these arguments and cites the causes as being attributed to the relative youth of the video game industry, as part of new media in general, and a resultant lack of knowledge and awareness about accessibility and audience design, factors which have been well established in AVT research and practice. These observations are indeed relevant to the wider development of new media, where such issues increasingly present a language and accessibility barrier to many current and potential users who are systematically disadvantaged and excluded.

5 Conclusion

In this chapter, we have reviewed the various industry standards that have been developed to ensure that high-quality subtitling and captioning are delivered to viewers regardless of their language or accessibility needs. While these standards have provided a comprehensive list of parameters that need to be addressed in order to achieve high quality, they lack the granularity, evidence base, and interoperability required to ensure widespread, global adoption across new media. To address these gaps, we have seen how AVT researchers are using a range of research methods, including eye-tracking and EEG, to better understand how diverse viewers process and interact with subtitled and captioned media. In developing the evidence base in this area, the likelihood of finding international standards and a wider range of applications of AVT is greatly increased, especially with regard to influencing policy and engaging with other disciplines, particularly those working in rapidly developing areas of language technology, namely MT and ASR. We have also seen how the rapid proliferation of new media and new technology poses a range of challenges to AVT stakeholders, while opening up a multitude of new opportunities in the face of growing consumer demand and regulatory requirements that require high-quality subtitling and captioning to be available to all.

While the benefits of AVT appear to be increasing in terms of visibility to those outside of the discipline (e.g. Gernsbacher 2015), the reliance on 'rules of thumb' over validated empirical guidelines remains a limitation to AVT research and practice, especially with regard to the development of a universally applicable measurement of quality. While it is indeed necessary to move beyond general guidelines and error-based metrics to achieve this, interdisciplinary collaboration between stakeholders can provide invaluable insights to enable this to happen.

Viewers may not be aware or willing to make use of subtitles and captions (e.g. Ivarsson and Carroll 1998), yet empirical evidence suggests that we can all benefit from well-designed subtitles and captions. Indeed, subtitles and captions can provide a valuable and cost-effective approach, especially when leveraged with new and emerging language technologies and evidence-based quality standards informed by widespread stakeholder input.

At a time when the availability and usability of AVT software, datasets, and communities continue to grow, there has never been a more promising time for meaningful engagement between language technology and AVT across the industry and academic sectors. Integration of language technologies and education about their strengths and limitations stand to be of great benefit to the AVT community, especially as more and more resources become available online (e.g. Igareda and Matamala 2011). Similarly, language technology stakeholders stand to benefit from engagement with AVT given the need to better understand the diverse range of user needs and scenarios as well as the complex and dynamic nature of audiovisual texts. It is through this interdisciplinary interaction between stakeholders on an international level (e.g. see Mikul 2014) that we stand the greatest chance of successfully addressing questions of quality, some of which have been articulated in this chapter, for current and future applications of subtitling and captioning.

References

Álvarez A, Martíınez-Hinarejos CD, Arzelus H, Balenciaga M, del Pozo A (2017) Improving the automatic segmentation of subtitles through conditional random field. Speech Comm 88:83–95

Apone T, Botkin B, Brooks M, Goldberg L (2011) Caption accuracy metrics project: research into automated error ranking of real-time captions in live television news programs. The Carl and Ruth Shapiro Family National Center for Accessible Media, Boston

Bentin S, Kutas M, Hillyard S (1993) Electrophysiological evidence for task effects on semantic priming in auditory word processing. Psychophysiology 30:161–169

Blake J (2015) YouTube: we know automatic subtitles aren't good enough, Newsbeat. Available via: http://www.bbc.co.uk/newsbeat/article/31004497/youtube-we-know-automatic-subtitles-arent-good-enough. Accessed 8 Aug 2017

Cho H, Shen L, Wilson K (2014) Perceived realism: dimensions and roles in narrative persuasion. Commun Res 41(6):828–851

D'Ydewalle G, De Bruycker W (2007) Eye movements of children and adults while reading television subtitles. Eur Psychol 12(3):196–205

D'Ydewalle G, Muylle P, van Rensbergen J (1985) Attention shifts in partially redundant information situations. In: Groner R, McConkie C, Menz C (eds) Eye movements and human information processing. Elsevier, Amsterdam, pp 375–384

D'Ydewalle G, Praet C, Verfaillie K, van Rensbergen JV (1991) Watching subtitled television: automatic reading behaviour. Commun Res 18(5):650–666

Dawson S (2015) Hamburger challenge. Available via: http://wwwyoutubecom/watch?v=CRPK8sy4Qqk. Accessed 9 Aug 2017

Díaz Cintas J (2013) Subtitling: theory, practice and research. In: Millán C, Bartrina F (eds) The Routledge handbook of translation studies. Routledge, London, pp 273–287

Díaz-Cintas J, Remael A (2014) Audiovisual translation: subtitling. Routledge, London

Doherty S (2016) The impact of translation technologies on the process and product of translation. Int J Commun 10:947–969

Doherty S, Kruger J-L (2018) The development of eye tracking in empirical research on subtitling and captioning. In: Dwyer T, Perkins C, Redmond S, Sita J (eds) Eye tracking the moving image. Bloomsbury, London, pp 46–64

Dumouchel P, Boulianne G, Brousseau J (2011) Measures for quality of closed captioning. In: Şerban A, Matamala A, Lavaur JM (eds) Audiovisual translation in close-up: practical and theoretical approaches. Peter Lang, Bern, pp 161–172

Fox W (2016) Integrated titles: an improved viewing experience? In: Hansen-Schirra S, Grucza S (eds) Eyetracking and applied linguistics. Language Science Press, Berlin, pp 5–30

Gambier Y (2013) The position of audiovisual translation studies. In: Millán-Varela C, Bartrina F (eds) The Routledge handbook of translation studies. Routledge, London, pp 45–59

Gaspari F, Almaghout H, Doherty S (2015) A survey of machine translation competences: insights for translation technology educators and practitioners. Perspect Stud Translatol 23(3):333–358

Gernsbacher MA (2015) Video captions benefit everyone. Policy Insight Behav Brain Sci 2(1):195–202

Green MC, Brock TC, Kaufman GF (2004) Understanding media enjoyment: the role of transportation into narrative worlds. Commun Theory 14(4):311–327

Gunter TC, Friederici AD (1999) Concerning the automaticity of syntactic processing. Psychophysiology 36(1):126–137

Harrenstien K (2009) Automatic captions in YouTube. Google, California. Available via: https://googleblog.blogspot.ie/2009/11/automatic-captions-in-youtube.html. Accessed 15 June 2017

Igareda P, Matamala A (2011) Developing a learning platform for AVT: challenges and solutions. JoSTrans 16:145–162

Ivarsson J, Carroll M (1998) Subtitling. TransEdit, Simrishamn

Jurafsky D, Martin JH (2009) Speech and language processing: an introduction to natural language processing, computational linguistics, and speech recognition, 2nd edn. Pearson Prentice Hall, Upper Saddle River

Just MA, Carpenter PA (1980) A theory of reading: from eye fixations to comprehension. Psychol Rev 87(4):329–354

Kalyuga S (2012) Instructional benefits of spoken words: a review of cognitive load factors. Educ Res Rev 7(2):145–159

Karamitroglou F (1998) A proposed set of subtitling standards in Europe. Trans J 2(2). Available via: http://translationjournal.net/journal/04stndrd.htm. Accessed 01 June 2017

Kruger J-L, Doherty S (2016) Measuring cognitive load in the presence of educational video: towards a multimodal methodology. Australas J Educ Technol 32(6):19–31

Kruger J-L, Steyn F (2014) Subtitles and eye tracking: reading and performance. Read Res Q 49(1):105–120

Kruger J-L, Soto-Sanfiel MT, Doherty S, Ibrahim R (2016) Towards a cognitive audiovisual translatology: subtitles and embodied cognition. In: Muñoz R (ed) Reembedding translation process research. John Benjamins, Amsterdam, pp 171–194

Kruger J-L, Doherty S, Ibrahim R (2017a) Electroencephalographic beta coherence as an objective measure of psychological immersion in film. Int J Trans 19:1–11

Kruger J-L, Doherty S, Sato-Sanfiel M (2017b) Original language subtitles: their effects on the native and foreign viewer. Comunicar 50(1):23–32

Kruger J-L, Doherty S, Fox W, de Lissa P (2018) Multimodal measurement of cognitive load during subtitle processing: same-language subtitles for foreign language viewers. In: Lacruz I, Jääskeläinen R (eds) New directions in cognitive and empirical translation process research. John Benjamins, Amsterdam, pp 267–294

Kubitschke L, Cullen K, Dolpin C, Larin S, Cederbom A (2013) Study on assessing and promoting e-accessibility. European Commission Directorate-General of Communications Networks, Content and Technology

Lison P, Tiedemann J (2016) OpenSubtitles2016: extracting large parallel corpora from movie and TV subtitles proceedings of the 10th international conference on language resources and evaluation, Portorož, Slovenia, pp 923–929

Lockrey M (2015) YouTube automatic captions score an incredible 95% accuracy rate! The deaf captioner, medium. Available via: https://medium.com/@mlockrey/youtube-s-incredible-95-accuracy-rate-on-auto-generated-captions-b059924765d5. Accessed 20 Jan 2017

Mangiron C (2013) Subtitling in game localisation: a descriptive study. Perspect Stud Translatol 21(1):42–56

Mangiron C (2016) Reception of game subtitles: an empirical study. Translator 22(1):72–93

Mayer RE, Moreno R (2003) Nine ways to reduce cognitive load in multimedia learning. Educ Psychol 38(1):43–52

McMains S, Kastner S (2009) Visual attention. Encyclopaedia of neuroscience. Springer, Berlin, pp 4296–4302

Mikul C (2014) Caption quality: international approaches to standards and measurement. Media Access Australia, Sydney

Nilsson N, Nordahl R, Serafin S (2016) Immersion revisited: a review of existing definitions of immersion and their relation to different theories of presence. Hum Technol 12(2):108–134

O'Hagan M (2009) Evolution of user-generated translation: Fansubs, translation hacking and crowdsourcing. J Int Localis 1(1):94–121

O'Hagan M (2013) The impact of new technologies on translation studies: a technological turn? In: Millán-Varela C, Bartrina F (eds) The Routledge handbook of translation studies. Routledge, London, pp 503–518

Ortiz-Boix C, Matamala A (2017) Assessing the quality of post-edited wildlife documentaries. Perspect Stud Trans Theory Pract 25(4):571–593

Perego E (2016) History, development, challenges and opportunities of empirical research in audiovisual translation. Across Lang Cult 17(2):155–162

Perego E, Del Missier F, Porta M, Mosconi M (2010) The cognitive effectiveness of subtitle processing. Media Psychol 13(3):243–272

Plass JL, Moreno R, Brünken R (2010) Cognitive load theory. Cambridge University Press, New York

Pollatsek A, Raney GE, LaGasse L, Rayner K (1993) The use of information below fixation in reading and in visual search. Can J Exp Psychol 47:179–200

Rajendran D, Duchowski A, Orero P, Martínez J, Romero-Fresco P (2013) Effects of text chunking on subtitling: a quantitative and qualitative examination. Perspect Stud Translatol 21(1):5–21

Romero-Fresco P (2016) Accessing communication: the quality of live subtitles in the UK. Lang Commun 49:56–69

Romero-Fresco P, Pérez JM (2015) Accuracy rate in live subtitling: the NER model. In: Díaz Cintas J, Baños Piñero R (eds) Audiovisual translation in a global context. Palgrave Macmillan, London, pp 28–50

Rossi S, Gugler MF, Friederici AD, Hahne A (2006) The impact of proficiency on syntactic second language processing of German and Italian: evidence from event-related potentials. J Cogn Neurosci 18(12):2030–2048

Sasamoto R, Doherty S (2016) Towards the optimal use of impact captions on TV programmes. In: O'Hagan M, Zhang Q (eds) Conflict and communication: a changing Asia in a globalising world. Nova Science Publishers, Hauppauge, pp 210–247

Smith AC, Monaghan P, Huettig F (2017) The multimodal nature of spoken word processing in the visual world: testing the predictions of alternative models of multimodal integration. J Mem Lang 93:276–303

Staub A, Rayner K (2007) Eye movements and on-line comprehension processes. In: Gaskell G (ed) Oxford handbook of psycholinguistics. Oxford University Press, Oxford, pp 327–342

Szarkowska A, Krejtz I, Pilipczuk O, Dutka Ł, Kruger J-L (2016) The effects of text editing and subtitle presentation rate on the comprehension and reading patterns of interlingual and intralingual subtitles among deaf, hard of hearing and hearing viewers. Across Lang Cult 17(2):183–204

Tal-Or N, Cohen J (2010) Understanding audience involvement: conceptualizing and manipulating identification and transportation. Poetics 38(4):402–418

Wald M, Bain K (2008) Universal access to communication and learning: the role of automatic speech recognition. Univ Access Inf Soc 6(4):435–447

Wissmath B, Weibel D, Groner R (2009) Dubbing or subtitling? Effects on spatial presence, transportation, flow, and enjoyment. J Media Psychol 21(3):114–125

Part III
Translation Quality Assessment in Practice

Machine Translation Quality Estimation: Applications and Future Perspectives

9

Lucia Specia and Kashif Shah

Abstract Predicting the quality of machine translation (MT) output is a topic that has been attracting significant attention. By automatically distinguishing bad from good quality translations, it has the potential to make MT more useful in a number of applications. In this chapter we review various practical applications where quality estimation (QE) at sentence level has shown positive results: filtering low quality cases from post-editing, selecting the best MT system when multiple options are available, improving MT performance by selecting additional parallel data, and sampling for quality assurance by humans. Finally, we discuss QE at other levels (word and document) and general challenges in the field, as well as perspectives for novel directions and applications.

Keywords Translation quality assessment · Principles to practice · Translation errors · Translation models · Post-editing effort · Statistical machine translation · Machine translation system ranking · Machine translation system selection · Quality estimation

1 Introduction

Machine Translation (MT) systems are becoming widely adopted both for gisting purposes and to produce professional quality translations. However, the quality of automatic translation is still below an acceptable level in many cases. This makes evident the need for automatic metrics for predicting the quality of a translated segment. These metrics are referred to as Quality Estimation (QE). The goal of QE is to provide an estimate on how good or reliable a translated text is without access to

L. Specia
Department of Computer Science, University of Sheffield, Sheffield, UK
e-mail: l.specia@sheffield.ac.uk

K. Shah
eBay Research, San Jose, CA, USA
e-mail: skshah@ebay.com

reference (human) translations. This is, therefore, different from standard evaluation methods where the task is to compare system translations with their reference counterparts, which are generally created by linguistic experts with knowledge of the languages involved. While MT systems can be evaluated using reference datasets and their average quality can be measured on those data points, it is known that the quality on individual inputs can vary considerably depending on a number of factors. QE is not aimed at estimating overall MT system performance, but rather performance on individual translations. The main motivation is to make applications more useful in real world settings, where information on the quality of each output is needed and reference outputs are not available. QE is aimed at MT systems in use. As such, QE metrics have several applications in the context of MT, which we discuss in this chapter. QE approaches also have the advantage of allowing for a flexible modelling of the concept of quality, depending, among other things, on the user or intended use of the MT system's output.

Work in QE for MT started in the early 2000s. Inspired by the confidence scores used in Speech Recognition, initial research explored information coming from the statistical MT models, such as word translation probabilities, language model scores and other statistical indicators. Back then it was called *confidence estimation*, a narrower term that reflects the fact that the statistical indicators used are related to the confidence of the MT system in the translation produced. A 6-week workshop on the topic at Johns Hopkins University in 2003 (Blatz et al. 2004) set as its goal the estimation of automatic metrics such as BLEU (Papineni et al. 2002) and WER (Word Error Rate) (Levenshtein 1966). These metrics are difficult to interpret, particularly at the sentence level. Given the metrics used and the fact that the overall quality of MT was considerably lower at the time, pinpointing the very few good quality MT segments was a much harder problem. As a consequence, results of multiple experiments proved unsuccessful. Also, no software or datasets were made available after the workshop.

A new surge of interest in the field started around 2010, motivated by the widespread use of MT systems in the translation industry, as a consequence of better translation quality, more user-friendly tools, and higher demand for translation. In order to improve the utility of MT in this scenario, a quantification of the quality of translated segments is needed. In a way, this quantification can be thought of as similar to "fuzzy match scores" from translation memory (TM) systems. However, QE work addresses this problem using more complex metrics that go beyond matching the source segment against previously translated data. In addition, QE can be useful for users other than professional translators, such as end-users reading translations for gisting, particularly those who cannot read the source language. Recent work focuses on estimating more interpretable metrics where "quality" is defined according to the task at hand, such as post-editing, gisting, sampling, etc. (see also Sect. 3.3 of Way in this volume).

A number of positive results have been reported. Examples include improving post-editing efficiency by filtering out low-quality segments which would require more effort or time to be corrected than translating from scratch (Specia et al. 2009; Specia 2011), selecting high-quality segments to be published as they are, without post-editing (Soricut and Echihabi 2010), selecting a translation from either an MT system or a TM for post-editing (He et al. 2010), selecting the best translation from multiple MT systems (Specia et al. 2010; Avramidis 2013), and highlighting sub-segments that need revision (Bach et al. 2011; Quang et al. 2014).

QE is generally addressed as a supervised machine learning task using a variety of algorithms to induce models from examples of translations described through a number of features and annotated for quality. For an overview of various algorithms and features we refer the reader to the WMT12–16[1] shared task on QE (Callison-Burch et al. 2012b; Bojar et al. 2013, 2014, 2015, 2016). Most of the research work lies on deciding which aspects of quality are more relevant for a given task and designing feature extractors for them. These can go from simple, language-independent features, to advanced, linguistically-motivated features. They can include features that rely on information from the MT system that generated the translations, as well as features that are independent of the way translations were produced. While simple features such as counts of tokens and language model scores can be easily extracted, feature engineering for more advanced and useful information can be very labour- and resource-intensive. Different feature sets are necessary for different language pairs or for optimisation against specific quality scores, where translations are created with different applications in mind (e.g. post-editing time vs translation adequacy).

In this chapter we focus on sentence-level experiments and results for what we believe are some of the most promising and practical applications of QE to date. Each of these applications has been developed around a specific objective:

- Estimate how much effort will be needed to post-edit a segment.
- Select among alternative translations produced by different MT systems.
- Decide whether the translation can be used for self-learning of MT systems.
- Select samples of translations for manual inspection.

In what follows, we first explain the general experimental settings, including features and learning algorithms, for the various QE applications to be covered (Sect. 2). For consistency purposes, across all datasets and applications we use the same feature sets and learning algorithms where possible. In the remainder of the chapter (Sects. 3, 4, 5, and 6), we present our work on the various above-mentioned applications and benchmark the results on freely available datasets.

2 Experimental Settings

Our experiments with all applications of QE are performed using QuEst++ (Specia et al. 2013, 2015a) – an open source framework for quality estimation containing

---

[1]The Workshop (now Conference) on Machine Translation runs annual competitive MT system evaluations for a range of tasks. See http://www.statmt.org/wmt17/ for the latest in the series.

a number of features, covering complexity, adequacy and, fluency of segments using a machine-learning algorithm. Amongst the learning algorithms available in QuEst++, we choose the Support Vector Regression algorithm given its promising performance in previous work.

2.1 Support Vector Regression (SVR)

SVR (Chang and Lin 2011) is the most commonly used algorithm for sentence-level QE. This is a very popular and powerful machine-learning algorithm used when the score to predict is numeric and distributed over an ordinal or continuous range, for example, post-editing time or Likert scores in {1,5}. To make our results comparable with most previous work, we use a kernel version of this algorithm with a radial basis function (RBF) kernel, which has been shown to perform very well in this task (Callison-Burch et al. 2012a). Kernel parameters are optimised using grid search with five-fold cross-validation.

2.1.1 Feature Sets

As feature sets, we consider the following for the sentence-level tasks:

- **BL**: 17 simple but effective baseline features that perform well across languages and were used as baseline in the WMT12–16 shared tasks on QE.
- **AF**: All features available in QuEst++ across the datasets, for example, 80 language and MT system-independent features for sentence-level prediction.

2.1.2 Evaluation Metrics

We use two main error metrics to evaluate our sentence level regression models: Mean Absolute Error (**MAE**), shown in Eq. 1 and Root Mean Squared Error (**RMSE**), shown in Eq. 2.

$$\text{MAE} = \frac{\sum_{i=1}^{N} |H(s_i) - V(s_i)|}{N} \tag{1}$$

$$\text{RMSE} = \sqrt{\frac{\sum_{i=1}^{N} (H(s_i) - V(s_i))^2}{N}} \tag{2}$$

where:

$N = |S|$ is the number of test instances
$H(s_i)$ is the predicted score for s_i
$V(s_i)$ is the human score for s_i

For the classification results, we use the standard **Accuracy** metric.

In addition, we use application-specific metrics, such as BLEU for MT system evaluation based on data selected through QE in Sect. 5.

2.1.3   Baselines

We compared our regression results with the **Mean** score, i.e., the score obtained by assigning the mean value of the training set labels to all test set instances. For classification experiments, we compared our results to the **Majority Class** score, i.e., the score obtained by assigning the most frequent label of the training set to all test set instances.

3   QE for Predicting Post-editing Effort

In this section we focus on QE for outbound purposes, i.e. a dissemination scenario. In this scenario, a judgement on the quality of translations has to take into account both the fluency and adequacy of such translations, and in some cases, it has to conform to style guides. MT is followed by manual post-editing and/or revision by human translators to achieve publishable quality. Our objective is to support human translators by designing QE methods to distinguish translations that are good enough for post-editing from those that are too bad, and so should be translated from scratch. A common distinction includes at least three levels of "effort": (i) translations that are good enough to be left untouched by human post-editors (but possibly still revised); (ii) translations which require further effort (post-editing) to be published; and (iii) translations that should better be discarded, as they require more effort from human translators to correct them than what is involved in manual translation from scratch. In the following we benchmark QE on various datasets annotated for post-editing effort in different ways.

3.1   Datasets

All datasets used in the experiments are available for download.[2] Statistics about these datasets are shown in Table 1. They differ in size, language pair and label for post-editing effort.

- **WMT14 (Task-1.1)** English-Spanish news sentence translations. The dataset contains news source sentences and their human translations, as well as three

[2]http://www.dcs.shef.ac.uk/~lucia/resources.html

Data	Languages	Training	Test	Label
WMT14	en-es	3,816	600	PEE 1–3
WMT12	en-es	1,832	422	PEE 1–5
EAMT11	en-es	900	64	PEE 1–4
EAMT11	fr-en	2,300	225	PEE 1–4
EAMT09-s_1	en-es	3,095	906	PEE 1–4
EAMT09-s_2	en-es	3,095	906	PEE 1–4
EAMT09-s_3	en-es	3,095	906	PEE 1–4
EAMT09-s_4	en-es	3,095	906	PEE 1–4

Table 1 Language pairs, number of training and test sentences and type of label in the datasets for the post-editing effort prediction

versions of MT output: by a statistical MT (SMT) system, a rule-based MT (RBMT) system and a hybrid system. Each translation was labelled by professional translators with 1–3 (lowest-highest) scores for perceived post-editing effort.

- **WMT12** English-Spanish sentence translations produced by a phrase-based (PB) Moses "baseline" system (Koehn et al. 2007),[3] and judged for post-editing effort in 1–5 (highest-lowest), taking a weighted average of three annotators.
- **EAMT11** English-Spanish (EAMT11 (en-es)) and French-English (EAMT11 (fr-en)) sentence translations produced by a PBSMT "baseline" Moses system and judged for post-editing effort in 1–4 (highest-lowest).
- **EAMT09** English sentences translated by four SMT systems into Spanish and scored for post-editing effort in 1–4 (highest-lowest). Systems are denoted by s_1–s_4.

3.2 Feature Selection

Given the large number of features available, it is often beneficial to select only the most relevant for the dataset at hand. We performed feature selection using Gaussian Processes, which has proved very effective in previous work (Shah et al. 2015). Gaussian Processes (GPs) (Rasmussen and Williams 2006) are a Bayesian non-parametric machine learning framework considered the state-of-the-art for regression. GPs have been used successfully for MT quality prediction (Shah et al. 2013), among other tasks. We use GPs with radial basis function (RBF) with automatic relevance determination, as in (3).

---

[3]http://www.statmt.org/moses/?n=Moses.Baseline

$$k(\mathbf{x}, \mathbf{x}') = \sigma_f^2 \exp\left(-\frac{1}{2}\sum_i^D \frac{x_i - x_i'}{l_i}\right) \qquad (3)$$

where the $k(\mathbf{x}, \mathbf{x}')$ is the kernel function between two data points $\mathbf{x}$ and $\mathbf{x}'$, and D is the number of features; σ_f and $l_i \geq 0$ are the kernel hyper-parameters, which control the covariance magnitude and the *length scales* of variation in each dimension, respectively. This is closely related to the RBF kernel used with SVR, except that each feature is scaled independently of the others, i.e. $l_i = l$ for SVR, while we allow for a vector of independent values. Following standard practice we also include an additive white-noise term in the kernel with variance σ_s^2. The kernel hyper-parameters ($\sigma_f, \sigma_n, \mathbf{l}$) are learned via gradient descent with a maximum of 100 iterations and cross-validation on the training set.

Feature selection is done by fitting per-feature RBF widths (also known as the *automatic relevance determination* kernel). The learned length scale hyper-parameters can be interpreted as the per-feature RBF widths which encode the importance of a feature: the narrower the RBF (the smaller the l_i), the more important a change in the feature value is to the model prediction. Therefore, the outcome of a model trained using GPs can be viewed as a list of features ranked by relevance, and this information can be used for feature selection by discarding the lowest-ranked (least useful) features. GPs on their own do not provide a cut-off point on this ranked list of features; instead this needs to be determined by evaluating loss on a separate dataset to determine the optimal number of features.

3.3   Results

The error scores for all datasets using SVR as the learning algorithm are reported in Table 2. It can be seen that adding more features (systems **AF**) improves the results in most cases as compared to the baseline system with 17 features **BL**. However, in most cases the improvements are not significant. This behaviour is to be expected as adding more features may bring more relevant information, but at the same time it makes the representation more sparse and the learning prone to overfitting.

Our experiments with feature selection using GPs led to significant further improvements in all cases. The **FS(GP)** figures are produced from selecting the fixed 17 top-ranked features (i.e. the same number as that of the baseline features). **FS(GP)** outperforms other systems despite using considerably fewer features (17 in all datasets). These are very promising results, as they show that it is possible to reduce the resources and overall computational complexity for training the models, while achieving similar or better performance.

Dataset	System	# Features	MAE	RMSE
EAMT11(en-es)	Mean	–	0.6027	0.7314
	BL	17	0.4867	0.6288
	AF	80	**0.4696**	0.5438
	FS(GP)	17	**0.4397**	**0.5224**
EAMT11(fr-en)	Mean	–	0.5411	0.6927
	BL	17	0.4387	0.6357
	AF	80	0.4275	0.6211
	FS(GP)	17	**0.4166**	**0.6176**
WMT12	Mean	–	0.8278	0.9898
	BL	17	0.6802	0.8192
	AF	80	0.6703	0.8373
	FS(GP)	17	**0.6224**	**0.7645**
WMT14	Mean	–	0.4585	0.6678
	BL	17	0.5241	0.6591
	AF	80	0.4896	0.6349
	FS(GP)	17	**0.4850**	**0.6331**
EAMT09-s_1	Mean	–	0.5382	0.7092
	BL	17	0.5294	0.6643
	AF	80	0.5235	0.6558
	FS(GP)	17	0.5045	**0.6392**
EAMT09-s_2	Mean	–	0.6854	0.7926
	BL	17	0.4604	0.5856
	AF	80	0.4734	0.5973
	FS(GP)	17	0.4514	**0.5735**
EAMT09-s_3	Mean	–	0.6753	0.7751
	BL	17	0.5321	0.6643
	AF	80	0.5437	0.6827
	FS(GP)	17	0.5130	0.6572
EAMT09-s_4	Mean	–	0.4990	0.6112
	BL	17	0.3583	0.4953
	AF	80	0.3569	0.5000
	FS(GP)	17	0.3383	0.4811

Table 2 Results with black-box features and SVR as learning algorithm. For each dataset, bold-faced figures are significantly better than all others (paired t-test with $p \leq 0.05$).

4 QE for System Selection

In this section the goal is to model quality estimation by contrasting the output of several translation sources for the same input sentence. The outcome of this process is a ranking of alternative translations based on their predicted quality. For the system selection application, we are more interested in correctly ranking the best translation at the top, as opposed to obtaining a complete ranking of all alternative translations. This top-ranked translation could either be provided to a human post-editor for revision, or used as is.

For all experiments, we use the features and settings for these experiments as those described in Sect. 2. We treat the problem as a machine-learning regression task, where SVR models are trained to estimate a continuous score within {1,3}. In the first round of experiments (Sect. 4.2) we evaluate different settings of these models following a standard regression setting, while in the second round of experiments we apply the models to select a given translation option for each segment and evaluate the outcome in terms of document-level translation quality (Sect. 4.3).

4.1 Datasets

The datasets used here are a superset of the **WMT14** dataset described in the previous section. They consist of news domain texts in four language pairs (Table 3): English-Spanish (**en-es**), Spanish-English (**es-en**), English-German (**en-de**), and German-English (**de-en**). For each language pair, the data contains a different number of source sentences and their human translations, as well as 2–3 versions of MT outputs: by an SMT system, an RBMT system and, for en-es/de only, a hybrid system. The translations were produced by top MT systems of each type (SMT, RBMT, and hybrid; hereafter **system2**, **system3**, **system4**) which participated in the translation shared task, plus the professional translation given as reference (**system1**).

Each translation in this dataset has been labelled by a professional translator with {1,3} scores for "perceived" post-editing effort, where:

- **1** = perfect translation, no editing needed.
- **2** = near miss translation: maximum of 2–3 errors, and possibly additional errors that can be easily fixed (capitalisation, punctuation).
- **3** = very low quality translation, cannot be easily fixed.

The distribution of true scores in both training and test sets is given in Figs. 1 and 2, for each language pair, and for each language pair and translation source (MT system or human), respectively.

Languages	# Training Src/Tgt	# Test Src/Tgt
en-es	954/3,816	150/600
en-de	350/1,400	150/600
de-en	350/1,050	150/450
es-en	350/1,050	150/450

Table 3 Number of training and test source (Src) and target (Tgt) sentences in each dataset for the system selection experiments

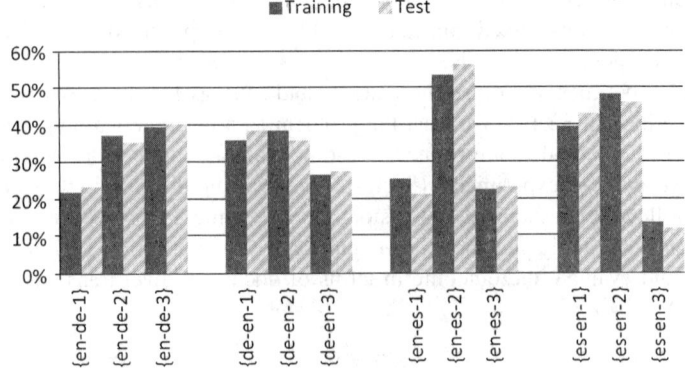

Fig. 1 Distribution of true scores by language pair

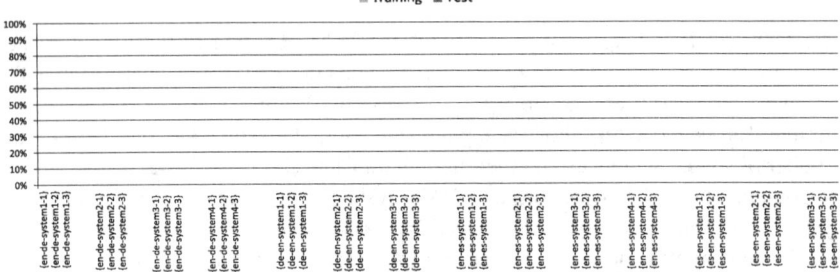

Fig. 2 Distribution of true scores for each MT system and language pair

4.2 Regression Results

For the standard regression evaluation, we compare prediction error for models trained (and tested) on pooled translations from all MT systems (and humans) together (Table 4), versus models trained on each dataset individually, considering two settings at test time:

- The system used to produce the translation is unknown (Table 5 blind setting), and so all models are applied, one by one, to predict the quality of this translation and the average prediction is used as output.
- The system is known and thus the model for the same translation system/human is used for prediction (Table 5 non-blind setting).

These two variants may be relevant depending on the application scenario. We consider a scenario where system identifiers are known by developers at model building time, but unknown at test time, to be very realistic, e.g. if QE is provided as a web service with pre-trained models. In all tables, **Mean** – assigning the mean

	System	# Features	MAE	RMSE
en-de	Mean	–	0.6831	0.7911
	BL	17	**0.6416**	**0.7620**
	AF	80	**0.6303**	**0.7616**
de-en	Mean	–	0.6705	0.7979
	BL	17	**0.6524**	**0.7791**
	AF	80	**0.6518**	**0.7682**
en-es	Mean	–	0.4585	0.6678
	BL	17	0.5240	0.6590
	AF	80	0.5092	0.6442
es-en	Mean	–	0.5825	0.6718
	BL	17	0.5736	0.6788
	AF	80	**0.5662**	**0.6663**

Table 4 SVR to build prediction models for each language pair combination, with all translation sources (including human) pooled together

of the training set labels to all test set instances – represents a strong baseline, given the large variation in scores across MT systems and human translators.

Comparing the two variants of the blind setting (Table 4 – blind training and test – and Table 5, blind test only), we see that pooling the data from multiple translation systems for blind model training leads to significantly better results than training models for individual translation sources but testing them in blind settings. This is likely to be due to the larger quantities of data available in the pooled models. In fact, the best results are observed with **en-es**, the largest dataset overall.

Comparing scores between blind versus non-blind test settings in Table 5, we observe a substantial difference in the scores for each of the individual translation system. This shows that the task is much more challenging when QE models are trained independently but the identifiers of the systems producing the test instances are not known.

There is also a considerable difference in the performance of individual models for different translation systems, which can be explained by the different distribution of scores (and also indicated by the performance of the **Mean** baseline). However, in general the prediction performance of the individual models seems less stable, and even worse than the baseline in several cases. Interestingly, the individual models trained on human translations only (system1) do even worse than individual models for MT systems. This can be an indication that the features used for quality prediction are not sufficient to model human translations.

In all cases, the use of all features (**AF**) instead of baseline features (**BL**) yields comparable or better results.

	System	# Features	Blind		Non-blind	
			MAE	RMSE	MAE	RMSE
en-de-system1	Mean	–	1.0351	1.2133	0.3552	0.4562
	BL	17	1.0487	1.2348	**0.3350**	0.4540
	AF	80	1.0510	1.2375	**0.3325**	0.4545
en-de-system2	Mean	–	0.7780	0.9339	0.4857	0.5487
	BL	17	**0.7006**	0.9499	**0.3615**	**0.4634**
	AF	80	**0.6924**	**0.9124**	**0.3570**	**0.4644**
en-de-system3	Mean	–	0.7369	0.8426	0.5577	0.6034
	BL	17	**0.6354**	**0.7950**	**0.4535**	**0.5363**
	AF	80	**0.6572**	0.8127	**0.4482**	**0.5245**
en-de-system4	Mean	–	0.7231	0.8215	0.5782	0.6433
	BL	17	**0.6438**	**0.7842**	**0.4912**	**0.5834**
	AF	80	**0.6386**	**0.7905**	**0.4818**	**0.5741**
de-en-system1	Mean	–	0.8594	1.0882	0.2506	0.3409
	BL	17	0.8747	1.1299	**0.2123**	0.3421
	AF	80	0.8747	1.1299	**0.2065**	0.3415
de-en-system2	Mean	–	0.7321	0.8484	0.5412	0.6678
	BL	17	**0.6897**	0.8330	**0.4745**	**0.5931**
	AF	80	0.7122	0.8509	**0.4604**	**0.5850**
de-en-system3	Mean	–	0.8137	0.9253	0.6000	0.6640
	BL	17	**0.7472**	**0.8903**	**0.4965**	**0.6011**
	AF	80	**0.7629**	0.9300	**0.4828**	**0.5901**
en-es-system1	Mean	–	0.8542	0.9923	0.3883	0.4353
	BL	17	0.8956	1.0480	**0.3633**	0.4390
	AF	80	0.8957	1.0480	**0.3519**	0.4381
en-es-system2	Mean	–	0.5567	0.6952	0.4232	0.5314
	BL	17	**0.5275**	0.6827	**0.3812**	**0.4951**
	AF	80	**0.5302**	0.6884	**0.3730**	**0.4893**
en-es-system3	Mean	–	0.5653	0.6998	0.4288	0.5213
	BL	17	**0.5155**	**0.6711**	**0.3821**	**0.4844**
	AF	80	**0.5184**	**0.6704**	**0.3714**	**0.4761**
en-es-system4	Mean	–	0.5573	0.6955	0.4300	0.5321
	BL	17	**0.5103**	**0.6680**	**0.4022**	**0.5162**
	AF	80	**0.5206**	**0.6727**	**0.3902**	**0.5016**
es-en-system1	Mean	–	0.6617	0.8307	0.3026	0.3916
	BL	17	0.6617	0.8307	0.3022	0.3917
	AF	80	0.6617	0.8308	0.3023	0.3915
es-en-system2	Mean	–	0.5637	0.6931	0.4494	0.6027
	BL	17	0.5588	0.7023	**0.4384**	0.6061
	AF	80	0.5567	0.7026	**0.4309**	0.6053
es-en-system3	Mean	–	0.6602	0.8129	0.4720	0.6245
	BL	17	0.7233	0.8621	0.4993	0.6220
	AF	80	0.6973	0.8435	0.4974	0.6198

Table 5 SVR to build individual prediction models for each language pair and translation source

4.3 System Selection Results

In what follows we turn to using the predictions from SVR models we have just described for system selection. The task consists of selecting, for each source segment, the best *machine* translation among all available: two or three depending on the language pair. For these experiments, we disregarded the human translations, as they do not tend to be present in settings for system selection, and would normally be better than the MT outputs in all cases. Another reason to rule out human translations from the selection is that they are used as references to compute BLEU scores of the selected sets of sentences, as explained below.

To provide an indication of the average quality of each MT system, Table 6 presents the BLEU scores on the QE test and training sets for individual MT systems. The bold-face figures for each language test set indicate the (BLEU) quality that would be achieved for that test set if the "best" system were selected on the basis of the average (BLEU) quality of the training set (i.e., no system selection). There is a significant variance in terms of quality scores, as measured by BLEU, among the outputs of 2–3 MT systems for each language pair, with training set quality being a good predictor of test set quality for all but **en-es**, once again, the largest dataset.

We measure the performance of the selected sets in two ways: (i) by computing the BLEU scores of the entire sets containing the supposedly best translations, using the human translation available in the datasets as reference, and (ii) by computing the accuracy of the selection process against the human labels, i.e., by computing the proportion of times both system selection and human agree (based on the pre-defined 1–3 human labels) that the sentence selected is the best among the 2–3 options (2–3 MT systems). We compare the results obtained from building pooled (all MT systems) against individual prediction models (one per MT system).

Table 7 shows the selection results with various models trained on MT translations only:

- **Best-SVR(I):** Best translation selected with regression model trained on data from individual MT systems, where prediction models are trained per MT system, and the translation selected for each source segment is the one with the

WMT14	system2		system3		system4	
	Test	Training	Test	Training	Test	Training
en-de	15.39	12.79	13.75	13.83	**17.04**	16.19
de-en	**27.96**	24.03	22.66	20.19	–	–
en-es	**25.89**	34.13	32.68	28.42	29.25	31.97
es-en	**37.83**	40.01	23.55	25.07	–	–

Table 6 BLEU scores of individual MT systems, without system selection. Bold-faced figures indicate scores obtained when selecting the best system on average (using BLEU scores for the training set).

	System	# Features	Best-SVR(I)	Best-SVR(P)
en-de	MC	–	16.14	15.55
	BL	17	17.20	17.05
	AF	80	**18.10**	17.55
de-en	MC	–	25.81	25.17
	BL	17	28.39	28.13
	AF	80	**28.75**	28.43
en-es	MC	–	30.88	30.29
	BL	17	32.92	32.81
	AF	80	**33.45**	33.25
es-en	MC	–	30.13	29.70
	BL	17	38.10	38.11
	AF	80	**38.73**	38.41

Table 7 BLEU scores on best selected translations (I = Individual, P = Pooled)

highest predicted score among these independent models. This requires knowing the source of the translations for training, but not for testing (blind test).

- **Best-SVR(P):** Best translation selected with regression model trained on pooled data from all MT systems. This assumes a *blind* setting where the source of the translations for both training and test sets is unknown, and thus pooling data is the only option for system selection.

Table 7 shows that the regression models trained on individual systems – **Best-SVR(I)** – with **AF** as feature set yield the best results, despite the fact that error scores (MAE and RMSE) for these individual systems are worse than for systems trained on pooled data. This is somewhat expected as knowing the system that produced the translation (i.e., training models for each MT system) adds a strong bias to the prediction problem towards the average quality of such a system, which is generally a decent quality predictor. We note, however, that the **Best-SVR(P)** models are not far behind in terms of performance. More important, we note the gains in BLEU scores as compared to the bold-face test set figures in Table 6, showing that our system selection approach leads to best-translated test sets rather than simply picking the MT system with best average quality (BLEU).

5   QE for Self-Training

One of the most efficient ways to improve the quality of an MT system is to supplement it with additional parallel training data. In some scenarios, monolingual data on either source or target languages (or both) can be abundant. However, parallel data has to be created by having humans translate monolingual content, which is an expensive process. Clever selection techniques to choose a subset with only the most useful sentences to translate from monolingual data can result in systems with higher quality using less training data. These techniques are usually referred to as Active Learning (AL) (Settles 2010).

The majority of AL methods for MT are based on sentence (dis)similarity with the training data, with particular focus on domain adaptation. Eck et al. (2005) suggest a TF-IDF metric to choose sentences with words absent in the training corpus. Ambati et al. (2010) propose a metric of informativeness relying on unseen n-grams.

Similar to the work described here, Banerjee et al. (2013) proposed a data selection guided by automatic QE to identify poorly-translated sentences in the target domain. They restrict the reference set to the sentences that were poorly translated by the baseline model instead of using the entire target-domain data as reference for data selection.

An alternative approach is to select source sentences based on their estimated translation quality by a baseline MT system before the addition of new data. It is assumed that if a sentence has been translated well with the existing data, it will not contribute to improving the translation quality. If, however, a sentence has been translated poorly, it might have words or phrases that are absent or incorrectly represented. Haffari et al. (2009) use features including n-grams and phrase frequency, MT model score, etc. to decide which sentences to select. Ananthakrishnan et al. (2010) build a pairwise classifier that ranks sentences according to the proportion of n-grams they contain that can cause errors. For quality estimation, Banerjee et al. (2013) train language models of well- and badly-translated sentences. The usefulness of a sentence is measured as the difference of its perplexities in these two language models.

Logacheva and Specia (2014) proposed a new quality-based AL technique which is based on a more complex and therefore potentially more reliable QE framework. It employs a wider range of features, which go beyond those used in previous work, covering information from both source and target sentences. The approach adds post-edited or reference translations for MT outputs predicted to have low quality.

In this section we describe a similar quality-informed strategy, but focus on the addition of new data that has been translated by MT, rather than human references. Machine-translated segments predicted to have high enough quality are added to the training corpus of an SMT system. Therefore, we rely only on monolingual data. The assumption is that the MT segments added to the training corpus can help by reinforcing statistics on existing data.

Another direction we investigate here is the potential of using translations from an RBMT system to supplement the training data of an existing (iteratively improved) SMT system. In this case, in addition to reinforcing statistics on existing data, translations can also provide new information to the SMT system, helping, for example, to deal with out-of-vocabulary words. We compare the improvements obtained by an SMT system enhanced with either SMT or RBMT data, as well as against the improvements obtained by an SMT system enhanced with additional reference translations instead of MT outputs as in Logacheva and Specia (2014).

5.1 Active Learning Strategy

Four sets of data are necessary in our experiments: (i) parallel sentences to train an initial, baseline SMT system (including a subset for tuning), (ii) an additional pool of parallel sentences to select from (or monolingual sentences only, in the case of adding machine-translated segments to the SMT training corpus), (iii) source-MT segment pairs labelled for quality to train a QE model, and (iv) a held-out parallel test set to evaluate the performance of the baseline and improved SMT systems. We describe these datasets in Sect. 5.4.

Once a QE model is trained, the active learning pipeline includes the following steps:

1. Train a baseline SMT system.
2. Translate the pool of active learning data.
3. Predict the quality for the pool of AL data.
4. Select top n sentences based on QE scores and a given selection criterion to add to the SMT training data.
5. Remove top n sentences from the pool of AL data.
6. Retrain the SMT models including the additional selected data.
7. Go to step 2 until the AL pool is empty.

The SMT models are retrained incrementally with the additional QE selected data. The selection criteria are explained in the next section.

5.2 Selection Criteria

One of the aims of this work is to compare the use of MT against the use of reference translations, i.e. translations produced by humans. We therefore consider two scenarios as bases for the type of data to be added to the SMT training corpus: (i) reference translation sentences, which simulate a real AL setting where we would resort to humans to provide a translation for poorly-translated segments, (ii) machine-translated sentences (by an SMT or an RBMT system), where we assume human intervention is not possible or too costly, and so resort to the **self-training** of the SMT systems with their own or third party MT outputs.

In the second scenario, machine translations can be noisy and lead to degradation in MT performance. However, our hypothesis is that by filtering the candidates with a QE-based AL selection, we will select higher quality data to be added to the SMT training data, leading to improvements in overall performance.

More specifically, we experiment with the following settings to select data from the AL pool:

- SMT translations (source sentences and their machine translations) for the translations predicted as having highest QE scores (scenario 2, above).

- References (source sentences and their references) for the translations predicted as having the lowest QE scores (scenario 1, above).
- RBMT translations (source sentences and their machine translations) for the translations predicted as having highest QE scores (scenario 2, above).

5.3 SMT Models

We use the Moses toolkit to train our SMT system with phrase-based models using 14 standard features.[4] These feature functions include phrase and lexical translation probabilities in both directions, seven features for a lexicalised distortion model, word and phrase penalties, and a target language model. MERT (Och 2003) is used to tune the weights of these feature functions. For simplicity, our experiments use only the QuEst 17 baseline features, i.e., the **BL** set.

5.4 Datasets

We assume a common real-world scenario that explores two types of data: a relatively small parallel dataset and an additional (often larger) pool of source language only sentences. We use the former to train a baseline SMT system, translate the latter using this baseline SMT system and then inject a subset of sentences selected as outlined in Sect. 5.2 (either a human translation or the automatic translation produced by the MT system) to the initial parallel corpus and retrain the SMT system. The following datasets were used in the experiments. Their statistics are given in Table 8:

- **SMT training:** To train the initial SMT models we randomly selected 70% of the News Commentary training data for two language pairs: en-de and de-en. We set aside 30% of the corpus as AL pool.
- **SMT tuning and test:** We used the official WMT14 (translation task) tuning and test sets.
- **QE training:** To train our QE models we used data provided for WMT14 QE Task 1.1 (both training and test sets pooled together). The QE dataset and its labels are explained in Sect. 4.1.

Before we turn to the AL experiments, we look at the quality of the different versions of the AL pool data (reference, SMT and RBMT translations) in two ways. We first measured the BLEU score obtained for the SMT translations in the entire $\sim$ 60k AL pool (produced by the baseline version of the SMT system with $\sim$140k parallel sentences) versus the BLEU score obtained for the RBMT translations in

---

[4]http://www.statmt.org/moses/?n=moses.baseline

Corpora	de-en	en-de
Initial data (baseline SMT system)		
Training – 70% of News Commentary corpus	140,900	140,900
Tuning – WMT newstest-2013	3,000	3,000
Test – WMT newstest-2014	3,000	3,000
Additional data (AL data)		
AL pool data – remaining 30% of News Commentary corpus	60,388	60,388
QE data		
Training QE models – WMT14 QE task	1,500	2,000

Table 8 Statistics of the datasets used for the self-learning experiments

	de-en	en-de
SMT translations	13.71	11.29
RBMT translations	13.30	11.09

Table 9 BLEU score for sentences in the AL pool against the reference translations. SMT translations are generated by the baseline SMT system (before any incremental learning)

	de-en	en-de
Source-reference	16.83	12.12
Source-SMT translations	14.99	10.84
Source-RBMT translations	14.66	10.70

Table 10 BLEU score for test sentences from models built with variants of the AL pool data only (~60 K parallel sentences)

the entire ~60k AL pool, both against the reference translations. These are shown in Table 9. The quality, in terms of BLEU, of both datasets is very similar, with the SMT translations achieving slightly higher figures for both languages.

Second, we built an SMT system using only the ~60k AL pool data for training, without incremental training with either the baseline SMT translations, the RBMT translations, or the reference translations. These models were tested on the official test set (WMT newstest-2014) and the results in terms of BLEU scores are shown in Table 10. Surprisingly, the SMT and RBMT translations seem equally useful as SMT parallel training corpora. We had hypothesised that SMT translations tend to be closer to the source segments than the latter in word order and style, leading to better word-alignment performance, which in turn leads to better translation models. This, however, does not seem to be the case with this dataset. Reference translations are clearly more helpful in building better SMT systems.

5.5 Results

We conducted a set of experiments to show the improvement rate of our main selection strategy (adding MT data) compared to reference/random data selection. With the **SMT translations**, at every iteration, based on quality predictions for translations in the AL pool produced by the current SMT system, batches of 10 K sentences from the pool with the predicted highest/lowest scores (depending upon MT or reference translation as selection criterion) were selected. These were added to the training data of the SMT system, which was then retrained using the **incremental training** option in Moses[5] to skip some of its initial, time-consuming steps. The selected sentences were removed from the AL pool. The new SMT system was applied to translate the held-out test set, and the performance was measured using BLEU. The process was repeated until the pool was empty. We note that the updated SMT system is also used to translate the remaining sentences in the AL pool.

RBMT translations were generated by the Lucy system, which is known to achieve the state-of-the-art performance for English↔German. The process here was slightly different: since the RBMT system cannot be easily updated based on quality predictions, the SMT system was updated with RBMT translations. Also different from the experiments with SMT translations, the AL pool was translated once, and each translation had its quality predicted also only once. The AL was then sorted by highest predicted quality and batches of 10 K (best-worst) were taken for every step and added to the SMT training corpus. As in the remaining experiments, the SMT system was retrained to translate the test set at every step.

In order to compare the impact of **SMT**, **RBMT** and (**Reference**) translations on SMT quality, we added these variants of translations to baseline SMT systems (10 K sentences at each iteration), starting with the baseline, using 70% of the News Commentary corpus. To evaluate the effectiveness of the QE predictions for the SMT translations, we also add a baseline that selects the 10 K batches of SMT translations randomly (**Random**). This allows us to contrast simply adding more data against adding more supposedly good quality data. Results are shown in Figs. 3 and 4, for each language pair. All BLEU figures are reported based on the test set. The BLEU scores show that adding more data significantly improves the results using all variants of the selection strategy.

Overall, as expected, the use of reference translations leads to better performance than using machine-translated segments. However, the performance obtained with the use of SMT translations follows closely behind. The use of SMT translations is even better than References for one particular step (iteration 3) with English-

---

[5] As detailed in http://www.statmt.org/moses/?n=Moses.AdvancedFeatures#ntoc37, instead of producing a phrase table with pre-calculated scores for all translations, the entire source and target corpora are stored in memory as a suffix array along with their alignments, and translation scores are calculated on the fly. When new training data is available, the word alignments are simply updated.

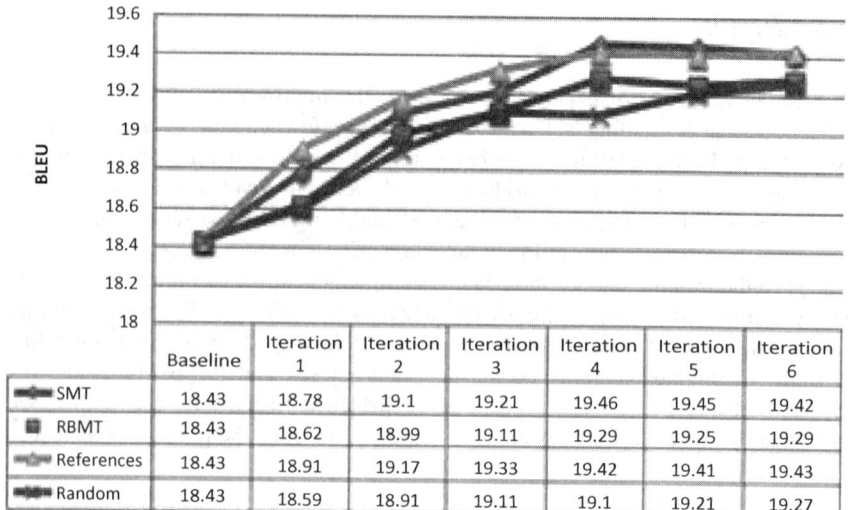

	Baseline	Iteration 1	Iteration 2	Iteration 3	Iteration 4	Iteration 5	Iteration 6
SMT	18.43	18.78	19.1	19.21	19.46	19.45	19.42
RBMT	18.43	18.62	18.99	19.11	19.29	19.25	19.29
References	18.43	18.91	19.17	19.33	19.42	19.41	19.43
Random	18.43	18.59	18.91	19.11	19.1	19.21	19.27

Fig. 3 Performance of de-en enhanced with data selected by different AL strategies

German translation. More importantly, the differences in the final scores (iteration 6) for SMT and References are virtually non-existent for de-en, and very marginal for en-de. This is a very positive result, as it shows that the same level of improvements can be obtained with machine-translated segments instead of reference translations. Another very interesting observation was that we observed that the performance for both language pairs is higher by using smaller amounts of data selected with QE rather than using the entire dataset. In particular, for de-en, at iteration 4 the BLEU score achieved is slightly superior to the score achieved when the entire AL pool is used (both with references and machine translations). This could indicate that some references may be noisy or difficult to align to their corresponding source segments, proving less helpful to the SMT system. The use of RBMT translations, on the other hand, does not seem very helpful, as its performance is close to or worse than that of randomly selecting SMT translations.

To highlight some important differences in terms of impact on SMT systems' performance with various settings, we look more closely at the following comparisons: The impact of each system can be observed in Figs. 3 and 4.

- **SMT vs. Reference:** In a first comparison between SMT translations and reference translations on SMT quality, it seems very encouraging that we get similar final scores (or very close) with both additional references and additional SMT data. SMT translations are much cheaper to obtain than reference translations. While our AL pool was relatively small, one could rely on much larger collections of monolingual data for this approach.

- **RBMT vs. Reference:** This comparison inspects the impact of RBMT systems versus reference translations on SMT quality. RBMT translations seem to

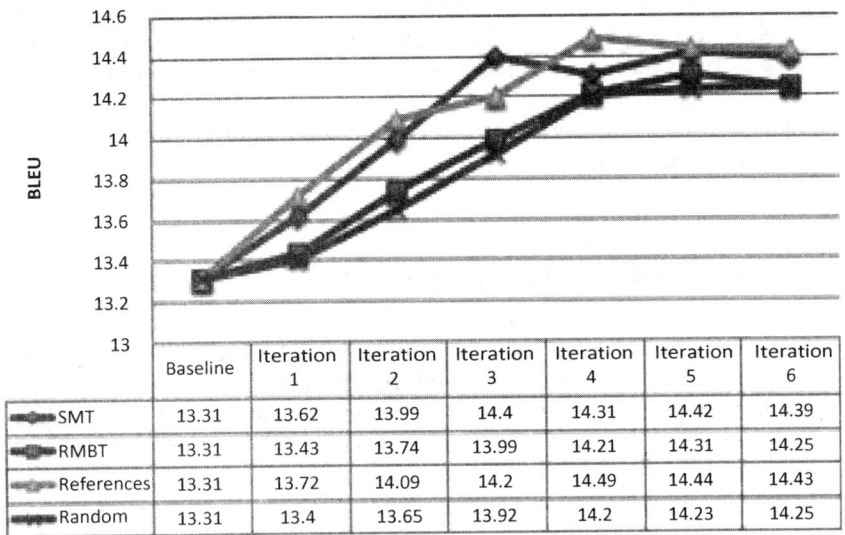

	Baseline	Iteration 1	Iteration 2	Iteration 3	Iteration 4	Iteration 5	Iteration 6
SMT	13.31	13.62	13.99	14.4	14.31	14.42	14.39
RMBT	13.31	13.43	13.74	13.99	14.21	14.31	14.25
References	13.31	13.72	14.09	14.2	14.49	14.44	14.43
Random	13.31	13.4	13.65	13.92	14.2	14.23	14.25

Fig. 4 Performance of en-de enhanced with data selected by different AL strategies

perform substantially worse than reference translations. We note that the RBMT system has not been customised in any manner to translate the type of data used in the experiments (news).

- **SMT vs. RBMT:** The improvements with SMT data are consistently higher than RBMT for both directions. One reason for that is the incremental versus static version of the experiments with both types of translations. As previously mentioned, in the RBMT setting, the translations in the remaining AL pool cannot be updated as the SMT system is updated, since they are generated from an RBMT system. Additionally, intuitively translations produced by RBMT systems are less close to the source segments than translations produced by SMT systems. The latter can thus be potentially more easily word-aligned by automatic tools, rendering them more useful to SMT retraining.
- **SMT vs. Random:** Here we compare our selection technique from SMT data against randomly selecting SMT data. From Figs. 3 and 4 we can see that our selection strategy with SMT data consistently outperforms random selection.
- **RBMT vs. Random:** Finally we compare our selection technique from RBMT data against randomly selecting data. RBMT data and random selection perform very similarly.

One final aspect investigated was the effects of incremental training, as opposed to batch training, on the final translation quality. We tested the performance of an SMT system built from the entire parallel corpus of source and reference translations, by simply concatenating the original ~140k and the additional ~60k segment pairs and training a batch model for it. For the batch mode, the scores obtained are 19.63 (de-en) and 14.65 (en-de). We recall that the BLEU scores obtained by these systems with the iterative AL setting (at the final iteration 6) are lower: 19.43 (de-en) and 14.43 (en-de). This shows that incremental learning leads to some performance degradation. If time is not an issue, one solution to this problem is to retrain the SMT models from scratch at every AL iteration, instead of using incremental training.

6 Sampling QE for Quality Assurance

Human assessment of translations for quality assurance purposes is a cognitively intensive and time-consuming task. While various assessment methods exist (e.g. the LISA QA model; see also the chapters by Popović and Lommel in this volume) that provide insight into translation quality, they cannot be implemented within the rapid development cycles that characterise the use of MT. Even with HT, quality assessment is often done on small samples of translations.

Traditionally, samples for quality assessment are selected at random. Random selection is a valid choice if enough data can be sampled for analysis, as this would reflect the natural distribution of errors across the entire set. However, more often than not, very small samples of translations are selected, potentially leaving out certain issues. In addition, for different purposes, it may be desirable to focus the assessments on the lower/higher quality cases translations. In this section we propose a quality-informed sampling method where translations estimated to have a certain level of quality (e.g. average, top or lower levels) are selected for human inspection. We contrast this method against random selection in terms of the number of selected translations that can be effectively assessed and the distribution of issues found.

We compare the task of quality assessment on data selected at random against data selected according to quality predictions for four language pairs. The two samples are given to human translators for error annotation using the Multidimensional Quality Metrics (MQM) error typology (see Lommel et al. (2014) and Lommel in this volume). Translations with quality predicted to be around average for the set are selected. This decision was based on the fact that translations with high quality do not require human inspection, and translations with very low quality are too hard – if not impossible – to have errors identified. One of our hypotheses was that translators could find more errors in samples of translations selected using QE, as many samples selected at random are too bad to be annotated. However, our analysis showed that this is not the case: the absolute number of errors found with randomly selected cases is still higher. Nevertheless, the error distributions in both types of samples were very similar. This indicates that samples with average quality, which are potentially easier and less time-consuming to annotate, still offer an advantage for human quality assessment over random samples.

6.1 Datasets

The datasets used for **training** the models were taken from official WMT14 task 1.1 on QE, which was described in Sect. 4.1. However, here we only use translations produced by the statistical phrase-based system. We train four QE models, one per language pair, with 500 instances for all but the en-es data, which has 1104 instances.

We apply the models to generate predictions for the WMT10–11 translation task **test sets**, taking only those segments whose source is originally in the language of interest (∼600 segments).

6.2 Sampling and Error Annotation

After training QE models for each of the datasets, we took a sample of 100 sentences whose quality predictions are the closest possible to 2 (good enough). The hypothesis here is that QE is helpful to select near-miss segments for manual inspection in order to perform systematic QE: perfect cases do not need to be inspected, worst cases are too bad to be inspected manually. It is worth mentioning that other selection criteria could be defined, such as selecting sentences with the lowest predicted quality. For comparison purposes, we selected a non-overlapping random sample of another 100 sentences.

For each language pair, we generated a combination of 100 QE-based and 100 random samples consisting of source segments and their translation. We gave these segments for annotation without disclosing the source of the sample. translate5 was used as annotation tool.[6] Each segment was annotated by four professional translators who received training on the annotation task and on translate5. Annotators were requested to annotate only cases with errors and mark segments that were too bad to be annotated as "fully unintelligible". In total, annotations were performed on 3,200 segments, i.e., 200 segments for four language pairs, with four annotators for each segment.

For human annotation we used a subset of MQM. This set of issues provides a reasonably comprehensive set of analytic issues that can be applied to spans within segments to identify specific issues at a fairly granular level. MQM issues are arranged in a hierarchy with more and less general types. A selection of core MQM issues which was designed specifically to analyse MT output is used here:

- **Accuracy**. Issues related to the relationship of the target and source content.

  - **Omission**. Content present in the source is improperly omitted in the target.

---

[6]http://test.translate5.net/

- **Mistranslation**. Content is translated with a different meaning from the source.
- **Untranslated**. Content present in the source remains in the source language.
- **Addition**. Content not present in the source has been added to the target text.

- **Fluency**. Issues related to the linguistic properties of the target language itself without regard to the fact that it is a translation.

  - **Spelling**. The text is misspelled (including capitalisation problems).
  - **Typography**. The text does not follow typographic conventions (other than spelling).
  - **Grammar**. There is a grammatical problem with the text.

    · **Word Form**. The text uses an incorrect word form.

      · **Part of speech**. The text uses the wrong part of speech.
      · **Agreement**. The text shows problems with number, gender, or case agreement.
      · **Tense/aspect/mood**. Verbs show incorrect tense, aspect, or mood.

    · **Word Order**. Portions of the text appear in the wrong order.
    · **Function word**. Function words (e.g. articles, prepositions) are used incorrectly

      · **Extraneous**. The text contains unneeded function words.
      · **Missing**. The text is missing needed function words.
      · **Incorrect**. The text uses function words incorrectly.

  - **Unintelligible**. The meaning of the text cannot be recovered. Used for cases in which a serious break-down of fluency has occurred.

As these issues are hierarchical in nature, if none of the subtypes for a given category apply, then the parent may be chosen. In addition to these categories, annotators were given an additional option to select: *fully unintelligible*. This annotation was used for cases where the annotators found the fluency or accuracy of the target segment so bad that they would not be able to identify individual errors in the translation.

6.3 Results and Analysis

In what follows we summarise the most important findings when comparing the annotation of QE-based samples versus random samples.

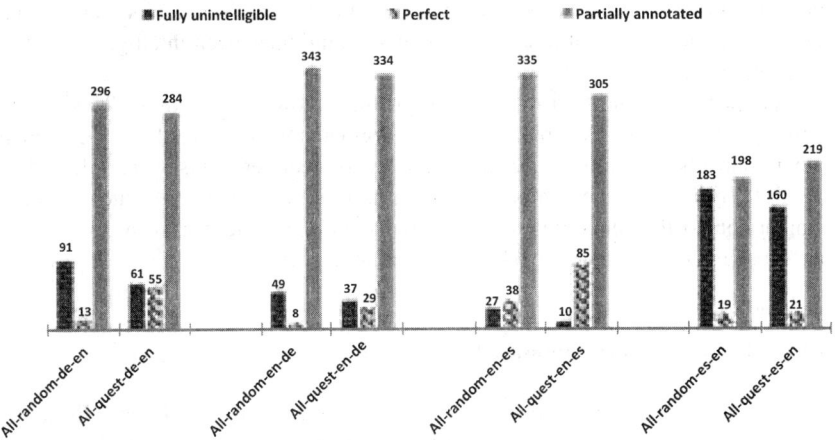

Fig. 5 Number of sentences (out of 400 per language pair) which are fully unintelligible, perfect or annotated for errors

6.3.1 Fully Unintelligible, Perfect and Annotated Segments

Figure 5 shows the number of three types of segments in each dataset, where "QuEst" represents the QE-based selection:

- **Perfect:** Segments that are not annotated at all as they are perfectly good translations.
- **Fully unintelligible:** Segments that are so bad that they cannot be annotated.
- **Annotated:** The remaining segments which are neither perfect nor fully unintelligible and are good enough for annotation.

Fewer fully unintelligible cases were found across all datasets with the QE-based sampler than the random sampler for en-es, de-en, and en-de. This finding is in line with our hypothesis that systematic quality evaluation can help in discarding segments which are too bad for annotation. However, in the case of es-en, we did not find the expected difference.

Although we are not certain why es-en results were different, annotators for this pair seem to have been much more critical of the output, annotating almost half of all segments as *fully unintelligible*. In previous annotation work,[7] we found that es-en translations were particularly prone to grammar problems, especially with incorrect subject and object pronouns, when compared to the other language pairs. Because Spanish is a "pro-drop" language with considerable verbal syncretism that relies on context for disambiguation, segments often lack sufficient syntactic and morphological information for proper translation without a consideration of their context. Since pronouns and verbal forms are particularly important for

---

[7]See QTLaunchPad Deliverable D1.3.1, "Barriers for High-Quality Machine Translation", p 15–20, at http://www.qt21.eu/launchpad/system/files/deliverables/QTLP-Deliverable-1_3_1-v2.0.pdf

understanding the meaning of sentences, it may be that annotators found many sentences unintelligible at first glance, which would have been intelligible in other language pairs.

As expected, the number of perfect segments is low in all datasets. This finding is true even for the QE sampler, given that segments were selected to have average rather than good quality. Nevertheless, more perfect segments were selected by QE than by the random sampler. As long as this number is still much lower in comparison to the remaining selected segments, it should not be a problem, as perfect segments can be easily skipped by annotators.

6.3.2   Total of Errors Annotated

The number of errors for each of the datasets, on a per-annotator basis, is shown in Fig. 6. The number of errors found in random samples is clearly larger than in QE samples, except for es-en, where the figures are very close, probably for the same reasons as noted above: the annotators were more critical in rejecting sentences outright. While different annotators annotated different numbers of errors, the relative differences in error counts between QE-based and random samples are maintained across annotators. For this analysis a fully unintelligible segment is counted as one error. However, those segments would most likely contain multiple errors had they been annotated. This may also explain the difference between annotators, as some annotators chose to mark more entire segments as unintelligible than others. Finally, it could also explain the case of es-en, where many of the segments were marked as fully unintelligible by all of the annotators. The fact that QE led to a higher proportion of "perfect" segments being sampled will naturally decrease the number of errors found in its samples.

For a more detailed analysis, we excluded from the counts the segments marked as fully unintelligible. The total number of errors per language pair (all annotators together) can be seen in Fig. 7. There is a clear drop in the number of errors for all language pairs, but the trend between random sampling and QE-based sampling is maintained: a higher number of errors is found with the randomly selected samples, except for es-en, where the number of errors in both samples is virtually the same: 648 (random) and 652 (QE). This is most likely a consequence of the fact that annotators discarded nearly 50% of the cases that are too complex to annotate in both samples, and thus the remaining sets in both cases will contain translations of similar levels of quality.

One important finding that stands out from Fig. 7 is the fact that, with the random sample, there are fewer segments annotated (more were rejected), but in absolute terms they contain more errors than the larger sets of segments selected by QE. Therefore, the proportion of errors per segment is much higher with random samples. Since we could not log annotation time, it is unclear whether annotating fewer segments with more errors is more time-consuming than annotating more segments with fewer errors. We can however hypothesise that samples with fewer errors per segment may lead to more consistent annotations, as multiple errors are often interrelated, making annotation harder and therefore more prone to mistakes and inconsistencies, particularly across annotators.

6.3.3 Distribution of Error Types

For a closer look at the overall distribution of errors, in Fig. 8 we combine annotations from all translators for each language pair and plot the proportion of each type of error, i.e., we normalise the counts of each error type by the total number of errors for that language pair (all annotators). The figures were obtained after excluding all segments marked as fully unintelligible. Across all datasets, mistranslation is the most common error type, followed by word order issues. A significant proportion of errors fall under the "unintelligible" category, particularly for es-en. This category covers unintelligible parts of a segment, as opposed to representing cases where the entire segment is too bad to be annotated. Given the small number of samples, particularly after excluding fully unintelligible cases, it is to be expected that certain types of errors will not be observed at all. Surprisingly however, this is only the case for very few error types, and these are mostly general error types, which work as fall back options when the exact error cannot be identified, such as the accuracy and fluency categories.

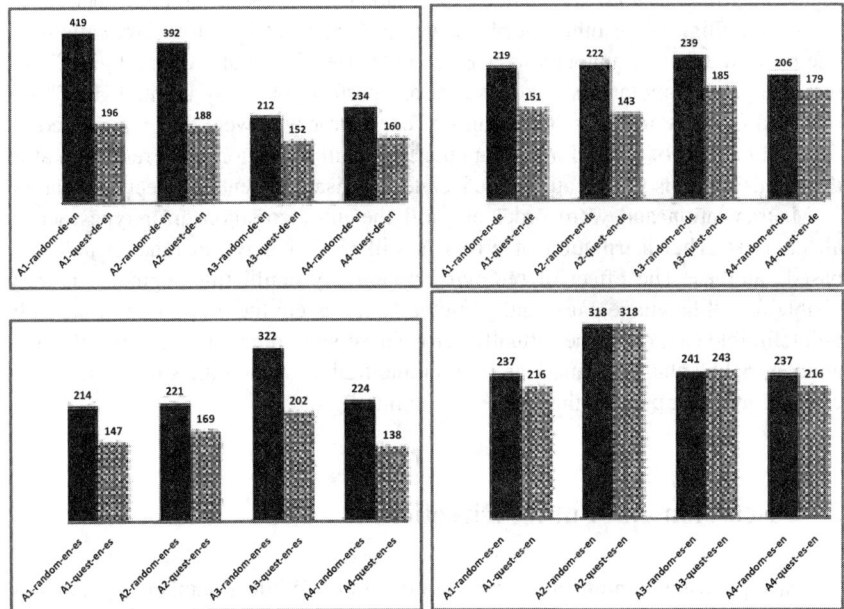

Fig. 6 Errors per dataset and annotator. Fully unintelligible segments count as one error.

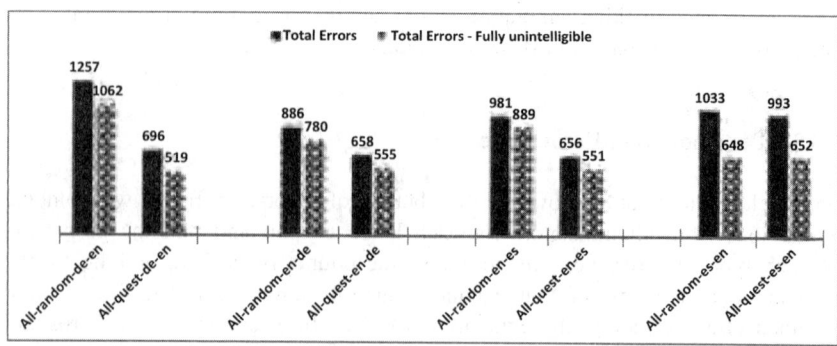

Fig. 7 Number of errors within all segments against number of errors within segments excluding those fully unintelligible, per language pair

Interestingly, the distribution of errors are very similar between random and QE-based samples. This shows that both sampling techniques will lead to spotting the same types of errors, in the same proportions. However, as was mentioned before, different annotators chose to annotate different segments, as they considered a different number of (potentially non-overlapping) fully unintelligible or perfect segments. In Fig. 9 we further analyse the error distributions by excluding all segments which at least one of the four annotators judged to be either perfect or fully unintelligible. In other words, given a segment and its four annotations, if one or more of these annotations was set as "perfect" or "fully unintelligible", the remaining 1–3 annotations were also set as "perfect" or "fully unintelligible" and removed from the analysis. The counts of each error type were thus normalised by the total number of errors for that language pair (all annotators) that remained after the exclusion. This was an attempt to isolate any disagreements between annotators.

Mistranslation and word order are still the most common error types across all datasets. The distribution of errors is still similar between random and QE-based samples. The effect of removing potentially conflicting segments is very visible for all language pairs, and particularly for es-en: the proportion of partially unintelligible cases became virtually zero. These were probably cases which some annotators had chosen to mark as fully unintelligible, while others had gone to the effort of marking parts of the segment as unintelligible.

7   Discussion and Future Directions

We have presented a number of applications of QE. While a number of evaluation campaigns and other benchmarking efforts have been made in recent years to measure progress in QE (we refer the reader to Callison-Burch et al. (2012b) and Bojar et al. (2013, 2014, 2015, 2016) for comprehensive experiments), our intention

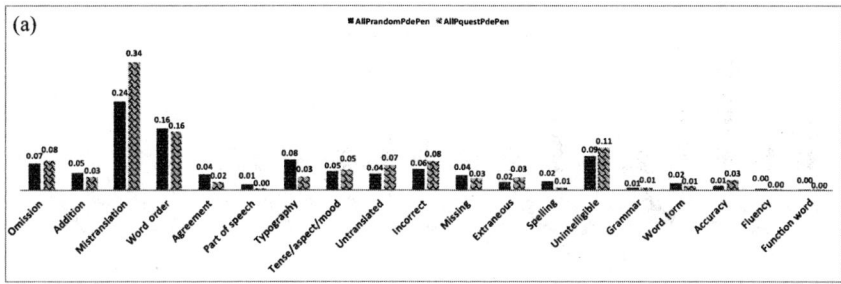

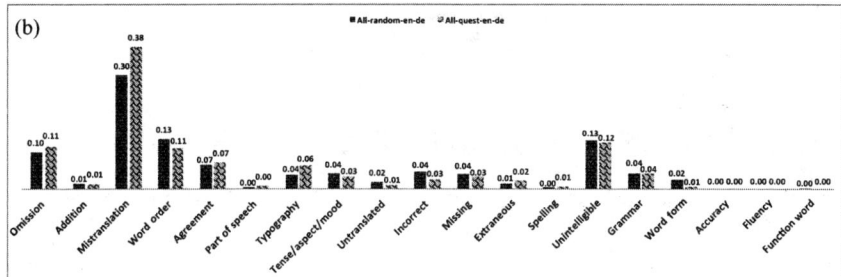

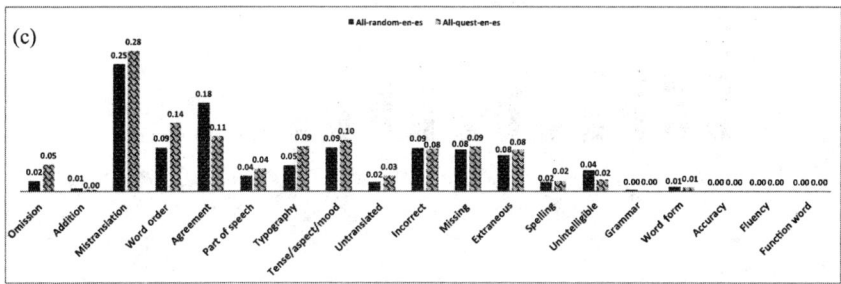

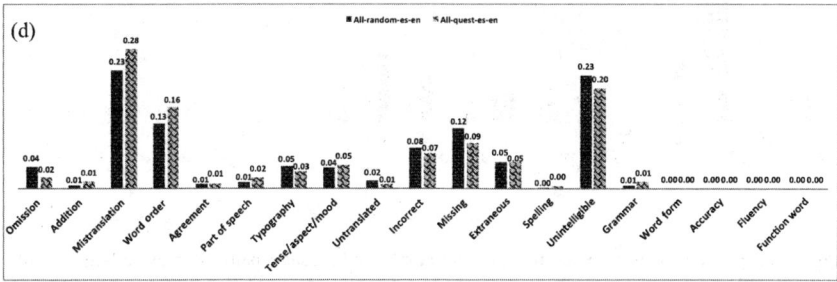

Fig. 8 Proportion of error types for all annotators per language pair, after excluding segments judged by at least one of the four annotators as perfect or fully unintelligible. (**a**) de-en. (**b**) en-de. (**c**) en-es. (**d**) es-en.

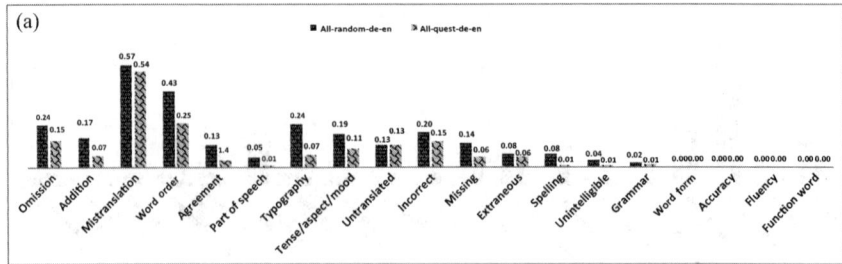

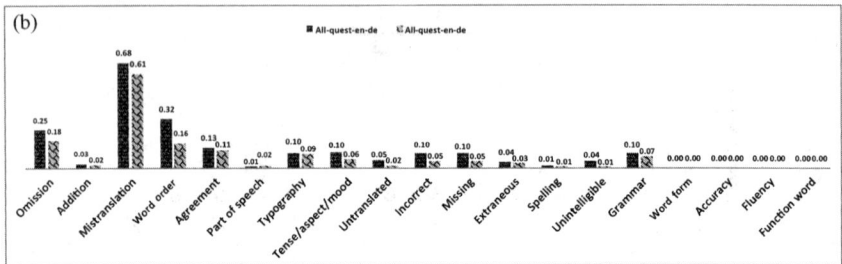

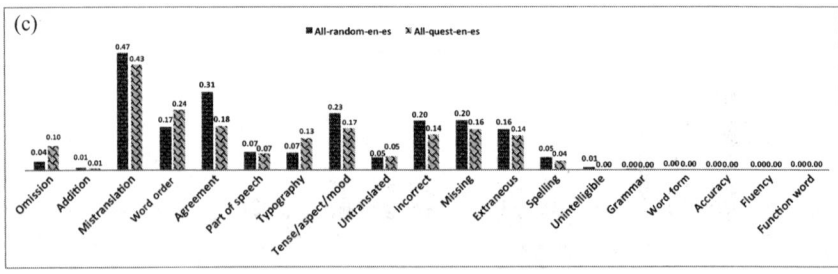

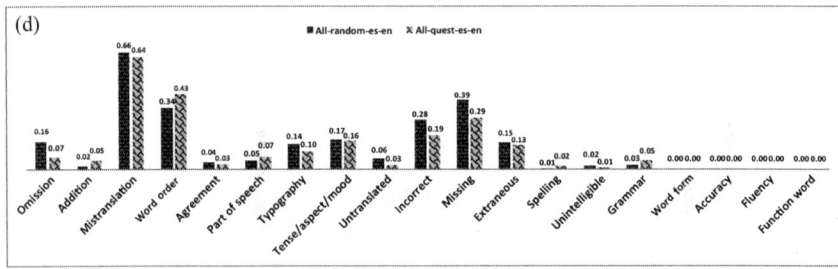

Fig. 9 Proportion of error types for all annotators per language pair, after excluding all fully unintelligible annotations as set by at least one annotator. (**a**) de-en. (**b**) en-de. (**c**) en-es. (**d**) es-en.

was to shed some light on promising practical uses of QE and on more intuitive evaluation approaches for these applications. Our focus was on sentence-level QE.

QE for predicting post-editing effort as described in Sect. 3 is perhaps the most widely studied variant of the task, with very clear application in the translation industry: translators are often required to post-edit the output of MT systems, but for many segments the effort required to fix the MT output is greater than that of translating the source segment from scratch. Filtering out these cases is very desirable to improve productivity and user experience. In addition, this information could be used to customise pricing of MT post-editing, as well as to estimate the time a post-editing job would require to be completed. Work done in this direction has showed promising results, but an important topic that is still to be researched is the investigation of the reliability and utility of quality labels in translation workflows. Preliminary experiments have been done in Turchi et al. (2015) and Specia (2011). The former focused on the usefulness of showing the translator a binary (good/bad) quality prediction for the sentence during post-editing, without performing any filtering on the MT output. The latter compared the time taken to post-edit sentences predicted to have high quality according to QE against sentences selected at random. While it showed that the QE-selected sentences can be post-edited in much shorter time, it did not factor in the translation from scratch of sentences predicted to have low quality.

The utility of QE for MT system selection can be more easily validated by checking the final quality of the selected dataset in terms of automatic metric scores such as BLEU, as was done in Sect. 4. As long as a reference set is provided to compute such metrics, this can be done automatically, without further human intervention. The results of the experiments presented in this chapter are very promising, showing that QE-selected sets are able to demonstrate improvements of up to 7.56 BLEU points over individual MT systems.

The same evaluation criterion can be used in the employment of QE for MT "self-learning" (Sect. 5). Our results using QE to select sentences predicted to have high enough quality to add to the SMT training corpus showed consistent improvements of around 1 BLEU point, which is virtually the same level of improvement obtained from adding the corresponding reference (human) translations to the SMT training corpus.

Work presented in Sect. 6 is a clear attempt to validate QE in a real-world application where the purpose is effective error annotation by human translators for quality assurance. The results of our experiments were, however, somewhat inconclusive, potentially due to the criterion used for the QE-based sampling: average quality translations. Future experiments should include selecting sets with different levels of quality, leading to a more general sample for quality assurance. This criterion is highly dependent on the objective of the error annotation process: finding the largest number of errors, annotating the largest number of segments, etc.

It is also important to mention that although we have focused on quality prediction for sentences, QE can be performed at other textual levels. QE has been gaining increasing attention at word and document levels. Word-level QE is useful for pinpointing specific errors in the words of a translated segment. It has various interesting applications, among others:

- Highlight words that need editing in post-editing tasks.
- Inform readers of portions of the sentence that are not reliable.
- Select the best words/phrases among options from multiple MT systems for system combination.
- Guide automatic post-editing.

Most of the work on word-level QE has focused on prediction of automatically derived labels. These are obtained mainly by aligning the MT output to its post-edited version, as has been done in most of the WMT shared tasks on QE (Bojar et al. 2013, 2015, 2016). To minimise the amount of annotated data that is needed and reduce data sparsity, errors are often conflated into one category, resulting in a binary classification task: correct versus incorrect target words. In 2014, the word-level QE shared task at WMT instead provided specific errors manually annotated according to 21 error categories from MQM. However, this introduced significant sparsity in the data, which made learning from it virtually impossible. Existing work exploits classification and sequence-labelling algorithms with a range of word-level and contextual features. Overall, this looks likely to remain a more challenging task. The context plays an important role in deciding whether a target word is an incorrect translation, but often words in context are also incorrect. A much larger number of examples is necessary to represent occurrences of target words in various contexts, and often the modelling is hindered by skewed class distributions: most words in a sentence tend to be correct.

Document-level QE focuses on more coarse-grained assessments to judge the overall quality of entire documents. While certain sentences are perfect in isolation, their combination in context may lead to an incoherent document. Conversely, while a sentence can be poor in isolation, when put in context it may benefit from information in surrounding sentences, leading to a good quality document. Document-level QE is needed particularly for gisting purposes where post-editing is not an option. An example application is quality prediction for translations of product reviews in order for readers to decide whether or not they are understandable and to select a subset of reviews for a given product that are good enough to be published. This level of prediction has been included in recent years as part of the WMT shared task on QE (Bojar et al. 2015, 2016), but has attracted very few participants.

Document-level QE is also very challenging as it requires annotations for quality at document level and modelling of discourse features (Scarton et al. 2015). No standard quality labels exist that capture all potential issues at document level. As for discourse features, very few processing tools are available to extract discourse-wide information. Moreover, the performance of existing tools (mostly for English) is negatively impacted by the various types of errors in the MT output.

Sentence-level QE, despite its popularity, is far from a solved problem. While extensive work has been done on feature engineering, this continues to be an active topic, with recent research showing the value of combinations of shallow and linguistically-motivated features (Bojar et al. 2016). Various approaches also explore neural models, including using them to generate features (Shah and Specia 2016) and to train prediction models (Kim and Lee 2016; Kim et al. 2017). Larger datasets have been produced in recent years (15K samples in WMT16 instead of 2.2K in WMT12), with additional post-editing data also used, where the edit distance between the original and revised MT output is taken as the quality label.

In recent years, a number of software toolkits have been made available to facilitate research and use of QE approaches. These include QuEst++ (Specia et al. 2015b), Marmot (Logacheva et al. 2016), WCE LIG (Servan et al. 2015), and Qualitative (Avramidis 2016). These tools generally differ in the feature set they extract and the type of machine-learning algorithms they provide, since they focus on different levels and types of prediction.

Overall, we believe that successful approaches to QE have immense potential to make MT more useful to end-users of various types. As a research area, many aspects of the problem require further investigation. Therefore, it is likely that QE at all levels will continue to be an active area of research, with continuing efforts by the community to push the field forward, ideally in collaboration with end-users to validate the proposed solutions.

Acknowledgements We thank Arle Lommel for his help with setting up and running the error annotation for the experiments in Sect. 6.

References

Ambati V, Vogel S, Carbonell J (2010) Active learning and crowd-sourcing for machine translation. In: Proceedings of the seventh international conference on language resources and evaluation (LREC 2010), 17–23 May 2010, Valletta, pp 2169–2174

Ananthakrishnan S, Prasad R, Stallard D, Natarajan P (2010) Discriminative sample selection for statistical machine translation. In: Proceedings of the 2010 conference on empirical methods in natural language processing (EMNLP-2010), MIT, Massachusetts, 9–11 Oct 2010, pp 626–635

Avramidis E (2013) Rankeval: open tool for evaluation of machine-learned ranking. Prague Bull Math Linguist (PBML) 100:63–72

Avramidis E (2016) Qualitative: python tool for MT quality estimation supporting server mode and hybrid MT. Prague Bull Math Linguist 106:147–158

Bach N, Huang F, Al-Onaizan Y (2011) Goodness: a method for measuring machine translation confidence. In: ACL11, Portland, pp 211–219

Banerjee P, Rubino R, Roturier J, van Genabith J (2013) Quality estimation-guided data selection for domain adaptation of SMT. In: MT summit XIV: Proceedings of the fourteenth machine translation summit, Nice, 2–6 Sept 2013. EAMT, pp 101–108

Blatz J, Fitzgerald E, Foster G, Gandrabur S, Goutte C, Kulesza A, Sanchis A, Ueffing N (2004) Confidence estimation for machine translation. In: Coling04, Geneva, pp 315–321

Bojar O, Buck C, Callison-Burch C, Federmann C, Haddow B, Koehn P, Monz C, Post M, Soricut R, Specia L (2013) Findings of the 2013 WMT. In: 8th WMT, Sofia, pp 1–44

Bojar O, Buck C, Federmann C, Haddow B, Koehn P, Monz C, Post M, Specia L (eds) (2014) Proceedings of the ninth workshop on statistical machine translation, Baltimore

Bojar O, Chatterjee R, Federmann C, Haddow B, Hokamp C, Huck M, Logacheva V, Pecina P (eds) (2015) Proceedings of the tenth workshop on statistical machine translation, Lisbon

Bojar O, Chatterjee R, Federmann C, Graham Y, Haddow B, Huck M, Jimeno Yepes A, Koehn P,
    Logacheva V, Monz C, Negri M, Neveol A, Neves M, Popel M, Post M, Rubino R, Scarton
    C, Specia L, Turchi, M, Verspoor K, Zampieri M (2016) Findings of the 2016 conference on
    machine translation. In: First conference on machine translation, volume 2: shared task papers,
    WMT, Berlin, pp 131–198
Callison-Burch C, Koehn P, Monz C, Post M, Soricut R, Specia L (2012a) Findings of the 2012
    WMT. In: WMT12, Montréal, pp 10–51
Callison-Burch C, Koehn P, Monz C, Post M, Soricut R, Specia L (eds) (2012b) Proceedings of
    the seventh workshop on statistical machine translation, Montréal
Chang CC, Lin CJ (2011) LIBSVM: a library for support vector machines. ACM Trans Intell Syst
    Technol (TIST) 2(3):27
Eck M, Vogel S, Waibel A (2005) Low cost portability for statistical machine translation based on
    N-gram frequency and TF-IDF. In: IWSLT 2005: proceedings of the international workshop on
    spoken language translation, Pittsburgh, 24–25 Oct 2005
Haffari G, Roy M, Sarkar A (2009) Active learning for statistical phrase-based machine translation.
    In: The 2009 annual conference of the North American chapter of the Association for
    Computational Linguistics. https://doi.org/10.3115/1620754.1620815
He Y, Ma Y, van Genabith J, Way A (2010) Bridging SMT and TM with translation recommenda-
    tion. In: ACL2010, Uppsala, pp 622–630
Kim H, Lee JH (2016) Recurrent neural network based translation quality estimation. In:
    Proceedings of the 1st conference on MT, pp 787–792
Kim H, Lee JH, Na SH (2017) Predictor-estimator using multilevel task learning with stack
    propagation for neural quality estimation. In: Proceedings of the 2nd conference on MT, pp
    562–568
Koehn P, Hoang H, Birch A, Callison-Burch C, Federico M, Bertoldi N, Cowan B, Shen W, Moran
    C, Zens R, Dyer C, Bojar O, Constantin A, Herbst E (2007) Moses: open source toolkit for
    statistical machine translation. In: 45th annual meeting of the Association for Computational
    Linguistics: demo and poster sessions, Prague, pp 177–180
Levenshtein VI (1966) Binary codes capable of correcting deletions, insertions
    and reversals. Sov Phys Dokl 10(8):707–710. https://www.bibsonomy.org/bibtex/
    220546d80ce76f58c6ef6ece9dd5f5056/jimregan
Logacheva V, Specia L (2014) A quality-based active sample selection strategy for statistical
    machine translation. In: Chair NCC, Choukri K, Declerck T, Loftsson H, Maegaard B, Mariani
    J, Moreno A, Odijk J, Piperidis S (eds) Proceedings of the ninth international conference
    on language resources and evaluation (LREC'14). European Language Resources Association
    (ELRA), Reykjavik
Logacheva V, Hokamp C, Specia L (2016) Marmot: a toolkit for translation quality estimation
    at the word level. In: Tenth international conference on language resources and evaluation,
    Portoroz, pp 3671–3674
Lommel A, Popovic M, Burchardt A (2014) Assessing inter-annotator agreement for translation
    error annotation. In: Automatic and manual metrics for operational translation evaluation
    workshop programme, p 5
Och FJ (2003) Minimum error rate training in statistical machine translation. In: Proceedings of the
    41st annual meeting on Association for Computational Linguistics, ACL '03, Sapporo, vol 1.
    Association for Computational Linguistics, Stroudsburg, pp 160–167. https://doi.org/10.3115/
    1075096.1075117
Papineni K, Roukos S, Ward T, Zhu WJ (2002) BLEU: a method for automatic evaluation of
    machine translation. In: ACL02, Philadelphia, pp 311–318
Quang LN, Laurent B, Benjamin L (2014) LIG system for word level QE task at WMT14. In:
    Workshop on machine translation (WMT)
Rasmussen CE, Williams CKI (2006) Gaussian processes for machine learning. The MIT Press,
    Cambridge, MA

Scarton C, Zampieri M, Vela M, van Genabith J, Specia L (2015) Searching for context: a study on document-level labels for translation quality estimation. In: 18th annual conference of the European Association for machine translation, Antalya, pp 121–128

Servan C, Le NT, Luong NQ, Lecouteux B, Besacier L (2015) An open source toolkit for word-level confidence estimation in machine translation. In: 12th international workshop on spoken language translation, Da Nang

Settles B (2010) Active learning literature survey. Computer sciences technical report 1648, University of Wisconsin, Madison

Shah K, Specia L (2016) Large-scale multitask learning for machine translation quality estimation. In: Conference of the North American chapter of the association for computational linguistics: human language technologies, San Diego, pp 558–567. http://www.aclweb.org/anthology/N16-1069

Shah K, Cohn T, Specia L (2013) An investigation on the effectiveness of features for translation quality estimation. In: Machine translation summit XIV, Nice, pp 167–174

Shah K, Cohn T, Specia L (2015) A Bayesian non-linear method for feature selection in machine translation quality estimation. Mach Translat 125. https://doi.org/10.1007/s10590-014-9164-x

Soricut R, Echihabi A (2010) TrustRank: inducing trust in automatic translations via ranking. In: ACL11, Uppsala, pp 612–621

Specia L (2011) Exploiting objective annotations for measuring translation post-editing effort. In: EAMT11, Leuven, pp 73–80

Specia L, Turchi M, Cancedda N, Dymetman M, Cristianini N (2009) Estimating the sentence-level quality of machine translation systems. In: EAMT09, Barcelona, pp 28–37

Specia L, Raj D, Turchi M (2010) Machine translation evaluation versus quality estimation. Mach Translat 24:39–50

Specia L, Shah K, Souza JGCD, Cohn T (2013, to appear) QuEst – a translation quality estimation framework. In: Proceedings of ACL demo session

Specia L, Paetzold G, Scarton C (2015a) Multi-level translation quality prediction with quest++. In: ACL-IJCNLP 2015 system demonstrations, Beijing, pp 115–120

Specia L, Paetzold GH, Scarton C (2015b) Multi-level translation quality prediction with quest++. In: Proceedings of the 53rd ACL

Turchi M, Negri M, Federico M (2015) MT quality estimation for computer-assisted translation: does it really help? In: 53rd annual meeting of the association for computational linguistics, Beijing, pp 530–535

Machine Translation and Self-post-editing for Academic Writing Support: Quality Explorations

10

Sharon O'Brien, Michel Simard, and Marie-Josée Goulet

Abstract Scholars who need to publish in English and who have English as a Foreign Language might consider and already be deploying free online MT engines to aid their writing processes. This raises the obvious question of whether MT is actually a useful aid for academic writing and what impact it might have on the quality of the written product. The work described in this chapter attempts to address these two broad questions. After a brief introduction, Sect. 2 reviews literature on three topics: English as a *lingua franca* in academic writing and the consequences this might have for individual authors and for academic disciplines, second-language writing, and the use of MT as a second-language writing aid. In Sect. 3, the methodology is presented. As will be detailed, the experiment involved ten participants, who were asked to write an abstract in their field of expertise. One half of the text was written in English, while the other half was written in their L1 and then machine-translated into English. Section 4 describes the results: subjective feedback of the participants acquired through a post-task survey, revision activity of a professional reviser, number and types of errors identified by a grammar-checking tool. The results suggest that MT and self-post-editing did not impact negatively on the text produced. However, the participants were divided in their opinions about which task was easier and whether they would consider using MT again for academic writing support. In Sect. 5, we offer a discussion on those results and provide future research ideas.

S. O'Brien
ADAPT Centre/School of Applied Language and Intercultural Studies, Dublin City University, Dublin, Ireland
e-mail: sharon.obrien@dcu.ie

M. Simard
National Research Council, Ottawa, ON, Canada
e-mail: Michel.Simard@cnrc-nrc.gc.ca

M.-J. Goulet
Université du Québec en Outaouais, Gatineau, QC, Canada
e-mail: marie-josee.goulet@uqo.ca

Keywords Translation quality assessment · Principles to practice · English as a
foreign language · Machine translation · Post-editing · Second-language writing
support · Self-post-editing · Academic writing

1 Introduction

This chapter presents an exploratory study of the potential of Machine Translation
(MT) and self-post-editing (self-PE) to support the academic writing process
for authors for whom English is a foreign language (EFL). Many scholars find
themselves in the position where they have to write in a foreign language (FL) in
order to publish and disseminate their research, which in turn is linked with career
success factors. As elaborated in Sect. 2, this language is predominantly English,
and having to write in EFL in order to be published arguably creates a disadvantage.

With recent improvements in MT technology and with free online MT engines
becoming available, the use of MT has become more pervasive both in general and
in the translation industry. However, MT is still not good enough to produce high-
quality output for all languages, all types of text, and in all contexts. Consequently,
post-editing, or the fixing of errors in MT output, has to take place if the MT output
is to be brought beyond 'gisting level' quality, i.e. a quality level that allows the
reader to get a basic idea, or gist, of the intended meaning.

The task of post-editing and its role in professional translation practice has
received much attention in the last while (see, for example, Garcia 2010, 2011;
Guerberof 2012; O'Brien et al. 2012, 2013, 2014a; Green et al. 2013; O'Brien
and Simard 2014, 2015; Gaspari et al. 2014; O'Brien et al. 2014b; Carl et al.
2015, among many others). Also, the use of MT by lay users has received some
attention (Hu et al. 2011; Tatsumi et al. 2012; Mitchell et al. 2014). To the best of
our knowledge, the use of MT by scholars for academic writing purposes has not
been studied to any extent. Yet, we assume that scholars who need to publish in
English and who have English as a Foreign Language might consider and already
be deploying free online MT engines to aid their writing processes. This raises
the obvious question of whether MT is actually a useful aid for academic writing
and what impact it might have on the quality of the written product. The work
described here attempts to address these two broad questions. Since no evidence
exists to demonstrate that these questions have already been researched, the study
is necessarily exploratory in nature. In our conclusion, we present plans for future
work that will go beyond the explorations here.

The structure of this chapter is as follows: In Sect. 2.1 we review literature on
the topic of English as a *lingua franca* in academic writing and the consequences
this might have for individual authors and for academic disciplines. In Sect. 2.2,
relevant literature on second-language writing is reviewed to give an overview of
the challenges involved in this activity. We then present the limited research to date
on the use of MT as a second-language writing aid. Following this overview of
relevant literature, we present the methodology for our exploratory study in Sect. 3,
followed by the results (Sect. 4). Our concluding section summarises the results and
outlines questions and ideas for expanding on this topic (Sect. 5).

2   Literature Review

2.1   English As Lingua franca in Academic Writing

English, according to Bennett (2013, 2014a, 2015), is indisputably the *lingua franca* of academia and non-native-English speakers are discriminated against by editors and referees of international journals. This point is emphasised by Flowerdew (2001) who suggests that non-native-speakers of English are not only disadvantaged, but that this disadvantage goes against natural justice and is likely to impoverish creation of knowledge. Flowerdew argues that by publishing work by non-native speakers of English in journals, focus can be removed from the dominant 'centre' and new perspectives can be attained.

Bennett (2014a) discusses the centripetal and centrifugal pulls that academics in the semi-periphery experience, with the former pulling them towards English-language international publication outlets and the latter pulling them towards more regional publications in their own language. The centripetal pull is gaining in strength as universities and government funding agencies link publications in international journals ever more closely with career advancement and funding. In a survey of 1717 Spanish researchers across different domains, a strong association was found between publication in English and the desire to be recognised and rewarded (López-Navarro et al. 2015).

The pressure to publish in English means that non-native speakers sometimes have to resort to the services of 'literacy brokers' (Lillis and Curry 2010; Bennett 2014a, b), that is editors, revisers, and translators, and sometimes academics from the same or from other disciplines, so that their articles can be made suitable for publication in international journals. According to a survey by Benfield and Feak (2006) for a specific medical journal, although the acceptance rate was the same for authors who were not native speakers of English, many more revisions were required for the articles submitted by this cohort. Literacy brokers may not, however, be a complete solution as they may not possess adequate domain knowledge and might have to enter into discussion with the author in order to clarify issues (Willey and Tanimoto 2015). Resorting to literacy brokers, then, costs time and money.

We are interested in investigating the role MT can play in the geopolitics of academic publishing. MT could facilitate the writing of academic articles in the L1, with subsequent automatic translation and self-PE. A potential advantage is that this process of L1 writing, MT and self-PE could lower the cognitive burden of writing in English and might remove the need for 'literacy brokers' in the publication cycle, thereby reducing publication time and cost. The assumption here is that an acceptable level of quality can be produced during this process and that is the specific question we wish to explore here: If MT is used in combination with self-PE, does it have a negative, positive or neutral effect on the quality of academic writing, when compared with text produced by the same author writing in EFL? We assume that if the quality is lower MT is not a useful academic writing aid for EFL writers.

2.2   Second-Language Writing

This section reviews some relevant studies on second-language writing and gives an overview of the challenges involved in this activity. First, Breuer (2015) examined the differences in the writing processes in L1 and FL academic writing. Her study involved ten L1 German students of English philology. The participants had to write two essays in L1 and two essays in FL, in two different contexts, that is, planning by note-taking and planning by freewriting. The analysis was focused on fluency, error types and revisions. The results show that freewriting in both languages had an enhancing effect, but this enhancing effect was stronger in L1. According to Breuer (2015), this result points to a stronger ability to think via writing in L1. However, the essays written in L1 did not contain fewer errors, nor was revision more effective.

Van Waes and Leijten (2015) also compared fluency in L1 and L2. Sixty-eight university students participated in their experiment, which consisted of writing one expository text in L1 (Dutch) and one expository text in L2 (English, French, German, or Spanish). Data was collected with Inputlog 5,[1] a keystroke-logging program developed to collect all keyboard and mouse activities during text production. To cite just a few results, the students typed more words per minute in their first language, they needed less pausing time than in L2, and the pausing time was shorter. In the conclusion, the authors affirm that the students were more productive when writing texts in L1, versus L2.

For their part, Hanauer and Englander (2011) approached the subject differently and asked 141 Mexican scientists (L1 Spanish) to reflect on the burden of writing academic papers in EFL. In a six-question survey, the participants had to rate, on a scale from 1 to 7, the difficulty, the dissatisfaction, and the anxiety to write academic papers in English and in Spanish. The results clearly show that all three aspects were rated higher for EFL and those statistics are highly significant. According to the authors, the study confirms that EFL academic writing can be challenging, and that this added burden of second-language academic writing is linguistic in nature. However, the authors admit that their "findings are limited to the self-reported and perceived burden of Mexican scientists and perhaps not to all scientists writing in a second language" (Hanauer and Englander, 2011). For example, there could be differences stemming from exposure to English, seniority, discipline, linguistic, and ethnic community.

From this brief review, we can conclude that not only is academic writing in EFL perceived as being a burden, but also that it may be easier to think in L1 while writing an academic paper and that writing in L1 may be more productive. These are reasonable justifications to explore the potential of MT and self-PE to support the academic writing process for authors for whom English is a foreign language.

---

[1]http://www.inputlog.net

2.3 MT and Second-Language Writing

Second-language teaching and learning has a long tradition of using technology for writing, for example grammar checkers (Omar et al. 2009; Cowan et al. 2014), text correctors (Zakaria et al. 2010), and visualisation tools (Nukoolkit et al. 2011). A meta-analysis of 59 studies published between 2000 and 2012 (Lin 2015) demonstrated that computer-mediated communication tools, such as blogs and wikis, have a positive effect on language learning, especially in the acquisition of writing skills. However, MT was not included in this meta-analysis. In this section, we summarise the main recent studies that focused on the use of MT in second-language writing.

Garcia and Pena (2011) aimed to discover whether Spanish learners would communicate better and learn more if they wrote directly in the L2 or with the help of MT. Their study involved 16 native speakers of English, of which 9 were beginner Spanish learners and 7 were early-intermediate. The experiment included 2 short writing tasks, of 50 words for beginners and 100 words for early intermediates. The participants used the MT Tradukka[2] interface and both tasks were timed, at 15 min each. The tests were screen-recorded (cursor movements and keyboard log), and two markers scored the final texts.

First, the analysis reveals that the beginners wrote more words with the help of MT. Also, on average the texts written with the help of MT obtained higher scores than the ones written directly in L2. According to Garcia and Pena (2011), these results suggest that MT could help the beginner learner to communicate more and to communicate better in the L2. In the second part of the analysis, the authors show that there are more pauses when the participants write directly in L2, compared with being assisted by MT. Taking pauses as an indication of effort, the authors conclude that it takes less effort to write in L2 with the help of MT. Furthermore, the authors did not find a definite pattern of edits, that is, there was a similar number of interventions made when writing with MT as when writing directly in L2. However, the analysis of the edits suggests that a relation exists between intermediate learners and a greater number of *successful* edits.

In his doctoral dissertation, O'Neill (2012) investigated the quantitative and qualitative effects of using online MT systems on L2 writing. The study was conducted with 32 university students having English as L1 and learning French as a second-language. The experiment included three different scenarios: participants who were allowed to use an online MT system for their writing after attending a training session on MT; participants who were permitted to use online MT for their writing, but who had received no prior training; and a control group whose participants had no training and were not allowed to use an online MT system. Participants were asked to write two short compositions, which were evaluated by raters (teachers of French as a second-language) using six features:

---

[2]http://tradukka.com

comprehensibility, content, spelling, syntax, grammar, and vocabulary. The results show that the global scores of the translation group that had received training were statistically higher on the second task as compared to the control group. Also, on both tasks, the translator groups significantly outperformed the control group on four of the six aspects evaluated. The participants' self-reports in the exit questionnaire indicated that the online MT system was used for varying purposes and to different extents, ranging from searching for isolated words to translating entire paragraphs. While we can assume that some post-editing was done in the latter case, the students' edits were not analysed in O'Neill (2012).

In Niño's study (2008), the experiment involved 32 participants, all advanced learners of Spanish and native speakers of English. Participants from the experimental group were given the source text in English and the raw MT output translated by *Systran Professional Standard 3.0* into Spanish. They were then asked to post-edit the text. Students in this group attended a ten-session course on MT post-editing. For their part, participants from the control group performed translation of the same source texts, from English into Spanish. The texts were manually corrected.[3] The results of this study indicate that the error types found in the post-edited MT output are not very different from those found in translation into the same target-language. Niño's analysis also shows that the scores of the students in both the post-editing and translation groups were very similar with regard to lexical, grammatical and discursive errors. Based on those results, we can conclude that MT post-editing into L2, at least for advanced learners of the target-language, does not produce lower quality outputs.

In conclusion, the studies summarised here demonstrate that the use of MT in second-language writing does not negatively impact the quality (Niño 2008). In fact, the use of MT has helped produce better quality texts (Garcia and Pena 2011; O'Neill 2012), and with less effort in one case (Garcia and Pena 2011).

2.4   General Conclusions from the Literature Review

The literature review presented here demonstrates that there are considerable challenges for academics who wish to, or are compelled to, publish in English when English is not their first language. A body of research exists on the use of technology in general as a language-learning aid, which suggests that technology has a positive effect on language learning, especially in the acquisition of writing skills. The few studies we could find on MT as an aid for second-language writing all suggest that MT does not have a negative impact on quality. However, we could not locate any research on the use of MT as a technological aid for the EFL academic writing process. This inspired the exploratory study, described below, which aims to discover whether MT might be a useful aid for the EFL writing process. We focus

---

[3]It is not explicitly stated in the paper, but we assume that the author corrected the texts herself.

in particular on the topic of quality to see if the text produced by EFL academic writers is the same, better or worse in terms of quality when compared with what those writers produce when writing directly in EFL.

3 Methodology

We designed an experiment with the goal of exploring the effect of using MT as an aid for writing academic texts in EFL. Following the granting of ethical approval, we recruited participants, and asked them to write a short (500-word) academic abstract in their field of expertise. This writing process took place in two distinct stages. During Stage 1, participants produced a first draft of their text: they were asked to write roughly one half of the text in English (their FL), and the rest in their native language (L1), with the order of production randomised. Then, in Stage 2, the part drafted in L1 was machine-translated into English, the full abstract was returned to the participant and we asked the participant to revise this new version, in order to produce a final version, entirely in English. We present below the details of this procedure.

3.1 Recruitment and Selection of Participants

In order to recruit participants, we sent emails to colleagues at Dublin City University, Université du Québec en Outaouais, and other universities and research centres. The email stated that we were exploring the potential benefits of using MT as a writing aid for early-stage researchers who are not native speakers of English, and that we were looking for academic researchers at PhD or early post-doc level who ordinarily have to write their research outputs in English. We estimated that participation would take approximately 4 hours of the participants' time, spread over a six-week period. Participants who completed all stages of the study would receive a 70-euro gift certificate for a well-known online retailer, as a compensation for their time. The invitation email provided a link to a website where interested candidates could fill in a short pre-participation survey. This questionnaire was designed to help us in selecting participants with appropriate and varied profiles, for example with regard to mother tongue and level of experience in academic writing. The pre-participation survey was also used to ask the potential candidates which of the following task(s) they would be willing to undertake:

- Write a 500 word summary of your PhD research,
- Write a 500 word abstract for a paper you are working on,
- Write a 500 word proposal for a future research project.

The pre-participation questionnaire is available in Appendix A.

3.2 Stage 1: Drafting

The experiment was divided into two stages. For each stage, participants were provided with detailed instructions. In Stage 1, participants were asked to write a 500-word abstract for a paper, PhD thesis or research proposal that they were working on. The nature of the text was determined based on each participant's preference (as formulated in the pre-task questionnaire); in the absence of a unique preference, we decided on the text type, aiming for diversity. We told the participants to treat this version as a first draft and that they would revise it at a later stage.

The participants were asked to divide their abstract into two parts, A and B, following the general structure outlined below:

Part A (approx. 250 words) should contain:

- Title: Give the (working) title that clearly indicates what the research is about,
- Background: Sentences putting the work in context,
- Motivation: Rationale for this research work.

Part B (approx. 250 words) should contain:

- Methods: Sentences that explain how the research was or will be done,
- Impact: Sentences that explain the (expected) impact of your findings for your domain, science and/or society.

Furthermore, participants were asked to write one part in their L1, the other in English. We provided each participant with personal instructions as to which part to write in which language: six of the ten participants were asked to write Part A in English and Part B in L1, the remaining four were asked to do the opposite. This was done to avoid the contents or the language order biasing the results.

Finally, the participants were asked to record the total time taken to write each part, and to note down any resources they used. They were allowed to use any resources available (dictionaries, spell-checker, etc.) to produce the abstract, except MT systems or colleagues/acquaintances.

3.3 Stage 2: Revision

Upon receiving the text produced by a participant, we used Google Translate[4] to translate into English the part written in L1, and substituted the result to produce a new version of the abstract, entirely in English. This new version was sent back to the participant, along with the instructions for Stage 2, explaining that the part of their abstract that was written in L1 had been machine-translated into English, and asking them to revise the text to create well-formed academic English for their

---

[4]https://translate.google.com

abstract. They were told to treat this revised abstract as a final version. We provided participants with the following revision guidelines:

- Aim for grammatically correct sentences,
- Ensure that terminology is correctly translated,
- Ensure that no information has been accidentally added, omitted or left untranslated,
- Apply the basic rules regarding spelling and punctuation.

The participants could also revise the part originally written in English, if they wished. If they did so, they were asked to record how much time this revision task took. As in Stage 1, the participants were allowed to use any resources available (dictionaries, spell-checker, etc.) to revise the abstract, except MT systems or colleagues/acquaintances, and they were asked to note down any resources they used.

3.4   Post-participation Survey

Upon receiving their revised abstract, each participant was asked to answer a short post-task questionnaire, intended to reflect their general impressions of the experience. The questions of this survey and the participants' answers are presented in the next section.

4   Results

The results are presented in four sections. Section 4.1 outlines the profiles of the participants in our experiment, as collected through the pre-task questionnaire. Section 4.2 provides results from the subjective feedback of the participants acquired through a post-task survey. In Sect. 4.3 we present results from the revision activity of a professional reviser, which we use as a form of quality assessment. The fourth Sect. 4.4, presents results from an automatic language-checking tool, Antidote, which is also used here as a form of contrastive quality assessment for the two parts written in L1 or EFL.

4.1   Participants' Profile

In practice, faced with the difficulty of recruiting enough candidates, we did not perform any selection, and all 14 candidates who filled in the pre-participation questionnaire were included as participants in the study, even though some did not entirely fit our initial criteria. Of these 14 participants, three did not complete all stages of the study, and one was discarded because they had not properly followed the instructions. Below is a summary of the profiles of the ten remaining participants.

Participants came from varied linguistic backgrounds. Their native languages (L1) were as follows: Arabic (1), Chinese (1), French (4), German (1), Romanian (1), or Spanish (2). They worked in one of the following research fields: applied engineering (1), biotechnology (3), chemistry (1), geology (1), marketing (1), psychology (2), and social sciences (1). Most participants were PhD students (7), but we also recruited one graduate assistant, one post-doctoral researcher, and one established faculty member. Half of our participants (5) had substantial experience in English academic writing, having written between 8 and 12 academic papers, posters or equivalent in English. The rest had little or no such experience (0 or 1 paper). When asked to self-rate their language competence in English, six candidates rated themselves as "Intermediate", one as "Intermediate-Advanced" and three as "Advanced". None of the participants rated themselves as "Beginner" or "Expert" (see descriptions for these labels in the pre-task questionnaire in Appendix A). Four of the ten participants reported that they had used MT previously to produce a first draft academic English text. Two participants wrote an abstract for an article, four wrote an abstract for their PhD thesis, and four wrote an abstract for a research proposal.

4.2   Post-task Survey Results

For space reasons, we do not report on all of the responses to the post-task survey in detail here, but summarise the most salient aspects (see Appendix B for full survey). Table 1 provides the number of minutes reported by the participants for both tasks. Participants P1, P3 and P9 did not follow the instructions to record the amount of time it took them to draft both sections of text, but the timings are available for all other participants.

As we can see, the drafting tasks did not vary substantially in the time required. The median time for L1 drafting was 44 min, while the median for EFL drafting was 45, though the ranges were large for both tasks (20–180 min for L1 drafting and 21–140 min for EFL drafting).

Task	Average	Median	Range
Time for L1 drafting (min)	63	44	20–180
Time for EFL drafting (min)	65	45	21–140
Time for L1 revision (min)	30	18.5	7–75
Time for EFL revision (min)	11	6.5	0–60

Table 1 Number of minutes reported by participants for drafting and revising in both tasks
EFL English as Foreign Language, *L1* first language of participant

Participant	Which section was easier to draft?	Which section was easier to revise?	Which section resulted in better quality?
P1	No difference	L1-MT/PE	No difference
P2	L2-EFL	L2-EFL	L2-EFL
P3	L2-EFL	No difference	No difference
P4	L2-EFL	L2-EFL	L2-EFL
P5	L1-MT/PE	No difference	No difference
P6	L2-EFL	L2-EFL	L2-EFL
P8	No difference	L1-MT/PE	No difference
P9	L2-EFL	L2-EFL	No difference
P11	L1-MT/PE	L2-EFL	No difference
P14	L1-MT/PE	L1-MT/PE	L1-MT/PE

Table 2 Results on the participants' perceptions on drafting and revising in L1-MT/PE and L2-EFL

For the revision/post-editing stage of the process, the temporal differences across the two tasks were more pronounced. For clarity and conciseness, we will refer to these revision processes in the following way: L1-MT/PE refers to the process of writing in the L1, followed by MT and self-post-editing; L2-EFL refers to the process of writing directly in English as a Foreign Language. The median time in minutes for revision of the part written in the L1-MT/PE was 18.5 (range: 7–75 min), whereas the median for revision of the part written in L2-EFL was only 6.5 min (range: 0–60). Nine out of ten participants took less time to revise the L2-EFL part than the L1-MT/PE part.

The post-task survey included questions about the perception of difficulty for drafting and revision for both tasks. Table 2 presents the results from this part of the survey. As shown in Table 2, half the participants found the L2-EFL task easier than the L1-MT/PE task. Three found it easier to draft in their L1, while two stated that the tasks were equal in terms of effort. Likewise, half the participants found revising the L2-EFL text easier than the L1-MT-PE text. Three found it easier to self-post-edit, while two stated that the revision tasks were equal in terms of effort.

Subjective evaluations by participants of the final quality of the texts they produced suggest that only three participants thought that the quality they produced was better for L2-EFL. One person thought the quality was better for L1-MT/PE and the remaining six felt that the quality produced was equal for both tasks.

These perceptions are correlated against three additional quality evaluations:

- Number of revisions implemented by a professional reviser for Parts A and B of each text (see Sect. 4.3),
- A ranking task performed by the reviser after she had carried out the revisions (see Sect. 4.3),
- Number and types of errors identified by Antidote, a grammar checking tool (see Sect. 4.4).

When asked what specific difficulties they encountered for the L1-MT/PE task, some participants mentioned that they were unused to typing in their L1 both from a cognitive perspective (i.e. thinking) and from a physical perspective (i.e. keyboarding) and that they struggled to find the appropriate terminology for their subject domain in their L1.

Participants were asked how likely they were to use MT and self-PE to write an academic text in English in the future, on a scale of 1–4 (1 = never again; 4 = every time). One person responded that they will never use MT for this purpose, four people are not likely to use MT frequently, based on this assessment (L1s: 2 = French, 1 = Spanish, 1 = Chinese), but four others (L1s: 1 = French, 1 = German, 1 = Romanian, 1 = Spanish) may use it often and one person (L1: French) said that they would use it every time.

It is obviously not possible to generalise with such a small cohort, but we can see from these results that the L1 does not seem to play a role in deciding whether or not MT would be used every time in the future for similar tasks, or not at all. At the same time, it is worth noting that the one participant who said that they would never use MT for this purpose again has Arabic as an L1 and commented on the vast differences in sentence structure between Arabic and English as a problem. Those who were in the middle (2 and 3) seemed somewhat surprised at the benefits of using MT, according to the comments they made.

Based on our post-task survey data, we can say that the ten participants had mixed views about the two different tasks. Some rated the first task easier while others thought the second was easier and others again found them both equal. The participants also had varied views on whether the first or second task produced better quality or were of equal quality. The two notable difficulties when writing in L1 was that the participants were not used to doing so, since English is the *lingua franca* for their domains, and they struggled with finding appropriate terminology in their L1s. The participants also had mixed views on whether they would use MT and PE for similar tasks again, but the majority seemed impressed by the quality and utility of the MT output.

4.3 Professional Reviser's Edits

The results presented in Sect. 4.2 are self-reported and rely on perception, with the exception of the times recorded for each task. To ensure a more objective quality evaluation of the abstracts, a professional reviser was engaged to revise each of the abstracts. This professional reviser is paid to do this kind of task on a regular basis.

The reviser was first asked to revise each abstract according to the following brief:

> We are looking for a surface revision, that is, grammar, orthography, punctuation, syntax, and major stylistic problems. We would like the abstracts to read well enough to be submitted to a scientific conference, for example.

The reviser was unaware of the L1 or EFL status of the authors of the abstracts. She was also unaware that one part of each abstract had been machine-translated and self-post-edited. For this task, each abstract was presented to her as a single text, without sections marked as Part A and Part B.

We present here an analysis of the edits performed by the professional reviser. Individual edits were identified by automatically computing the *edit distance* between each participant's final version of his/her abstract, and the reviser's corresponding final version. This was done using a variant of the Wagner and Fischer (1974) algorithm for determining the minimal number of edits (insertions, deletions or substitutions) required to produce the revised version. This procedure is similar to what is used in typical text-comparison software, such as Microsoft Word's version comparison function, or online tools such as DiffChecker.[5] For this analysis, we considered edit operations over whole word tokens: deleting a word, inserting a word or changing a word each count for a single edit operation. Furthermore, we considered punctuation marks as individual words: inserting or deleting a comma, or changing a period into a question mark, also counts as a single edit operation. Table 3 presents the results of this analysis.

For the L1-MT/PE parts, the total number of edits by the professional reviser across all abstracts was 178, whereas for the L2-EFL parts, the total number of edits was 239. This represents changes to 6.9% (L1) and 8.3% (EFL) of the total number of tokens in each part, across all abstracts (see Table 3). We conclude from this that the number of edits made by the professional reviser for both text parts do not differ substantially, which suggests that both parts were of comparable quality.

	L1-MT/PE part			L2-EFL part		
Participant	No. of words	No. of edits	No. of edits/no. of words (%)	No. of words	No. of edits	No. of edits/no. of words (%)
P1	248	2	0.8	360	22	6.1
P2	299	50	16.7	285	21	7.4
P3	295	12	4.1	289	25	8.6
P4	282	2	0.7	337	10	3.0
P5	251	24	9.6	266	15	5.6
P6	273	12	4.4	264	21	8.0
P8	251	13	5.2	278	47	16.9
P9	248	27	10.9	258	30	11.6
P11	233	13	5.6	289	35	12.1
P14	187	23	12.3	240	13	5.4
Total	**2567**	**178**	**6.9**	**2866**	**239**	**8.3**

Table 3 Number of edits made by the professional reviser, for each part of the texts

---

[5]https://www.diffchecker.com/

Participant	Which part is better quality according to the reviser?	Which part is better quality according to the participant?	Agreement?
P1	No difference	No difference	Yes
P2	L2-EFL	L2-EFL	Yes
P3	No difference	No difference	Yes
P4	L2-EFL	L2-EFL	Yes
P5	No difference	No difference	Yes
P6	No difference	L2-EFL	No
P8	L1-MT/PE	No difference	No
P9	No difference	No difference	Yes
P11	L1-MT/PE	No difference	No
P14	L2-EFL	L1-MT/PE	No

Table 4 Participants' and reviser's quality ratings

On completion of this task, the professional reviser was given a second task. The abstracts were returned to her with Parts A and B marked this time. The brief she was given was as follows:

> Please read the following text and evaluate the quality of each part. You should not concentrate on the content or on the structure of the text, but rather on its linguistic form. For example, you can use the following criteria: grammar, syntax, orthography, punctuation, style, idiomaticity, appropriate level of language, etc.

Please indicate whether:

- Part A is of better quality than Part B,
- Part B is of better quality than Part A,
- There is no difference in quality between Part A and Part B.

Please do the evaluation without referring to your previous corrections.

In Table 4, we present the results from this evaluation and compare them with the participants' evaluation.

For five abstracts, the professional reviser stated that there was no difference in terms of quality. In three cases, she judged the part produced by L2-EFL to be of better quality and in two cases, she judged the part produced using L1-MT/PE to be of better quality.

When we compare the reviser's perceptions with the quality ratings given by the participants, we note a good level of agreement, i.e. the reviser and participants agree in six cases (P1, P2, P3, P4, P5, P9), as illustrated in Table 4.

By quantifying the number of edits made by the professional reviser, we conclude that there are no substantial differences between those parts of the abstracts written in L1 and those written in EFL. However, we note that the range for number of edits is relatively large (2–50 for L1-MT/PE and 10–47 for L2-EFL), suggesting that individuals and/or language combinations may well be a factor here. The professional reviser's assessment suggests that there is no evidence that one writing method systematically produces better quality than the other. Furthermore, this assessment reflected that of the participants themselves. We take from this that the use of MT and self-PE as a writing aid did not negatively affect the perceived quality of the written product for this particular set of participants and texts.

4.4 Errors Reported by an Automatic Grammar and Style Checker (Antidote)

Antidote[6] is an automatic grammar and style checker available for both French and English. It includes an automatic grammar and style checker, detailed dictionaries and built-in style guidelines. The version used in this study was V.9 for English.

Antidote was used as an additional, and objective, measure of quality since both measures mentioned above involve an element of subjectivity. Furthermore, it is not unrealistic that, for L1 and EFL, writers might use this kind of tool to check for issues when writing for academic publication (see for example Omar et al. 2009; Zakaria et al. 2010; Cowan et al. 2014).

The three error types identified by Antidote which we deemed to be relevant for this study were 'Language', 'Typography' and 'Style'. For the 'Language' category, the error types reported are 'errors', 'unknown words' and 'ambiguities'. 'Errors' refer to cases such as singular/plural mismatch, incorrect compounding (when words should form compounds but do not, or vice versa), incorrect hyphenation and spelling (in general and depending on the dictionary selected: American or British English). Unknown words are words that are not in Antidote's dictionaries and ambiguities are occurrences where ambiguity could arise, when a word is not hyphenated as a modifier, 'decision-making' vs. 'decision making' for example. The 'Typography' category picks up on missing or unnecessary spaces, e.g. missing space before a measurement unit such as 'mm', and on nested parentheses. Style is a somewhat more subjective category that highlights, for example, repetition of words, nested phrases, passive voice, informal register, regionalisms, and use of commonplace verbs. Whether or not these are treated as errors largely depends on the language, writing conventions in general, text type and accepted practice in a domain.

We ran Antidote for Parts A and B for each abstract and recorded all of the errors reported in a spreadsheet. The version of abstract used was that version before the professional reviser implemented any corrections as we assumed that the latter version should, theoretically, not contain *any* errors. We then assessed whether the error was, in fact, a 'valid' error (i.e. the precision of the tool). For instance, when Antidote proposed that 'are' should be corrected to 'is' under the category of 'Language', we viewed the context. If this was a valid correction, it was counted as such. If not, it was counted as an invalid correction. If a word was listed as 'unknown', this was counted as a valid error if it was a typo, for example, but not if it was a specialised term that was simply not in Antidote's dictionary (e.g. 'polymerizable'). If in doubt about the validity of the word, we checked via a Google search to see if it arose in the context of the abstract domain. The same strategy was used for the error categories 'Typography' and 'Style'. In this way, data was collected on the total number of errors recorded for each error type and the number of valid errors. Table 5 presents the results of this analysis.

---

[6]http://www.antidote.info/antidote

		Total	Average	Median	Range
L1-MT/PE					
Language	No. of errors reported by Antidote	109	10.9	10	4–19
	No. of valid errors	22	2.2	1.5	0–7
	Total no. of words	2341			
Typography	No. of errors reported by Antidote	18	1.8	0.5	0–8
	No. of valid errors	8	0.8	0	0–3
Style	No. of errors reported by Antidote	228	22.8	23.5	13–33
	No. of valid errors	0	0	0	0–0
L2-EFL					
Language	No. of errors reported by Antidote	154	15.4	13.5	5–34
	No. of valid errors	30	3	3	1–6
	Total no. of words	2596			
Typography	No. of errors reported by Antidote	50	5	1	0–22
	No. of valid errors	23	2.3	1	0–17
Style	No. of errors reported by Antidote	261	26.1	26	16–40
	No. of valid errors	1	0.1	0	0–1

Table 5 Analysis of errors from Antidote

Text production type	Total no. of words produced	Total no. of valid errors	Normalised error count per 1000 words
L1-MT/PE	2567	30	11.7
L2-EFL	2866	54	18.8

Table 6 Normalised valid error count per 1000 words

Language Errors

For those parts of the abstracts that were written in L1-MT/PE, the median number of valid errors reported by Antidote was 1.5 (range 0–7). The median for the parts drafted in L2-EFL was higher at 3 (range 1–6).

Typography Errors

For this category, the median number of valid errors reported by Antidote for the L1-MT/PE sections was 0 (range 0–3); for the L2-EFL sections, the median was 1 (range 0–17).

Stylistic Errors

We judged the stylistic errors reported by Antidote to be largely invalid and so the medians for both parts of the abstracts was zero.

Since the L1-MT/PE and L2-EFL parts of the abstracts vary in the total number of words produced across all participants, we also present figures on valid errors per total number of words produced in Table 6. This shows that the normalised valid error count per 1000 words is lower for L1-MT/PE text production (11.7 vs. 18.8).

The sample is too small to carry out any meaningful tests for statistical significance. However, in summary, we can see that the Antidote analysis suggests that there are no major differences in quality (from an Antidote perspective) between the abstract parts written across the two processes. In fact, the median number of language and typography errors is slightly higher for the L2-EFL passages. Also, the normalised valid error count per 1000 words is lower for L1-MT/PE text production. These results further consolidate the results of the subjective quality evaluations of the participants themselves and of the professional reviser, as respectively reported in Sects. 4.2 and 4.3.

As an aside, we draw attention to the fact that the percentage of valid errors reported by Antidote was quite low, i.e. its precision for this test was not high. For instance, the percentage of valid errors for the category 'Language' was 20.2% for L1-MT/PE passages and 19.5% for L2-EFL passages. For Typography, the figures were 44.4% and 46.0% respectively. Although these figures are low from a precision perspective, their similarity across the two passage types at least indicates a reliable and consistent performance by the tool. It was beyond our scope to also test for recall of the tool.

4.5   Summary of Results

To summarise the results presented in this section:

- The median times for drafting were not substantially different between L1-MT/PE and L2-EFL, but the revision times and number of revisions implemented were greater for the L1-MT/PE sections (see Sect. 4.2). When combined, this could suggest that drafting and revising in L1 with MT and self-PE might be more time-consuming, at least in initial stages where authors have not become familiar with this task.
- Half the participants found drafting in the L1 easier than drafting in EFL. However, half the participants found revising the text they had drafted in English easier than self-PE of the text drafted in their L1 (see Sect. 4.2).
- Six thought that the quality produced for both tasks was equal, three thought that the L2-EFL process produced better quality and the professional reviser mostly agreed with this assessment (see Sect. 4.2).
- Five participants were likely to use MT again to support their writing process (see Sect. 4.2).
- Concerning the number of edits made by the professional reviser, there were no substantial differences between those parts of the abstracts written in L1-MT/PE and those written in L2-EFL (see Sect. 4.3).
- The Antidote analysis confirms that there are no major differences in quality across the two processes (see Sect. 4.4).

5   Discussion and Future Research Ideas

This exploratory study has focused mainly on the impact that the process of MT and self-PE might have on quality. With participants working in different domains and with different L1s, we found that MT and self-PE did not impact negatively on the text produced. However, the participants were divided in their opinions about which task was easier and whether they would consider using MT again for academic writing support.

In our literature review, we highlighted some of the issues surrounding the topic of English as a *lingua franca* for international academic publishing, suggesting that MT could act as an aid for EFL academic writers and that it might offer some advantages, such as reducing cognitive burden. It needs to be investigated further whether MT and self-PE can in fact reduce the cognitive burden of writing in EFL; MT and post-editing have been shown to reduce 'effort' (technical, temporal and cognitive) for translation, but effects vary according to the individual and depend on the MT engine, language pair, text type and context. It is to be expected that this would also be true for MT as a writing aid. In the experiment presented in this chapter, some participants mentioned that writing in their L1 was difficult because they were not used to doing so and did not know their disciplinary terminology in their L1. If writers are unfamiliar with academic text production in their L1 due to the fact that their education and practice in the discipline has been through English, and if this is coupled with a lack of knowledge of, or a deficiency in, discipline-specific terminology, then MT cannot be expected to plug such gaps. On the other hand, academic authors could presumably acquire expertise in discipline-specific writing in their L1 through practice. The issue of terminological deficiency and 'borrowing' of words from English is a considerable one that we do not intend to delve into here, but if academics are only writing in English it is certain that terminology gaps will not be plugged. If they write at least some of the time in their L1, more attention might be given to terminology gaps. Furthermore, not only would the author become more used to writing in her L1, but we would expect that the effect of MT and self-PE would change over time as the writer becomes more acclimatised to the process and the MT system learns from the edits implemented and becomes more tuned to the specific domain. The L1, its closeness to English, the potential success of MT for that language, and the availability of specialised terminology for the L1 in the research domain all seem to be factors that could influence the adoption of MT for academic writing support. These are factors that could be investigated more thoroughly in future research. It is our intention to build on this exploratory study to investigate in a more in-depth manner the potential of MT as an academic writing aid for EFL writers. Some potential paths include tracking people over time as they become used to writing in L1 with MT and self-PE to see if they become more comfortable and efficient in this task and if they eventually surpass the quality they can produce while writing in EFL.

What also needs to be investigated is the impact that MT and self-PE might have on the rhetorical structure of the text. As pointed out by others, academic genres differ across languages (Swales 2004; Bennett 2014a, b; Breuer 2015) and articles written by non-native English speakers are often rejected on the grounds that they do not meet linguistic or rhetorical expectations (Lillis and Curry 2010). An article may be written in an L1 according to the rhetorical norm expectations for that language (and, indeed, for that discipline), but the MT systems of today can only translate words and phrases; they cannot *transform* the text to meet the genre requirements of the target-language, English, and of the particular domain. In fact, MT systems still struggle to resolve discourse-level (coherence and cohesion) demands, never mind demands based on rhetorical norms. Some MT researchers have addressed this problem (Marcu et al. 2000), but existing implementations of these ideas are still restricted to the sentence level (Tu et al. 2013, Hardmeier et al. 2015). More recent approaches to MT, such as those based on neural networks, aim at a deeper treatment of the translation process (Bahdanau et al. 2014). These approaches appear promising in this regard, but going beyond the sentence level is still a major challenge for MT (Pouget-Abadie et al. 2014, Li et al. 2015). The question therefore remains open: could MT facilitate both of these demands (language and genre) to such an extent that the burden is lower on the EFL writer?

It is a well-known fact from years of Controlled Language (CL) research that MT systems perform best when sentences are shorter than approximately 25 words and the fewer referential pronouns there are in a sentence, the better. Although CL research was mostly driven by the Rule-Based MT paradigm, there is still evidence to suggest that short sentences can be more easily processed by Statistical MT systems (Doherty 2012). The English language is quite suited to this type of writing, but other languages, especially Romance languages, recognise long sentences and indirect rather than direct presentation of 'factual' information as markers of sophisticated and mature writing (Bennett 2013: 175). This type of writing would clearly present additional challenges to a technology that is already challenged considerably and might limit the usefulness of MT as an academic writing aid. It may be the case, then, that MT would be useful only in circumstances where the author is willing to 'write for' MT, and only using the type of rhetorical structure that is expected for English Academic Discourse. Additionally, it may be the case that MT will only be useful for 'scientific' discourse, as opposed to humanities and social science discourse; these are all open questions that require further investigation. On the basis of the exploratory study presented here, where multiple L1s were included and authors were not instructed to 'write for MT', we believe that the potential is considerable. What is more, of the ten abstracts analysed, seven were in the scientific domain but three were in the broad domain of humanities and social science (topics included: marketing, crisis management and trust), which further suggests that MT's usefulness as a writing aid is not necessarily limited to scientific discourse. In any case, an increase in inter- and transdisciplinarity would topple the overly simplistic dichotomy of scientific vs. humanities and social science 'discourses'. Whether MT as an academic writing aid is more useful for empirically-oriented research paradigms (sciences) rather than constructivist paradigms (humanities and social science) and their associated discourse types is an interesting question that needs to be addressed. Whether MT is only useful as an academic writing aid if the author is willing to write with MT and English as a target-language in mind, i.e. shorter sentences, fewer referential pronouns, using expected rhetorical structure for English Academic Discourse publications, is another topic that could be explored.

If MT does indeed have potential as a writing aid for EFL writers, another question that emerges is what mode of interaction suits the academic writing process best? In our exploration, we selected the more typical, punctuated process: write first, machine-translate, self-post-edit. An alternative mode is interactive writing and translation. In this mode, the writer would write in her L1 and the MT system would translate phrases in real-time, updating suggestions as phrases were accepted, rejected or revised (Foster et al. 1997; Langlais et al. 2000; Foster et al. 2002; González-Rubio et al. 2010; González-Rubio et al. 2013). Without doubt, each mode would impact on the cognitive process and on the product in different ways. Also, one mode might suit one writer while the alternative mode suits another. We would also like to investigate whether interactive MT is a more desirable mode compared with the more staged process we implemented in the study described above. The nature of the L1, its sentence structure, terminological completeness, and way of presenting knowledge might also have an impact on which mode is best.

The practicality and usefulness of free, generic MT engines compared with customised, domain-specific engines also deserves attention. The quality produced and utility of MT as an academic writing aid could be investigated further through traditional metrics (e.g. revision tracking), but also through measures such as readability (using readability indices and/or eye tracking), number and nature of peer review comments, and even publication acceptance metrics.

The analysis we present here is an initial exploratory study, with a focus on quality assessment. As a follow up, and in order to do a more detailed analysis, we annotated the number and types of revisions implemented by the professional reviser across both texts, focusing on the type of operation involved (e.g. addition), the linguistic unit affected (e.g. adjective) and the dimension (e.g. syntax). The results of this analysis can be read (in French) in Goulet et al. (2017). Furthermore, in order to investigate the utility of MT as a writing aid in more detail, we conducted a similar study, focusing on one L1 (Spanish) and on one specific discipline (Medicine). The results of that study can be found in Parra Escartín et al. (2017).

Acknowledgments This project was partly funded by the ADAPT Centre for Digital Content Technology, which is funded under the Science Foundation Ireland Research Centres Programme (Grant 13/RC/2106) and is co-funded under the European Regional Development Fund.

Appendices

Appendix A: Pre-task Questionnaire

[Questions marked with a "*" are required]

1. Please provide us with your email address here *
   Your email address will allow us to contact you should you qualify for the next
   stage of the study. We will not disclose your email address or any other personal
   data provided by you to us to any third party. No information given here will be
   associated with your responses in any publications on this study.
2. What is your first language (mother tongue)? *
3. What is your current field of study?
4. Please indicate approximately the level you are at in your academic career *
   Tick the option that is most relevant to you. Select only one.

   - PhD student
   - Post-doctoral researcher
   - Early stage faculty staff (between 1 and 5 years)
   - Established faculty (5+ full-time years of experience as faculty staff)
   - Other (specify):

5. How many academic papers have you published in English? *
   For example: conference papers, journal articles, workshop papers, posters, oral
   presentations etc. Please do not count papers co-authored by a native speaker
   of English.

6.a Please rate your academic English writing competence *
   If you participate in this study, you will be asked to write a 500-word academic
   text in English, on a subject with which you are familiar. How do you rate
   your competence at writing this sort of text? Please select only one option – the
   option that best matches your current competences.

   - Beginner: I can write a short, simple academic text, for example a summary
     of a chapter I have read in an academic book.
   - Intermediate: I can write extended text on my domain specialisation, such
     as an academic assignment, short conference paper or abstract. I can use an
     appropriate register. I can publish that paper with some editorial help from a
     native speaker of English.
   - Advanced: I can express myself in clear, well-structured academic text,
     expressing points of view at some length. I can write about complex subjects
     in an academic article. I can select a style and register appropriate to the
     reader in mind. I can write sentences that are mostly grammatical and need
     only minor editing from an editor.
   - Expert: My writing skills in academic English are indistinguishable from
     those of any native speaker of English in my academic field.
   - Other:

6.b How easy do you rate the task of writing academic texts in English? *

   1 = very difficult, 2 = difficult, 3 = easy, 4 = very easy

7. Have you ever resorted to a professional reviser when writing an academic text
   in English? *

8.a Have you ever used Machine Translation to produce a first draft academic English text before? *

Examples of Machine Translation (automated translation) include: Google Translate, Bing Translator, Reverso, Systran, etc.

8.b If yes, how easy do you rate the task of post-editing English, i.e. revising a machine translated text?

1 = very difficult, 2 = difficult, 3 = easy, 4 = very easy; if you don't know, just leave this blank

9. Which of the following writing tasks could you undertake in the next 4–6 weeks? *

Tick all that apply.

- A 500 word summary of your PhD research
- A 500 word abstract for a paper you are working on
- A 500 word proposal for a future research project

10. Do you consent to participate in this study? *

This is a pre-task survey to aid with the selection of participants. To indicate that you consent to participate in the event that you are selected, please TICK ALL THE FOLLOWING STATEMENTS:

- I have read the Plain Language Statement (available at https://sites.google.com/site/selfpostediting/pre-questionnaire)
- I understand the information provided.
- I have had an opportunity to ask questions and discuss this study.
- I have received satisfactory answers to all my questions.
- Should this study include an interview, I am aware that it may be audio-recorded.
- I consent to take part in this research project.
- I understand that I will receive an Amazon voucher to the value of 100 euros (or equivalent in another currency) ONLY if I complete all stages of the study.

Appendix B: Post-task Questionnaire

* Required

1. Please provide us with your email address here *
This information is required to link your answers with the previous questionnaire.
2. Which DRAFTING task did you find easier? *
Reminder: By DRAFTING we refer to the first stage of the task when you initially wrote your text.

- Drafting the text in my first language was easier.
- Drafting the text in English was easier.
- Both were equal in terms of effort.

3. Which REVISION task did you find easier, revising the text drafted in English, or revising the text drafted in your first language and then machine translated? * Reminder: By REVISION we refer to the second stage of the task when you produced the final version of your draft.

- Revising the text I drafted in English was easier.
- Revising the text I drafted in my first language, which was then machine translated, was easier.
- Both were equal in terms of effort.

4. What specific difficulties did you encounter when drafting/revising in English? *

(for example: sentence structure issues, terminology issues . . . ?)

5. What specific difficulties did you encounter when drafting in your first language and revising the machine translation? *

(for example: sentence structure issues, terminology issues . . . ?)

6.a Which task produced the better QUALITY text, in your opinion? * Please specify: drafting/revising in English OR drafting in my first language and revising the machine translation.

- Drafting/Revising in English.
- Drafting in my first language and revising the machine translation.
- Both were equivalent in terms of quality.

6.b Please explain your choice for the previous question. *

7. What language tools or resources (e.g. dictionaries, spell-checker, etc.) did you use to produce your text for both tasks? * Please list as many as you can remember.

8.a On a scale of 1–4, how likely are you to use Machine Translation and Revision to write an academic text in English in the future? *

(1=Never again, 4=Every time)

8.b Please explain your reasons for your decision in the previous question.

9. Would you be happy to participate in an interview to explore further your opinions and questions? * We will contact you by email should you qualify for an interview.

References

Bahdanau D, Cho K, Bengio Y (2014) Neural machine translation by jointly learning to align and translate. arXiv preprint arXiv:14090473

Benfield JR, Feak CB (2006) How authors can cope with the burden of English as an international language. Chest 129(6):1728–1730

Bennett K (2013) English as a lingua franca in academia. Interpret Trans Train 7(2):169–193

Bennett K (2014a) The political and economic infrastructure of academic practice: the 'semi-periphery' as a category for social and linguistic analysis. In: Bennett K (ed) The semi-periphery of academic writing: discourses, communities and practices. Palgrave Macmillan, London, pp 1–12

Bennett K (2014b) Conclusion: combating the centripetal pull in academic writing. In: Bennett K (ed) The semi-periphery of academic writing: discourses, communities and practices. Palgrave Macmillan, London, pp 240–246

Bennett K (2015) Towards an epistemological monoculture: mechanisms of epistemicide in European research publication. In: Plo R, Pérez-Llantada C (eds) English as an academic and research language (English in Europe vol 2). De Gruyter Mouton, Berlin, pp 9–35

Breuer EO (2015) First language versus foreign language: Fluency, errors and revision processes in foreign language academic writing. Peter Lang Edition, Frankfurt am Main

Carl M, Gutermuth S, Hansen-Schirra S (2015) Post-editing machine translation: efficiency, strategies, and revision processes in professional translation settings. In: Ferreira A, Schwieter JW (eds) Psycholinguistic and cognitive inquiries into translation and interpreting. John Benjamins, Amsterdam, pp 145–174

Cowan R, Choo J, Lee GS (2014) ICALL for improving Korean L2 writers' ability to edit grammatical errors. Lang Learn Technol 18(3):193–207

Doherty S (2012) Investigating the effects of controlled language on the reading and comprehension of machine translated texts: a mixed-methods approach. Dissertation, Dublin City University

Flowerdew J (2001) Attitudes of journal editors to non-native speaker contributions. TESOL Q 35(1):121–150

Foster G, Isabelle P, Plamondon P (1997) Target-text mediated interactive machine translation. Mach Trans 12(1–2):175–194

Foster G, Langlais P, Lapalme G (2002) User-friendly text prediction for translators. In: Proceedings of the 2002 conference on empirical methods in natural language processing, Philadelphia, July 2002, pp 148–155

Garcia I (2010) Is machine translation ready yet? Target 22(1):7–21

Garcia I (2011) Translating by post-editing: is it the way forward? Mach Trans 25:217–237

Garcia I, Pena MI (2011) Machine translation-assisted language learning: writing for beginners Computer. Assist Lang Learn 24(5):471–487

Gaspari F, Toral A, Naskar SK, Groves D, Way A (2014) Perception vs reality: measuring machine translation post-editing productivity. In: Proceedings of the Third workshop on Post-Editing Technology and Practice (WPTP3), Conference for the Association for Machine Translation in the Americas (AMTA), Vancouver, pp 60–72

González-Rubio J, Ortiz-Martínez D, Casacuberta F (2010) Balancing user effort and translation error in interactive machine translation via confidence measures. In: Proceedings of the ACL 2010 conference short papers, Uppsala, Sweden, pp 173–177

González-Rubio J, Ortiz-Martínez D, Benedí JM, Casacuberta F (2013) Interactive machine translation using hierarchical translation models. In: Proceedings of the conference on empirical methods in natural language processing, Seattle, Washington, DC, pp 244–254

Goulet MJ, Simard M, Parra Escartín C, O'Brien S (2017) La traduction automatique comme outil d'aide à la redaction scientifique en Anglais language seconde: résultats d'une étude exploratoire sur la qualité linguistique. ASp – La revue de la Groupe d'Étude et de Recherche en Anglais de Spécialité 72:5–28

Green S, Heer J, Manning CD (2013) The efficacy of human post-editing for language translation. In: Proceedings of the SIGCHI conference on human factors in computing systems, Paris, France, pp 439–448

Guerberof A (2012) Productivity and quality in the post-editing of output from translation memories and machine translation. Dissertation, Universitat Rovira i Virgili

Hanauer DI, Englander K (2011) Quantifying the burden of writing research articles in a second language: data from Mexican scientists. Writ Commun 28(4):403–416

Hardmeier C, Nakov P, Stymne S, Tiedemann J, Versley Y, Cettolo M (2015) Pronoun-focused MT and cross-lingual pronoun prediction: findings of the 2015 DiscoMT shared task on pronoun translation. In: Second workshop on discourse in Machine Translation (DiscoMT), Lisbon, pp 1–16

Hu C, Bederson BB, Resnik P, Kronrod Y (2011) MonoTrans2: a new human computation system to support monolingual translation. In: Proceedings of the SIG-CHI conference on human factors in computing systems, Vancouver, pp 1133–1136

Langlais P, Foster G, Lapalme G (2000) TransType: a computer-aided translation typing system. In: Proceedings of the NAACL-ANLP workshop on embedded machine translation systems, Seattle, Washington, DC, pp 46–51

Li J, Luong MT, Jurafsky D (2015) A hierarchical neural autoencoder for paragraphs and documents. In: Proceedings of the 53rd annual meeting of the Association for Computational Linguistics and the 7th international joint conference on natural language processing, Beijing, pp 1106–1115

Lillis T, Curry MJ (2010) Academic writing in a global context: the politics and practices of publishing in English. Routledge, London

Lin H (2015) A meta-synthesis of empirical research on the effectiveness of computer-mediated communication (CMC) in SLA. Lang Learn Technol 19(2):85–117

López-Navarro I, Moreno AI, Quintanilla MÁ, Rey-Rocha J (2015) Why do I publish research articles in English instead of my own language? Differences in Spanish researchers' motivations across scientific domains. Scientometrics 103:939–976

Marcu D, Carlson L, Watanabe M (2000) The automatic translation of discourse structures. In: Proceedings of the 1st North American chapter of the Association for Computational Linguistics conference, Seattle, Washington, DC, pp 9–17

Mitchell L, O'Brien S, Roturier J (2014) Quality evaluation in community post-editing. Mach Trans 28(3–4):237–262

Niño A (2008) Evaluating the use of machine translation post-editing in the foreign language class. Comput Assist Lang Learn 21(1):29–49

Nukoolkit C, Chansripiboon P, Mongkolnam P, Todd RW (2011) Text cohesion visualizer. In: The 6th international conference on Computer Science and Education (ICCSE 2011), Singapore, pp 205–209

O'Brien S, Simard M (eds) (2014) Machine Translation, special issue on post-editing. 28:159–329

O'Brien S, Simard M (eds) (2015) Proceedings of the fourth workshop on Post-Editing Technology and Practice (WPTP4), Workshop held at the MT Summit 2015, Miami

O'Brien S, Simard M, Specia L (eds) (2012) Proceedings of the first workshop on Post-Editing Technology and Practice (WPTP1), Workshop held at the Association for Machine Translation in the Americas conference (AMTA), San Diego

O'Brien S, Simard M, Specia L (eds) (2013) Proceedings of the second workshop on Post-Editing Technology and Practice (WPTP2), Workshop held at the European Association for Machine Translation conference (EAMT), Nice

O'Brien S, Simard M, Specia L (eds) (2014a) Proceedings of the third workshop on Post-Editing Technology and Practice (WPTP3), Workshop held at the conference for the Association for Machine Translation in the Americas (AMTA), Vancouver

O'Brien S, Balling LW, Carl M, Simard M, Specia L (eds) (2014b) Post-editing of machine translation: Processes and applications. Cambridge Scholars Publishing, Newcastle-Upon-Tyne

O'Neill EM (2012) The effect of online translators on L2 writing in French. Dissertation, University of Illinois at Urbana-Champaign

Omar N, Razali NAM, Darus S (2009) Automated grammar checking of tenses for ESL writing. Lecture notes in computer science. Springer, Heidelberg, pp 475–482

Parra Escartín C, O'Brien S, Goulet MJ (2017) Machine translation as an academic writing aid for medical practitioners. In: Proceedings of the Machine Translation Summit XVI, Nagoya, pp 254–267

Pouget-Abadie J, Bahdanau D, van Merriënboer B, Cho K, Bengio Y (2014) Overcoming the curse of sentence length for neural machine translation using automatic segmentation. arXiv preprint arXiv:14091257

Swales J (2004) Research genres: explorations and applications. Cambridge University Press, New York

Tatsumi M, Aikawa T, Yamamoto K, Isahara H (2012) How good is crowd post-editing? Its potential and limitations. In: Proceedings of the first workshop on Post-Editing Technology and Practice (WPTP3), Conference for the Association for Machine Translation in the Americas (AMTA), San Diego, pp 69–77

Tu M, Zhou Y, Zong C (2013) A novel translation framework based on rhetorical structure theory. In: Proceedings of the 51st annual meeting of the Association for Computational Linguistics, Sofia, Bulgaria, pp 370–374

Van Waes L, Leijten M (2015) Fluency in writing: a multidimensional perspective on writing fluency applied to L1 and L2. Comput Compos 38:79–95

Wagner RA, Fischer MJ (1974) The string-to-string correction problem. J ACM 21(1):168–173

Willey I, Tanimoto K (2015) "We're drifting into strange territory here": what think-aloud protocols reveal about convenience editing. J Second Lang Writ 27:63–83

Zakaria TNT, Aziz MJA, Rizan TN, Maasum TN (2010) Transformation of L2 writers to correct English: the need for a computer-assisted writing tool. In: Proceedings of the international symposium on Information Technology – System Development and Application and Knowledge Society, Kuala Lumpur, Malaysia, pp 1508–1513

What Level of Quality Can Neural Machine Translation Attain on Literary Text?

11

Antonio Toral and Andy Way

Abstract Given the rise of the new neural approach to machine translation (NMT) and its promising performance on different text types, we assess the translation quality it can attain on what is perceived to be the greatest challenge for MT: literary text. Specifically, we target novels, arguably the most popular type of literary text. We build a literary-adapted NMT system for the English-to-Catalan translation direction and evaluate it against a system pertaining to the previous dominant paradigm in MT: statistical phrase-based MT (PBSMT). To this end, for the first time we train MT systems, both NMT and PBSMT, on large amounts of literary text (over 100 million words) and evaluate them on a set of 12 widely known novels spanning from the 1920s to the present day. According to the BLEU automatic evaluation metric, NMT is significantly better than PBSMT ($p < 0.01$) on all the novels considered. Overall, NMT results in a 11% relative improvement (3 points absolute) over PBSMT. A complementary human evaluation on three of the books shows that between 17% and 34% of the translations, depending on the book, produced by NMT (versus 8% and 20% with PBSMT) are perceived by native speakers of the target language to be of equivalent quality to translations produced by a professional human translator.

Keywords Translation quality assessment · Principles to practice · Literature translation · Neural machine translation · Pairwise ranking · Phrase-based statistical machine translation

A. Toral
Faculty of Arts, Center for Language and Cognition, University of Groningen, Groningen, The Netherlands
e-mail: a.toral.ruiz@rug.nl

A. Way
ADAPT Centre/School of Computing, Dublin City University, Dublin, Ireland
e-mail: andy.way@adaptcentre.ie

1 Introduction

Literary text is considered to be the greatest challenge for machine translation (MT). According to perceived wisdom, despite the tremendous progress in the field of statistical MT over the past two decades, there is no prospect of machines being useful in (assisting with) the translation of this type of content.

However, we believe that the recent emergence of two unrelated technologies opens a window of opportunity to explore this topic:

1. The electronic book: the market share of e-books is continuously growing,[1] as a result of which there is a wide availability of books in digital format, including original novels and their translations. Because the main resource required to train statistical MT systems is bilingual parallel text, we are now able to build MT systems tailored to novels. This should result in better performance, as it has been shown in MT research again and again that for a statistical MT engine to perform optimally it should be trained on similar data to the data it is applied to, e.g. Pecina et al. (2014).

2. Neural MT: NMT is a new approach to statistical MT, which, while having been introduced only very recently,[2] has already shown great potential, as there is evidence that it can attain better translation quality than the dominant approach to date, namely phrase-based statistical MT (PBSMT). This has been shown for a number of language pairs and domains, including transcribed speeches (Luong and Manning 2015), newswire (Sánchez-Cartagena and Toral 2016) and United Nations documents (Junczys-Dowmunt et al. 2016). Beyond its generally positive performance, NMT is of particular interest for literary texts due to the following two findings:

   • Its performance seems to be especially promising for lexically-rich texts (Bentivogli et al. 2016), which is the case with literary texts.
   • There are claims that NMT "can, rather than do a literal translation, find the cultural equivalent in another language".[3]

With respect to the last point, literal (but not word-for-word) translations are deemed acceptable for domains for which PBSMT is already widely used in industry, such as technical documentation, as the aim of the translation process here is purely to carry over the meaning of the source sentence to the target language, without necessarily reflecting any stylistic niceties of the target language. In contrast, literal translations are not at all suitable for literary texts because

---

[1] For example, in the US the market share of e-books surpassed that of printed books for fiction in 2014, http://www.ingenta.com/blog-article/adding-up-the-invisible-ebook-market-analysis-of-author-earnings-january-2015-2/

[2] Working models of NMT have only recently been introduced, but from a theoretical perspective, very similar models can be traced back two decades (Forcada and Ñeco 1997).

[3] http://events.technologyreview.com/video/watch/alan-packer-understanding-language/

the expectations of the reader are considerably higher; it is not sufficient for the translation to merely preserve the meaning, as it should also preserve the reading experience of the original text.

In this chapter we aim to assess the performance that can be offered by state-of-the-art MT for literary texts. To this end we train PBSMT and NMT systems for the first time on large amounts of literary texts (over 100 million words) and evaluate them on a set of 12 widely known novels that span from the 1920s to the beginning of the twenty-first century.

The rest of the chapter is organised as follows. In the following section, we provide an overview of the research carried out in the field of MT targeting literary texts. Next, we outline our experimental set-up (Sect. 3) and provide technical details of the PBSMT and NMT systems built (Sect. 4). Subsequently we evaluate and analyse the translations produced by both MT systems (Sect. 5). Finally, we conclude and outline lines of future work in Sect. 6.

2   State-of-the-Art in MT of Literary Text

There has been recent interest in the Computational Linguistics community regarding the processing of literary text. The best example is the establishment of an annual workshop (Computational Linguistics for Literature) in 2012, which has run ever since. A popular strand of research concerns the automatic identification of text snippets that convey figurative devices, such as metaphor (Shutova et al. 2013), idioms (Li and Sporleder 2010), humour and irony (Reyes 2013), applied to monolingual text. Conversely, there has been a rather limited amount of work on applying MT to literary texts, as we now survey.

Genzel et al. (2010) constrained SMT systems for poetry to produce French-to-English translations that obey length, meter, and rhyming rules. Form is preserved at the price of producing considerably lower-quality translations; the score according to the BLEU automatic evaluation metric (Papineni et al. 2002) (see the papers by Castilho et al. and Way in this volume for more details of this metric) decreases by around 50%, although it should be noted that their evaluation was not on poetry but on news.

Greene et al. (2010) translated poetry, choosing target output realisations that conform to the desired rhythmic patterns. Specifically, they translated Dante's *Divine Comedy* from Italian sonnets into English iambic pentameter. Instead of constraining the SMT system, as done by Genzel et al. (2010), they passed its output lattice through a device that maps words to sequences of stressed and unstressed syllables. These sequences were finally filtered with an iambic pentameter acceptor.

Voigt and Jurafsky (2012) examined the role of referential cohesion in translation and found that literary texts have more dense reference chains. They concluded that incorporating discourse features beyond the level of the sentence (Hardmeier 2014) is an important research focus for applying MT to literary texts.

Jones and Irvine (2013) used general-domain MT systems to translate samples of French literature (prose and poetry) into English. They then used qualitative analysis grounded in translation theory on the MT output to assess the potential of MT in literary translation and to address what makes literary translation particularly difficult.

Besacier (2014) used MT followed by post-editing (by non-professional translators) to translate a short story from English into French. Such a workflow was deemed a useful low-cost alternative for translating literary works, albeit at the expense of lower translation quality.

Our recent work (Toral and Way 2015b) contributed to the state-of-the-art in two dimensions. First, we conducted a comparative analysis on the translatability of literary text according to narrowness of the domain and freedom of translation, which is more general and complementary to the analysis by Voigt and Jurafsky (2012). Second, related to Besacier (2014), we evaluated MT for literary text. There were two differences though; first, Besacier (2014) translated a short story, while we translated a novel; second, their MT systems were evaluated against a post-edited reference produced by non-professional translators, while we evaluated our MT systems against the translation produced by a professional translator.

This work builds upon our previous study (Toral and Way 2015b), the following being the main differences between the two: we now train a literary-adapted MT system under the NMT paradigm (while previously we used PBSMT), the translation direction considered is more challenging as the languages are more distant (English-to-Catalan versus Spanish-to-Catalan), we conduct a considerably broader evaluation (12 books now versus just one in the previous work), and we analyse the results with respect to a set of textual features of each novel.

3   Experimental Set-Up

This section covers the experimental settings. We explain the motivation for the language pair chosen for this chapter (Sect. 3.1), describe the data sets used in our experiments (Sect. 3.2) and finally the tools that were utilised (Sect. 3.3).

3.1   Language Pair

In general, it is widely accepted that the quality attainable by MT correlates with the level of relatedness between the pair of languages involved. This is because translations between related languages should be more literal, and complex phenomena (such as metaphorical expressions) might simply transfer rather straightforwardly to the target language, while they are more likely to require complex translations between unrelated languages.

In our previous work (Toral and Way 2015a,b), we considered a closely-related language pair (Spanish-to-Catalan), where both languages belong to the same family (Romance). We built a literary-adapted PBSMT system and used it to translate a novel from an internationally renowned author, Ruiz Zafón. We concluded that our system could be useful to assist with the translation of this kind of text due to the following two findings.

1. For a random subset of sentences from the novel, we asked native speakers to rank the translations coming from the MT system against those from a professional translator (i.e. taken from the published novel in the target language), although they did not know which were which. For over 60% of the sentences, native speakers found both translations to be of the same quality (Toral and Way 2015b).

2. The previous evaluation was carried out at the sentence level, so it might be argued that this is somewhat limited as it does not take context beyond the sentence into account. Accordingly, we subsequently analysed 3 representative passages (up to 10 consecutive sentences): one of average MT quality (i.e. the quality of this passage is similar to the quality obtained by MT on the whole novel, as measured with BLEU), another of high quality (i.e. its BLEU score is similar to the average BLEU score of the 20% highest-scoring passages), and finally, one of low quality (i.e. its BLEU score is similar to the average BLEU score of the 20% lowest-scoring passages). For the passages of high and average quality, we showed that the MT output requires only a few character edits to match the professional translation (Toral and Way 2015a).

Encouraged by the positive results obtained on a closely-related language pair, we have now decided to explore the potential for a less-related pair, correspondingly a more challenging task. The language pair in this study is English-to-Catalan, where the two languages involved belong to different families (Germanic and Romance, respectively).

We choose Catalan as the target language as an example of a mid-size European language.[4] These are languages into which a significant number of novels have been translated; we have easily identified over 200 English e-books available in Catalan. Nonetheless, this number is very low compared to the amount of books translated into 'major' European languages (such as German, French, Italian, or Spanish). Concerning mid-size European languages, because there is (i) a reasonable amount of data available to train literary-adapted MT systems and also (ii) room to have more novels translated if the output translations produced by MT are deemed useful to assist translators, we believe this is a sensible choice of target language type for this line of research.

---

[4]With this term we refer to European languages with around 5–10 million speakers, as is the case of many other languages in Europe, such as Danish, Serbian, Czech, etc.

| Dataset | # sentences | # tokens | |
		English	Catalan
Training parallel (in-domain)	1,086,623	16,876,830	18,302,284
Training parallel (OpenSubs)	402,775	3,577,109	3,381,241
Training monolingual (in-domain)	5,306,055	–	100,426,922
Training monolingual (in-domain)	13,841,542	210,337,379	–
Training monolingual (web)	16,516,799	–	486,961,317
Development	2,000	34,562	38,114

Table 1 Number of sentences and tokens (source and target sides) in the training and development data sets

3.2 Data Sets

3.2.1 Training and Development Data

We use parallel and monolingual in-domain data for training. The parallel data comprises 133 parallel novels (over one million sentence pairs), while the monolingual data consists of around 1,000 books written in Catalan (over five million sentences) and around 1,600 books in English[5] (over 13 million sentences). In addition, we use out-of-domain datasets, namely OpenSubtitles[6] as parallel data (around 400,000 sentence pairs) and monolingual Catalan data (around 16 million sentences) crawled from the web (Ljubešić and Toral 2014). The development data consists of 2,000 sentence pairs randomly selected from the in-domain parallel training data and removed from the latter data set. Quantitative details of the training and development data sets are shown in Table 1.

3.2.2 Test Data

We test our systems on 12 English novels and their professional translations into Catalan. In so doing we aim to build up a representative sample of literary fiction, encompassing novels from different periods (from the 1920s to the present day) and genres and targeted at different audiences. Details are provided in Table 2. For each novel, aside from the number of sentences and tokens (i.e. words) that it contains, we also show the portion of the source book (percentage of sentences) that was evaluated.[7]

---

[5]While our experiments are for the English-to-Catalan language pair, we also use English monolingual data to generate synthetic data for our NMT system (see Sect. 4.2).

[6]http://opus.lingfil.uu.se/OpenSubtitles.php

[7]In order to build the test sets we sentence-align the source and target versions of the books. We keep the subset of sentence pairs whose alignment score is above a certain threshold. See Sect. 3.3.1 for further details.

Author, book and year	% sentences	# sentences	# tokens	
			English	Catalan
Auster's *Sunset Park* (2010)	75.43%	2,167	70,285	73,541
Collins' *Hunger Games #3* (2010)	73.36%	7,287	103,306	112,255
Golding's *Lord of the Flies* (1954)	82.93%	5,195	64,634	69,807
Hemingway's *The Old Man and the Sea* (1952)	76.01%	1,461	24,233	25,765
Highsmith's *Ripley Under Water* (1991)	65.86%	5,981	84,339	94,565
Hosseini's *A Thousand Splendid Suns* (2007)	67.54%	6,619	97,728	105,989
Joyce's *Ulysses* (1922)	46.65%	11,182	136,250	159,460
Kerouac's *On the Road* (1957)	76.35%	5,944	106,409	111,562
Orwell's *1984* (1949)	68.23%	4,852	84,062	90,545
Rowling's *Harry Potter #7* (2007)	69.61%	10,958	186,624	209,524
Salinger's *The Catcher in the Rye* (1951)	76.57%	5,591	77,717	77,371
Tolkien's *The Lord of the Rings #3* (1955)	66.60%	6,209	114,847	129,671

Table 2 Percentage of sentences used from the original data set and number of sentences and tokens in the novels that make up the test set

Author	# books	# sentence pairs	# tokens (English)
Auster	2	6,831	145,195
Collins	2	15,315	216,658
Golding	0	0	0
Hemingway	0	0	0
Highsmith	4	27,024	382,565
Hosseini	1	7,672	105,040
Joyce	2	8,762	146,525
Kerouac	0	0	0
Orwell	2	4,068	88,372
Rowling	6	50,000	836,942
Salinger	4	8,350	141,389
Tolkien	3	23,713	397,328

Table 3 Number of books in the training set, together with their overall number of sentence pairs and source-side tokens for each writer that is also represented in the test set

Whilst obviously none of the novels in the test set is included in the training data, the latter dataset may contain other novels from writers represented in the test set. For example, the test set contains the 7th book in the *Harry Potter* series from Rowling, while the training set contains the previous six books in that series. Table 3 shows, for each writer represented in the test set, how many books appear in the training set from this writer, and how many sentence pairs and tokens (source side) these books amount to.

3.3   Tools

We have leveraged state-of-the-art techniques in the field through the pervasive use of open-source tools throughout the different stages of our experimentation, namely preprocessing, MT experimentation and evaluation, as detailed in the remainder of this section.

3.3.1   Preprocessing

The datasets (see Sect. 3.2) are preprocessed in order to make them suitable for MT. In-domain data is extracted from e-books and converted to plain text with Calibre support tools,[8] then sentence-split with NLTK (Bird 2006) and Freeling (Padró and Stanilovsky 2012) for English and Catalan, respectively, subsequently tokenised with Moses' scripts (Koehn et al. 2007) and Freeling, for English and Catalan, respectively, and finally sentence-aligned with Hunalign (Varga et al. 2005). Sentence alignment is carried out on lowercased text, in order to reduce data sparsity, with the assistance of a bilingual dictionary extracted from the Catalan–English Apertium rule-based MT system.[9] Following empirical observations, we keep aligned sentences with confidence scores higher than 0.3 and 0.5 for the training and test sets, respectively.

Subsequently, all datasets are truecased and normalised in terms of punctuation with Moses' scripts. Finally, in the parallel training data we discard sentence pairs where either of the sides has fewer than 1 or more than 80 tokens.

3.3.2   MT Toolkits and Evaluation

PBSMT systems are trained with version 3 of the Moses toolkit, while NMT systems are trained with Nematus (Sennrich et al. 2017).[10] For both paradigms default settings are used, unless mentioned otherwise in the description of the experiments (see Sects. 4.1 and 4.2 for PBSMT and NMT, respectively).

Automatic evaluation is carried out with the BLEU metric and is case-insensitive. Multi-bleu as implemented in Moses 3.0 is used for evaluating the development set while mteval (13a) is used to evaluate the test set. Statistical significance of the difference between systems is computed with paired bootstrap resampling (Koehn 2004) ($p \leq 0.01$, 1 000 iterations).[11] Human evaluation is rank-based and is performed with the Appraise tool (Federmann 2012).[12]

---

[8] https://calibre-ebook.com/

[9] http://sourceforge.net/projects/apertium/files/apertium-en-ca/0.9.3/

[10] https://github.com/rsennrich/nematus

[11] http://www.cs.cmu.edu/~ark/MT/paired_bootstrap_v13a.tar.gz

[12] https://github.com/cfedermann/Appraise

4 MT Systems

4.1 PBSMT System

The PBSMT system is trained on both the in-domain and out-of-domain parallel datasets by means of linear interpolation (Sennrich 2012) and uses three reordering models (lexical- and phrase-based as well as hierarchical). In addition, the system makes use of additional feature functions based on the operation sequence model (OSM) (Durrani et al. 2011) and language models based not only on surface n-grams but also on continuous space n-grams (NPLM) (Vaswani et al. 2013). The OSM and NPLM models are built on the in-domain parallel data (both sides in the case of OSM and only the target side for NPLM). The vocabulary size for NPLM is set to 100,000. Surface-form n-gram language models are built on the in-domain and out-of-domain datasets with KenLM (Heafield 2011) and then linearly interpolated with SRILM (Stolcke 2002). Tuning is carried out with batch MIRA (Cherry and Foster 2012).

During development we tuned PBSMT systems using different subsets of the components previously introduced in order to assess their effect on translation quality as measured by the BLEU evaluation metric. Table 4 shows the results, where we start with a baseline trained on in-domain data (in) both for the translation model (TM) and the language model (LM) and we measure the effect of the following:

- Adding NPLM, both using 4- and 5-g, which results in absolute improvements of 0.57 and 0.75 BLEU points, respectively.
- Adding OSM (+0.4).
- Adding linearly interpolated out-domain data both for the TM and the LM (+0.14).

4.2 NMT System

Due to the lack of established domain-adaptation techniques for NMT at the time when this system was built, our NMT system was trained solely on in-domain data. Specifically, we trained our NMT system on the concatenation of the parallel in-domain training data and a synthetic corpus obtained by machine-translating the Catalan in-domain monolingual training data into English.

TM	LM	OSM	NPLM	BLEU
in	in	–	–	0.3344
in	in	–	4-g	0.3401
in	in	–	5-g	0.3419
in	in	y	5-g	0.3459
inIout	inIout	y	5-g	0.3473

Table 4 Performance of different configurations of the PBSMT system on the development set

We use additional parallel data in which the source side is synthetic (machine-translated from the target language), as this has been reported to be a successful way of integrating target-language monolingual data into NMT (Sennrich et al. 2015) (see also Footnotes 12 and 25 in Way's chapter in this volume for a discussion on "back-translation"). The in-domain monolingual training data for Catalan is translated into English by means of a Catalan-to-English PBSMT system built for this purpose. This PBSMT system is based on the PBSMT system described in Sect. 4.1. Aside from reversing the translation direction, this PBSMT system is trained on the same datasets and has the same components, except for the following, which are not used: out-of-domain training data (both parallel and monolingual) and NPLM. The reason not to use these components has to do with an efficiency versus translation quality trade-off; this system needs to be fast as it is used to translate over five million sentences (i.e. the in-domain monolingual training data for Catalan), and taking the example of NPLM, this is a rather computationally expensive component to run.

We limit the source and target vocabularies to the 50,000 most frequent tokens in the respective sides of the training data. Training is then run until convergence, with models being saved every 3 h.[13] Each model is evaluated on the development set using BLEU in order to track performance over training time and find out when the training reaches convergence.

Figure 1 shows the results. We can observe that performance increases very quickly in the first iterations, going from 0.0251 BLEU points for model 1 (i.e. after 3 h of training) to 0.2999 for model 12 (i.e. after 36 h), after which it grows slowly to reach its maximum (0.3356) for model 53 and then plateaus.

We select the four models with the highest BLEU scores. These are, in descending order, 53 (0.3356 points), 76 (0.3333), 74 (0.3322) and 69 (0.3314). We trained these models for 12 h with the embeddings frozen (i.e. the whole network keeps being trained except the first layer (embeddings) which is fixed). We then evaluate ensembles of these four models 'as is' as well as with the additional training for 12 h with fixed embeddings. Their BLEU scores are 0.3561 (2.05 points absolute higher than the best individual system, a 6.1% relative improvement) and 0.3555 (1.99 points absolute higher than the best individual system, 5.9% relative), respectively. In other words, ensembling led to a substantial improvement, but fixing embeddings – reported to provide further improvements in several experiments in the literature – did not increase performance in our set-up.

Subsequently, we tried to improve upon this NMT system by implementing the following two functionalities:

1. Using subwords rather than words as translation units. Specifically, we segmented the training data into characters and performed 90,000 operations jointly on both the source and target languages (Sennrich et al. 2016b). These operations iteratively join the most frequent pair of segments. This results in a score of 0.3689 (1.28 points absolute higher than the initial NMT ensemble, a 3.6% relative improvement).

---

[13]Training is performed on an NVIDIA Tesla K20X GPU.

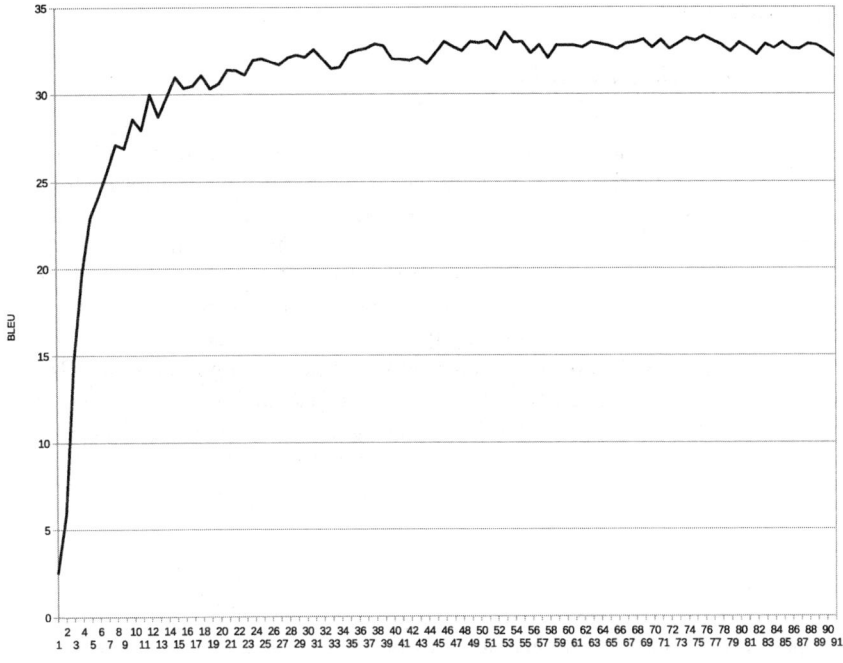

Fig. 1 BLEU scores obtained by the NMT models on the development set

2. Producing an *n*-best list and reranking it with a right-to-left NMT system (Sennrich et al. 2016a). We trained a so-called right-to-left system, with almost the same settings, the only difference being that the target sentences of the training data are reversed at the word level. We then produced an *n*-best list containing the top-50 translations with the previous model and re-ranked it with the right-to-left model. This leads to a BLEU score of 0.3948 (2.59 points higher than the previous system, a 7% relative improvement), and almost 6 BLEU points better (a 17.6% relative improvement) than the best individual system.

Due to the fact that we use the same dataset for development in the PBSMT and NMT paradigms, we are able to compare their results. When doing so, however, one should take into account that any such comparison would be unfair to NMT. This is because in the development of PBSMT, the system is optimising its log-linear weights to obtain the highest performance on the development set. Conversely, in the development of NMT we use the development set for validation, i.e. the system is not optimised on the development set. Despite this bias towards PBSMT, we observe that the score obtained by the best NMT system (0.3948, ensemble, using subword units and re-ranked with a right-to-left model) is notably higher (4.75 points, a 13.7% relative improvement) than the score achieved by the best PBSMT system (0.3473, all components, see Table 4).

5   Evaluation

5.1   Automatic Evaluation

As previously mentioned in Sect. 3.3.2, we automatically evaluate the MT systems using the BLEU metric. Table 5 shows the BLEU scores obtained for each novel in the test set with both PBSMT and NMT. The results across the different novels show a very high degree of variability, indicating that fiction is far from a monolithic domain. In fact scores go from a low of 0.1611 (PBSMT for *Ulysses*) to the highest of 0.3892 (NMT for *Harry Potter #7*), which more than doubles the first figure.

As for the performance obtained by the two paradigms that we compare in this chapter, NMT beats PBSMT by a statistically significant margin for all novels. On average, NMT outperforms PBSMT by 10.67% relative and 3 points absolute. The improvement brought about by NMT compared to PBSMT varies widely depending on the book, going from 3.11% (Auster's *Sunset Park*) to 14% (Collins' *Hunger Games #3*).

5.1.1   Analysis

We performed a set of additional analyses in order to obtain further insights from the output translations and, especially to try to find the reason why NMT, while outperforming PBSMT for all the novels, does so by rather diverging margins (from a minimum of 3.11% to a maximum of 14%, see Table 5).

Novel	PBSMT	NMT	Relative improvement (%)
Auster's *Sunset Park* (2010)	0.3735	0.3851	3.11
Collins' *Hunger Games #3* (2010)	0.3322	0.3787	14.00
Golding's *Lord of the Flies* (1954)	0.2196	0.2451	11.61
Hemingway's *The Old Man and the Sea* (1952)	0.2559	0.2829	10.55
Highsmith's *Ripley Under Water* (1991)	0.2485	0.2762	11.15
Hosseini's *A Thousand Splendid Suns* (2007)	0.3422	0.3715	8.56
Joyce's *Ulysses* (1922)	0.1611	0.1794	11.36
Kerouac's *On the Road* (1957)	0.3248	0.3572	9.98
Orwell's *1984* (1949)	0.2978	0.3306	11.01
Rowling's *Harry Potter #7* (2007)	0.3558	0.3892	9.39
Salinger's *The Catcher in the Rye* (1951)	0.3255	0.3695	13.52
Tolkien's *The Lord of the Rings #3* (1955)	0.2537	0.2888	13.84
Average	0.2909	0.3212	10.67

Table 5 BLEU scores obtained by PBSMT and NMT for each of the books that make up the test set. NMT outperforms PBSMT by a statistically significant margin ($p < 0.01$) on all books

More specifically, we considered three characteristics of the source-side of each novel in the test set (lexical richness, novelty with respect to the training data, and average sentence length) and studied whether any of these features correlates to some extent with the performance of the PBSMT and NMT systems and/or with the relative improvement of NMT over PBSMT. The motivation to use these three features is as follows:

- Lexical richness has been already studied in relation to NMT, and there are indications that this MT paradigm has "an edge especially on lexically rich texts" (Bentivogli et al. 2016).
- There is evidence that NMT's performance degrades with sentence length (Toral and Sánchez-Cartagena 2017).
- Despite, to the best of our knowledge, the lack of empirical evidence, it is still the perceived wisdom that NMT is better at generalising than PBSMT, and so it should perform better than the latter especially on data that is unrelated to the training data.

Lexical Richness

We use type-token ratio (TTR) as a proxy to measure lexical richness. The higher the ratio, the less repetitive the text and hence it can be considered lexically more varied, and thus richer. To measure this we calculate the TTR on the source side of each novel. As they have different sizes, we calculate the TTR for each novel on a random subset of sentences that amount to approximately n words, n being 20,000, a slightly lower number to the number of words contained in the smallest novel in our dataset, *The Old Man and the Sea* with 24,233 words.

Sentence Length

We measure the average sentence length of each novel as the ratio between its total number of tokens and its number of sentences. Both these values were reported in Table 2.

Novelty with Respect to the Training Data

We use n-gram overlap to measure the novelty of a novel with respect to the training data. Concretely, we consider the unique n-grams ($n = 4$) in the parallel training data and in each novel, and calculate the overlap as the ratio between the size of the intersection and the number of unique n-grams in the training set. The higher the overlap, the less novelty that the novel presents with respect to the training data. As in the analysis concerning lexical richness, we consider 20,000 words from randomly selected sentences for each novel.

Novel	TTR	Avg. sentence length	Overlap
Auster's *Sunset Park* (2010)	0.1865	**32.434**	0.368
Collins' *Hunger Games #3* (2010)	0.1716	14.177	0.393
Golding's *Lord of the Flies* (1954)	0.1368	12.442	0.370
Hemingway's *The Old Man and the Sea* (1952)	0.1041	16.587	0.371
Highsmith's *Ripley Under Water* (1991)	0.1492	14.101	0.404
Hosseini's *A Thousand Splendid Suns* (2007)	0.1840	14.765	0.377
Joyce's *Ulysses* (1922)	**0.2761**	12.185	**0.216**
Kerouac's *On the Road* (1957)	0.1765	17.902	0.335
Orwell's *1984* (1949)	0.1831	17.325	0.343
Rowling's *Harry Potter #7* (2007)	0.1665	17.031	0.433
Salinger's *The Catcher in the Rye* (1951)	0.1040	13.900	0.448
Tolkien's *The Lord of the Rings #3* (1955)	0.1436	18.497	0.368

Table 6 TTR, average sentence length and 4-g overlap for the source side of the 12 novels that make up the test set. The highest TTR and average sentence length as well as the lowest n-gram overlap values are shown in bold

BLEU	TTR	Avg. sentence length	Overlap
PBSMT	–	–	$r = 0.62, p < 0.05$
NMT	–	–	$r = 0.66, p < 0.01$
Rel. diff	–	$\rho = -0.45^{a}, p = 0.07$	–

Table 7 Correlations between the BLEU scores for NMT, PBSMT and their relative difference and the other metrics considered (TTR, average sentence length and 4-g overlap) for the 12 novels that make up the test set. Empty cells mean that no significant correlation was found
[a]A significant parametric Pearson correlation was found ($r = -0.78, p < 0.01$) but the assumption that both variables come from a bivariate normal distribution was not met, hence the reason why a non-parametric Spearman correlation is shown instead

Results

Table 6 shows the values for each novel and for each of the three features analysed. We can clearly observe an outlier in the data for all the three variables reported. *Ulysses* has the highest TTR by far at 0.276 and is also the novel with the lowest overlap by a wide margin (0.216). As for sentence length, the value for *Sunset Park* (32.434) is over 10 points higher than the value for any other novel.

Table 7 shows the significant correlations between the BLEU scores (for PBSMT, NMT and the relative difference between both, see Table 5) and the three variables analysed (TTR, average sentence length and n-gram overlap). Each of the significant correlations is then plotted, including its regression line and its 95% confidence region, in Figs. 2, 3 and 4.

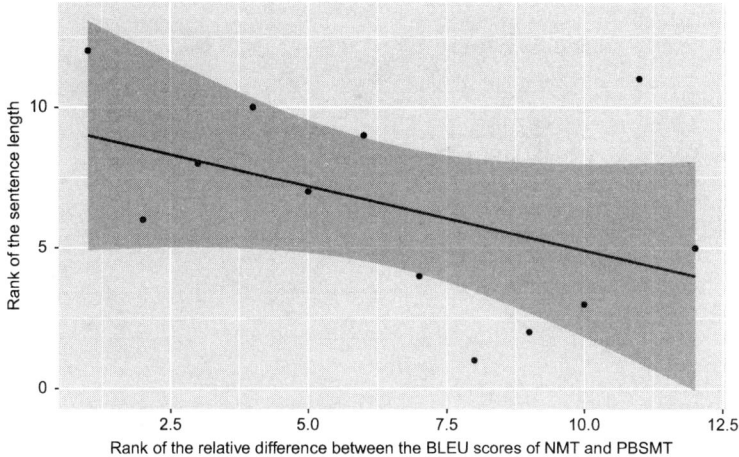

Fig. 2 Spearman correlation between the relative difference between the BLEU scores of the NMT and PBSMT systems and sentence length

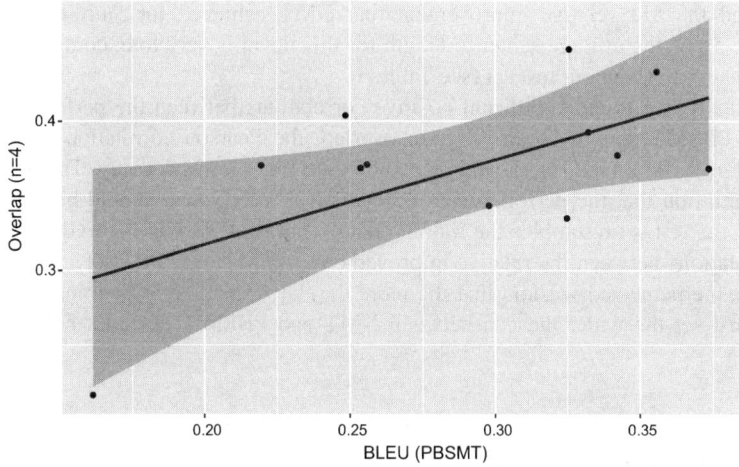

Fig. 3 Pearson correlation between the BLEU score of the PBSMT system and 4-g overlap

While Bentivogli et al. (2016) found a moderate correlation ($r = 0.73$) between TTR and the gains by NMT over PBSMT (measured with mTER – multi-reference TER (Snover et al. 2006) – on transcribed speeches), there is no significant correlation in our set-up.

With respect to sentence length (see Fig. 2), we observe a negative correlation ($\rho = -0.45$), meaning that the relative improvement of NMT over PBSMT decreases with sentence length. This corroborates the findings in previous work (Toral and Sánchez-Cartagena 2017) and appears to be the main reason

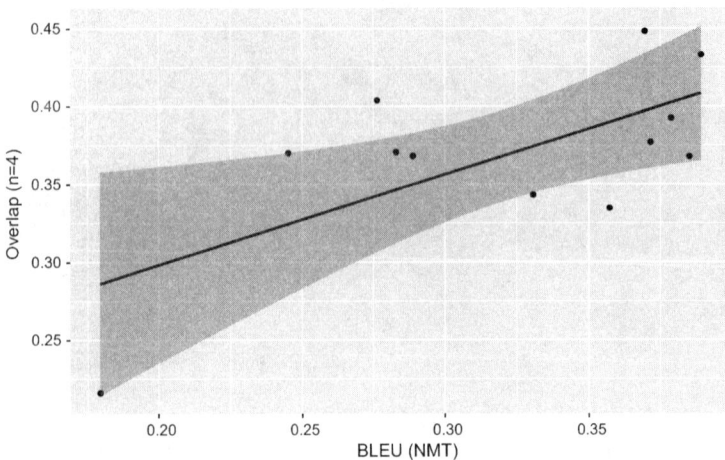

Fig. 4 Pearson correlation between the BLEU score of the NMT system and 4-g overlap

behind the low relative improvement that NMT achieved for *Sunset Park* (see Table 5), as the average sentence length for this novel is very long compared to all the other novels in our test set (see Table 6).

Finally, we found significant positive correlations between the performance of both PBSMT and NMT and n-gram overlap, the Pearson correlation coefficient being $r = 0.62$ (see Fig. 3) and $r = 0.66$ (see Fig. 4), respectively. This matches the intuition that the performance of a statistical MT system should be better the more the test set resembles the training data. That said, we did not find significant correlations between the relative improvement of NMT over PBSMT and overlap. Thus, the perceived wisdom that the more unrelated the data to be translated from the test set the wider the gap between NMT and PBSMT, does not hold for our set-up.

5.2 Human Evaluation

We also conducted a manual evaluation, in order to gain further insights. A common procedure (e.g. conducted in the annual MT shared task at WMT)[14] consists of ranking the translations produced by different MT systems (see also Section 3.4 in Castilho et al. in this volume). Given the source and target sides of the reference (human) translations, and two or more outputs from MT systems, these outputs are ranked according to their quality, e.g. in terms of adequacy and/or fluency.

---

[14]e.g. http://www.statmt.org/wmt17/translation-task.html

In our experiment, we are not only interested in comparing two MT systems – PBSMT and NMT – to each other, but also with respect to the human reference translation. Hence, we conduct the rank-based manual evaluation in a slightly modified setting; we do not provide the target of the reference translation as reference but as one of the translations to be ranked. The evaluator thus is provided with the source-side of the reference and three translations, one being the human translation and the other two the translations produced by the PBSMT and NMT systems. The evaluator of course does not know which is which. Moreover, in order to avoid any bias with respect to MT, they are not told whether the translations are human or automatic.

This human evaluation is conducted for three of the books used in the automatic evaluation: Orwell's *1984*, Rowling's *Harry Potter #7* and Salinger's *The Catcher in the Rye*. For each of these books, the sentences in 10 randomly selected passages were ranked. Each passage is made of 10 contiguous sentences, the motivation being to provide the annotator with context beyond the sentence level. Therefore, sentences 1–10 (passage 1) are contiguous in the book, then there is a jump to a second passage contained in sentences 11–20, and so forth.

All the annotations were carried out by two native Catalan speakers with an advanced level of English. They both have a background in linguistics but no in-depth knowledge of statistical MT (again, to avoid any bias with respect to MT). Comprehensive instructions were provided to the evaluators in their native language, in order to minimise ambiguity and thus foster high inter-annotator agreement. Here we reproduce the translation into English of the evaluation instructions:

Given three translations, the task is to rank them:

- Rank a translation *A* higher (rank 1) than a translation *B* (rank 2), if the first translation is better than the second.
- Rank two translations *A* and *B* equally (rank 1 for both *A* and *B*), if both have an equivalent quality.
- Use the highest rank possible, e.g. if there are three translations *A*, *B* and *C*, and the quality of *A* and *B* is equivalent and both are better than *C*, then they should be ranked as follows: *A* = rank 1, *B* = rank 1, *C* = rank 2. Do NOT use lower rankings, e.g.: *A* = rank 2, *B* = rank 2, *C* = rank 3.

Please follow the following guidelines to decide that a translation is better than another:

- Above anything else: the meaning of the original is understood, all the information is preserved and, if possible, the translation sounds natural.
- If all translations preserve the meaning to a similar extent, you might compare the number of errors (e.g. lexical, syntax, etc) in each translation.
- If for a given set of translations, you cannot decide how to rank them, you can skip that set by pressing the button "flag error".

Figure 5 shows a snapshot of the manual evaluation process. In this example the annotator is asked to rank three translations for the second sentence from the first passage of Salinger's *The Catcher in the Rye*.

All of a sudden, he sald, "For Chrissake, Holden. **This is about a goddam baseball glove.**" Cold as hell.   NA NA NA

O Rank 1 O Rank 2 O Rank 3
Alxò és sobre un guant do beisbol.

O Rank 1 O Rank 2 O Rank 3
Alxò va d'un cony de guant de beisbol.

O Rank 1 O Rank 2 O Rank 3
Es tracta d'un col de guant de beisbol.

Submit   Reset   Flag Error

Fig. 5 Snapshot from the manual evaluation process

5.2.1 Inter-annotator Agreement

The inter-annotator agreement in terms of Fleiss' Kappa (Fleiss 1971) is 0.22 for Orwell, 0.18 for Rowling and 0.38 for Salinger. The values for Orwell and Salinger fall in the band of fair agreement $[0.21, 0.4]$ (Landis and Koch 1977) while that for Rowling is at the higher end of slight agreement $[0.01, 0.2]$. For the sake of comparison, the average inter-annotator agreement at WMT for the closest language direction to ours (English-to-French) over the last four editions in which that language direction was considered is 0.29, see Table 4 in Bojar et al. (2016).

5.2.2 Pairwise Rankings

From the sets of annotations (rankings between three translations), we extract all pairwise rankings, i.e. the rankings for each pair of translations. Given two translations A and B, the pairwise ranking will be $A > B$ if translation A was ranked higher than B, $A < B$ if A was ranked lower than B, and $A = B$ if both were ranked equally.

It is worth mentioning that while the PBSMT translations consistently cover the source sentences, this is not always the case for the other two translations. NMT has a tendency towards omission errors (Klubička et al. 2017). The human translation sometimes does not cover the source sentence fully either. This may be due to a choice of the translator, e.g. to translate the sentence in a way that diverges notably from the source. There are also some cases where the human translation is

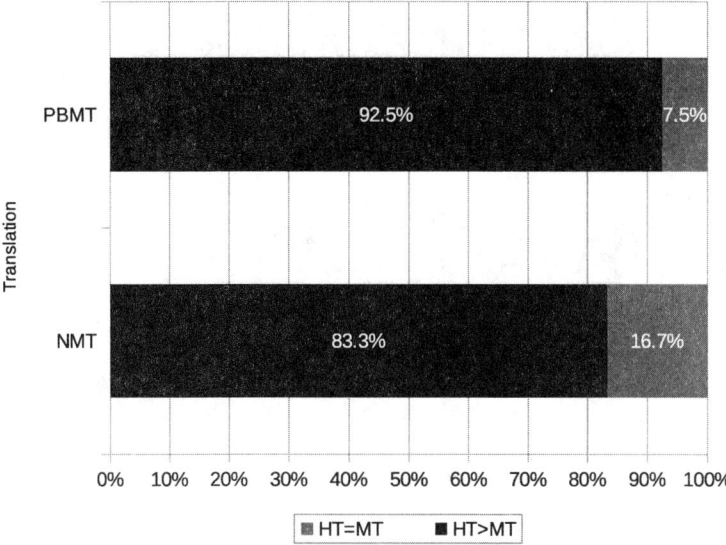

Fig. 6 Pairwise rankings between HT and MT for Orwell's *1984*

misaligned[15] and so it is unrelated to the source sentence. Most cases in which the human translation is ranked lower than MT (PBSMT or NMT) are due to either of these two reasons. It is clearly unjustifiable to rank the human translation lower than MT in these cases, so we remove these pairwise rankings, i.e. $A < B$ where A is the human translation and B corresponds to the translation produced by either MT system.[16]

Figures 6, 7 and 8 show the pairwise rankings between each MT system and the human translation (HT) for Orwell's, Rowling's and Salinger's books. In all three books, the percentage of sentences where the annotators perceive the MT translation to be of equivalent quality to the human translation is considerably higher for NMT compared to PBSMT: 16.7% vs. 7.5% for Orwell's, 31.8% vs. 18.1% for Rowling's and 34.3% vs. 19.8% for Salinger's. In other words, if NMT translations were to be used to assist a professional translator (e.g. by means of post-editing), then around one third of the sentences for Rowling and Salinger's and one sixth for Orwell's would not need any correction.

---

[15] As mentioned in Sect. 3.3.1, the source novels and their human translations were sentence-aligned automatically. The empirically set confidence threshold results in most alignments being correct, but some are erroneous.

[16] While the majority of HT<MT cases are unjustified, not all of them are. By removing these rankings, the results are slightly biased in favour of HT and thus overly conservative with respect to the potential of MT.

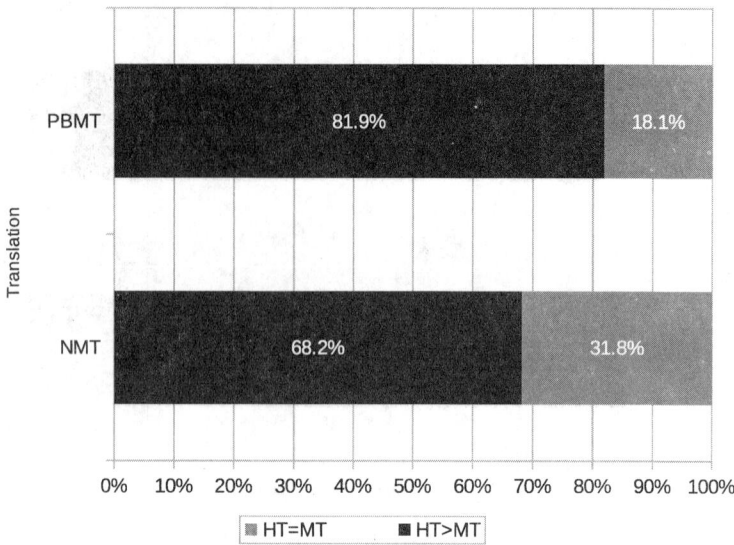

Fig. 7 Pairwise rankings between HT and MT for Rowling's *Harry Potter #7*

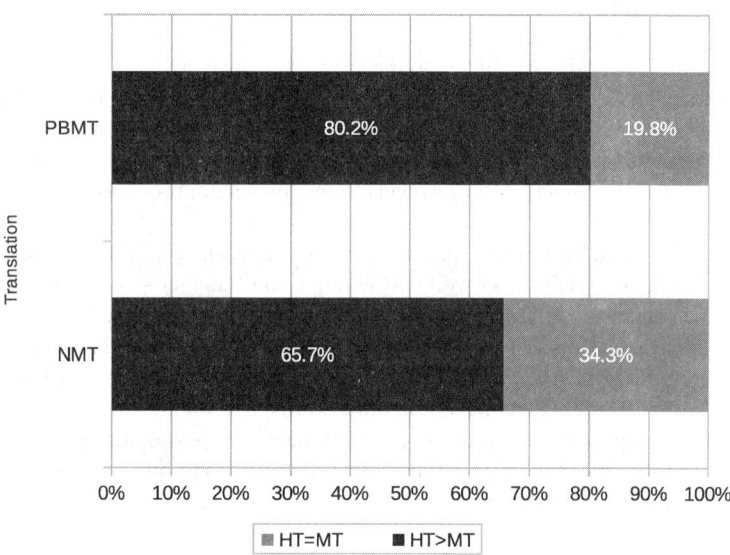

Fig. 8 Pairwise rankings between HT and MT for Salinger's *The Catcher in the Rye*

Having looked at pairwise rankings between MT and human translations, we move our attention now to the pairwise rankings between the two types of MT systems. The results for all three books are depicted in Fig. 9. In all the books

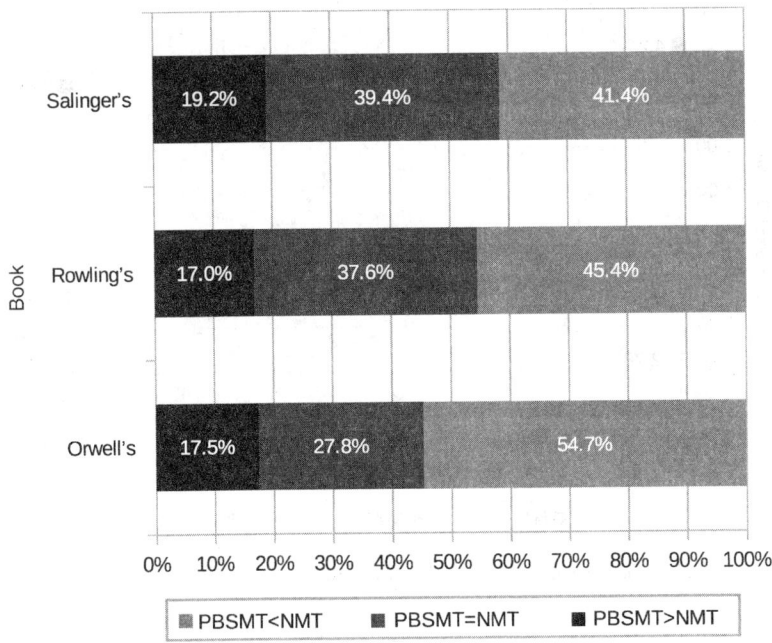

Fig. 9 Pairwise rankings between PBSMT and NMT

the trends are similar. The biggest chunk (41.4%, 54.7%) corresponds to cases where NMT translations are ranked higher than PBSMT's (PBSMT<NMT). The second relates to translations by both systems which are ranked equally (27.8%, 39.4%), (PBSMT = NMT). Finally, the smallest chunk (less than 20% in all three books) signifies translations for which PBSMT is ranked higher than NMT (PBSMT > NMT).

5.2.3 Overall Human Scores

In addition to the pairwise rankings, we derive an overall score for each translation type (HT, NMT and PBSMT) and novel based on the rankings. To this end we use the TrueSkill method adapted to MT evaluation (Sakaguchi et al. 2014) following its usage at WMT15,[17] i.e. we run 1,000 iterations of the rankings recorded with Appraise followed by clustering ($p < 0.05$).

Figure 10 depicts the results. For all three books considered, all the translation types are put in different clusters, meaning that the differences between every pair of translation types are significant. The ordering of the translation types corroborates that seen in the pairwise analysis (see Sect. 5.2.2), namely human translations come on top, followed by NMT outputs and finally, in third place, PBSMT outputs.

---

[17]https://github.com/mjpost/wmt15

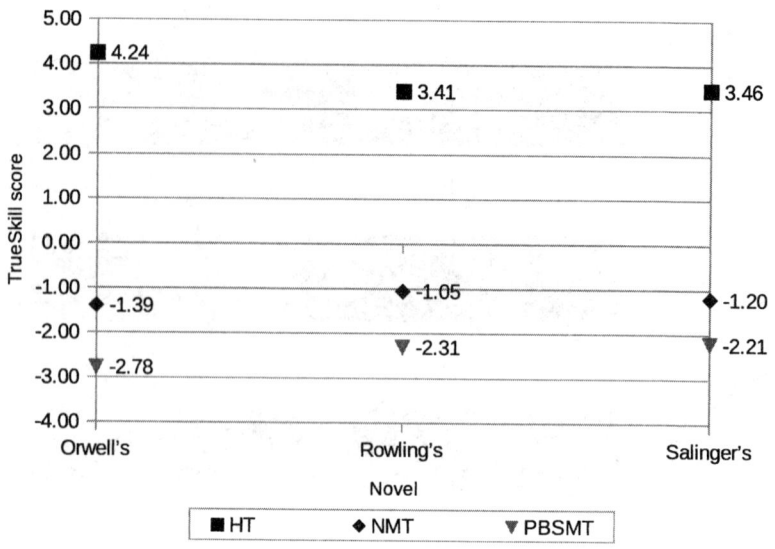

Fig. 10 Overall human evaluation scores with TrueSkill

If we consider PBSMT's score as a baseline, the score given to the human translations as a gold standard, and the distance between the two as the potential room for improvement for MT, we could interpret NMT's score as the progress made in our journey towards better translation quality for novels, departing from PBSMT and targeting human translations as the goal to be reached ultimately. Using this analogy, although there is still a long way to go, with NMT we have covered already a considerable part of the journey: 20%, 22% and 18% for Orwell's, Rowling's and Salinger's books, respectively; while it may not yet be a case of *A Thousand Splendid Suns*, it can be said with confidence that we are *On The Road*!

6   Conclusions and Future Work

This chapter has assessed the quality attainable for novels by the two most common paradigms to MT at present, NMT and PBSMT. To this end, we built the first in-domain PBSMT and NMT systems for literary text by training them on large amounts of parallel novels. We then automatically evaluated the translation quality of the resulting systems on a set of 12 widely known novels spanning from the 1920s to the present day. The results proved favourable for NMT, which outperformed PBSMT by a significant margin for all the 12 novels.

We then delved deeper into the results by analysing the effect of three features of each novel: its lexical richness, its degree of novelty with respect to the training data, and its average sentence length. Only for the last feature did we find a meaningful correlation with NMT relative improvement over PBSMT, which corroborates the tendency for improvements in NMT over PBSMT to decrease with sentence length. This seems to be the main reason behind NMT achieving a relatively low improvement over PBSMT for one of the novels, but we note that particular novel to be a considerable outlier in terms of sentence length.

We have also conducted a human evaluation, where we manually ranked the translations produced by NMT, PBSMT, as well as the human translations for three of the books. Again, NMT outperformed PBSMT. For two out of the three books native speakers perceived NMT translations to be of equivalent quality to those of human translations in around one third of the cases (one fifth for PBSMT).

As for future work, we would like to assess the feasibility of using MT to assist with the translation of literary text. To that end, we plan to carry out an experiment in which we integrate MT into the workflow of professional literary translators by means of post-editing and assess its impact in the translation process (e.g. temporal and technical effort) as well as in the translation result (e.g. quality and reading experience of the resulting translation).

Acknowledgements Carme Armentano and Álvaro Bellón ranked the translations used for the human evaluation. The research leading to these results has received funding from the European Association for Machine Translation through its 2015 sponsorship of activities programme (project PiPeNovel). The second author is supported by the ADAPT Centre for Digital Content Technology, funded under the SFI Research Centres Programme (Grant 13/RC/2106).We would like to thank the Center for Information Technology of the University of Groningen and the Irish Centre for High-End Computing (http://www.ichec.ie) for providing computational infrastructure.

References

Bentivogli L, Bisazza A, Cettolo M, Federico M (2016) Neural versus phrase-based machine translation quality: a case study. In: Proceedings of the 2016 conference on empirical methods in natural language processing, Austin, pp 257–267

Besacier L (2014) Traduction automatisée d'une oeuvre littéraire: une étude pilote. In: Traitement automatique du langage naturel (TALN), Marseille, http://hal.inria.fr/hal-01003944

Bird S (2006) NLTK: the natural language toolkit. In: Proceedings of the COLING/ACL on interactive presentation sessions, Sydney, pp 69–72

Bojar O, Chatterjee R, Federmann C, Graham Y, Haddow B, Huck M, Jimeno Yepes A, Koehn P, Logacheva V, Monz C, Negri M, Neveol A, Neves M, Popel M, Post M, Rubino R, Scarton C, Specia L, Turchi M, Verspoor K, Zampieri M (2016) Findings of the 2016 conference on machine translation. In: Proceedings of the first conference on machine translation, Berlin, pp 131–198

Cherry C, Foster G (2012) Batch tuning strategies for statistical machine translation. In: Proceedings of the 2012 conference of the North American chapter of the Association for Computational Linguistics: human language technologies, Montréal, pp 427–436

Durrani N, Schmid H, Fraser A (2011) A joint sequence translation model with integrated reordering. In: Proceedings of the 49th annual meeting of the Association for Computational Linguistics: human language technologies, vol 1, Portland, pp 1045–1054

Federmann C (2012) Appraise: an open-source toolkit for manual evaluation of machine translation output. Prague Bull Math Linguist 98:25–35

Fleiss JL (1971) Measuring nominal scale agreement among many raters. Psychol Bull 76(5): 378–382

Forcada ML, Ñeco RP (1997) Recursive hetero-associative memories for translation. In: Proceedings of the biological and artificial computation: from neuroscience to technology: international work-conference on artificial and natural neural networks, IWANN'97 Lanzarote, 4–6 June 1997. Springer, Berlin/Heidelberg, pp 453–462

Genzel D, Uszkoreit J, Och F (2010) "Poetic" statistical machine translation: rhyme and meter. In: Proceedings of the 2010 conference on empirical methods in natural language processing, Cambridge, pp 158–166

Greene E, Bodrumlu T, Knight K (2010) Automatic analysis of rhythmic poetry with applications to generation and translation. In: Proceedings of the 2010 conference on empirical methods in natural language processing, Cambridge, pp 524–533

Hardmeier C (2014) Discourse in statistical machine translation. PhD thesis, University of Uppsala

Heafield K (2011) Kenlm: faster and smaller language model queries. In: Proceedings of the sixth workshop on statistical machine translation, Edinburgh, pp 187–197

Jones R, Irvine A (2013) The (un)faithful machine translator. In: Proceedings of the 7th workshop on language technology for cultural heritage, social sciences, and humanities, Sofia, pp 96–101

Junczys-Dowmunt M, Dwojak T, Hoang H (2016) Is neural machine translation ready for deployment? A case study on 30 translation directions. arXiv preprint arXiv:161001108

Klubička F, Toral A, Sánchez-Cartagena VM (2017) Fine-grained human evaluation of neural versus phrase-based machine translation. Prague Bull Math Linguist 108:121–132

Koehn P (2004) Statistical significance tests for machine translation evaluation. In: Proceedings of the conference on empirical methods in natural language processing, Barcelona, vol 4, pp 388–395

Koehn P, Hoang H, Birch A, Callison-Burch C, Federico M, Bertoldi N, Cowan B, Shen W, Moran C, Zens R, Dyer C, Bojar O, Constantin A, Herbst E (2007) Moses: open source toolkit for statistical machine translation. In: Proceedings of the 45th annual meeting of the ACL on interactive poster and demonstration sessions, Prague, pp 177–180

Landis RJ, Koch GG (1977) The measurement of observer agreement for categorical data. Biometrics 33(1):159–174

Li L, Sporleder C (2010) Using Gaussian mixture models to detect figurative language in context. In: Human language technologies: the 2010 annual conference of the North American chapter of the Association for Computational Linguistics, Los Angeles, pp 297–300

Ljubešić N, Toral A (2014) caWaC – a Web corpus of Catalan and its application to language modeling and machine translation. In: Proceedings of the ninth international conference on language resources and evaluation (LREC'14), Reykjavik, pp 1728–1732

Luong MT, Manning CD (2015) Stanford neural machine translation systems for spoken language domain. In: Proceedings of the international workshop on spoken language translation, Da Nang, pp 76–79

Padró L, Stanilovsky E (2012) Freeling 3.0: towards wider multilinguality. In: Proceedings of the eighth international conference on language resources and evaluation (LREC-2012), Istanbul, pp 2473–2479

Papineni K, Roukos S, Ward T, Zhu WJ (2002) Bleu: a method for automatic evaluation of machine translation. In: Proceedings of the 40th annual meeting of Association for Computational Linguistics, Philadelphia, pp 311–318

Pecina P, Toral A, Papavassiliou V, Prokopidis P, Tamchyna A, Way A, van Genabith J (2014) Domain adaptation of statistical machine translation with domain-focused web crawling. Lang Resour Eval 49(1):147–193

Reyes A (2013) Linguistic-based patterns for figurative language processing: the case of humor recognition and irony detection. Procesamiento del Lenguaje Natural 50:107–109

Sakaguchi K, Post M, Van Durme B (2014) Efficient elicitation of annotations for human evaluation of machine translation. In: Proceedings of the ninth workshop on statistical machine translation, Baltimore, pp 1–11

Sánchez-Cartagena VM, Toral A (2016) Abu-Matran at WMT 2016 translation task: deep learning, morphological segmentation and tuning on character sequences. In: Proceedings of the first conference on machine translation, Berlin, pp 362–370

Sennrich R (2012) Perplexity minimization for translation model domain adaptation in statistical machine translation. In: Proceedings of the 13th conference of the European chapter of the Association for Computational Linguistics, Avignon, pp 539–549

Sennrich R, Haddow B, Birch A (2015) Improving neural machine translation models with monolingual data. arXiv preprint arXiv:151106709

Sennrich R, Haddow B, Birch A (2016a) Edinburgh neural machine translation systems for WMT 16. In: Proceedings of the first conference on machine translation, Berlin, pp 371–376

Sennrich R, Haddow B, Birch A (2016b) Neural machine translation of rare words with subword units. In: Proceedings of the 54th annual meeting of the Association for Computational Linguistics, Berlin. Long papers, vol 1, pp 1715–1725

Sennrich R, Firat O, Cho K, Birch A, Haddow B, Hitschler J, Junczys-Dowmunt M, Läubli S, Miceli Barone AV, Mokry J, Nadejde M (2017) Nematus: a toolkit for neural machine translation. In: Proceedings of the software demonstrations of the 15th conference of the European chapter of the Association for Computational Linguistics, Valencia, pp 65–68

Shutova E, Teufel S, Korhonen A (2013) Statistical metaphor processing. Comput Linguist 39(2):301–353

Snover M, Dorr B, Schwartz R, Micciulla L, Makhoul J (2006) A study of translation edit rate with targeted human annotation. In: AMTA 2006: proceedings of the 7th conference of the association for machine translation in the Americas, "Visions for the Future of Machine Translation", Cambridge, pp 223–231

Stolcke A (2002) SRILM-an extensible language modeling toolkit. In: Proceedings of the 7th international conference on spoken language processing (ICSLP 2002), Denver, pp 901–904

Toral A, Sánchez-Cartagena VM (2017) A multifaceted evaluation of neural versus phrase-based machine translation for 9 language directions. In: Proceedings of the 15th conference of the European chapter of the Association for Computational Linguistics: volume 1, Long Papers, Valencia, pp 1063–1073

Toral A, Way A (2015a) Machine-assisted translation of literary text: a case study. Translat Spaces 4:241–268

Toral A, Way A (2015b) Translating literary text between related languages using SMT. In: Proceedings of the fourth workshop on computational linguistics for literature, Denver, pp 123–132

Varga D, Halaácsy P, Kornai A, Nagy V, Németh L, Trón V (2005) Parallel corpora for medium density languages. In: International conference RANLP-2005, recent advances in natural language processing, proceedings, Borovets, pp 590–596

Vaswani A, Zhao Y, Fossum V, Chiang D (2013) Decoding with large-scale neural language models improves translation. In: Proceedings of the 2013 conference on empirical methods in natural language processing, Seattle, pp 1387–1392

Voigt R, Jurafsky D (2012) Towards a literary machine translation: the role of referential cohesion. In: Proceedings of the NAACL-HLT 2012 workshop on computational linguistics for literature, Montrèal, pp 18–25